RECENT PERSPECTIVES ON EARLY CHILDHOOD
EDUCATION AND CARE IN CANADA

Edited by Nina Howe and Larry Prochner

Early childhood education is critical for preparing children for success in formal school settings, and is a topic of major concern in many Western and developing countries. This volume brings together research in this area to inform ECEC practitioners and students, policy makers, curriculum specialists, and program developers on the latest ideas and advances in the field.

Recent Perspectives on Early Childhood Education and Care in Canada is divided into three main parts. The first focuses on recent history (since 1950), social policy, economics of child care, and issues related to provincial regulations and policies. The second focuses on issues related to new directions in programs for children, curriculum, and teachers. The final part addresses recent developments in government involvement in early childhood education and care that are unique to Canada. Bringing together a distinguished group of contributors, the volume presents a wealth of new research and analysis to further public discussion and to help policy makers shape better decisions for Canadian families.

NINA HOWE is Concordia University Research Chair in Early Childhood Development and a professor in the Department of Education at Concordia University.

LARRY PROCHNER is a professor in the Department of Elementary Education at the University of Alberta.

Recent Perspectives on Early Childhood Education and Care in Canada

EDITED BY NINA HOWE AND LARRY PROCHNER

UNIVERSITY OF TORONTO PRESS
Toronto Buffalo London

© University of Toronto Press 2012
Toronto Buffalo London
www.utppublishing.com
Printed in Canada

ISBN 978-1-4426-4520-2 (cloth)
ISBN 978-1-4426-1331-7 (paper)

Printed on acid-free, 100% post-consumer recycled paper with
vegetable-based inks.

Library and Archives Canada Cataloguing in Publicaton

Recent perspectives on early childhood education and care in Canada / edited
by Nina Howe and Larry Prochner.

Includes bibliographical references and index.
ISBN 978-1-4426-4520-2 (bound). ISBN 978-1-4426-1331-7 (pbk.)

1. Early childhood education – Canada. 2. Child care services –
Canada. I. Howe, Nina, 1951– II. Prochner, Larry, 1956–

LB1139.3.C3R43 2012   372.210971   C2012-903935-7

This book has been published with the help of a grant from the Canadian
Federation for the Humanities and Social Sciences, through the Aid to
Scholarly Publications Program, using funds provided by the Social Sciences
and Humanities Research Council of Canada.

University of Toronto Press acknowledges the financial assistance to its
publishing program of the Canada Council for the Arts and the
Ontario Arts Council.

 Canada Council   Conseil des Arts
for the Arts   du Canada    ONTARIO ARTS COUNCIL
CONSEIL DES ARTS DE L'ONTARIO

University of Toronto Press acknowledges the financial support of the
Government of Canada through the Canada Book Fund for its publishing
activities.

Contents

Acknowledgments

We wish to thank the following units for their generous financial support of the workshop on which this book is based: the Department of Education, Centre for Research in Human Development (CRDH), the Faculty of Arts and Sciences, and the vice-president research and graduate studies, Concordia University. We also thank the Social Sciences and Humanities Research Council of Canada (Aid to Workshops Program) for their generous support. The CRDH support was particularly generous and went well beyond their financial contribution. In particular, the planning and organization of the workshop would not have been possible without the outstanding work of Donna Craven, CRDH administrator, whose expertise made the workshop a reality. She was ably assisted by Pierre-Étienne Mercier's technical expertise and Michelle Cormier's bookkeeping efforts. In addition, CRDH generously provided Knowledge Transfer Fellowships for two doctoral students (Sandra Della Porta, Education, and Paula Ruttle, Psychology) to assist their training in this area. Sandra was an excellent assistant in the preparation of the Concordia University and the Social Sciences and Humanities Research Council of Canada grant applications. We are deeply grateful to Sandra and Paula for their chairing of the Student Organizing Committee, whose members were instrumental in helping to plan and run all aspects of the workshop. They were assisted by an amazing group of students whose efforts were widely applauded by the workshop participants and included Shireen Abuhatoum, Allyson Funamoto, Vanessa Rayner, Lina Saldariagga, and Brittany Scott. We also thank Louise Dandurand, vice-president research and graduate studies, and Brian Lewis, dean, Faculty of Arts and Sciences, who both took time out of their busy schedules to welcome participants at the workshop. Both Sandra and Paula have been invaluable and insightful editors of the chapters that appear in the book. Their enthusiastic, willing, and professional collaboration on this project has been a joy to witness. Finally, we would like to acknowledge the support and encouragement we received from our families; special thanks to the Howe-Bukowski family (Bill, Ana, and Nick) and to the Prochner family (Barb and Isabel).

RECENT PERSPECTIVES ON EARLY CHILDHOOD
EDUCATION AND CARE IN CANADA

Introduction

NINA HOWE AND LARRY PROCHNER

Early childhood learning, education, care, and development is a topic of major concern in many Western and developing countries, and it is now recognized as critical for preparing children for success in more formal school settings, as well as giving children an optimal start in life. As such, early learning and education have become a major focus of governments, policy makers, and of course, researchers. Furthermore, there is a tremendous need to train students in the field of early childhood education and care (ECEC), so as to advance their understanding of the critical issues and to prepare them to enter employment in a variety of fields that influence the provision of early learning and educational experiences for children.

Clearly, raising healthy, competent, and well-educated children has immediate and long-term social, cultural, and economic benefits for any society; in our case, the focus is on Canada. The early years are critical for children's healthy social-emotional and psychological development and for success in formal (e.g., schools) and informal (e.g., interacting with peers on the playground) settings. Healthy child development requires the active and positive involvement of many dedicated persons (e.g., parents, family and community members, teachers, day care educators, psychologists, researchers, policy makers): thus, our book is addressed to a wide, but committed audience. We hope that the chapters, as described below, will inform policy makers, curriculum designers, college and university instructors, practitioners' teaching practices, developers of intervention programs created to address issues of local and national importance, and of course, students.

A close examination of ECEC reveals that the field has been defined by three major traditions or perspectives on critical issues, which are sometimes distinct but often overlap. This intersection or overlap between the three traditions creates rich opportunities for research, policy initiatives, designing and implementing intervention programs, training early childhood educators, and other professionals. The first tradition is child care, which has been defined as a service for parents (both public and private) that typically focuses on the *care* provided for children and, thus, nurturing their health, well-being, and social and cognitive development. The second tradition is *education*, which focuses on children's early learning, social and cognitive development, and school readiness and is delivered in early years' classrooms (e.g., pre-school, nursery school, kindergarten, or early elementary grades). The third tradition is that of *development*, which sometimes takes (1) an epidemiological perspective with a focus on health, economics, safety, and parenting/family support and/or (2) a child development perspective with a focus on at-risk populations, atypical development, prevention, and intervention programs. These three traditions are evident in varying degrees in the chapters in this book, for example, the issue of care is covered by Friendly and Prentice, Jacobs and Adrien, and Heydon, whereas issues related to education are found in the chapters by Prochner and Robertson and Langford. Issues related to development are prominent in the chapters by Pelletier and Peters, Howell-Moneta, and Petrunka. Nevertheless, the overlap between traditions is very striking in many of the chapters and indicates a rich and dynamic field of study. Finally, to some degree the age range of children covered under these three traditions has varied, but for our purposes, we would include children from birth to about age 8 years of age.

This book emanated from a small workshop titled 'New Directions in Early Childhood Education,' held at Concordia University, 12–13 March 2010. The contributors were asked to provide a draft of their chapters prior to the workshop so that the three Canadian commentators (Hillel Goelman, Alan Pence, and Carl Corter) and our international commentator (Helen Penn) could reflect on the chapters and begin to prepare some informed discussion. This promoted a lively and dynamic conversation between the authors and our invited audience composed of researchers, graduate students, community college instructors, child care centre directors and educators, policy makers, provincial civil servants responsible for child care, and other interested parties. The workshop, generously supported by Concordia University and the Social Science and Humanities Research Council of Canada, allowed for an intellectually stimulating exchange of ideas and active participation by the authors and the audience. This resulted in conceptually stronger written contributions, which are gathered together into this volume. We hope that our readers will enjoy the various contributions and be prompted to ask further research questions and to critique, promote, and advance the well-being of ECEC programs in Canada. Currently, Canada has a patchwork of provincial and federal initiatives that barely meet the needs of Canadian families, rather than a universal, publicly funded, high-quality system. Our hope is that this book will further the public discussion on the very slow road to creating a high-quality early childhood experience for Canadian children and families, a worthy but distant goal, at least as seen in 2012.

The book is organized into three parts, each of which focuses on a specific theme; the thematically linked chapters in each part are followed by a commentary by a leading Canadian expert in the ECEC field. The three themes are (1) historical and contemporary issues, (2) children, curriculum, and teachers, and (3) government initiatives and involvement in the ECEC field. Finally, Helen Penn, from the United Kingdom, provides an international perspective in her concluding commentary.

Part I introduces historical and contemporary perspectives on ECEC. The four chapters focus on recent history (since 1950), social policy, the economics of child care, and issues related to provincial regulations and policies. Larry Prochner and Lynne Robertson's opening chapter addresses key developments in ECEC in the 1950s and 1960s. Following an active period for ECEC during the Second World War, the following fifteen years or so were a quiet time of retrenchment given that many women opted to stay at home with their young children. Prochner and Robertson analyse this period by describing seven dimensions: ethos, teaching, learning, settings, curriculum, assessment, and diversity. They proceed to analyse innovations that renewed the field, beginning in the 1960s, specifically the notion of enrolling children in pre-schools as a strategy for reducing poverty and supporting child care as a strategy for labour market equity. The authors outline three major themes evident in more recent years: the integration of services for children and families, the international inspiration for ideas about curriculum, and recent efforts to focus ECEC on school readiness. This chapter provides the foundation for the book and raises a number of issues that are taken up in subsequent chapters.

In chapter 2, Martha Friendly and Susan Prentice provide an analysis of how the political structures and ideas explain the way that ECEC has developed in Canada. They review the ten benchmarks of quality ECEC services as defined in the 2008 ECEC Report Card issued by UNICEF and indicate how Canada achieved a failing grade. Employing regime theory, the authors discuss the way that ECEC is organized, financed, and delivered in Canada with a particular emphasis on our privatized financing of child care, the marketized and mixed economy for providing services, and the liberal welfare approach to providing government services for ECEC. Finally, they consider how Canada's style of federalism has restrained the creation of policy initiatives to build and sustain a coherent system of ECEC, particularly since 2000. This chapter offers an excellent context for understanding how Canadian approaches to early childhood education and care are similar and also different from international approaches.

In chapter 3, Gordon Cleveland presents an economic analysis of Canadian ECEC services and policies, while also drawing on international research. This analysis helps to place the Canadian situation into an international context. He focuses on current scholarly and policy evidence regarding the costs and benefits of ECEC services with an emphasis on how the benefits are closely associated with the quality of the services. Cleveland also examines how the costs and benefits of investing in ECEC programs are linked to particular policy reforms, the institutional structure of service delivery, and the behavioural incentives associated with such reforms. He concludes with an economic interpretation of the ways that ECEC policy reforms can maximize benefits while deterring factors associated with costs.

The final and fourth chapter in Part I, by Ellen Jacobs and Emmanuelle Adrien, examines provincial and territorial regulations and policies for child care. The authors provide a detailed examination of regulations, monitoring systems, and exemptions in the ten provinces and three territories regarding educator pre-service training (type, level), in-service professional development, and child care programming and/or curriculum. Regulations for programming and curriculum are analysed according to various criteria (e.g., developmental appropriateness, behavioural guidance, cultural sensitivity). In addition, the authors examine links between early childhood education (ECE) training programs and provincial regulations regarding qualified staff.

Part I concludes with an insightful commentary by Hillel Goelman on the four chapters. He conceptualizes these chapters as the 'geology' of ECEC pointing out that the specific 'history, policy, economics, and curriculum issues account for the unique configurations, the possibilities and the limitations currently faced in ECEC in Canada today.'

The five chapters in Part II address issues that are related to new directions in programs for children, curriculum, and teachers. These chapters address diversity issues, intergenerational programming, frameworks for early education and learning, child care quality, and in-service professional development for early childhood educators. Clearly, these topics are at the heart of delivering high-quality programs and early learning experiences for children, and the chapters cover a range of interesting initiatives and approaches.

Chapter 5, by Veronica Pacini-Ketchabaw and Judith Bernhard, opens Part II by examining issues facing newcomers to Canada and services (e.g., child care) available to assist their adjustment to a new culture and society. The authors employ anti-racist and transnational feminist theory as a foundation for moving beyond the historical Canadian approach to immigration (i.e., multiculturalism) and for considering more sensitive approaches to providing services for newcomers. They critique multicultural perspectives on newcomers and then discuss studies that have employed anti-racist and transnational feminist perspectives as alternative approaches to providing ECEC services.

In chapter 6, Rachel Heydon examines intergenerational programming from a critical curriculum studies' perspective by describing the nature, form, and type of such programs and the derived benefits for both children and seniors. Using a critical theoretical framework, she describes her research on the value of intergenerational programming in two sites and analyses the benefits for young and elderly learners and their teachers. Based on her research, Heydon concludes with some practical advice for creating optimal learning opportunities for both young and elderly participants in intergenerational programs.

Recent provincial initiatives in developing early learning curriculum frameworks are the focus of chapter 7 by Rachel Langford. Led by Quebec in 1997, four other provinces (New Brunswick, Ontario, Saskatchewan, and British Columbia) have recently developed curriculum frameworks that define their specific educational philosophy and are intended as guides for early childhood educators' practices, but are not prescribed curricula. Langford analyses the theoretical approach and social context of each framework, particularly in reference to international approaches to curriculum (e.g., Te Whāriki, New Zealand; Reggio Emilia, Italy) that have greatly influenced Canadian efforts. In this way, Langford is able to contextualize Canadian approaches within a more global movement. In addition, Langford examines the development, purpose, and content of the frameworks, as well as the recommendations regarding practical tools for educators. Finally, the process of implementation and evaluation of each framework is reviewed including the issue of bringing pre-service and in-service educators up-to-date on the new frameworks.

In chapter 8, Alan Pence and Veronica Pacini-Ketchabaw provide a reconceptualist approach to ECEC, with a focus on the Investigating Quality Project developed by the authors in British Columbia. The project arose out of a critique of current practices and was designed to initiate new ways of thinking about ECE research and practice, which were inspired by post-structuralist thought and international developments, particularly those in New Zealand, Italy, and Sweden. Although these international influences are strong, it is clear that the B.C. project is uniquely Canadian as it attempts to address the needs of the local population. The authors describe the development and discourse involved in the Investigating Quality Project and its impact on the implementation of the provincial curriculum framework, as well as the implications for practice.

Nina Howe and Ellen Jacobs, in chapter 9, focus on in-service professional development for early childhood educators. In-service professional development is one means of keeping educators abreast of new developments in the field (e.g., constructivist approaches to curriculum) and helping them to refine their pedagogical skills. The authors critique typical methods of in-service professional development (e.g., workshops, short courses) and report two case studies drawn from a larger intervention program. The program employed expert mentors to work individually with educators to enhance their understanding and implementation of a constructivist curriculum. The journal of one mentor, who worked with two educators, was analysed to identify the key elements of mentoring and provide an in-depth understanding of this process. The authors discuss the issue of the generalizability of their findings and the implications for practice.

Alan Pence submits an intriguing commentary on Part II using his own personal history as an educator, researcher, and thinker to describe and analyse changes in the field since the 1960s. He integrates his commentary on the chapters into this analysis in insightful ways to illustrate his points.

Part III highlights uniquely Canadian municipal, provincial, territorial, and federal government programs and initiatives in ECEC that reflect the sometimes ambivalent, but often well-meaning attempts by government to better the lives of Canadian children and families. The four chapters in this part of the book highlight efforts at establishing a provincial system of child care in Quebec, community-based early prevention and intervention programs, municipal programs for establishing integrated models for delivering ECEC services, and federal investments in enhancing Indigenous capacity via culturally based early childhood services.

Christa Japel, in chapter 10, provides a critical analysis of Quebec's attempt to establish a child care system. She employs the Canadian standards, namely, the QUAD principles (quality, universality, accessibility, and developmentally appropriate programs) to assess the Quebec program; these principles were announced by the federal government in 2004 to establish a national system of early learning and child care, but this direction has not been supported by the current Conservative government. Japel critically reviews research studies demonstrating that the Quebec child care system generally only minimally meets (or fails to meet) the four QUAD principles, although some studies have identified positive child outcomes (i.e., cognitive development, behavioural adjustment). Finally, Japel calls for strengthening provincial regulations for child care, teacher training, and support in order to increase the quality of the care provided for Quebec children and families.

In chapter 11, Ray Peters, Angela Howell-Moneta, and Kelly Petrunka outline community-based early prevention and intervention programs aimed at improving the quality of life for vulnerable Canadian children and families. They describe and critique a number of federal programs (e.g., the Canada Prenatal Nutrition Program) and provincial programs (e.g., Communities Raising Children community groups in New Brunswick; Best Start Networks and Community Health Groups in Ontario), many of which have not been empirically evaluated. The authors focus on Ontario's Better Beginnings Better Futures Project that has been extensively evaluated. Initiated in 1991 in eight communities, longitudinal studies of Better Beginnings Better Futures programs demonstrated the long-term cost effectiveness of community-based projects implemented when children were aged 4 to 8 years rather than for younger children. The authors discuss reasons for the long-term success of the programs for older children.

In chapter 12, Jessica Ball provides a history of First Nations, Métis, and Inuit communities' initiatives to develop culturally based ECEC programs in the past two decades. Federal funding for Aboriginal Head Start, starting in 1995, initiated the growth of capacity of Indigenous Peoples in Canada to create child care programs that address children's cognitive, Indigenous language, and cultural development, as well as health, nutrition, and social support. Ball describes community-based initiatives to develop child care that incorporate Indigenous values and culture and that address local needs. Issues related to the creation of bicultural, community-based post-secondary education programs to support Indigenous capacity by training qualified early childhood educators are also covered.

Chapter 13, by Janette Pelletier, introduces the 'school-as-hub' model of delivering integrated early childhood services (i.e., child care, kindergarten, public health services, recreation, family literacy) in a single school setting. She describes two projects (Toronto First Duty, Peel Best Start) that highlight the integration of child care, parenting, and kindergarten services; both programs were created by partnerships with municipal governments, school boards, and other social services agencies. Pelletier identifies how the demonstration project in Toronto First Duty informed the development of the provincial program, Best Start, specifically in the region of Peel. The process of establishing these centres, accompanying challenges, and policy implications are also addressed.

Carl Corter's commentary for Part III identifies several common themes evident in these four chapters. He highlights the broad developmental aims that guide many of the programs, how research contributes to policy development for government, and the value of research for creating a deeper understanding of the processes and outcomes of programs and the implementation of policy. But Corter also notes the disconnect evident in key dimensions that impact how programs are delivered across jurisdictional boundaries, between different social services (e.g., education and health care), and between services, families, and communities.

In a Postscript to this book, Helen Penn, from the University of East London, offers an international perspective on ECEC in Canada. She participated in the OECD's 2006 Starting Strong Report that compared the quality of early childhood education and care services in twenty Western countries. Penn was specifically involved in the evaluation of Canada's performance, thus we invited her to provide a final commentary for the book. Penn frames her comments from a European perspective as she assesses Canadian developments in ECEC and at times her position on some issues varies from that of the chapter authors. In particular, she contrasts the 'slow road' of Canadian developments with those in the European Union and elsewhere and poses the key question of why is Canada so slow in accepting that ECEC is part of a modern-day society.

Our hope is that the dynamic discussions of the pertinent issues covered in this book will advance our understanding of the current status of early childhood education and care in Canada by building on previous and current successes to examine the lessons learned for future developments. In sum, nothing is more important to Canada – to its people, its economy, its culture, and its well-being – than the healthy development and well-being of its young children. The past decade of research has taught Canada's health care experts, educators, policy makers, and politicians that physical and psychological health must be promoted in the early childhood classroom rather than being repaired later in the clinic or emergency room. Clearly, Canada cannot afford to simply hope that 'nature' or standard practices will create the successful individuals who will ensure our country's future.

References

Organisation for Economic Co-operation and Development. (2006). *Starting strong II: Early childhood education and care*. Paris: OECD.

PART I

Historical and Contemporary Perspectives

1 Early Childhood Education and Care in Canada in the 1950s and 1960s: Retrenchment and Renewal

LARRY PROCHNER AND LYNNE ROBERTSON

British education historian Harold Silver described developments in infant education in the nineteenth century as 'a series of fresh starts' (1965, p. 145). The radical approach to early education envisioned by Robert Owen and established in his factory village in Scotland was taken up and added to by educators in various locations across a period of several decades. However, the original purpose of infant schools as a compensatory program providing care and education for young children, and their basic form – learning via play interspersed with formal lessons – remained essentially the same. This chapter examines early childhood education and care (ECEC) in Canada in the 1950s and 1960s, almost a century and a half on from the infant school experiments, as a further example of a 'fresh start' for ECEC: in terms of the retrenchment of ideas, programs, and policies in early education and child care following the Second World War, and the renewal of the 1960s. The chapter sets the stage for the remaining chapters in this book by providing a foundation on which to assess recent directions such as integrated early childhood services, which comprise yet another 'fresh start.'

Retrenchment

The years immediately following the Second World War were marked by a sharp rise in the birth rate in Canada – a trend popularly known as the baby boom, which started in 1946 and ended in 1962 (Owram, 1996). One result was increased attention to children in terms of their schooling as well as their growth and development in general. Experts weighed in with opinions, most of which included the judgment that the best place for mothers and children was the home.

In *The Common Sense Book of Baby and Child Care*, first published in 1946, Benjamin Spock urged mothers to follow baby's lead in most situations. To do so mothers had to be ever watchful and remain at home with their children. Spock claimed that 'the average day nursery or "baby farm" is no good' for children due to the lack of attention and affection provided by caregivers (p. 485). For those parents needing help, he urged the creation of 'guidance nurseries' supplemented by 'itinerant nursery school teachers who will move from neighborhood to neighborhood, showing children how to have fun with each other, and showing parents how to get along with their children' (Spock, 1949, p. 857).

According to the historian Peter Stearns (2003), the result of such expert advice among the middle class was anxious parents who feared that a misstep in child rearing would have lifelong consequences for their youngster. As Stearns describes, children were portrayed as needing to be safeguarded from a long list of dangers – including comic books, pool halls, obesity, school failure, and sexual predators – as well as requiring discipline, often termed *guidance*. In this view, institutional child care was a further danger, creating a risk condition that would ultimately hinder a child's attachment to mother. Half-day pre-school programs, on the other hand, played a preventive part in mental health, supplementing but not interfering with family ties.

The large number of young families in this period led to a housing crisis and consequent construction boom in Canada. Newly developed suburbs had infrastructure and services for families with young children, including schools. Half of the public schools in Edmonton operating in 2010 opened between 1950 and 1970 (O'Donnell, 2010, p. A7). Although the Winnipeg School Division built few new schools in the period 1955 to 1965, additions were constructed in almost thirty established schools (Chafe, 1967). The additional classes needed teachers, and traditional teacher education programs could not keep up. 'Emergency training' programs, consisting of a summer course, prepared teachers for the classroom in September (Owram, 1996).

In contrast to the growth in schools, centre-based child care became more limited (Prentice, 1989), in a process of retrenchment. Social service agencies and organizations such as the Child Welfare League of America (CWLA) and the National Association of Nursery Education (NANE) were largely critical of existing provisions run by charities. At a meeting sponsored by the U.S. Children's Bureau in 1944, leading thinkers on child welfare and development united to condemn group child care (*New York Times*, 1944). Among them were the director of the CWLA, Arnold Gesell of Yale University, and Benjamin Spock, who was in the process of writing the first edition of his child care manual.

In this environment, many charity-run child care centres closed and the development of new day nurseries was curtailed. At the same time, the need for more child care spaces grew. Child care was targeted at children from poor families and those whose mothers had to work outside the home due to the illness of the father, or divorce; it was not regarded as a normal support for families in general. The Edmonton Crèche closed its doors in 1964 when its board determined that clients outside of these categories were using its services (Prochner, 2000). In Toronto, in the 1950s, junior kindergartens were planned as a cheaper alternative, 'eliminating the necessity of costly day nursery supervision' (*Globe and Mail*, 1956).

In 1965, the death of a 3-year-old boy in Toronto, who was left at home alone while his mother worked as a school crossing-guard, led child care advocates to call for more support for municipal day nurseries (*Globe and Mail*, 1965, 20 Feb. and 25 March). In her editorial after the inquest into the death, journalist Barbara Frum (1965) quoted Ontario Welfare Minister Louis Cecile, who believed that 'working wives are creating many social problems' (p. W4), in addition to placing children at physical risk.

The situation in Alberta provides an example of how change during the period was sparked by increased urbanization and industrialization. The growth of the petroleum industry following the discovery of oil at Leduc in 1947 impacted the education sector in the form of new buildings, higher salaries for teachers, and additional facilities such as libraries. The changes raised questions regarding the role of school in society and the value of traditional versus progressive educational practices. The Faculty of Education at the University of Alberta and the Provincial Department of Education were seen as hotbeds of progressive thinking. A retreat from traditional approaches was cause for concern for some academics, notably Hilda Neatby at the University of Saskatchewan. Neatby's critique of progressive education, provocatively titled *So Little for the Mind* (1953), charged that Canadian schools failed to provide intellectual training. In support of her argument, she drew heavily on examples from provincial curricula rather than from actual schools.

While child-centred philosophies dominated academic writing and were represented in curriculum documents, they did not reflect the

Table 1.1. Kindergarten in Public Schools in Canada in 1960

Province	Legislation	Financial assistance available from Department of Education	Kindergarten-aged children who attended public kindergarten (%)
Newfoundland	Permissive[a]	Yes	NA
Prince Edward Island	Permissive	No	0
Nova Scotia	Required[b]	Yes	87
New Brunswick	Permissive	No	1
Quebec[c]	Permissive	Yes	54
Ontario	Permissive	Yes	61
Manitoba	Permissive	Yes	19
Saskatchewan	Permissive	Yes	10
Alberta	Permissive	No	1
British Columbia	Permissive	Yes	11

Source: British Columbia. Royal Commission on Education. (1960). *Report of the Pre-Primary Education Committee to the Royal Commission on Education*. Victoria, BC: Queen's Printer.
NA = not available.
[a]In permissive legislation, local government has the option of implementing provincial policy.
[b]Called the Primary Grade or Grade Primary.
[c]Data in original study collected for Protestant schools only.

situation in most classrooms, which continued to follow more traditional approaches to teaching and learning. This was the reality that Sutherland (1997) found evidence for in his study of adults' memories of school. As he recounts, 'If my informants are to be believed, then all the changes that took place in education outside the classroom had very little effect on what went on behind its doors' (p. 219).

Curriculum changes implemented in the years following the Second World War did place more emphasis on science education, but development towards progressive approaches to teaching and learning was slow. One indicator of the slow pace of change was the stagnant development of kindergarten programs after some initial growth in services (see Table 1.1). The rash of surveys and reports initiated by government agencies in the same period was more concerned with taking stock of education and sampling views than on initiating reforms (Royal Commissions on Education in Alberta, 1959; British Columbia, 1960; Manitoba, 1959; Ontario, 1951; Quebec, 1966).

In the following section, pre-school child care and kindergarten in the period are profiled in relation to six dimensions: ethos, teaching, learning, settings, curriculum, assessment, and diversity. Information is drawn from textbooks, academic writing, education policy and curriculum documents, and government reports. The textbooks reviewed are mainly American. In this period, as in earlier times, Canadian developments in child care, nursery school, and kindergarten education closely followed those in the United States (Prochner, 2009). As one example, when the Winnipeg Public Schools reviewed their programs in 1948, they brought in experts from the University of Chicago. The result was the *Reavis Report*, which was highly critical of many aspects of the work of the Winnipeg Public Schools, noting the lack of materials and the poor accommodation in their kindergartens (University of Chicago, 1948).

In contrast to the situation with public kindergartens, nursery school education for children younger than school age continued to be dominated by the writings of William Blatz and the staff at the Institute of Child Study in Toronto, as it was known from the 1920s. Thus, Blatz's *Understanding the Young Child*, first published in 1944, was republished in 1962. Similarly, *The Adult and the Nursery School Child*, by Margaret Fletcher, the long-time head teacher at the Institute of Child Study nursery school, was published in 1958 and issued in a second edition in 1974. This later edition also included a useful contribution from Dorothy Millichamp (1974), assistant director at the Institute for almost three decades, who provided a history of pre-school teaching from the 1920s to the 1970s as an epilogue, with Blatz's security theory (1966) placed front and centre.

Textbooks varied in the terminology they used to describe school-based early childhood settings, but most emphasized the connection between kindergarten and Grade 1. Logan (1960) referred to *kindergarten and primary classrooms*. Some used the old term *kindergarten-primary*. Imhoff (1959) described both settings as *early elementary education*, whereas Lambert (1960) referred to a field of *early childhood education* (ECE), a term that first appeared in the 1920s (Pickett & Boren, 1923). Child care for children of working parents was variously called *day care* or *day nursery care*, and in a few cases, by the older name, *crèche* care. The educational program in pre-school child care was influenced by ideas from kindergarten education for older children and nursery school training for the younger ones.

Ethos

John Dewey's (1963) philosophy of education, which stressed children's activity and cooperative group living, dominated thinking in ECE in the period. The esteemed place that Dewey held at the time is illustrated by Lambert (1960), who called Dewey 'perhaps the greatest educational philosopher of our time . . . it was he who thought of children as active rather than passive beings; he who gave emphasis to learning by doing, to the use of all the senses in learning' (p. 12). She went on to suggest that 'because the child rather than subject matter has been the chief concern of the primary grades, educators in this area have felt relatively freer to explore new ideas' (p. 12).

However, in a number of descriptions of ECE in the period, the philosophical foundations of kindergarten-primary education were implicit rather than clearly articulated. Where philosophical statements were made, schools were described as sites for adjustment or 'modification of behavior' for successful living in a democratic society (Heffernan, 1959, p. 1). In order to further children's adjustment to school, there was a concern for continuity between home and school experiences, with nursery schools and kindergartens playing a lead role. Echoing a historical theme, nursery schools were considered a support for parents, 'extending and supplementing the work of the mother' (UNESCO, 1953, p. 9), whereas kindergartens were oriented towards building foundations for learning. Education from kindergarten to Grade 3 highlighted a 'whole child' approach with attention to social, emotional, and intellectual development.

Children were considered to be psychologically vulnerable and easily damaged by the harsh realities of the world. As 'immature and tender young beings' (Rudolph & Cohen, 1964, p. 377) children needed adult protection. The importance of early experience for future growth was highlighted, particularly as it impacted emotional development. Maternal care was identified as crucial for normal infant development. Experts judged the prospects for children growing up in institutions to be extremely bleak (Bowlby, 1953; Spitz, 1949). Although the focus of concern over non-familial care was on residential or foster care (Child Welfare League of America, 1962), day nursery care was caught in the same critique. Day nursery care could be justified for poor children, but not as a normal service for the children of all working parents, and certainly not for infants.

Similar beliefs contributed to the model of maternal teaching used in kindergarten, and contributed to the isolation of the kindergarten program within elementary schools. In some cases, kindergarten classrooms were physically separate with their own entrances and playgrounds. However, while teachers were warned not to make their kindergarten-primary classrooms 'hothouses' that forced their tender plants to bloom, they were also to guard against treating kindergarten as a 'pleasurable *entr'acte* before the important business of skill learning' in primary school (Rudolph & Cohen, 1964, p. 3). This approach was reflected in the Alberta Department of Education's description of the program in its *Kindergarten Manual* in 1963: 'Kindergarten has ceased to be regarded as a play school or nursery school and has drawn closer to the publicly supported primary schools of our continent' (p. 3).

The emergence of wartime nurseries in Canada during the Second World War meant that nursery education was more influential than kindergarten in child care developments in the 1950s. Staff and graduates from the Institute of Child Study set up the Ontario wartime nurseries program, helped write the Ontario Day Nurseries Act after the war, and served as directors of the provincial Day Nurseries Branch (Prochner, 1996). Whereas nursery education theory focused on developing children's independence and security in the manner described by Blatz (1966), kindergarten education was mainly concerned with peer group socialization and preparation for learning in primary school. Child care in the 1950s and 1960s nevertheless continued as a social welfare service, although with a concern for children's mental and physical health, a trajectory established in the 1920s. Toronto's West End Crèche, for example, underwent a fairly easy transition from a day nursery to a treatment centre for children with autism in the late 1950s (Prochner, 1997). Day care was justified as a specialized service – approved by experts for children from impoverished families or who had special needs – and not as a universal family support.

Teaching

A general lack of philosophical or theoretical thinking in the ECEC field left the way open for a grounding in the psychology of child development. However, the area of child development itself was not well defined or respected, making it reliant on other disciplines for ideas, and 'dependent on the nursery school movement' for its status (Beatty, 2009, p. 446). Hymes (1955) described the field of child development as 'steal[ing] from other disciplines what it can use. But it does not steal everything. It is very selective, a kind of gentleman thief' (p. 3). Teachers' professional knowledge was based in typical child development. Although development was considered in its component parts (physical, social, emotional, cognitive), teachers were called upon to concern themselves with the *whole child*. The aim was to understand what children had in common rather than what made them unique. Teachers used their knowledge of child development as a 'basis for planning,' in order to time their interventions 'at the right psychological moment' (Logan, 1960, cited in Alberta Department of Education, 1963, p. 3).

Teachers were urged to focus on children's mental health as a preventive measure (Hymes, 1955). Based on the view that all children had the potential for emotional disturbance, early childhood education (ECE) was focused on locating problems or potential problems and fixing or pre-empting them at an early stage. This outcome was more efficiently achieved if teachers first built relationships with children, so teachers were advised to take steps to ensure that children liked them and to develop a rapport (Foster & Headley, 1966; Hymes, 1955).

Although teaching philosophies were not always described in the literature, personal and professional qualities of teachers were elaborated in great detail (Foster & Headley, 1966, pp. 53–64). Teachers should be professionally prepared with specific training in early childhood education, have 'a pleasingly modulated voice,' a 'ready smile' and a 'merry laugh,' 'unbounded patience,' and be equitable in their treatment of children, avoiding favouritism.

The term used for the role of child care workers differed from those for staff of kindergarten or nursery school – sometimes they were termed teachers, but they could also be caregivers or nurses depending on the children's age and the type of program. The national standards for wartime day nurseries in Canada indicated that staff must be 'inherently equipped' to care for children (Ryan, 1942, p. 46). The Child Welfare League of America's day care consultant, Dorothy Boguslawski (1966), noted that although 'good will and love for children are most important . . . they are not a safeguard for the knowledge needed to educate, care for, and safeguard groups of young children' (p. 44). Desirable personal characteristics for educators in child care were 'a warm, sympathetic, friendly personality,' 'self-confidence,' 'dependability and stability,' 'ability to accept supervision,' and 'good health' (pp. 48–49).

There was no general agreement that younger children required a greater number of adult caregivers or more individual attention. In the day nurseries operated by the City of Toronto in the 1950s, the provincial regulations concerning the staff:child ratio were commonly interpreted as setting the maximum, not minimum number of staff (Day Nursery Committee of the Toronto Welfare Council, 1953). Individual attention would have been difficult or impossible in Alberta's standards: regulations in the mid-1960s required one adult for ten children under the age of 2 years, and one for twenty children aged 2 to 7 years (Social Planning Council of Calgary, 1967).

Learning

Theories of learning in pre-school child care and kindergarten hinged on developmental characteristics of children: how children learned or the way they benefited from experience was related to their age and stage. The approach was drawn from the work of Arnold Gesell and his colleagues, who charted milestones of development in children from birth to the age of 10 years (Gesell, 1940; Gesell & Ilg, 1946). Gesell's ideas were the basis for a series of films created by the National Film Board of Canada in the 1950s (Crawley Films & Crawley, 1951, 1953, 1954, 1956), which remained in active distribution until the 1980s (Evans, 1991). The philosophical orientation was maturationist, meaning that children were believed to develop or mature in a predictable manner according to a genetically driven plan. Teachers supported development but could not hurry it along, and characteristics of each age were clearly laid out. Logan's (1960) list of the developmental characteristics of a 5-year-old reflected the maturationist view: 'The five-year-old loves kindergarten, his teacher, and life. Being good is easy for him, for he is not looking for new worlds to conquer. He is content to do what he can do. He is a good boy, satisfied with himself, with his world, and with the adults around him. He goes confidently to and from kindergarten. He has completed the first long lap on the pathway to maturity' (p. 47).

Children learned from experiences within clear limits set by their stage of development. The 5-year-old described above was unlikely to experiment, preferring familiar activities (Logan, 1960). A 4-year-old would learn via sensory experiences with finger-paint, sand, or water. By age 4.5 years, the same child would prefer less tactile pursuits, such as 'painting and books' (p. 47). Such changes were considered rules rather than general guidelines as to how the child would develop. Hymes (1955) described the process as a 'chain of inheritance [that] sets each child's speed. This chain has the power, not the child' (pp. 54–55); to this we add, neither did the teacher.

Logan listed the following six principles of learning from a maturationist standpoint:

1 Learning is continuous, occurring across time and settings.
2 Each child develops at his or her own rate, which cannot be rushed.
3 Learning is optimum when adjusted to level of maturity, and is based on individual readiness. 'The teacher who tries to force learning before the child has reached the essential general maturity is unwise.'
4 Efficient learning is related to pupil purpose, meaning that the child must share the goal.
5 Children learn best through concrete situations in the form of real-life problems that connect the school with the community.
6 Efficient learning maximizes understanding whereas rote learning achieved through rewards or punishment is 'unsatisfying' for children. (1960, p. 59)

The actual process of learning was described in behavioural terms involving drive, cue, response, and reward. Learning could be measured according to 'a change in performance or behavior' resulting from 'training, practice or observation' (Landreth 1958, cited in Logan, 1960, p. 57). In Imhoff's (1959) view, learning was also seen to occur through imaginative and purposeful play. From this perspective, play was a natural way for children to explore their world and express their creativity and emotions. It was also a forum for developing skills in sharing, cooperating and making friends. In the elementary school, teachers were advised to use structured play as a teaching strategy, emphasizing its value in furthering problem solving and thinking skills.

Setting

Writing within the philosophy of the time, Imhoff defined the educational environment as 'the physical and psychological setting . . . in which the learning experiences take place' (1959, p. 147). The main setting for kindergarten was a classroom within a school, with special activities occurring in the school library, gymnasium, and playground. Characteristics of high-quality classrooms were adequate space, concern for the aesthetics and organization of the space, and the appropriateness of the educational materials. Classrooms were ideally located on the ground floor of the school with a large enough space for group play and cooperative activities. The room should be clean and brightly lit with an abundance of storage space. Room colours should be subdued because it was believed that 'children react to color, and too much color can play havoc' (Logan, 1960, p. 419). The classroom should be organized using 'interest centres' (Logan, 1960) or 'activity areas' (Foster & Headley, 1966). Typical centres were a doll corner, science centre, library corner, music centre, arithmetic corner, workbench, sand table, block centre, and art centre. Teachers provided a variety of simultaneous activities from which the children could choose, although they were generally required to rotate among the activities to assure their balanced development. Educational materials and equipment supported learning across developmental and subject area domains. The Alberta Department of Education highlighted in particular that 'a piano and/or record player are essential' (1963, p. 5).

In creating this environment, the aim was to dampen emotional responses while providing structured opportunities for social development. Care was taken not to overstimulate children by having large groups in too small a space. Where the outdoor play area was adjacent to the classroom, the classroom and the outdoor area could be used at the same time. Furnishings should be child-sized and moveable. Foster and Headley specified the precise distance, 7.5 inches, between the height of the chair seat and the kindergarten table (1966, p. 97).

Child care centre facilities were frequently in shared or rented space in church basements or other community facilities. Developed for child care settings in some provinces after the Second World War, licensing standards set minimum requirements for educator training, staff:child ratios, space and facilities and outdoor play space, eating, rest, and hygiene, in addition to including recommendations for educational and developmental programming. As explained by Boguslawski: 'Communities require licenses for restaurants, beauty parlors, barber shops, veterinarians, pet shops, etc., to assure minimal health protection. Where the young children of our community are concerned, such protection is vitally important because not only the health but the psychological development of the children is at stake' (1966, p. 11). Furnishings and equipment were required to be adequate but could be simple and in limited quantities. As noted in the recommendations of a Canadian report, 'a child can keep himself amused by very little' (Family Services Association of Edmonton, 1966, p. 15).

Curriculum

The program content, by which we mean what children were intended to learn, was organized as curricula in relation to the developmental characteristics of children (Imhoff, 1959). Knowing that children matured at different rates and that development could not be hastened, teachers should plan a range of learning experiences adapted to individual needs. Children played a role in shaping the curriculum in so far as they selected from available experiences.

Logan described four common ways to organize curricula in kindergarten and primary classrooms: according to separate subjects; in 'broad fields' or cutting across subjects; as 'problems of living' pertinent to the children; and through the 'activity curriculum' centred on children's interests (1960, p. 109). An activity curriculum was recommended for kindergarten, while an integrated, problem-based curriculum was recommended for the primary grades. The aim for primary grades was to organize learning experiences 'in some meaningful fashion,' which need not follow traditional subject areas as in later grades (p. 113). Table 1.2 lists typical topics used as curriculum organizers in kindergarten to Grade 3. As it shows, topics were repeated over several grades, and discrete subject area work was added in later grades.

In whatever way the curriculum was organized, there were common guidelines for determining a high-quality program. In particular, it should be 'varied, flexible, based on firsthand experience, free and creative, timed to children's readiness, and characterized by a rhythm of active and quiet periods. It offers continued opportunity for individual and group growth in functional knowledge, group rapport, and process skills. It fosters total personality growth' (Imhoff, 1959, p. 201). These program requirements meant that students were not to learn content by rote. Moreover, the historical bias against teaching reading in kindergarten was continued in the 1950s. Experience was the basis for reading, and rushing children to reading narrowed their experience. In the view of Rudolph and Cohen, 'the learning of symbols without enough general background of experience to comprehend what the

Table 1.2. Typical Topics Used as Curriculum Organizers, Kindergarten to Grade 3

Kindergarten	Grade 1	Grade 2	Grade 3
Airplanes	A grocery store	Our community	Living in our community
Boats	Family life at school	Our neighbour-hood	Living in contrasting cultures
A toy shop	Our school	Transportation	Discovering ways to meet basic needs for food, shelter, clothing
Caring for pets	Community helpers	Communication	How our community began and grew
Creative dramatization	The neighbour-hood	Food production	Ways of communicating
Birthday parties	Transportation	The farm	Methods of transportation
Holidays	The farm	The dairy	Life in a primitive community
Gardening	Safety	The post office	Children in other lands
Living together at home	Healthful living	Pets	The grocery store
Our playhouse	Our pets	Health and safety	The school bank
Mother hen and chicks	Animals, homes	Planting seeds	The city hall
The zoo	How plants and animals live	Weather	The post office
The circus	The seasons	People who help us	A truck-farm neighbour-hood
The train	Puppet shows	Numbers	How nature works for us
The rhythm band	Our flower garden	Spelling	Indian life
Trips to the park	Indians	How animals live in winter	Why air and water are important
Writing a letter	Our circus	The policeman	Arithmetic
Reading readiness	A toy shop	The janitor	Cursive writing
Writing readiness	Reading experience	A beehive	Language and spelling
Number readiness	Charts	The market	Music and art
Rhythms	Numbers	The store	Reading
Thrift	Writing	Writing	
Safety club	Rhythm	Dancing	
Outdoor guides	Dramatics	The fire station	
	Spelling	Reading	
	Sharing	Indians	

Source: Logan (1960, p. 115).

symbols stand for is so much wasted effort' (1964, p. 8). As one expert claimed at a Nursery Education Conference in Toronto in 1965, 'when Johnny is ready to put c, a, t, together to spell cat, he will do it on his own' (*Globe and Mail*, 1965, 19 May). The Alberta Department of Education *Kindergarten Manual* included a bolded warning: 'a formal reading program has no place in kindergarten. There are more important things to be accomplished at this level' (1963, p. 29). Priorities changed dramatically in Grade 1, where considerable time was devoted to reading and other literacy activities (as seen in Table 1.2).

Kindergarten, a film produced by the National Film Board of Canada, documents a day in an actual kindergarten in Montreal in 1962 (Daly & Côté, 1962). The film was made for television, and used to popularize the idea of public school kindergarten in Canada, as the historian Brian Low (2002) describes. The children are shown at play and in group activities in a program with few intellectual challenges. In his synopsis of the afternoon activities, Low conveys the tone of the program:

> The children return to the circle upon hearing their teacher strike a chord repeatedly on the classroom piano. Back in the circle, they discuss their fears, especially about fires and being stuck in elevators. At the end of the discussion, a black girl leads them all in a 'thank you prayer.' The children sing 'Taxi Song' and play 'block scramble.' They play with 'asbestos clay,' and they settle down to peruse special children's newspapers. One happy boy wears a bow tie; a girl who has newly emigrated from France is in tears because she cannot understand what is being said. During free time the children play house. Girls are observed playing with dolls and toy irons; boys are filmed playing in rocking chairs and talking on toy telephones. One girl is filmed pulling boys into a playhouse. 'Little Myrtle has been known to have six husbands at any one time,' the narrator remarks. (pp. 107–108)

Day care had a 'daily living curriculum' and a general concern for children's physical care, which helped structure the overall program. Boguslawski noted that in day care, learning integrated these various concerns: 'Because the child's education goes on all day, every day, it is a misnomer to designate one part of the daily activities as the "educational program"' (1966, p. 58).

Expert knowledge regarding educational and developmental programming in child care drew heavily on ideas from nursery and kindergarten education. This borrowing was strategic and a way to legitimize day care as 'good for children' (Rose, 1999). It was also advantageous for the pre-school movement. In the opinion of a Toronto social worker, when wartime child care began, 'the nursery school turned to day care to meet its goals' (Touzel, 1992). Ethel Beer (1940), writing about pre-school education programming in child care, bemoaned the lack of child care specialists from within the field itself: 'The potentiality of the day nursery is great if it will establish its own standards. To-day its weakness is that it has to go out of its own ranks for leadership to determine its policies. This is because the few authorities there are hide under other professions' (p. 150). She then urged that 'the day nursery must ferret them out and claim them' (ibid.).

As discussed by Foster, in her review of publications on day care by the Child Welfare League of America, Beer's ambitions for day care were not realized to any significant extent: 'child development specialists long hesitated to support even the concept of day care centres, and very little has been written about them' (1971, p. 57). An exception was Caldwell and Richmond's (1965) 'growth-inducing program for day care' or 'programmed day care' in Syracuse, New York, designed to improve the 'educability' (p. 135) of impoverished children from birth to the age of 3 years. In the 1990s, Caldwell (1991) called the approach 'educare.' In describing the Syracuse program's aims, Caldwell and Richmond used language hitherto reserved for experimental nursery schools: 'The programmed environment will attempt to develop powers of sensory and perceptual discrimination, an orientation toward activity, and the feeling of mastery and personal accomplishment which appear so essential for the development of a favorable self-concept' (p. 139). Activities were to include 'learning 'games' similar to classical laboratory studies of visual and auditory discrimination,' although 'the leitmotiv will be to permit development of the child's own natural curiosity and interest in his environment' (p. 140). The authors believed programmed day care 'need not resemble the toxic institutional environment' (p. 138). Instead, 'the basic hypothesis to be tested is that an appropriate environment can be programmed which will offset any developmental detriment associated with maternal separation and possibly add a degree of environmental enrichment frequently not available in families of limited social, economic, and cultural resources' (p. 141). They developed conditions for care in an institution that ameliorated the possible negative effect of the setting and improved on the home environment. The Syracuse program has been identified as 'playing a major role in the creation of Head Start' (Kirst, 2008; Mabie, 2001, p. 40).

Assessment

Although assessment of children's learning in kindergarten was more often called evaluation in the 1950s and 1960s, here we will use the modern-day term. Assessment was done in relation to evidence of progress towards meeting clearly defined pre-set goals and objectives (Lambert, 1960). Principles of assessment were that it was comprehensive, continuous, individualized, and done in cooperation with teachers, specialists, and parents (Lambert, 1960; Logan, 1960). Evaluation involved analysing information collected through observations, anecdotal records, checklists, interviews, personality and ability tests, sociometric measures (e.g., sociograms), and achievement tests. Achievement tests were ideally related to what children in individual classrooms had experienced and were teacher-constructed rather than standardized across school districts.

Foster and Headley (1966) recommended that kindergarten teachers keep samples of student work in 'cumulative record folders' as a means of determining changes over time. The folders could be used for communicating a child's progress with her or his parents. Parent conferences were recommended as a modern approach to home–school relations, and one means of reporting student progress to parents (Imhoff, 1959). Another such means was through report cards, although Lambert cautioned that they 'often served to alienate' parents (1960, p. 261). The Association for Childhood Education International (ACEI) recommended that teachers use a variety of methods including parent conferences and 'modified report cards' with broad objectives and narrative reports (cited in Lambert, 1960, p. 262). The practice was varied. The kindergarten report card used in the Grand Prairie School District in 1964–65 included space for narrative comments concerning physical, social, emotional, and intellectual development with no set objectives (personal collection). The report card used in Regina public schools that is summarized in Table 1.3 evaluated 'Habits and Attitudes' and 'Abilities.' In a modification of the report card viewed by the authors, the teacher rated 'Abilities' as 'satisfactory,' 'unsatisfactory,' or 'improving.'

Evaluations reporting grades only were inconsistent with a maturationist view in which each child 'begins at a different point and has a different potential for growth' (Lambert, 1960, p. 263). This view influenced ideas concerning student promotion and retention. Hymes (1955) noted that 'many wise schools have no failure [student retention] in their first three grades' because children mature at different

Table 1.3. Regina Public Schools Kindergarten Progress Report, 1963–1964

Habits and Attitudes	Abilities
The following lists show certain habits, attitudes, and abilities desirable for good citizenship and conducive to the child's development	In our Kindergartens we cover a definite program in Language, Number Work, Reading Readiness, and Handwork. Your child's capabilities will be commented upon in the remarks below as well as some observations on his habits and attitudes.
Enjoys group play	Language (expresses ideas well; speaks distinctly)
Is careful of property	Number Work
Is self-reliant	Reading Readiness
Is willing to share with others	Special Abilities
Obeys cheerfully and promptly	
Is attentive	
Has good work habits	
Is courteous	
Has self-control	
Makes an effort to improve	
Observes the Health Rules	

Larry Prochner, personal archive.

rates (p. 130). Children enter Grade 1 at different levels of maturity, and they cannot all reach the same point by the end of the year. If teachers make demands for more complex thinking, the differences will be even greater, leading Lambert to comment that 'children become more unlike rather than alike with good teaching' (p. 370). Research discouraged retention as it was thought to be ineffective in terms of a student's eventual academic achievement and had the potential to lead to behavioural problems (Kline & Brareson, 1929; Witty & Wilkins, 1948).

Children's physical development was the focus of assessment in child care, which was undertaken by visiting physicians, dentists, and public health nurses. With young children gathered together in institutions, opportunities for early developmental assessment were opened such that, where anomalies were identified, interventions could be made before 'potentially serious deviations' become 'internalized or fixed' (Family Services Association of Edmonton, 1966, p. 6). Child care teachers used record keeping to aid planning and as a means of communicating information about a child's day to parents. Information for planning was drawn from admission interviews with parents and child observations were recorded in 'on the spot notes' (Child Welfare League of America, 1966, p. 13). Records also included 'family history, progress regarding the child's adjustment, relationship with other children and teachers, specific procedures for the child's special needs and up to date entries regarding the child's current behavior' (Family Services Association of Edmonton, 1966, p. 19). Child care was also a context for remedial work with parents, and social workers offered counselling, casework services, and parent education groups for adult family members.

Diversity

Cultural diversity was downplayed in the period under review: assimilation was believed to be good for everyone, and schools offered possibilities for socializing newcomers according to Anglo-Canadian norms (see the chapter by Pacini-Ketchabaw & Bernhard in this volume). However, it was believed that educating all children was a social responsibility in a democratic society, and particular attention was paid to children with special learning needs, who were classed as 'exceptional children' in contrast to 'typical children' (Lambert, 1960, p. 68). In some cases, depending in part on the type of special need, exceptional children spent a portion of the day in a specialized teaching room, with their remaining time in a regular classroom. This was termed 'partial segregation' and was recommended for children with some types of visual impairments. 'Slow learners' (Logan, 1960) could be placed in either a special facility or a regular classroom. If the latter option was chosen, repeating kindergarten was recommended. Teachers in regular classrooms were advised to adjust their teaching strategies when working with exceptional children, for example, to give 'praise for work that shows any indication of worth' (p. 390).

Some special needs were considered pervasive, affecting all children to some extent; thus, for example, speech pathologists attended to children in regular schools to deal with speech defects. Teachers were responsible for early identification of special needs, because 'unless they are identified early, the disability may grow' and impair the child's education (Lambert, 1960, p. 85). Specialized and segregated education facilities existed for children with a range of other learning needs.

Similar developments took place in day nurseries, where children were available for testing and evaluation at a much younger age (Prochner, 1997). In some cases, children with special needs were integrated into regular day nursery care programs; in others, specialized crèche care was offered.

Renewal

A new wave of early childhood education and care programs developed in the early to mid-1960s, first in the United States and then in Canada, marking what was characterized by Shane as a 'renaissance of interest in the very young' (1969, p. 369). Factors involved in creating this interest were new or rediscovered ideas in psychology, the civil rights movement, and U.S. President Johnson's War on Poverty legislation that funded the Head Start pre-school program. In Canada, Liberal governments in the 1960s introduced universal medical insurance and a national pension plan, but no pre-schools. The Special Senate Committee on Poverty (Canada, 1969–1970) recommended a national child care program (but it was never developed) as an anti-poverty initiative (Finkel, 2006).

In the same period, international agencies were concerned for the well-being of children in the developing world: the United Nations adopted the Declaration of the Rights of the Child in 1959, and declared the 1960s the Decade of Development. In 1963, the United Nations International Children's Fund (UNICEF) released its landmark report, *Children of the Developing Countries*, which emphasized a whole child approach through health, nutrition, and educational programs to protecting vulnerable children and preparing them for the future. In the 1950s, UNICEF began using schools as community hubs for services supporting child health, such as feeding and vaccination programs (Jones, 2004). There was, however, little emphasis in international development work on pre-school programs, although day care was promoted as a support for working mothers and a means of child protection (UNICEF, 1963).

The renewed interest in the very young was matched by a shift in the image of the child. In his book *Intelligence and Experience*, psychologist Joseph McVicker Hunt (1961) questioned the relevance of the maturationist view of development – or standing back and waiting for development to happen (Weber, 1970, p. 13) – and proposed instead that experience played the greater role. In his view, all development, including intellectual development, was influenced by experience.

Hunt drew on Jean Piaget's research, which up to this point had been unpopular with North American psychologists due to its clinical methodology and U.S. psychology's focus on learning theory (Beatty, 2009). Piaget had maintained for decades that children created ideas about how the world works through their active exploration with people and the physical world (Piaget, 1952). In Hunt's words, 'It is relatively clear that experience, defined as the organism's encounters with his environment, is continually building into the developing human organism a hierarchy of operations for processing information and for coping with circumstances' (1961, p. 247). For Hunt, attention to the match between a child's existing thinking and new challenges presented by the environment was a key to learning. If the match was perfect, little learning would occur; if the divide between them was too wide, the child might become frustrated.

Pre-school as a Strategy for Reducing Poverty

Other psychologists drew attention to the role of experience in development (Bloom, 1964), further nudging the pendulum's swing from nature to nurture. A similar proposition was applied to social problems, such as poverty, that were once believed to have genetic roots. The American Civil Rights Movement sought equal opportunity for those who were historically oppressed. Government responded with poverty reduction strategies that sought to disrupt generational poverty by increasing children's educational opportunities and other initiatives. One result was Project Head Start established in the United States in 1965 (at the time it was popularly called Operation Head Start). This was accompanied by a number of other intervention programs for young children considered 'culturally disadvantaged' due to poverty. Programs for children with poverty as a risk condition existed from the nineteenth century and focused mainly on preparation for school and imparting Anglo-Canadian values to new immigrants (Prochner, 2009). Later programs aimed to increase IQ as well as to introduce children to the expectations of the school system and 'middle class values' (Palmer, 1966, p. 2).

In 1963, a group of Canadian educational leaders toured intervention programs for poor children in sixteen cities in the United States with a grant from the Ford Foundation. The Ford Foundation's involvement in pre-school education and its role in stimulating the Head Start initiative are described in detail by Vinovskis (2005). The aim of the study tour was to learn from the experience in order to introduce similar programs in Canada. Many of the U.S. programs they visited included a nursery school component. The aims of a Baltimore pre-school were typical: 'to accelerate the achievement of children who are limited in their development by environmental factors, to increase parental understanding, and to mobilize community resources to assist children and adults in depressed areas' (Quick, 1964, p. 83). How to achieve such aims, however, was not clear. Although, in time, a variety of program models were developed and tested, initial planning was haphazard. As the historian Alice O'Connor describes, 'from its inception . . . Head Start had violated almost every principle of rational planning and systematic decision making associated with systems analysis' (2002, p. 187).

Project Head Start was announced in the United States in January 1965 (Vinovskis, 2005). Canadian nursery school teachers learned details about the program later that year at a conference in Toronto organized by the Nursery Education Association of Ontario and the U.S.-based Midwestern Association for Nursery Education. A newspaper report on the conference noted that similar government-sponsored programs were not available in Canada and that 'several Canadian delegates expressed bitterness about the dearth of municipal nursery care' (*Globe and Mail*, 1965, 10 May). A report in the *Globe and Mail* during Head Start's first summer suggested that 'it would be surprising if a similar project did not shortly find its way into the Canadian anti-poverty program of the Pearson Government' (MacDonald, 1965, p. 7). Although no nationwide program emerged, Canadians were not content to watch these initiatives across the border, and in some cases, provincial governments filled the gap.

Ontario Education Minister William Davis, speaking in the Provincial Legislature in June 1965, stated, 'Early training is particularly important for poor or deprived children, such as those in rundown urban areas and some Indian and Eskimo communities' (quoted in *Globe and Mail*, 1965, 3 June); American Indian Head Start was part of the original Head Start Initiative in 1965. In November, Davis announced the creation of an 'education, economic and social centre' as a pilot project located in Moosonee for First Nations families (*Globe and Mail*, 1965, 23 Nov.). When the centre opened in 1967, it included a nursery school in which children would be taught English and prepared for Grade 1. In 1966, the Ontario government begun funding pre-schools on reserves, and the importance of 'reserve nursery schools' was highlighted in a report on education prepared for the federal Department of Indian

Affairs (Hawthorn, 1967; Lowe, 2000). Nursery schools were described as an essential head start for First Nations children in the same way as for African-American children in the United States, without which school success was threatened: 'The Indian child is not ready to use the tools of the school until he familiarizes himself with them, and while he is engaged in this task, his White peers are learning skills such as reading and writing' (Hawthorn, 1967, p. 148).

Government financial support did not mean that projects always followed government guidelines. A spirit of resistance was evident in the Inglewood Community Pre-School Pilot Project, an experimental pre-school in inner-city Calgary funded by the Department of Education in Alberta in 1970 (Alberta Department of Education, Inglewood Community Association & Educorps, 1971). The Department's aim was to compare community pre-school programs with those operated by local school districts (de Nance, 2009). Guidelines for proposals specified that the pre-schools should '(1) select disadvantaged children, (2) diagnose their disadvantages, [and] (3) design a program to change the children "through personal development . . . to enable each child to adapt successfully to . . . elementary school life"' (quoted in Alberta Department of Education et al., 1971, p. 4). Early on, the project's organizers decided that they 'felt free to ignore the demand that their proposal "must be governed by the government's guidelines," (assumptions),' in particular, the notion that problems resided within the child. They reasoned that among the range of factors, including 'the child, the home and parents, the community, and the elementary school . . . [t]he child seemed the least problematic' (p. 5). The objective was 'the development of a pre-school environment, curriculum, and community participation system to the point where the Project and the community participants had arrived at a mutual understanding of shared goals' (p. 1). The project report noted that 'while the Project is innovative in its composite, there is not really anything new about the individual pieces that make it up' (p. 1). Inspiration for the children's program was eclectic, drawn from the Government of Ontario's Hall-Dennis Report (Provincial Committee on Aims and Objectives of Education in the Schools of Ontario, 1968), Head Start and experimental pre-schools in the United States, the British Infant School, and the ideas of psychoanalyst Susan Isaacs. The result was a pre-school that combined 'play theory with freedom of choice, freedom of movement and freedom of speech' (Alberta Department of Education et al., 1971, p. 1).

Some researchers believed compensatory pre-schools could not achieve their goals in the context of such a play-based educational program, and a number of alternatives developed including Bereiter and Englemann's (1966) Academically Oriented Preschool program. A conference on pre-school education organized by the Department of Applied Psychology at the recently opened Ontario Institute for Studies in Education showcased their work. As department chair David Brison explained in his introduction to the conference proceedings, 'preschool education provides an example of the application of psychological theory and methods to educational problems' (1968, p. 1). Although behavioural psychology had been influential in kindergarten and nursery education for decades, some researchers' bold assertions that traditional approaches were useless or even harmful caused a rift in the pre-school field. A reporter's interpretation of Bereiter and Englemann's (1966) approach in the *Globe and Mail* was typical: 'Disadvantaged children get plenty of the equivalent of finger-painting through playing in the mud (unlike most middle-class children) and plenty of freedom through being left alone while mother works. What disadvantaged children need, [Bereiter and Englemann] insist, is a no-nonsense diet of learning' (*Globe and Mail*, 1967, 18 March).

Another sector of education affected by the American Civil Rights Movement was special education. The concept of normalization – or normalized living for persons with disabilities – was a basis for de-institutionalization (Winzer, 2005). However, changes in education were slow, and special day schools and residential schools continued to be the usual placement for students with disabilities in the early to mid-1960s.

At the same time, schools were identified as playing a lead role in perpetuating social problems such as racial and class inequalities, problems Mayer called a 'scandal of modern education for slum children' (1964, p. 33). If experience was a key to development, the quality of experience was important. A new wave of reports on the international scene urged reform to increase the relevance of schooling (Coleman, 1966; Plowden, 1967) and address the 'crisis in the classroom' (Silberman, 1970). However, the renewed interest in early childhood education was not matched with new ideas concerning curriculum or pedagogy: Maria Montessori's (2004) method, for example, although neglected by mainstream education in the United States and Canada for fifty years, was dusted off and given new life in the 1960s. As Barbara Beatty explains, such prolonged experiments with ideas were due to the 'insulation and isolation of preschools from the norms of elementary and secondary education' (2009, p. 444).

In 1971, Bettye Caldwell challenged that while 'the [ECEC] field is being looked to as offering the most hopeful solution to many of our social problems associated with poverty and family disorganization,' within the field there was a vacuum of new ideas, an absence of philosophical thinking, and resistance to innovation (p. 251). Evelyn Weber, writing in 1970, called kindergarten 'the no-man's land of education today' (p. 2). There was a concern that early childhood education had lost its way, that the 'time has come to seek a new direction for kindergarten education' (Robison & Spodek, 1965, p. 1).

Child care was caught up in the rush of excitement and call for reform, although many of the programs initiated in the era were half-day school-readiness programs for poor children. Moreover, high-profile child development researchers focused attention on changing individual children rather than addressing social problems – the cause of consternation for the organizers of Calgary's Inglewood Community Pre-School. This trend in child development followed the more general course of what O'Connor calls 'poverty knowledge,' in which poverty is seen as a product of 'individual failings rather than structural inequality' (2002, p. 4). Burton White, head of the Preschool Project at Harvard, observed that 'the original concept behind the [U.S.] Government's project Head Start was that "something's wrong with these children at age 6. There was no appreciation of how early that something comes about"' (quoted in Pines, 1969, p. 12). Caldwell and Richmond, describing their experimental day care program at the State University of New York in Syracuse, suggested that of the three ways to improve school success for poor children – changing learning materials, changing teaching, or changing children – 'attempting to change the child himself in some way so as to make him more receptive to the whole learning process . . . is in many ways the most hopeful of all' (1965, p. 134).

Child Care as a Strategy for Labour Market Equity

In 1972, the Canadian government created the National Day-Care Information Centre within Health and Welfare Canada. The purpose of the Centre was to 'stimulate research on day care services for children and to promote development of standards in the day care field' (*Globe and Mail,* 1972, 2 Aug.). It was headed by social worker Howard Clifford, who had been director of Day Care Services for the City of Edmonton. Clifford (1973) noted what he believed to be new trends in thinking in Canadian child care: a heightened interest in day care as a service to women working outside the home; concerns over the impact of infant child care on development; and a move away from a 'one size fits all approach' through the provision of family-based care, sick child care, and care reflecting the cultural diversity of families. Although he may have been overly optimistic in his assessment of the changes, the 1960s had at least increased the attention paid to the potential for child care to support the needs of the labour market by enabling women's greater participation in it, mirroring international trends.

In 1960, a national conference on day care was organized by U.S. government agencies and held in Washington, DC. The aim was to 'call the country's attention to the potential for positive living that daycare services provide both now and in the future' with the focus on women's labour force participation (U.S. Department of Health, Education, and Welfare & U.S. Department of Labor, 1961, pp. 1–2). The conference signalled the beginning of a shift in attitude among leaders in day care, social work, and government regarding child care as a normal support for working mothers. It is notable that there was no mention in the report of 'educational or developmental programming' or any particular benefits for children. There were, however, concerns over the possible negative impact of child care on children's development. In contrast, the children's educational program was considered at a meeting on day care sponsored by the United Nations and World Health Organization in 1962. The delegates, who represented a mainly European perspective, stressed that child care must attend to more than children's physical needs, so that 'their minds are . . . fully exercised and in no danger of being warped by their stay in them' (World Health Organization, 1964, p. 7).

Canadian reports on child care in the 1960s drew upon this literature (Canadian Welfare Council, 1968), and a spate of local surveys highlighted the large gap between need and available services (e.g., Family Services Association of Edmonton, 1966; Hamilton Social Planning and Research Council, 1967; Social Planning Council of Calgary, 1967; Social Planning Council of Metropolitan Toronto, 1968). There was a change in awareness of the need for child care as a means to achieve gender equity, if not in its availability. Nevertheless, the critical judgment of mothers and their motivations for wanting child care remained, even among those speaking in their support. A report by Family Services Association of Edmonton noted: 'If the mother is working out of economic necessity, there does not seem to be much incidence of disturbance in the child's development, provided he receives adequate substitute care. When the mother works for material gain only, the effect on the child is more damaging and there is a higher incidence of disturbed children in families. This mother is working out of her own need, rather than the child's' (1966, p. 5). A more positive view was evident in submissions to the Royal Commission on the Status of Women in Canada in 1968. The majority of written submissions to the Commission on the topic of employment linked child care to employment equity for women (Timpson, 2001, p. 32). When the final report was released, it included a call for 'immediate action,' with the claim that 'the time is past when society can refuse to provide community child services in the hope of dissuading mothers from leaving their children and going to work' (Royal Commission on the Status of Women in Canada, 1970, p. 163).

This claim, too, was optimistic, and changes in support were incremental at best. In 1966, the federal government had introduced the Canada Assistance Plan, increasing federal transfers to the provincial and territorial social programs through cost-sharing programs to develop services designed to lessen, remove, or prevent the causes of poverty, child neglect, or dependence on public assistance (Friendly, 2000; Government of Canada, 1966). Although this policy boosted regional support for day care programs, federal reimbursement was available only through fee subsidization for low income families using regulated, non-profit child care services. During this period, regional governments enhanced child care regulations, but most provinces did not include pre-schools in their mandate, and did not include regulations for infant centre care. Other federal initiatives included the Local Initiatives Program in 1970, which supported the creation of additional day care centres. However, the number of licensed child care spaces remained inadequate, and the National Council of Welfare reported a continuing 'child care crisis' at the end of the 1980s (1988, p. 3).

Conclusion

The review of ECEC in the 1950s and 1960s reveals points of innovation, retrenchment, and renewal of policies and services. In the summary comments that follow, we note three general themes: the integration of services, the source of ideas, and school readiness.

Attention to integration of services was a characteristic of pre-school programs in the 1960s: health care, education, and social welfare professionals converged on young children and their families to moderate or eliminate the effects of poverty. As described by Frederick Elkin in his keynote address at the Canadian Conference on Day Care in 1971, 'when we think of community institutions, we also realize that one thing they are *not*, is independent' of one another (Canadian Council on Social Development, 1972, p. 10; original emphasis).

There was also integration of ideas across child care and kindergarten concerning the curriculum or the content of the program. Day care leaders emphasized the benefits of educational day care as applicable to all children, not only to those from deprived circumstances. Pre-school and kindergarten programs were implemented within day nurseries (Varga, 1997; Woitte, 2006). The shift in nomenclature to categorize pre-school child care staff as teachers was one outcome of this development. Some experts recommended avoiding the term *day care* altogether, preferring instead full-day pre-school centres 'because of the welfare stigma attached to the day care terminology' (Ryan, 1970, p. 64). Pre-school advocates succeeded in gaining public support for the conclusion that early education had been 'good for all' in earlier decades. By the 1950s and 1960s, there were rarely claims that part-day pre-school – offered in the context of nursery school or kindergarten – was harmful for children's development.

We see attention to educational and developmental programming in child care programs in current provincial early learning frameworks, provincial child care standards, and early childhood educator training programs. The implementation of full-day kindergarten in some jurisdictions provides a default child care service within an educational setting. The co-location of combinations of child care, pre-schools, and kindergarten, generally in schools, is becoming more common. In small communities or on reserves, the pre-school, day care services and/or Head Start–type programs are often located in health or community centres (see the chapter by Jessica Ball in this volume). An attempt to integrate care and educational services in an urban context is described by Janette Pelletier in this volume. Change is also evident in the shift of programs to education ministries from social services, child and family departments, and privately funded organizations.

The second theme was the source of influences on and ideas in ECEC in Canada. In the 1950s and 1960s, Canadian programs followed trends in the United States. As psychologist Thomas Ryan observed in 1970, with 'a few notable exceptions, research on the effects of altering the early experiences of young children is virtually non-existent in Canada' (p. 62). The view has expanded in the current situation to include Canadian research as well as interest in international models and approaches beyond the United States (see the chapter by Alan Pence and Veronica Pacini-Ketchabaw in this volume). There has also been attention to developing local, community-based approaches (Ball & Pence, 2006). Consideration of recent developments in Canada from an international perspective has led to reflection on how the nation measures up to international standards. Canada's poor performance on the UNICEF report card (UNICEF, 2008) is referred to in several chapters in this volume.

The third theme concerns the role of pre-school programs in preparing children for formal education, and what counts as preparation. Experts in the 1950s emphasized the value of pre-school for children's social adjustment. In the 1960s, school readiness for academic activities was considered imperative mainly for children deemed at-risk of school failure due to poverty or 'cultural deprivation.' In recent years, kindergarten especially but also other pre-school programs have increasingly adopted school readiness as a goal. Beth Graue (2009) observes that, as a result, pre-school and kindergarten programs have been 'recalibrated,' such that an 'increasing numbers of teachers say their students are not prepared for the rigors of kindergarten's new structure.' This trend has the potential to increase the gap between students, with elite nursery schools and kindergartens focusing on academic preparation and poverty pre-schools offering skill-based programs (Lubeck, 1985; Polakow, 2007).

In the 2000s, we see burgeoning interest in early childhood programs worldwide, not only as a social uplift for poor children, but for all, which Kirp has identified in the United States as a 'movement for universal preschool' (2007, p. 6). Kirp further points out that the movement is defined by the educational benefits of pre-kindergarten programs and that it has not resulted in additional government interest or support for child care. A similar situation exists in Canada: although kindergarten programs are now part of public schooling in all provinces and territories, there remain major issues concerning availability and affordability in the child care world.

References

Alberta Department of Education. (1963). *Kindergarten manual*. Edmonton: Author.

Alberta Department of Education, Inglewood Community Association, & Educorps. (1971). *The Inglewood Project.* Calgary: Inglewood Community Pre-School Pilot Project.

Alberta. Royal Commission on Education. (1959). *Report of the Royal Commission on Education in Alberta.* Edmonton: Queen's Printer.

Ball, J., & Pence, A. (2006). *Supporting Indigenous children's development: Community–university partnerships.* Vancouver: UBC Press.

Beatty, B. (2009). Transitory connections: The reception and rejection of Jean Piaget's psychology in the Nursery School Movement in the 1920s and 1930s. *History of Education Quarterly, 49,* 442–464.

Beer, E. (1940). Preschool education in the day nursery. *School and Society, 51,* 150.

Bereiter, C., & Englemann, S. (1966). *Teaching disadvantaged children in the preschool.* Englewood Cliffs, NJ: Prentice-Hall.

Blatz, W.E. (1944). *Understanding the young child.* London: University of London Press.

Blatz, W.E. (1962). *Understanding the young child.* London: University of London Press.

Blatz, W.E. (1966). *Human security: Some reflections.* Toronto: University of Toronto Press.

Bloom, B.S. (1964). *Stability and change in human characteristics.* New York: Wiley.

Boguslawski, D. Beers. (1966). *Guide for establishing and operating day care centres for young children.* Washington, DC: Child Welfare League of America.

Bowlby, J. (1953). *Child care and the growth of love.* London: Penguin.

Brison, D.W. (1968). Introduction. In D.W. Brison & J. Hill (Eds.), *Psychology and early childhood education: Papers presented at the OISE Conference on Preschool Education, 15–17 Nov., 1966* (pp. 1–4). Toronto: Ontario Institute for Studies in Education.

British Columbia. Royal Commission on Education. (1960). *Report of the Royal Commission on Education.* Victoria, BC: Queen's Printer.

Caldwell, B. (1971). On reformulating the concept of early childhood education – some whys needing wherefores. In R.H. Anderson & H.G. Shane (Eds.), *As the twig is bent: Readings in early childhood education* (pp. 251–260). Boston, MA: Houghton Mifflin.

Caldwell, B. (1991). Educare: New product, new future. *Journal of Developmental and Behavioral Pediatrics, 12,* 199–205.

Caldwell, B., & Richmond, J.B. (1965). Programmed day care for the very young child – a preliminary report. *Child Welfare, 44,* 134–142.

Canada. Senate of Canada. (1969–1970). *Proceedings of the Special Senate Committee on Poverty.* Ottawa: Queen's Printer.

Canadian Council on Social Development. (1972). *Proceedings, Canadian Conference on Day Care, 20–23 June 1971*. Ottawa. Ottawa: Author.

Canadian Welfare Council. (1968). *The day care of children in Canada*. Ottawa: Author.

Chafe, J.W. (1967). *An apple for the teacher: A centennial history of the Winnipeg School Division*. Winnipeg: Winnipeg School Division no. 1.

Child Welfare League of America. (1962). *Maternal deprivation*. New York: Author.

Child Welfare League of America. (1966). *A guide for teacher recording in day care centers*. New York: Author.

Clifford, H. (1973). *Current trends and issues in day care in Canada*. Paper presented at the Northwest Regional Conference of the Child Welfare League of America, Edmonton, 10–13 June 1973. ERIC Doc. No. ED 087551.

Coleman, J.S. (1966). *The Coleman Report: Equality of educational opportunity*. Washington, DC: National Centre for Educational Statistics.

Crawley Films Limited (Producer) & Crawley, J. (Director). (1951). *The terrible twos and trusting threes*. [Motion Picture]. Ottawa: National Film Board of Canada (NFB).

Crawley Films Limited (Producer) & Crawley, J. (Director). (1953). *The frustrating fours and fascinating fives*. [Motion Picture]. Ottawa: NFB.

Crawley Films Limited (Producer) & Crawley, J. (Director). (1954). *From sociable six to noisy nine*. [Motion Picture]. Ottawa: NFB.

Crawley Films Limited (Producer) & Crawley, J. (Director). (1956). *From ten to twelve*. [Motion Picture]. Ottawa: NFB.

Daly, T. (Producer) & Côté, G.L. (Director) (1962). *Kindergarten*. Ottawa: NFB. Retrieved from http://www.nfb.ca/film/Kindergarten.

Day Nursery Committee of the Toronto Welfare Council. (1953, 23 Oct.). *Day Nursery Committee minutes*, SC 40, Box 9, file 9, Toronto Welfare Council, City of Toronto Archives.

de Nance, J. (2009). *Kindergarten in Alberta*. Unpublished ms., University of Alberta.

Dewey, J. (1963). *Experience and education*. New York: Collier.

Evans, G. (1991). *In the national interest: A chronicle of the National Film Board of Canada from 1949 to 1989*. Toronto: University of Toronto Press.

Family Services Association of Edmonton. (1966). *Day Care Study*. Edmonton: Author.

Finkel, A. (2006). *Social policy and practice in Canada: A history*. Waterloo, ON: Wilfrid Laurier University Press.

Fletcher, M.I. (1958). *The adult and the nursery school child*. 2nd ed. Toronto: University of Toronto Press, 1974.

Foster, G.W. (1971). The Child Welfare League of America publications on day care. *Child Care Quarterly, 1,* 56–61.

Foster, J.C., & Headley, N.E. (1966). *Education in the kindergarten.* 4th ed. New York: American Book Co.

Foster, L.E. (1975). *A sociological analysis of the Royal Commission on Education in Alberta, 1957–1959.* Unpublished doctoral dissertation, University of Alberta.

Friendly, M. (2000). Child care as a social policy issue. In L. Prochner & N. Howe, *Early childhood care and education in Canada* (pp. 252–272). Vancouver: UBC Press.

Frum, B. (1965, 24 June). Citing cost of day care centres excuse to cover up prejudice, nursery director says. *Globe and Mail,* p. W4.

Gesell, A. (1940). *The first five years of life.* New York: Harper & Bros.

Gesell, A., & Ilg, F.L. (1946). *The child from five to ten.* New York: Harper & Bros.

Globe and Mail. (1956, 30 May). Metro will study. p. 5.

Globe and Mail. (1965, 20 Feb.). Boy's mother working as he is asphyxiated in West Toronto fire. p. 5.

Globe and Mail. (1965, 25 March). Jury recommends working mothers prove children cared for. p. W2.

Globe and Mail. (1965, 10 May). U.S. to provide classes for underprivileged child. p. 12.

Globe and Mail. (1965, 19 May). Teaching babies to read harmful to school work, instructors say. p. 12.

Globe and Mail. (1965, 3 June). School from 4 to 18 may be considered. p. 42.

Globe and Mail. (1965, 23 Nov.). A most hopeful experiment. p. 6.

Globe and Mail. (1967, 18 March). Junior kindergarten set for Metro boom. p. 41.

Globe and Mail. (1972, 2 Aug.). Information centre on day care planned. p. 10.

Government of Canada. (1966). *Canada Assistance Plan.* Ottawa: Author.

Graue, B. (2009). Reimagining kindergarten. *School Administrator, 66*(10), 10–15. Retrieved from http://www.aasa.org/SchoolAdministratorArticle.aspx?id=8450.

Hamilton Social Planning and Research Council. (1967). *Report on the provision of day nursery care in Hamilton.* Hamilton, ON: Author.

Hawthorn, H.B. (Ed.). (1967). *A survey of the contemporary Indians of Canada: Economic, political, education needs and policies.* (Part 2). Ottawa: Indian Affairs Branch.

Heffernan, H. (Ed.). (1959). *Guiding the young child: Kindergarten to grade three.* 2nd ed. Boston: D.C. Heath.

Hunt, J.M. (1961). *Intelligence and experience.* New York: Ronald Press Co.

Hymes, J.L. (1955). *A child development point of view.* Englewood Cliffs, NJ: Prentice-Hall.

Imhoff, M.M. (1959). *Early elementary education.* New York: Appleton-Century Crofts.

Jones, P.W. (2004). *The United Nations and education: Multilateralism, development and globalisation.* New York: Routledge/Falmer.

Kirp, D.L. (2007). *The sandbox investment: The preschool movement and kids-first politics.* Cambridge, MA: Harvard University Press.

Kirst, S. (2008, 4 Aug.). A founder recalls launch of Head Start. *The Post Standard* (Syracuse). Retrieved from http://www.syracuse.com.

Kline, V., & Brareson, E. (1929). Trial promotion versus failure. *Educational Research Bulletin, 8,* 6–11.

Lambert, H.M. (1960). *Early childhood education.* Boston, MA: Allyn & Bacon.

Landreth, C. (1958). *The psychology of childhood.* New York: Alfred A. Knopf.

Logan, L.M. (1960). *Teaching the young child: Methods of preschool and primary education.* Boston, MA: Houghton Mifflin.

Low, B.J. (2002). *NFB kids: Portrayals of children by the National Film Board of Canada, 1939–89.* Waterloo, ON: Wilfrid Laurier University Press.

Lowe, E. (2000). Child care heritage: Interviews with pioneers. *Interaction, 14*(2), 33–36.

Lubeck, S. (1985). *Sandbox society: Early childhood education in black and white America.* Philadelphia, PA: Falmer.

Mabie, G.E. (2001). A life with young learners: An interview with Bettye M. Caldwell. *Educational Forum, 66*(1), 40–49.

MacDonald, B. (1965, July 26). An education for the deprived. *Globe and Mail,* p. 7.

Manitoba. Royal Commission on Education. (1959). *Report of the Royal Commission on Education.* Winnipeg: Queen's Printer.

Mayer, M. (1964). Schools, slums, and Montessori. *Commentary, 37*(6), 33–39.

Millichamp, D.A. (1974). Preschool teaching – An historical perspective [Epilogue]. In M.I. Fletcher, *The adult and the nursery school child* (2nd ed.) (pp. 77–92). Toronto: University of Toronto Press.

Montessori, M. (2004). *The Montessori method: The origins of and education innovation: Including an abridged and annotated edition of Maria Montessori's The Montessori method,* G.L. Gutek (Ed.). Lanham, MD: Rowman & Littlefield.

National Council of Welfare. (1988). *Child care: A better alternative.* Ottawa: Ministry of Supply and Services Canada.

Neatby, H. (1953). *So little for the mind.* Toronto: Clarke Irwin.

New York Times. (1944, 12 July). Group day care of infants is hit. p. 16.

O'Connor, A. (2002). *Poverty knowledge: Social science, social policy, and the poor in twentieth-century U.S. history*. Princeton, NJ: Princeton University Press.

O'Donnell, S. (2010, 15 March). Capilano's fortunes have seen boom, bust. *Edmonton Journal*, p. A7.

Ontario. Royal Commission on Education. (1951). *Report of the Royal Commission on Education in Ontario, 1950*. Toronto: B. Johnston, Printer to the King.

Owram, D. (1996). *Born at the right time: A history of the baby boom in Canada*. Toronto: University of Toronto Press.

Palmer, J.A. (1966). *The effects of junior kindergarten on achievement: The first five years*. Toronto: Research Department, Board of Education for the City of Toronto.

Piaget, J. (1952). *The origins of intelligence in children*. New York: International Universities Press.

Pickett, L.H., & Boren, D. (1923). *Early childhood education*. Yonkers-on-Hudson, NY: World Book Co.

Pines, M. (1969, July 7). Researchers find growth period before 4 most important. *Globe and Mail*, p. 12.

Plowden, B. (1967). *The Plowden Report (1967): Children and their primary schools*. London: Her Majesty's Stationery Office.

Polakow, V. (2007). *Who cares for our children? The child care crisis in the other America*. New York: Teachers College Press.

Prentice, S. (1989). Workers, mothers, reds: Toronto's postwar daycare fight. *Studies in Political Economy: A Socialist Review, 30*, 115–141.

Prochner, L. (1996). 'Share their care Mrs Warworker': Wartime day nurseries in Ontario and Quebec, 1942–1945. *Canadian Journal of Research in Early Childhood Education, 5*(1), 115–126.

Prochner, L. (1997). The development of the Day Treatment Centre for Emotionally Disturbed Children at the West End Crèche, Toronto. *Canadian Bulletin of Medical History, 14*, 1–25.

Prochner, L. (2000). A history of early education and child care in Canada, 1820–1966. In L. Prochner & N. Howe (Eds.), *Early childhood care and education in Canada* (pp. 11–65). Vancouver: UBC Press.

Prochner, L. (2009). *A history of early childhood education in Canada, Australia, and New Zealand*. Vancouver: UBC Press.

Provincial Committee on Aims and Objectives of Education in the Schools of Ontario. (1968). *Living and learning*. Toronto: Publications Office, Department of Education.

Quebec. Royal Commission of Inquiry on Education. (1966). *Report of the Royal Commission of Inquiry on Education in the Province of Quebec*. Quebec: Government Printer.

Quick, E.J. (1964). *New opportunities for the culturally disadvantaged.* Toronto: Canadian Education Association.

Robison, H.F., & Spodek, B. (1965). *New directions in the kindergarten.* New York: Teachers College Press.

Rose, E. (1999). *A mother's job: The history of day care, 1890–1960.* New York: Oxford University Press.

Royal Commission on the Status of Women in Canada. (1970). *Report of the Royal Commission on the Status of Women in Canada.* Ottawa: Information Canada.

Rudolph, M., & Cohen, D.H. (1964). *Kindergarten: A year of learning.* New York: Meridith.

Ryan, K. (1942). Share their care, Mrs War Worker, with your able and willing helper, the day nursery. *Canadian Home Journal, 39*(16), 44–46.

Ryan, T. (1970). Poverty and young children: A brief submitted to the Special Senate Committee on Poverty Canada. In Senate of Canada, *Proceedings of the Special Senate Committee on Poverty,* no. 21 (pp. 21.25–21.26). Ottawa: Queen's Printer.

Shane, H.G. (1969). The renaissance of early childhood education. *Phi Delta Kappan, 50*(7), 369, 412–413.

Silberman, C.E. (1970). *Crisis in the classroom: The remaking of American education.* New York: Random House.

Silver, H. (1965). *The concept of popular education: A study of ideas and social movements in the early nineteenth century.* London: MacGibbon & Kee.

Social Planning Council of Calgary. (1967). *Day care study: The present pattern of day care in Calgary.* Calgary: Author.

Social Planning Council of Metropolitan Toronto, Committee on Day Care of Children. (1968). *Day care for children in Metropolitan Toronto.* Toronto: Author.

Spitz, R. (1949). The effects of institution residence (*Hospitalisme*): An inquiry into the genesis of psychopathic states in early childhood. *Revue Française de Psychanalyse, 13,* 397–425.

Spock, B. (1946). *The common sense book of baby and child care.* New York: Duell, Sloan, & Pearce.

Spock, B. (1949). The Child Health Institute in Rochester Minnesota. *American Journal of Public Health, 39,* 854–857.

Stearns, P. (2003). *Anxious parents: A history of modern childrearing in America.* New York: New York University Press.

Sutherland, N. (1997). *Growing up: Childhood in English Canada from the Great War to the age of television.* Toronto: University of Toronto Press.

Timpson, A.M. (2001). *Driven apart: Women's employment equality and child care in Canadian public policy.* Vancouver: UBC Press.

Touzel, B. (1992, 23 March). Interview by L. Prochner, Toronto.

United Nations Children's Fund (UNICEF). (1963). *Children of the developing countries: A report.* Cleveland, OH: World Publishing Co.

United Nations Children's Fund (UNICEF). (2008). *The child care transition: A league table of early childhood education and care in economically advanced countries.* Innocenti Report Card, 8. Florence, Italy: Innocenti Research Centre.

United Nations Educational, Scientific and Cultural Organization (UNESCO). (1953). *Mental hygiene in the nursery school.* Paris: Author.

University of Chicago. (1948). *Report of the directed self survey, Winnipeg public schools.* Chicago, IL: Department of Education, Committee on Field Services, University of Chicago.

U.S. Department of Health, Education, and Welfare & U.S. Department of Labor. (1961). *Day care services: Form and substance.* Washington, DC: U.S. Government Printing Office.

Varga, D. (1997). *Constructing the child: A history of Canadian day care.* Toronto: Lorimer.

Vinovskis, M.A. (2005). *The birth of Head Start: Preschool education policies in the Kennedy and Johnson administrations.* Chicago, IL: University of Chicago Press.

Weber, E. (1970). *Early childhood education: Perspectives on change.* Worthington, OH: Charles A. Jones.

Winzer, M.A. (2005). *Children with exceptionalities in Canadian classrooms.* 7th ed. Toronto: Prentice-Hall.

Witty, P., & Wilkins, L. (1948). Promotion and grouping policy for the elementary school. *American School Board Journal, 66,* 37–38.

Woitte, S.L. (2006). *Daycare kindergarten in Alberta: A case study.* Unpublished doctoral dissertation, University of Calgary.

World Health Organization. (1964). *Care of children in day care centres.* Geneva: Author.

2 Provision, Policy, and Politics in Early Childhood Education and Care in Canada

MARTHA FRIENDLY AND SUSAN PRENTICE

Political ideas and structures are key to understanding why and how early childhood education and care (ECEC) in Canada has developed the way it has, offering an explanation for why there has been so much resistance to policy change. This chapter addresses quality and access through the lens of provision, beginning with an overview of services using ten benchmarks developed by UNICEF's Innocenti Research Centre. We go on to examine ideological and structural factors that affect ECEC in Canada. To do this, we use regime theory to explore how ECEC is organized, financed, and delivered. Canada's privatized approach to financing child care, its marketized mixed economy of service provision, and divided approaches for early childhood education and child care are all consistent with the limited government approach to social programs that characterizes what are called *liberal welfare regimes*. We further examine how Canada's brand of federalism has encumbered the development of coherent and sustained policy approaches to ECEC concluding with an analysis of ECEC politics since 2000, especially as they are linked both to ideology and federalism. Politics are key, as they determine what ECEC provision is ultimately like 'on the ground' – whether, how, and what kind of ECEC is available for Canadian families and young children.

Provision: What We Have

In the beginning of the 2000s, Canada took part in an international study carried out by the Organization for Economic Co-operation and Development (OECD). This study provided the first comparison of our ECEC programs with those in other developed, affluent countries. The study included twenty OECD member countries that volunteered to be part of the research (see OECD, 2006). Four international experts assessed Canada using a set of protocols and questions as a common framework across countries for reviewing data; information from interviews with policy makers, service providers and advocates; and observations from visits to child care centres and kindergartens. The team's key conclusion was that Canada is considerably behind almost all other OECD countries in providing early childhood education and care programs (OECD, 2004).

The OECD Canada review confirmed what Canadian researchers, analysts, and advocates had long maintained: ECEC in Canada is a hodgepodge, a patchwork, unplanned, inadequate, and less than effective for children and families (see, e.g., Cooke et al., 1986; Child Care Advocacy Association of Canada, 2004; Friendly & Prentice, 2009). The OECD made fifteen broad recommendations covering all aspects of ECEC programs from national policy to pedagogy to financing to diversity. Recommendations were addressed to the federal and provincial governments and followed from the report's summary statement that 'national and provincial policy for the early education and care of young children in Canada is still in its initial stages' (OECD, 2004, p. 6).

Canada has fourteen separate jurisdictions (in addition to First Nations and municipal governments in Ontario) responsible for ECEC provision and policy – ten provinces, three territories, and the federal government. Each has multiple programs for child care, kindergarten, and other areas intended to meet an assortment of objectives including child development, women's equality, health promotion, poverty reduction, and supporting parents in the parenting role; there is no national policy, framework, or approach.

One characteristic of Canada's ECEC provision is that – unlike most countries with more developed ECEC programs – child care and kindergarten have been treated quite separately. Until very recently, child care and early childhood education (ECE) programs for 3- and 4-year-olds such as nursery schools were typically the responsibility of provincial/territorial social service departments, while education ministries took responsibility for kindergarten for children from 4 or 5 years of age. With the growing involvement of the education sector in early childhood programs Canada-wide (called 'the most important trend in [Canadian] ECEC'; Beach & Flanagan, 2010), this historical division appears to be shifting. While the shift to 'child care' and 'early childhood education' as an integrated or seamless program is still in the early stages in Canada, by 2010, six provinces/territories had situated child care and kindergarten within the same department – education – and six jurisdictions were offering full school-day kindergarten, at least for 5-year-olds.

Each province/territory has a statute shaping regulated child care (centre-based full-day child care, regulated family child care, school-aged child care, and, usually, nursery or pre-schools), regulations for operation of services, and a variety of funding arrangements. Provincial/territorial governments also have responsibility for public kindergarten that primarily operates part-time, usually 2.5 hours a day, every other day, or, at best, for a school-day for 5-year-olds under ministries of education. Generally, kindergarten programs covering 5-year-olds (and 4-year-olds in Ontario) are treated as a public responsibility while child care and ECEC for children younger than 5 years tend to be treated as private family responsibilities in that there is no obligation for governments to provide services or public financing.

The federal government's direct role in ECEC is restricted to programs for which the federal government assumes responsibility – Aboriginal people on-reserve, military families, and newcomers to Canada. In this capacity, the federal government provides and finances some ECEC programs for these special populations. Otherwise, the federal government's current role in early childhood education and care is restricted to limited financing through transfer payments to provinces and some funding to individual families (see chapter by Jessica Ball in this volume for an analysis of Aboriginal ECEC programs). For detailed descriptions and information about federal and provincial/territorial ECEC programs, see Beach et al. (2009).

Canadian national data show that participation in an ECEC program or extra-parental arrangement of some kind has become the norm for pre-school-aged children. According to Statistics Canada (2005), the proportion of children aged 6 months to 5 years who were in some form of extra-parental child care or ECEC increased significantly from the 1980s until at least 2004; during the same period more child care–using families shifted to child care centres and relative care from unregulated care.

Cleveland et al. (2008) found that nearly 80 per cent of pre-school-aged children with mothers who were employed or studying are in some form of non-parental child care (including unregulated family child care and ECEC including kindergarten) on a regular basis. Almost half of these children are in organized programs, such as regulated child care, nursery school, pre-school, or kindergarten. Kindergarten programs, which developed mostly during the four decades from the 1950s to the 1980s, are set up to provide broad (universal) coverage for age-eligible children. By the late 1990s, virtually all 5-year-olds and some 4-year-olds in most of Canada attended public kindergarten on a part-day basis. There are, however, no reliable, current data on whether kindergartens meet parents' needs for child care or whether or not they are high quality enough to be defined as early childhood education.

A national study that collected quality data in regulated child care centres and family child care homes in 1998 concluded that while child care centres generally offered 'physically safe environments that protect children's health and safety, staffed by warm, supportive adults,' only one-third of centres and regulated family child care homes were of high enough quality to 'support and encourage children's social, language and cognitive development.' Indeed, most regulated child care was at best mediocre in quality, and in about 7 per cent of centres was at such a low level of quality that the researchers believed it could have a negative impact on children's development (Goelman et al., 2001). Several other studies of child care quality carried out in Quebec, Toronto, and Atlantic Canada have produced largely similar results, but Canadian data on quality are quite limited (Cleveland et al., 2008; Japel, Tremblay, & Côté, 2005; Lyon & Canning, 1995).

Despite the ever-increasing rate of mothers' participation in the labour force (which has increased annually since the 1980s) and considerable research showing that the quality of ECEC programs is of key importance for child development, the establishment of ECEC programs that meet both children's and parents' needs has proceeded slowly. In 2008, many or most of the more than 70 per cent of Canada's pre-school-aged children with both parents or a single parent in the paid labour force were presumed to be in a child care arrangement with an unregulated family child care provider, in-home caregiver, or a relative, for at least part of their parents' working hours, often for all or the majority of their non-parental time (Friendly, 2008).

The OECD's analysis confirmed that neither Canada as a whole, nor the provinces and territories that have the jurisdictional responsibility, have developed ECEC systems (with the possible exception of Quebec). The international ECEC specialists who reviewed Canada observed multiple ECEC programs under disconnected administrations and rationales; their report remarked there was neither national policy nor financing, and provincial policy and financing were limited as well. Furthermore, neither the federal government nor the provinces had set out goals and objectives or financed programs in enough detail to deliver high quality or equitable access (OECD, 2004).

By and large, Canadian ECEC policy and funding arrangements are weak and ineffectual. ECEC programs are limited in number and coverage, and often precarious, operated by underfinanced community groups or by relatively small-time entrepreneurs. What this means for children and families is that there are few good ECEC options in most of Canada. While most mothers with young children are in the paid labour force, many or most children with working parents spend all day or a large part of their day in unregulated child care arrangements of unknown quality. Regulated child care is expensive, availability is insufficient, and the quality is usually too mediocre to be considered consistently educational or developmental. Parent fees are expected to cover most of the costs of child care programs, so regulated care is often inaccessible to poor, modest-, and middle-income families, most of whom do not qualify for Canada's ineffectual and antiquated fee subsidy systems. Kindergarten is separated from child care philosophically, administratively, and programmatically, and is generally (outside Ontario) not available to children under age 5 years.

International ECEC Benchmarks: How Canada's Provinces and Territories Fare

In the mid-2000s, UNICEF's Innocenti Research Centre (IRC), based in Florence, Italy, compared ECEC provision across twenty-five of the world's most affluent countries as part of a series of 'report cards' on key issues affecting children (UNICEF, 2008). The IRC report cards take a children's rights perspective, an orientation consistent with the United Nations Convention on the Rights of the Child (CRC). The ECEC report card, number eight in the series, provides an extensive analysis of the role of child care in modern life and draws on research from a variety of perspectives. Its centrepiece is a set of ten indicators or minimum benchmarks for ECEC provision designed to address the key policy issues of quality and access.

The IRC found that Canada was tied with Ireland as the lowest scoring of the twenty-five countries. Sweden met all ten benchmarks, followed by Iceland (at nine), while Denmark, Finland, France, and Norway all met eight benchmarks. Only Australia, Canada, and Ireland met fewer than three (UNICEF, 2008; Table 1 in the IRC report card shows each country's scores on the ten benchmarks). Canada met just one benchmark: Canada's score in the UNICEF league table was a composite across provinces, as are the scores of the other federated countries (i.e., United States, Australia, Germany, Switzerland, Austria, Spain) in which ECEC programs are determined by sub-national units such as provinces or states.

The following sections examine each of the UNICEF national benchmarks and criteria for achievement and then apply each indicator across Canada's provinces and territories. This analysis treats each province and territory as its own entity; note that the section uses provincial/territorial data from Beach et al. (2009) for almost all of the benchmarks, and other sources used are indicated. Overall, despite modest variations, Canada's jurisdictions are much more similar to than different from one another.

Benchmark 1: A Minimum Entitlement to Paid Parental Leave

UNICEF's criteria state (2008, p. 13): 'The minimum proposed standard is that, on the birth of a child, one parent be entitled to leave of at least a year (to include prenatal leave) at 50 per cent of salary (subject to upper and lower limits). For parents who are unemployed or self-employed, the income entitlement should not be less than the minimum wage or the level of social assistance. At least two weeks parental leave should be specifically reserved for fathers.'

Comment

In Canada, maternity and parental leave benefits (payments) are a federal responsibility, while leave provisions are determined by the provinces/territories. Canada met the payment and duration requirements, but failed to earn a point because designated father leave is not provided in most provinces. Table 2.1 provides an assessment of whether each province's leave provisions meet this benchmark. Although the provinces/territories generally meet the minimum duration and payment provisions, only Quebec meets the criterion of designated father leave.

Table 2.1. Canada's Provinces/Territories Regarding UNICEF Benchmark 1: Minimum Entitlement to Paid Parental Leave

Province/Territory	Achieved?	Comment
Newfoundland and Labrador	No	
Prince Edward Island	No	
Nova Scotia	No	
New Brunswick	No	
Quebec	Yes	Only province to provide designated father leave
Ontario	No	
Manitoba	No	
Saskatchewan	No	
Alberta	No	
British Columbia	No	
Northwest Territories	No	
Nunavut	No	
Yukon	No	

Sources: Statistics Canada (2010a, 2010b).

Benchmark 2: A National Plan with Priority for Disadvantaged Children

UNICEF's criteria state (2008, p. 13): 'All countries going through the child care transition should have undertaken extensive research and evolved a coherent national strategy to ensure that the benefits of early childhood education and care are fully available, especially to disadvantaged children. This dimension of early childhood services cannot currently be assessed and compared in a satisfactory way. Rather than omit such a critical factor, Benchmark 2 records, as a proxy measure, whether governments have at least drawn up a national plan for the organization and financing of early childhood services.'

Comment

Canada as a whole has no national strategy for the organization and financing of early childhood services – no national ECEC program, policy,

Table 2.2. Canada's Provinces/Territories Regarding UNICEF Benchmark 2:
Comprehensive Plans

Province/Territory	Achieved?	Comment
Newfoundland and Labrador	No	NL has said it will develop such a plan.
Prince Edward Island	No	PEI tabled a detailed provincial plan in 2010.
Nova Scotia	No	
New Brunswick	No	
Quebec	No	QC's relatively comprehensive plan, developed a decade ago, made considerable progress but then slowed down far short of meeting the goal of full access.
Ontario	No	ON is in the first stages of implementing a comprehensive plan but it is not in place nor has ON adopted the goal of full access except for 4- and 5-year-olds.
Manitoba	No	MB has adopted a 5-year planning cycle for child care but has not integrated care and education nor adopted the goal of full access.
Saskatchewan	No	
Alberta	No	
British Columbia	No	
Northwest Territories	No	
Nunavut	No	
Yukon	No	

Source: Beach et al. (2009).

or approach, so Canada did not achieve this benchmark. Table 2.2 provides an assessment of whether or not each province has, at the least, devised a provincial plan for the organization and financing of early childhood services and is making progress towards achieving the plan.

Benchmark 3: A Minimum Level of Child Care Provision for Children under 3 Years of Age

UNICEF's criteria state (2008, p. 13): 'The minimum proposed is that subsidized and regulated child care services should be available for at least 25 per cent of children 0–3 years.'

Table 2.3. Canada's Provinces/Territories Regarding UNICEF Benchmark 3:
Subsidized and Regulated Child Care for 25% of Children <3 Years of Age

Province/Territory	Achieved?	Comment
Newfoundland and Labrador	No	
Prince Edward Island	No	
Nova Scotia	No	
New Brunswick	No	
Quebec	?	QC may be the only province achieving this, considering availability of a mix of funded centres and family child care. Year-of-age data not available.
Ontario	No	
Manitoba	No	
Saskatchewan	No	
Alberta	No	
British Columbia	No	
Northwest Territories	No	
Nunavut	No	
Yukon	No	

Source: Beach et al. (2009).

Comment

Most Canadian provinces provide less than 25 per cent coverage for children aged 0 to 5 years (data for 0–3 years are not available, so can only be inferred); however, only Quebec and Manitoba fund virtually all regulated spaces, as shown in Table 2.3, so the benchmark of regulated and *subsidized* services is generally not met.

Benchmark 4: A Minimum Level of Access for 4-Year-Olds

UNICEF's criteria state (2008, p. 14): 'The minimum proposed is that at least 80 per cent of four-year-olds participate in publicly subsidized and accredited early education services for a minimum of 15 hours per week.'

Table 2.4. Canada's Provinces/Territories Regarding UNICEF Benchmark 4:
Participation of 80% of 4-Year-Olds in Funded Early Childhood Education

Province/Territory	Achieved?	Comment
Newfoundland and Labrador	No	
Prince Edward Island	No	
Nova Scotia	No	
New Brunswick	No	
Quebec	No	QC does not provide widespread 4-year-old kindergarten, and 0–4 child care centre coverage does not appear high enough to bring QC up to the indicator.
Ontario	Yes	ON is the only province to provide virtually universal access to 4-year-old kindergarten, mostly part-day but slated to become full school-day for all by 2014.
Manitoba	No	
Saskatchewan	No	
Alberta	No	
British Columbia	No	
Northwest Territories	No	
Nunavut	No	
Yukon	No	

Source: Beach et al. (2009).

Comment

Overall, Canada did not meet this benchmark. Table 2.4 assesses participation of 4-year-olds in at least part-day kindergarten or funded child care or nursery school. There are no data by year of age to determine what proportion of 4-year-olds are in regulated child care, so it is necessary to estimate. The benchmark stipulates 'publicly subsidized' early childhood services, an important component of accessibility. Most regulated child care in Canada, outside Quebec and perhaps Manitoba, does not meet this funding criterion.

Table 2.5. Canada's Provinces/Territories Regarding UNICEF Benchmark 5: Minimum Early Childhood Education Training Requirements (80% in Centres and Family Child Care Have at Least a Basic Course)

Province/Territory	Achieved?	Comment
Newfoundland and Labrador	Yes	One person PSE; others basic course
Prince Edward Island	No	
Nova Scotia	No	
New Brunswick	No	
Quebec	Yes, qualified	2/3 (66%) of centre staff required to have PSE
Ontario	No	
Manitoba	Yes, qualified	2/3 of centre staff required to have PSE; others basic course within one year
Saskatchewan	Yes	30% PSE; others basic course
Alberta	No	25% PSE; others basic course
British Columbia	Yes	Sole province to require PSE (one year) for all centre staff
Northwest Territories	No	
Nunavut	No	
Yukon	Yes	30% PSE; others basic course

Source: Beach et al. (2009).
PSE = post-secondary education.

Benchmark 5: A Minimum Level of Training for All Staff

UNICEF's criteria state (2008, p. 14): 'The minimum proposed is that at least 80 per cent of staff having significant contact with young children, including neighbourhood and home-based child carers, should have relevant training. As a minimum, all staff should complete an induction course. A move towards pay and working conditions in line with the wider teaching or social care professions should also be envisaged.'

Comment

Canada as a whole did not meet this benchmark, as shown by Table 2.5. Only British Columbia requires all staff to have post-secondary training (see chapter by Ellen Jacobs and Emmanuelle Adrien in this volume). Only a few provinces require a majority of staff in centres to have relevant (i.e., ECE or equivalent) early childhood training at a post-secondary level for children 0 to 6 years of age (and several have much lower requirements for school-aged children). Several provinces have regulations that require all centre staff to have a minimum course and others now require regulated family child care providers to have a minimum course (generally considered to be an 'induction course'). While Canada's ECEC training requirements are low by international standards, this is an area in which there has been improvement in recent years. Low wages and poor working conditions in child care, however, remain a key problem in all regions of Canada.

Benchmark 6: A Minimum Proportion of Staff with Higher Level Education and Training

UNICEF's criteria state (2008, p. 14): 'The minimum proposed is that at least 50 per cent of staff in early education centres supported and accredited by governmental agencies should have a minimum of three years tertiary education with a recognized qualification in early childhood studies or a related field.'

Comment

In the Canadian context, this benchmark is interpreted to refer to kindergartens ('early education centres') for 4- and 5-year-olds. While all provinces and territories require at least three years tertiary education for kindergarten teachers (essentially, a university degree) whether or not the teachers are required to have an early childhood qualification or equivalent is, at best, ambiguous, as shown in Table 2.6. Generally, an ECE background is not required for Canadian kindergarten teachers.

Benchmark 7: A Minimum Staff-to-Child Ratio

UNICEF's criteria state (2008, p. 14): 'The minimum proposed is that the ratio of pre-school children (four- to five-year-olds) to trained staff (educators and assistants) should not be greater than 15 to 1, and that group size should not exceed 24.'

Table 2.6. Canada's Provinces/Territories Regarding UNICEF Benchmark 6: Minimum 50% Teachers in Kindergartens Required to Have a University Degree in an Early Childhood–Related Field

Province/Territory	Achieved?	Comment
Newfoundland and Labrador	No	
Prince Edward Island	Yes	PEI kindergarten is shifting from child care centres to public kindergartens, and a university degree with an early childhood emphasis is envisioned.
Nova Scotia	No	
New Brunswick	No	
Quebec	No	
Ontario	Yes	ON is phasing in universal full-day early childhood programs for 4- and 5-year-olds, with one degreed teacher and one registered ECE per class.
Manitoba	No	
Saskatchewan	No	
Alberta	No	
British Columbia	No	
Northwest Territories	No	
Nunavut	No	
Yukon	No	

Source: Beach et al. (2009).

Comment

Canada did not meet this benchmark, which was interpreted here to apply to kindergarten-like ECEC programs, as in most countries most 4- and 5-year-olds are in kindergarten. Provinces/territories generally do not apply staff-to-child ratios in kindergarten legislation, although these are required by child care regulations. Where information is available about kindergarten class size, adult:child ratios appear to be poorer than recommended (see Table 2.7).

Table 2.7. Canada's Provinces/Territories Regarding UNICEF Benchmark 7: Minimum Staff–Child Ratio for 4- and 5-Year-Olds in Kindergarten Better than 15:1; Group Size Fewer than 25 Children

Province/Territory	Achieved?	Comment
Newfoundland and Labrador	No	
Prince Edward Island	No	
Nova Scotia	No	
New Brunswick	No	
Quebec	No	
Ontario	?	ON is bringing in full-day 4- and 5-year-old kindergarten programs; the adult:child average ratio is envisioned to more or less meet this criterion.
Manitoba	No	
Saskatchewan	No	
Alberta	No	
British Columbia	No	
Northwest Territories	No	
Nunavut	No	
Yukon	No	

Source: Beach et al. (2009).

Benchmark 8: A Minimum Level of Public Funding

UNICEF's criteria state (2008, p. 14): 'The suggested minimum is that the level of public spending on early childhood education and care (for children aged 0 to 6 years) should not be less than 1 per cent of Gross Domestic Product (GDP).'

Comment

This benchmark originates with the European Union's cross-national work and has come to be regarded as the international standard (European Commission Childcare Network, 1995). In Canada, public spending data for ECEC ought to include both regulated child care for

Table 2.8. Canada's Provinces/Territories Regarding UNICEF Benchmark 8: Minimum 1% of Provincial (Territorial) Domestic Product (PDP) Spent in Public Funding of Regulated Child Care and Kindergarten for Ages 0–6 Years

Province/Territory	Achieved?	Actual (%)
Newfoundland and Labrador	No	0.09
Prince Edward Island	No	0.16
Nova Scotia	No	0.14
New Brunswick	No	0.28
Quebec	No	0.70
Ontario	No	0.28
Manitoba	No	0.30
Saskatchewan	No	0.10
Alberta	No	0.07
British Columbia	No	0.16
Northwest Territories	No	0.16
Nunavut	No	0.22
Yukon	No	0.35

Source: Beach et al. (2009).

children aged 0 to 6 years and kindergarten, as these are separate programs, and Table 2.8 is calculated on that basis. Note that data are not always available to disentangle spending for children under and over 6 years of age, so the figures in the table generally include regulated school-aged child care for children 6 to 12 years of age. Notwithstanding this conservative assumption, Canada is far below the benchmark. Table 2.8 uses provincial/territorial figures as a percentage of provincial domestic product (PDP) to show that no province/territory meets this benchmark. In 2008, Canada as a whole spent less than 0.3 per cent of GDP on child care and kindergarten programs combined.

Benchmark 9: A Low Level of Child Poverty

UNICEF's criteria state (2008, p. 8): 'Specifically, a child poverty rate of less than 10 per cent. The definition of child poverty is that used by the OECD – the percentage of children growing up in families in

Table 2.9. Canada's Provinces/Territories Regarding UNICEF Benchmark 9: Less than 10% Children Aged 0–12 Years Living below the Low Income Cut-Off, 2006 Provinces/ Territories

Province/Territory	Achieved?	Actual (%)
Newfoundland and Labrador	No	16.7
Prince Edward Island	No	13.9
Nova Scotia	No	13.2
New Brunswick	No	16.7
Quebec	No	14.3
Ontario	No	17.1
Manitoba	No	20.1
Saskatchewan	No	23.7
Alberta	No	11.5
British Columbia	No	22.3
Northwest Territories	NA	NA
Nunavut	NA	NA
Yukon	NA	NA

Source: Beach et al. (2009).
NA = not available.

which income, adjusted for family size, is less than 50 per cent of median income.'

Comment

Table 2.9 shows the percentage of children living below Statistics Canada's low income cut-off (LICO) in 2006, a standard measure of children living in poverty that uses the concept of 'relative poverty' for ages 0 to 12 years (used because age breakdowns are not available in some provinces). Canada as a whole did not achieve this benchmark.

The UNICEF report card notes that it is important to consider ECEC programs in a wider policy context, as UNICEF did when it included a child poverty measure (Benchmark 9) and access to basic health care as a proxy for universality and access for low income children (Benchmark 10). UNICEF explained that its assessment package was 'supplemented by two further indicators designed to acknowledge and reflect wider social and economic factors critical to the efficacy of early childhood services' (UNICEF, 2008, p. 8).

Benchmark 10: Universal Outreach

UNICEF criteria state (2008, p. 8):

> To reinforce one of the central tenets of this report – that early childhood services should also be available to the children of disadvantaged families – this last benchmark attempts to measure and compare demonstrated national commitment to that ideal. As no direct measure is currently possible, the suggested proxy measure is the extent to which basic child health services have been made available to the most marginalized and difficult-to-reach families.
>
> Specifically, the benchmark of 'universal outreach' is considered to have been met if a country has fulfilled at least two of the following three requirements: (a) the rate of infant mortality is less than 4 per 1,000 live births, (b) the proportion of babies born with low birth weight (below 2,500 grams) is less than 6 per cent, and (c) the immunization rate for 12- to 23-month-olds (averaged over measles, polio and DPT3 vaccination) is higher than 95 per cent.

Comment

Canada as a whole failed to earn this point, because it met only one of the three requirements at the time of the report card's compilation. The 2004 low birth weight figure for Canada just barely met the criterion (less than 6% below 2,500 grams), but slipped in 2005 to 6 per cent. Canada's average immunization rate (measles, polio, and DPT3) of 92.3 per cent failed to meet the UNICEF benchmark of 95 per cent. The Canada-wide infant mortality rate in the 2008 UNICEF report (2004 data) of 5.3 deaths per 1,000 births also did not meet the minimum benchmark of fewer than 4.0 deaths per 1,000 births (it improved slightly to 5.1 in 2007). Table 2.10 provides provincial/territorial breakdowns for low birth rate and infant mortality (note that immunization rates are not available by province/territory).

Summary

In summary, Canada's early childhood situation at both national and provincial levels includes a list of concerns that have remained largely unchanged for more than twenty years and which fall far below international standards. High user fees exclude many children. Poor or

Table 2.10. Canada's Provinces/Territories Regarding UNICEF Benchmark 10: Low Birth Weight (Less than 2,500 g) and Infant Mortality, 2007

Province/Territory	Low birth weight (%)	Achieved?	Infant mortality (deaths per 1,000)	Achieved?
Newfoundland and Labrador	5.9	Yes	7.5	No
Prince Edward Island	5.4	Yes	5.0	No
Nova Scotia	6.3	No	3.3	Yes
New Brunswick	6.0	No	4.3	No
Quebec	5.6	Yes	4.5	No
Ontario	6.2	No	5.2	No
Manitoba	5.4	Yes	7.3	No
Saskatchewan	5.7	Yes	5.8	No
Alberta	6.6	No	6.0	No
British Columbia	5.6	Yes	4.0	Yes
Northwest Territories	3.7	Yes	4.1	No
Nunavut	8.4	No	15.1	No
Yukon	3.7	Yes	8.5	No

Sources: Statistics Canada (2010a, 2010b).

uninspired program quality and restrictive age or other eligibility criteria in kindergarten have failed to keep up with developments in knowledge about the importance of good learning environments in early childhood. Infant care, inclusive programs for children with special needs, and programs for Aboriginal, rural, and remote communities are in especially short supply. Compounding these problems, ECEC programs are often not scheduled to coincide with parents' work lives, although most mothers work outside the home.

Policy and Welfare Regime Ideology: Why Canada Is Not Sweden

Examining the ways in which advanced capitalist countries approach social policy reveals significant differences and commonalities between regimes. This approach originated in the late 1980s, with the work of Danish sociologist Gøsta Esping-Andersen, who identified three main approaches to social welfare. Esping-Andersen's (1990) approach offers a useful and explanatory typology of the 'three worlds of welfare' by finding common patterns in what are termed *conservative, liberal,* and *social democratic regimes.* Many researchers have used welfare regime theory to understand ECEC policy (see, e.g., Meyers & Gornick, 2003; Morgan, 2003; Turgeon, 2009; White, 2008; Wincott, 2006).

According to welfare regime theory, social policies help reinforce patterns of relations among and between individuals and families, the market, and the state. The small 'l' liberal regime type, found primarily in the main English-speaking countries – the United States, Australia, Britain, Ireland, and New Zealand; the small 'c' corporatist countries – Germany, France, Spain, Italy; and the social democratic welfare states – the Nordic countries of Sweden, Norway, Finland, and Denmark – constitute the three main regime types.

In this model, the conservative or corporatist welfare states are characterized by social insurance models and are based on a male breadwinner paradigm. In these countries, ECEC is likely to be oriented to an education approach, as it indeed is in France, Spain, Austria, and other similar countries, with coverage to meet working mothers' needs for child care a possible area of weakness. The corporatist countries can be seen as 'woman-unfriendly,' tending to the patriarchal but paradoxically – as can be seen from the UNICEF report card in the previous section – generally providing better quality, more accessible ECEC programs than the liberal regimes.

Liberal (or liberal democratic) welfare states are likely to be inclined to resist what is defined as 'undue' intervention in family life, as well as significant interference in the private sector. In liberal regimes, like Canada, there is likely to be strong commitment to the privacy of the family and the primacy of the marketplace. This means that rather than being planned, organized, and delivered by government, social programs tend to be privatized, relegated to the marketplace, and employing individualized financing schemes. Consequently, liberal welfare regimes generally tend to have low levels of social provision.

Residualism is another liberal element. Liberal welfare states tend to emphasize the targeting of social programs to low-income families along with eligibility testing rather than universal entitlements. In liberal welfare regimes such as Canada, the United States, Australia, and the United Kingdom, users of a social program are often stigmatized, and services are seen as being mainly for the poor or disadvantaged rather than an entitlement for citizens (Friendly & Prentice, 2009). Liberal welfare states are also likely to be 'woman-unfriendly' – failing to actively promote work/family balance and doing little to support child care (Hernes, 1987). Thus, liberal states have been more likely to promote traditional sexual division of paid and unpaid labour, although in practice, most countries, regardless of their welfare regime type, now have much higher rates of women's labour force participation than they did even a decade ago.

Around the world, the liberal regimes – Canada, the United States, the United Kingdom, Australia, New Zealand, and Ireland – all share a common approach to child care that includes a preference for targeted, rather than universal services as well as fragmentation of early childhood education and care. In all these countries, child care funding and delivery is privatized. ECEC services are characterized by high parent fees, and public dollars are primarily directed through individualized forms such as tax breaks, parent cheques, or fee subsidies based on family eligibility rather than as funding to a system. From the perspective of governance, or ownership of child care programs, liberal democratic countries primarily rely on private ownership of organized child care, usually on a mixture (sometimes called a 'mixed economy of child care') of private non-profit and private for-profit programs with their track record of dubious quality (Cleveland et al., 2007) and considerable dependence on unregulated family child care or in-own-home care. Not surprisingly, none of the liberal welfare states achieve high levels of quality or access to child care.

While child care in liberal welfare states is mostly market driven and private, public, universal systems of kindergarten under education departments coexist with child care as disconnected, parallel programs. As Meyers and Gornick (2003) describe, public education tends to be valued in the liberal countries, consistent with what some consider to be a dominant conviction (in the United States, at least) that education has the capacity to be the great social leveller. This conviction has been challenged by such commentators as American education expert Christopher Jencks and his colleagues (1972). In this approach, while early education is primarily publicly funded and publicly delivered, child care tends to be relegated to the stigmatized welfare sector, a pattern into which Canada fits quite neatly, with our tradition of public kindergarten and private child care delivery (Prentice, 2006).

In contrast, the social democratic states do an excellent job of supporting families, supporting women's equality, promoting children's rights, and providing social welfare overall. It is no surprise that in UNICEF's Innocenti Research Centre report on ECEC, the Nordic countries were all (together with France and Iceland) at the very top of the league table, with Sweden the only country to meet all ten indicators (UNICEF, 2008, see Table 1).

Canadian Federalism

Canada's status as a federation has considerable explanatory value vis-à-vis the state of Canadian ECEC policy and programs. A federation is a system of government in which power and authority are divided between the national government (in this case, the federal government, or 'Ottawa') and sub-national units (the provinces and territories). However, countries that operate as federations (e.g., the United States, Australia, Brazil, Switzerland, Austria, Germany, Switzerland, Belgium, and Argentina) differ from one another in multiple ways. One of the most important differences is the relative strength of the national and sub-national governments, that is, the degree to which they are centralized or decentralized, and which responsibilities are national or sub-national. Among federations, Canada is considered to be quite decentralized (though not as decentralized as Switzerland, for example).

The Constitution Act of 1867 established a number of federal powers (public debt, the Criminal Code, regulation of trade and commerce, taxation, and national defence) and some provincial powers as well (including hospitals, justice, marriage, and corporate affairs). The Act has a section on education, which is perhaps, the most jealously guarded provincial responsibility. Although education tends to be a sub-national responsibility in federations, it is noteworthy that Canada is the sole federation that has no national department of education or any federal involvement in education whatsoever (Wallner, 2010).

Social programs are generally assumed to be provincial responsibilities, although some programs providing cash or payments to individual Canadians – pensions, unemployment insurance, and the Universal Child Care Benefit (UCCB) introduced by the Conservatives in 2006, for example, are exceptions. While responsibility for individual transfers for social purposes is somewhat ambiguous, development and provision of social or health care services are considered to be unambiguously a provincial responsibility.

Friendly and White describe this situation: 'Under the Constitution Act, 1867, substantive jurisdictional authority over social policies such as child care has been deemed to lie with provincial governments. Child care, like other social policy matters, is not one of the enumerated heads of federal jurisdiction . . . of the Constitution Act. As with other social policy matters, it has been deemed to lie under 92(13): a matter of "property and civil rights" for provincial governments. If one conceptualizes child care as part of education policy, then constitutional jurisdiction would also lie with provincial governments' (2008, p. 188). It is also interesting to note that although provinces have been free to establish, or fail to establish, whatever ECEC services they choose, provinces have not chosen to establish high-quality, widely accessible ECEC systems (with the partial exception of Quebec). Friendly and White (2008) point out that this failure challenges what is often regarded as one of the strengths of decentralization in federations: acting as 'laboratories of innovation.'

In the Canadian federation, Ottawa's leadership in areas under provincial jurisdiction, such as health care, has traditionally been linked to how it distributes money. The federal government's main social policy lever in areas of provincial jurisdiction is its spending power, arising from the fact that, in Canada, the federal government has had the most far-reaching ability to raise funds through taxation. Spending power has allowed the federal government to shape social policy indirectly through the use of financial incentives, something the federal government chose to do quite extensively until the 1990s (White, 2008).

Historically, driven by both ideology and politics, Ottawa has sometimes chosen to use its spending power to try to influence what provinces do, while at other times, Ottawa has handed over transfer payments to the provinces with few or no conditions on how the money is spent. While these arrangements are usually negotiated, not unilaterally handed down, over the years, spending power has been one of the federal government's main tools in establishing a vision of Canada.

By the mid-1990s, and more specifically, with the watershed 1995 federal budget, the use of the federal spending power as an instrument of federal policy leadership became increasingly contested as a result of federal spending cutbacks and a near-victory for Quebec separatists in the 1995 sovereignty referendum (Boismenu & Graefe, 2004; Doherty, Friendly, & Oloman, 1998).

Federalism is a dynamic relationship between the levels of government in any federation. The 'strings' or conditions the federal government imposes or negotiates in areas of provincial jurisdiction are almost always contested by the provinces. The relative strengths of the federal government and the provinces have undoubtedly shifted multiple times over the years. In the modern era, ECEC came onto the national public agenda as Canada was entering a decentralizing phase, a timing that has undoubtedly had an impact. At other times, there has been more emphasis on a stronger role for Ottawa (Cameron & Simeon, 2002). During the eras of Prime Ministers Pearson and Trudeau, the federal government usually took the lead in developing national social programs. More recently, especially since the mid-1990s, there has been considerable devolution of power to the provinces. Since then, Ottawa has often found it more and more difficult to – or has chosen not to – intervene on provincial turf.

Friendly and White (2008), writing about the impact of Canada's particular approach to federalism on child care, noted the rapid shifts in how federalism has been practised in the 2000s and the interplay between ideology and federalism. They echo Fritz Scharpf's observation that federalism can create joint decision traps that take us very far from substantive policy making (1988).

In summary, both ideology and institutional political arrangements play key roles in how and why ECEC has developed as it has in Canada. The answer to the question 'Why is Canada not Sweden?' lies in history, culture, and politics that together have shaped today's ECEC situation across Canada.

Politics: On and Off the Political Agenda in the New Millennium

Politics is about both ideas or ideology and institutional arrangements. Over the years, political ideology and Canadian federalism have significantly affected development of Canadian ECEC. Neither of these has been uniform historically or regionally. What has been reflected in politics is whatever approach to federalism is dominant regarding social welfare and, increasingly, education. As we have described in the preceding section, although there have been an array of regional and time-linked variations, both of these policy factors have significantly shaped ECEC in Canada.

Historically, Canada's initiative during the Second World War to establish day nurseries so women could be employed in essential wartime industries required provincial participation, but it was led by the federal government of the day (Prentice, 1989). In 1966, when Ottawa introduced the federal-provincial cost-sharing Canada Assistance Plan (CAP), it paved the way for the development of child care as a residual, targeted welfare service under provincial legislation. During the 1980s, federal governments, both Liberal and Progressive Conservative, studied child care twice, each time in connection with the idea of bringing in a national child care program with provincial participation. However, neither effort was ultimately successful. A federal Liberal government elected in 1993 promised significant expansion of child care (although not a national program), but then abandoned it when the government ethos shifted to cost-cutting and devolution of responsibility for social policy making to provinces in the wake of fears about Quebec separatism and budget deficits. Such limited public funding for child care as was available from the federal government was, instead, subsumed under a 1995 block fund comprising the federal government's whole contribution to all social service, health care, and post-secondary education spending. This represented a significant policy shift in the use of the federal spending power as, in contrast to the previous cost-shared Canada Assistance Plan, provinces were free to use the block grants any way they chose (Friendly, 2001).

In this environment, the late 1990s, with its erosion of social programs, child care failed to progress in most of Canada (with the exception of Quebec). Without the impetus of federal policy, leadership, and funding, variation among the provinces grew rapidly. In the 1990s, Canada edged into what is called *executive federalism*, with a more limited role for Parliament and a greater role for federal and provincial ministers (executives).

New millennium policy making and child care politics began in earnest in 2003 with the Multilateral Agreement (MLA) on Early Learning and Child Care. Led by Liberal federal Human Resources Minister Jane Stewart, it was, like most Canadian policy making in this period of executive federalism, executed by an agreement among federal and provincial ministers, not by national legislation. Providing federal transfer payments to provinces under limited specified conditions, the ECEC MLA is quite significant because it represents the first federal funding earmarked for child care programs since the Second World War and a reversal of the 'Anything but Child Care' (ABC) environment of the late 1990s (Friendly, 2001).

During the 2004 federal election, Paul Martin, the new Liberal leader, promised a 'truly national system of early learning and child care,' sending a signal that the federal Liberals were re-engaged in social policy making regarding services and willing to spend money and take leadership. The promise of the 'truly national system' was much constrained, however, by the decentralizing direction that had been set in motion in the 1990s by Prime Minister Paul Martin's own government (Friendly, 2001).

While Paul Martin's federal government committed a fairly hefty (for Canada) initial budget of about $1 billion per year for the first five years of the new program, they found themselves constrained by the devolved conditions that had come to define federal/provincial relations. Some provinces contested even the modest conditions – a stated plan of action, regulation, and public reporting – upon which federal Human Resources Minister Ken Dryden had insisted. Eventually, as child care advocates urged the federal government to take a stronger stand on the details of provincial ECEC programs, a series of bilateral agreements were hammered out with all provinces. But before the bilateral agreements could get underway, the minority Liberal government was defeated in a general election (Friendly & White, 2008).

The 2006 election of the Conservatives, with Stephen Harper as leader, saw a profound break in federal/provincial policy making. The new federal government's first activity upon taking the oath of office was to unilaterally cancel the formal agreements signed between each province and the federal government, an unprecedented action; the Manitoba Minister of Family Services and Housing called it 'one of the biggest U-turns in modern day social policy' (Bailey, 2007). In addition, the Conservative early childhood initiatives that replaced the Liberal plan sharply moved away from the idea of accountability for public expenditures (Anderson & Findley, 2007).

The cancellation of the ECEC program was part of a broader abdication of a thirty-year role for the federal government's support for civil society groups, research, and social justice programs as part of women's equality (Canadian Feminist Alliance for International Action & the Canadian Labour Congress, 2010). At the same time, financial support for ECEC research and organizations were cancelled, too.

This was truly a new era for Canadian ECEC. Since the Second World War, Liberal and Progressive Conservative federal governments had exercised their policy leadership capacity and spending power. While, overall, Ottawa's role in shaping national priorities has diminished over the past three decades, with an increase in provincial power, liberal (or neo-liberal) ideas about a reduced role for government in social welfare have been part of a more and more rightward direction for Canada. In the latter part of the 2000s, with the four-year minority tenure of the Harper government, federal ECEC policies first stalled, and then went backward as the first real possibility of a national ECEC program ended in 2006. Paradoxically, while finding good child care remains as elusive as ever for parents, there is heightened interest among provincial governments across Canada and among Opposition parties in developing new policies and programs for young children (see chapter by Rachel Langford in this volume on early learning frameworks). The Childcare Resource and Research Unit, releasing its bi-annual report, *Early Childhood Education and Care in Canada 2008*, noted that – in the absence of federal interest or funds – while expansion of funds and spaces had slowed in all provinces, a number of jurisdictions had new education-linked initiatives, indicating, for the first time in most instances, a cross-Canada shift towards a more early education-focused ECEC perspective (Beach et al., 2009).

Politics Matter

In Canada, views about the private nature of family responsibilities have often gone hand-in-hand with political commitments to a smaller and decentralized government and more individual responsibility than is typically found in European, especially social democratic, countries. At the same time, Canada has had a stronger tradition of supporting the public good and collective responsibility than has typically been found in the United States or Australia.

It is noteworthy that a unified social movement, which began by calling for 'more child care, better child care,' has been part of the politics of Canadian child care since the 1970s. Widespread community-based advocacy for a universal ECEC system is unique to Canada. While there are advocates for child care elsewhere, especially in the other liberal welfare states, the Canadian alliance among a broad range of civil society groups with a long-term common goal of a universal child care system fits the definition of a real social movement in a way that advocacy in other countries does not. Over the years, the child care movement has appealed to Canada's more activist view of government, urging Ottawa to take a lead role in building a universal ECEC system and to play a prominent role in ECEC by identifying the key issues, developing policy strategies, and in making child care a public issue (Friendly & Prentice, 2009).

Conclusion

How policy ideas and structures about early childhood education and care are translated into politics ultimately determines how ECEC is provided 'on the ground' for families and children. Today, despite an ever-more devolved federalism and the ascendance of neo-liberal ideas about governments and social welfare, most Canadian families have changed. Most children have a working mother, so the historical male breadwinner family is both increasingly rare and no longer universally desired. At the same time, more Canadians have come to understand the developmental or educational value of good quality ECEC programs; public opinion polls show that Canadians generally favour more public solutions (Environics Research Group, 2006).

In Canada, ECEC comes to the policy table well after the glory days of welfare state expansion. Some of the politics have to do with institutional arrangements, especially federalism, and a liberal welfare ideology that emphasizes individualized funding arrangements and privatized child care delivery. These are political in the sense that Canada has been engaged in devolution and privatization. Alongside such formal political arrangements are ideas about families and children, preferences for gender equality, a tension between the idea that we should care for our neighbours but look out for ourselves – such beliefs are part of political culture and common sense. In this climate of multiple and conflicting needs, ideologies, and anxiety about the future, the next iterations of Canadian ECEC developments are likely to prove as interesting and tangled as those of the 2000s.

References

Anderson, L., & Findley, T. (2007). *Making the connections: Using public reporting to track the progress on child care services in Canada.* Ottawa: Child Care Advocacy Association of Canada.

Bailey, S. (2007). *Child care groups say Tory 'U-turn' far from enough.* 16 March 2007. Winnipeg: Winnipeg Free Press. Retrieved from 7http://findarticles.com/p/articles/mi_8029/is_20070316/ai_n42581050/.

Beach, J., Friendly, M., Ferns, C., Prabhu, N., & Forer, B. (2009). *Early childhood education and child care in Canada 2008.* Toronto: Childcare Resource and Research Unit, University of Toronto.

Boismenu, G., & Graefe, P. (2004). The new federal tool belt: Attempts to rebuild social policy leadership. *Canadian Public Policy, 30*(1), 71–89.

Cameron, D., & R. Simeon. 2002. Intergovernmental relations in Canada: The emergence of collaborative federalism. *Publius, 32*(2), 49–71.

Canadian Feminist Alliance for International Action & the Canadian Labour Congress. (2010). *Reality check. Women in Canada and the Beijing Declaration and Platform for Action fifteen years on. A Canadian civil society response.*

Ottawa: Authors. Retrieved from http://www.canadianlabour.ca/sites/
default/files/2010–02–22-Canada-Beijing15-NGO-Report-EN.pdf.

Child Care Advocacy Association of Canada. (2004). *From patchwork to frame-work: A child care strategy for Canada*. Ottawa: Author.

Cleveland, G., Forer, B., Hyatt, D., Japel, C., & Krashinsky, M. (2007). *An eco-nomic perspective on the current and future role of non-profit provision of early learning and child care services in Canada*. University of Toronto, University of British Columbia, & Université du Québec à Montréal. Retrieved from http://childcarepolicy.net/documents/final-report-FINAL-print.pdf.

Cleveland, G., Forer, B., Hyatt, D., Japel, C., & Krashinsky, M. (2008). New evidence about child care in Canada: Use patterns, affordability and quality. *Choices, 14*(2). Montreal: Institute for Research on Public Policy (IRPP).

Cooke, K., London, J., Edwards, R., & Rose-Lizée, R. (1986). *Report of the Task Force on Child Care*. Ottawa: Status of Women Canada.

Doherty, G., Friendly, M., & Oloman, M. (1998). *Women's support, women's work: Child care in an era of deficit reduction, devolution, downsizing, and deregu-lation*. Ottawa: Status of Women Canada.

Environics Research Group. (2006). *Final report. Canadians' attitudes toward na-tional child care policy*. Conducted for the Child Care Advocacy Association of Canada. Retrieved from http://www.ccaac.ca/pdf/resources/Reports/Public_Opinion_on_Child_Care_Policy.pdf.

Esping-Andersen, G. (1990). *The three worlds of welfare capitalism*. Cambridge: Polity Press & Princeton, NJ: Princeton University Press, 1990.

European Commission Childcare Network. (1995). *Quality targets in services for young children*. (Reprinted with permission in 2005 as a Quality by Design working document) Toronto: Childcare Resource and Research Unit, University of Toronto.

Flanagan, K. & Beach, J. (2010). *Examining the human resource implications of emerging issues in early childhood education and care: Integration of ECEC and Education Report* prepared for the Child Care Human Resources Sector Council (unpublished). Ottawa.

Friendly, M. (2001). Child care and Canadian federalism in the 1990s: Canary in a coal mine. In G. Cleveland & M. Krashinsky (Eds.), *Our children's fu-ture: Child care policy in Canada* (pp. 25–61). Toronto: University of Toronto Press.

Friendly, M. (2008). Canada's legacy of inaction on early childhood education and child care. *Policy Options, 29*(8): 62–67 Montreal: IRPP.

Friendly, M., & Prentice, S. (2009). *About Canada: Childcare*. Winnipeg: Fernwood.

Friendly, M., & White, L. (2008). From multilateralism to bilateralism to unilat-erism in three short years. Child care in Canadian federalism 2003–2006.

In H. Bakvis & G. Skogsted (Eds.), *Canadian federalism: Performance, effectiveness, and legitimacy* (pp. 182–204). Don Mills, ON: Oxford University Press.

Goelman, H., Doherty, G., Lero, D., LaGrange, A., & Tougas, J. (2001). *You bet I care! Caring and learning environments – Quality in child care centres across Canada.* Guelph, ON: Centre for Families, Work & Well-being, University of Guelph.

Hernes, H. (1987). *Welfare states and woman power: Essays in state feminism.* Oslo: Norwegian University Press.

Japel, C., Tremblay, R.E., & Côté, S. (2005). Quality counts! Assessing the quality of daycare services based on the Quebec Longitudinal Study of Child Development. *Choices, 11*(5). Montreal: IRPP.

Jencks, C., Smith, M., Acland, H., Bane, M.J., Cohen, D., Gintis, H., Heyns, B., & Michelson, S. (1972). *Inequality: A Reassessment of the effect of family and schooling in America.* New York: Basic Books.

Lyon, M., & Canning, P. (1995). *The Atlantic Day Care Study.* Halifax: Mount St Vincent University.

Meyers, M.K., & Gornick, J. C. (2003). Public or private responsibility? Early childhood education and care, inequality, and the welfare state. *Journal of Comparative Family Studies, 34*(3), 379–415.

Morgan, K.J. (2003). Child care and the liberal welfare regime: A review essay. *Review of Policy Research, 20,* 743–748.

Organization for Economic Co-operation and Development. (2004). *Canada country note.* Paris: Author.

Organization for Economic Co-operation and Development. (2006). *Starting strong II.* Paris: Author.

Prentice, S. (1989). Workers, mothers, reds: Toronto's postwar childcare fight. *Studies in Political Economy, 30,* 115–141.

Prentice, S. (2006). Childcare, co-production and the third sector in Canada. *Public Management Review, 8,* 521–536.

Scharpf, F.W. (1988). The joint-decision trap: Lessons from German federalism and European integration. *Public Administration, 66,* 239–278.

Statistics Canada. (2005). Child care: 1996–2001. *The Daily.* Ottawa: Author. Retrieved from http://www.statcan.ca/Daily/English/050207/d050207b.htm.

Statistics Canada. (2010a). *Live birth by birth weight (less than 2500 grams) and sex, Canada, provinces and territories, annual* (CANSIM table 102–444509). Retrieved from http://www.statcan.gc.ca/pub/84f0210x/2007000/tablesectlist-listetableauxsect-eng.htm.

Statistics Canada. (2010b). *Infant mortality rates, by province and territory.* CANSIM, table 102–0504 and Catalogue no. 84F0211X. Retrieved from http://www.statcan.gc.ca/bsolc/olc-cel/olc-cel?lang=eng&catno=84F0210X.

Turgeon, L. (2009). *Tax, time and territory: The development of early childhood education and child care in Canada and Great Britain.* Unpublished doctoral dissertation, University of Toronto.

United Nations Children's Fund (UNICEF). (2008). *The child care transition.* Innocenti Report Card 8, 2008. Florence, Italy: Innocenti Research Centre. Retrieved from http://www.unicef.ca/portal/Secure/Community/502/WCM/HELP/take_action/Advocacy/rc8.pdf.

Wallner, J. Beyond national standards: Reconciling tensions between federalism and the welfare state. *Publius, 40*(4), 646–671.

White, L. (2008*). Continuity and change in OECD early childhood education and care (ECEC) regimes: Where does Canada fit?* Paper presented at the 80th annual conference, Canadian Political Science Association. Vancouver. Retrieved from http://www.cpsa-acsp.ca/papers-2008/White,%20Linda.pdf.

Wincott, D. (2006). Paradoxes of New Labour social policy: Toward universal child care in Europe's 'most liberal' welfare regime? *Social Politics: International Studies in Gender, State & Society, 13,* 286–312.

3 The Economics of Early Childhood Education and Care in Canada

GORDON CLEVELAND

This chapter presents an economic perspective on early childhood education and care (ECEC) services and policy in Canada. The economic rationale for public investment in and regulation of ECEC services is based on an analysis of market failures if markets are left on their own. This chapter discusses up-to-date academic and policy evidence about the magnitudes of both the costs and benefits of early childhood education and care services, and the uncertainty about the size of the costs and benefits, now and in the future. Benefits are strongly dependent on quality of ECEC services. In general, the costs and benefits of investment in ECEC are highly dependent on the details of policy reforms (especially the quality of services supported), the institutional details of service delivery, and the behavioural incentives provided by those reforms. This chapter considers how policy reforms in ECEC can seek to maximize the excess of benefits over costs.

Economists believe goods (or services) give benefits to the consumers of those goods. Because goods are costly to produce, and therefore to purchase, the consumer has to weigh the value of the benefits against the costs and decide whether to purchase a good. In other words, every consumer does a cost-benefit analysis each time he or she makes a purchase. This is the source of economists' love affair with markets: when markets are working well (when they are competitive), the results are good. Consumers act to maximize the surplus of benefits over the costs of that economic activity. When each consumer behaves this way, and when markets are competitive so producers have no ability to manipulate this process, economists will argue that any government interference in the market will just make results worse, because it cannot improve them. Economic resources will be allocated such that the surplus of benefits over costs is as high as possible.

From an economist's perspective, early childhood education and care services are unusual for several reasons. First, it is not the direct consumer of the service (i.e., the child) who decides whether the benefits are sufficient to make the purchase worthwhile. There is a chance, therefore, that the parents, who make the purchase, may not have good information about the quality and characteristics of the early childhood service being used. Thus, their evaluation of benefits may be faulty.

Second, the demand for ECEC services is partially a derived demand – derived from the need or desire of parents to be employed for pay. This benefit is received by parents, but is very much constrained by the amount of extra income that it permits families to earn. Since, in our society, women are still considered to be the primary caregivers for children in most families, child care usually facilitates the mother's employment. To the extent that mothers' incomes are low, there is strong downward pressure on the amount that families are willing to spend on child care services.

The third unusual feature of ECEC services is that there may be substantial public benefits from the quality of the services. Because children are our future adult population, there is a strong public interest in ensuring that their cognitive (e.g., linguistic and numerical) and non-cognitive (e.g., social, emotional, behavioural) skills develop at optimal rates. This means that even if parents are perfectly informed about the quality of the ECEC services their child is using, they may not fully take into account the benefits provided to society at large (such as higher future productivity, higher future tax payments, lower probability of crime, lower probability of problems in school) from spending more on quality programs when children are young.

The fourth unusual feature of ECEC services is that there may be substantial public benefits from increasing the quantity of these services, and inducing additional women to join the labour market. There are a number of barriers to women's labour force participation that restrict the supply of female labour below what economists would consider to be its efficient level. Work disincentives built into social assistance benefit schemes play this role for many single parents or low-income two-parent families. Because income taxation reduces the marginal returns to the last hour of paid work, income taxation has similar effects. Gender discrimination in labour markets, artificially lowering the wages of and opportunities for women because of their role in raising children, may also act as a barrier to women's labour force participation.

In short, early childhood education and care services are not the typical good of free-market economic theory. The special features of ECEC mean that free markets are unlikely to provide the optimal quantity and quality of these services for children and families. The language that economists use to describe this problem is 'market failure.' When markets fail to allocate resources optimally, there is the possibility that government intervention in markets, or even government provision of ECEC services, will produce better results.

Cost-Benefit Analysis

Cost-benefit analysis is the main tool that economists use to calculate whether a particular public investment (or, more generally, government spending or regulatory change, etc.) is worthwhile. To most non-economists, cost-benefit analysis is some kind of magic mumbo-jumbo that is very helpful when it supports something they want, and clearly wrong when it does not. To economists, cost-benefit analysis is a way of mimicking a market calculation of costs and benefits in situations where the market fails to do the calculation properly.

Investment in ECEC can take different forms. Governments can provide services themselves (e.g., kindergarten and junior kindergarten, municipal child care centres, Aboriginal Head Start). Governments can regulate privately provided services to improve their quality and reliability, or to set a maximum price or limit price increases. And governments can subsidize services in a variety of ways in order to change the effective price, quality, and availability of services for some, many, or all families. In addition, governments can provide maternity, paternity, and parental benefits to allow parents to care for their own young children while their jobs are protected.

Analysing these kinds of ECEC investments using cost-benefit analysis can be very complicated in its details, but conceptually it is quite straightforward. Cost-benefit analysis derives directly from economists' concern about resource allocation. At any point in time, a society has an approximately fixed amount of productive resources (labour with different skills, natural resources, and capital equipment) at its disposal. Those resources can be allocated so that they deliver the maximum benefits to society's participants, or not. If all goods were private goods and all markets were perfectly competitive, the natural process of buying and selling would ensure that resources were well allocated to the production of different goods and services, but, as we have seen, market failure exists (and may be widespread in services such as education and health care).

A cost-benefit analysis is a way of taking a particular project (e.g., the Confederation Bridge to Prince Edward Island, a new airport for Toronto, full-day integrated ECEC services for 4- and 5-year-old children in Ontario) and trying to calculate all of the benefits (both private and public) and all of the costs (in theory, the cost of any resource is measured by the benefits that would have been produced by using that resource in the best alternative way). Those benefits and costs, which are received over time, can be discounted back to the present to determine whether the discounted benefits exceed the discounted costs. Discounting is required because benefits received in the future are worth less, and costs incurred in the future are less burdensome, than benefits and costs today. If benefits exceed costs, an economist will conclude that the investment is worthwhile; in other words, the proposed expenditure would be a good, productive way to spend society's scarce resources.

There is no guarantee that any particular proposed ECEC investment will survive this cost-benefit criterion. It is entirely possible that while we recognize that private markets for early childhood education and care will suffer from market failure, we might decide that some particular proposal is not a sensible way to spend society's resources. For instance, a particular ECEC proposal (e.g., giving families $5,000 for each child to spend on any non-parental child care of their choice) could be good for encouraging mothers' labour force participation, but it might well not provide sufficient financial support and incentives to purchase the kind and quality of ECEC services needed to generate a positive developmental environment for children. The benefits might not exceed the costs. The details of any ECEC proposal matter a great deal, and they will affect the cost-benefit calculation.

The other aspect of cost-benefit analysis that is not widely understood is that generally it does not take equity factors into account. A cost-benefit analysis uses existing market realities when it is seeking to measure benefits; part of that existing market reality is the existing distribution of income, opportunities, and life situations. Ignoring equity issues is usually problematic when considering government policy; many government policies are designed to correct perceived or possible inequities. So this is a weakness of cost-benefit analysis. It does not provide a complete and adequate assessment of the effects of a particular policy change. Instead, cost-benefit analysis is designed to answer a relatively narrow, but important, question about economic efficiency: Is this proposed project justified because it will correct a market failure and improve the allocation of society's resources? It is not designed to answer whether that proposed project would contribute to making society more equitable.

Of course, equity concerns are prominent among the reasons for recommending reforms to government ECEC policies. Many people believe that families with children are not given sufficient support in Canadian society; that is an equity issue. Many people believe that children should, as much as possible, be given equal opportunities to succeed in life, independent of the circumstances into which they were born; that is an equity issue. Economists have no special ability to give advice about policies that will promote equity goals. Their silence should not be interpreted as meaning that equity goals are unimportant (or even that economists believe that equity goals are unimportant). Any proposed ECEC policy reform will have effects on both economic efficiency and equity; a cost-benefit analysis only provides insight on efficiency effects. The implication is that a proposed ECEC policy that passes a cost-benefit test and also improves social equity will have very desirable results.

Are the Benefits of ECEC Greater than the Costs?

One way in which to answer this question – are the benefits of early childhood education and care greater than the costs? – is to look at cost-benefit studies of ECEC written by different authors. There are only a small number of full or partial cost-benefit analyses of early childhood education and care programs. The best known, which has been updated as children have aged, is the cost-benefit analysis of the Perry Preschool Program (Barnett, 1985, 1996; Belfield et al., 2006). In addition, there have been cost-benefit analyses of the Abecedarian program (Masse & Barnett, 2002) and of the Chicago Child-Parent Centers Project (Reynolds et al., 2002). All of these were programs involving largely disadvantaged African-American children in the United States. Ludwig and Phillips (2007) have recently written a cost-benefit analysis of the U.S. Head Start programs, which involve close to one million 3- to 5-year-old disadvantaged children a year.

There are other cost-benefit calculations that use the results of the above programs to project what the costs and benefits would be if these programs became available to a wider population of disadvantaged or low-income children. These include studies by Lynn Karoly and her colleagues at the RAND Corporation (Karoly & Bigelow, 2005; Karoly et al., 1998; Kilburn & Karoly, 2008) and by Robert Lynch (2004), as well as calculations made by the Federal Reserve Bank of Minneapolis (Grunewald & Rolnick, 2003). Finally, there are studies that try to calculate the costs and benefits of universal child care programs. These include Cleveland and Krashinsky (1998, 2003) and, in the United Kingdom, PricewaterhouseCoopers (2003, 2004).

All of these studies find that early childhood development programs can have a positive impact on children that are higher than their costs. The projected returns, stated as a proportion of the costs, are sometimes quite large. In the case of the Perry Preschool Program these returns are variously 7.16:1, 8.74:1, and when the children reached 40 years of age about 17:1. Karoly et al. (1998) recalculated the shorter-term Perry Preschool benefit:cost ratio by eliminating some controversial calculations of the reduction-of-crime benefits to find a ratio of 4.1:1. Heckman and his colleagues (2010) have thoroughly reviewed and checked the rate of return from the Perry Preschool Program, which they estimate at between 7 per cent and 10 per cent per year. Masse and Barnett (2002) reported that the Abecedarian project delivers a return of 3.78:1. The Chicago Child-Parent Centers was found (Reynolds et al., 2002) to deliver a return of 7.14:1. Since any benefit:cost ratio exceeding 1:1 is an investment that is worthwhile, these studies are, on the face of it, very convincing.

The benefit-cost analysis of the Abecedarian Early Childhood Intervention (Masse & Barnett, 2002) described the nature of the effects of this five-year program. The lives of children and their mothers were positively affected, and the benefits for children were both cognitive and behavioural. In particular, for children, there were improved measures of intelligence and achievement over the long term, leading to higher earnings and fringe benefits. There were lower levels of grade retention and placement of children in special education classes, leading to cost savings in elementary and secondary education. Mothers gained through improved employment and earnings made possible by access to early childhood services. Children who had participated in the intensive high-quality ECEC services of Abecedarian were less likely to smoke and had improved child health as a result. Finally, there was reduced use of social assistance by Abecedarian children.

The costs of providing intensive high-quality child care in the Abecedarian program were high. For infants, there was one staff member to every three children; for 2- and 3-year-olds, there were two staff members for every seven children; for 4- and 5-year-olds, the ratio was one to six. All staff were paid competitive public school salaries. Nevertheless, the value of the benefits, discounted back to the present, was found to be considerably higher than the costs.

However, there are many caveats. All four of these well-known projects serve or served a quite disadvantaged clientele, and the first two were quite small. Perry Preschool provided one or two years of part-time pre-school to 3- and 4-year-old children during the school term in Ypsilanti, Michigan, between 1962 and 1967. The program included parenting support in the form of ninety-minute home visits once a week. Only fifty-eight children received this treatment and about an equal number of control children were followed by the study. All of the children recruited to the study were African-American, came from low-SES families, and scored less than 85 on an IQ test.

The Abecedarian Study began in North Carolina in 1972 and included 112 children born between 1972 and 1977; all of them scored high on a high-risk index for delayed cognitive development. The average characteristics of this group of children on program entry included the following: maternal education of about ten years, maternal IQ of 85, 75 per cent single-parent families, and 55 per cent of families on social assistance. These children were randomly assigned to treatment and control groups. Treatment involved high-quality, full-day, centre-based child care from infancy until school age, following a curriculum that emphasized language development called Partners in Learning.

The Chicago Child-Parent Centers was a larger program, now serving about 5,000 children annually in an inner-city area in a large urban setting. This program offered a half-day pre-school program to 3- and 4-year-old children living in disadvantaged neighbourhoods, and encouraged parental involvement in classroom activities, field trips, and adult education classes. The program emphasized reading and language, but also provided free breakfasts and lunches and comprehensive health and social services. This was not a random-assignment study; instead, the comparison group was chosen retrospectively.

Head Start is either a part-day or full-day pre-school program in the United States offered to 3- to 5-year-old children whose families meet certain criteria of economic disadvantage. The majority of children are African-American and/or Hispanic, but there are many children from poor, white families as well. This program began in the 1960s and continues, now with nearly one million children per year receiving services. Because of its large size, and its funding as a federal–local matching grant program, there is considerable heterogeneity in the type and quality of program offered in different parts of the United States. In general, there are substantial supplementary services (e.g., health, early identification, meals, parent education) offered in addition to pre-school services.

Taking just these four sets of cost-benefit studies, it is not clear what inferences we should draw about the value of early childhood education and care services in Canada. Both the Perry Preschool and Abecedarian programs refer to the provision of high-quality (i.e., well-trained teachers, favourable ratios of children to teachers) services to highly disadvantaged populations of children in the United States. This might imply that similar returns could be gained from providing high-quality services to vulnerable populations in Canada; these studies do not, however, provide evidence about the economic returns we should expect from providing ordinary ECEC to middle-class populations in Canada.

The cost-benefit studies of the Chicago Child-Parent Centers program and Head Start are more promising because the child populations served are broader (while still being highly targeted programs). However, while the Chicago results are strongly positive, the benefit:cost-calculus for Head Start (Ludwig & Phillips, 2007) is uncertain (the study is based on a recent experimental evaluation and some of the estimated parameters of child effects are statistically insignificant, although positive). Further, the tested treatment is, typically, a half-day pre-school program for 3- or 4-year-old children, rather than a high-quality, full-day, ECEC program for ordinary children from infancy to school age.

The second group of cost-benefit studies leans heavily on the first. Karoly and Bigelow (2005) adjusted the returns found by the Chicago Child-Parent Centers program, assuming that returns would be lower for children from higher-SES backgrounds and higher for children from lower-SES backgrounds. By summing up these adjusted returns, they made a projection of the returns expected from a one-year universal program of part-day pre-school for 4-year-olds in California.

Lynch (2004) provided calculations of the costs and benefits that would come from providing a high-quality early childhood development (ECD) program to the 20 per cent of 3- and 4-year-olds in the United States who live in poverty. Lynch argues that the Perry Preschool results would likely apply to a large nationwide program of the type he recommends; he predicts 'exceptional returns.'

The Federal Reserve Bank of Minneapolis (Grunewald & Rolnick, 2003) conducted similar types of calculations to find a 16 per cent annual rate of return to providing early childhood services – of which one-quarter (4%) is a private return and three-quarters (12%) is a public return. They recommended a program to serve 3- and 4-year-old children living in poverty in Minnesota.

The final group of cost-benefit studies seeks to make calculations about the costs and benefits of universal child care programs available to children from 2 to 5 years of age in one case (Cleveland & Krashinsky, 1998, 2003), and for children aged 1 to 4 years in another case (PricewaterhouseCoopers, 2003, 2004). Cleveland and Krashinsky provide a thorough review of economic studies of effects of children to argue their case that returns would be positive for both disadvantaged and typical children across Canada. Their numerical estimate of benefits is based on these studies and on the willingness of relatively affluent families to pay for ECEC services. Putting together the differential benefits for children already using full-day regulated care, those currently using informal care, and those who currently are cared for exclusively by parents, Cleveland and Krashinsky calculated the marginal social benefits of a universal good-quality child care program to be twice as high as the marginal social costs.

PricewaterhouseCoopers (2004) modelled the costs and benefits of a universal high-quality child care program of the Swedish or Danish type applied to the United Kingdom. Their calculations were based on clearly stated assumptions (employment and earnings effects for mothers, higher future productivity for children receiving care, reduced social assistance and related benefits, costs per full-time space); they provided sensitivity tests to show which of these assumptions were particularly important to the final cost-benefit results. Some potential benefits (e.g., reduction in child poverty, improvements in gender equity, increased equity in children's life chances) were deliberately ignored because of the difficulty of making credible assumptions; this was also true of some potential costs (e.g., emotional costs for some parents of foregone time with children; potential negative emotional effects for some children). Measuring costs and benefits in British pounds (GBP), PricewaterhouseCoopers found that the shorter-term benefits barely exceeded costs (10.3 billion GBP vs. 9.8 billion GBP), but that the longer-term benefits (including the increased productivity and earnings of children) exceeded costs by 40 billion GBP (in 2003 prices) over a sixty-five-year period.

The sensitivity analysis by PricewaterhouseCoopers is particularly interesting. They find, for instance, that a one percentage point fall in the assumed female employment rate (assumed to rise to 81 per cent for 35- to 49-year-old women) would shift the net present value by about 45 billion GBP and make the investment marginally negative. The assumed productivity effects on children are also important; assuming that they are the same as other children, rather than 2 per cent more productive, reduces the net present value by about 30 billion GBP. The assumed costs of care are likewise important to the calculation of benefits and costs. An increase in assumed costs by 10 per cent (from the current level of 6,500 GBP per full-time place per year) reduces the net present value close to zero.

What Do Other Studies Tell Us about the Effects of ECEC on Children?

The effects of early childhood education and care on children depend on the type of care (public kindergarten, centre-based child care, regulated family child care, informal care) and especially on the quality of that care (with quality measures reflecting safety and health issues, of course, but especially the warmth, the child-centredness, and the educational/developmental content of that care). Beyond that, the effects on children depend on the age and other characteristics (gender seems to be important, but also, apparently, the socio-economic background of the family and the parenting abilities and interest of the parents).

Random assignment studies are the 'gold standard' for judging the effects on children because they deal with the problem of separating family selection effects (careful choice of good quality child care by caring, well-resourced families) from the actual effects of early childhood education. Some more recent studies have used different techniques to solve this problem.

For instance, Gormley and colleagues (2005) used a regression discontinuity design to control for selection bias by comparing children using universal 4-year-old pre-kindergarten in Tulsa, Oklahoma, with those children just excluded from pre-kindergarten because of their age. The effects they find are very strong, and not affected by narrowing the age bands considered until the treatment and control groups are of virtually identical ages. Using nationally normed test instruments (Woodcock-Johnson sub-tests for letter-identification [pre-reading], spelling [pre-writing], and applied problems [pre-math]), the authors reported effect sizes from one year of attending a very good quality pre-kindergarten program of 0.79 of a standard deviation for pre-reading, 0.64 of a standard deviation for pre-writing, and 0.38 of a standard deviation for pre-math. Strong positive effects were found for both disadvantaged and middle-class children, and for children from different racial and ethnic groups (with, in general, somewhat larger effects for disadvantaged and both Black and Hispanic children, but substantial positive effects for all children).

The Oklahoma results were partly due to the very high quality of the pre-kindergarten services provided in the schools by teachers who had both a teaching certificate and a certificate in early childhood education (ECE), and who were paid at public school rates. Classroom sizes were capped at twenty children, and, with one lesser-trained assistant, this meant that staff:child ratios were 1:10.

A similar pattern has, however, been found in other pre-kindergarten programs. Barnett and colleagues (2005) replicated the regression discontinuity design in the study of pre-kindergarten programs in five U.S. states: Michigan, South Carolina, New Jersey, West Virginia, and Oklahoma. Some of these programs are universal and some targeted, but not as well resourced as the Tulsa program. In all five states, they found substantial gains in both pre-reading and pre-math skills.

Magnuson, Ruhm, and Waldfogel (2007a) analysed average quality pre-kindergartens in the Early Childhood Longitudinal Study – Kindergarten Cohort (ECLS-K) and found improved reading and math skills for children attending pre-kindergarten. These pre-school effects did not persist in small and high instruction classrooms because, in that environment, other children are able to catch up. However, in large and low instruction classrooms, the pre-school advantage continued to exist, largely due to continuing low performance in that environment of children cared for exclusively by parents (Magnuson, Ruhm, & Waldfogel, 2007b).

Of course, these results are for pre-kindergarten (generally provided in schools), rather than child care or other pre-schools. However, there is good evidence that child care can have positive cognitive effects too, even in the United States where average quality is acknowledged to be low. The NICHD studies (by the Early Child Care Research Network for the National Institute of Child Health and Human Development, henceforth NICHD-ECCRN) are well-resourced studies of everyday child care in the United States. Using multiple types of controls for selection bias, NICHD and Duncan (2003) conclude that the effects of quality are relatively small (0.04 to 0.08 of a standard deviation on cognitive outcomes for children), but that, in addition, use of centre-based care in the third and fourth year of a child's life has an independent effect of about 0.25 on cognitive and academic achievement outcomes. Taken together, the NICHD estimate of the effect of a good quality centre-based program would be substantial (less than half the size of the effects of parenting or home environment or being in poverty, but still sizeable).

Other studies of centre-based programs include various studies of Head Start by Janet Currie and her colleagues (Currie & Thomas, 1995, 1999; Garces, Thomas, & Currie, 2002). Head Start children are a targeted low-income group. Head Start programs are more heterogeneous than state-guided pre-kindergarten programs would be, delivered to approximately one million children per year in the United States.

These studies are well designed to account for selection bias; the main technique used is sibling fixed effects. In other words, the control group for the effect of Head Start is composed of the sibling of each Head Start attendee who did not attend Head Start. This controls for unmeasured family characteristics that might affect both Head Start enrolment and child outcomes. Currie and Thomas (1995) documented long-term (i.e., into the early school years) positive effects on school achievement for white Head Start attendees, but not for African-American children. In a second paper, Currie and Thomas (1999) reported long-term positive effects on school achievement for Hispanics. In a follow-up study of effects at age 21, Garces, Thomas, and Currie (2002) found white children who attended Head Start were more likely to complete high school and to attend college, and to earn more than other white children who did not attend Head Start. Black children did not have the same school achievement gains, but were significantly less likely to be arrested for criminal activity than similar children who did not attend Head Start.

Finally, a recent study examined the long-term effects of the introduction of universal access to early childhood education and care for 3- to 6-year-olds in Norway in the 1970s. A difference-in-differences design, based on differential implementation of the program across various Norwegian municipalities, found strong positive effects on long-term child outcomes. An increase of 17,500 child care spaces resulted in about 6,200 additional years of education measured thirty years later. There were also significant increases in labour market participation for these children by the time they had reached their early 30s, and reduced welfare dependency (Havnes & Mogstad, 2009). Havnes and Mogstad reported that these universal child care services, with particularly strong effects for girls and children from lower income families, also had the effect of equalizing opportunities for children at school entry.

In summary, there are good reasons to believe that some forms of centre-based child care or pre-school or pre-kindergarten can have important positive effects on children, whether these children are disadvantaged and from low-income and from single-parent families or whether these children are from middle-income and two-parent families. The effect sizes appear to be dependent on two main factors: the quality and type of child care/early education they did receive and the quality (support and stimulation) of the care the children would have alternatively received (often related to the family situation of the child) if they had not been enrolled in such a program. The age, and perhaps the gender, of the child moderates both of these factors, and the persistence of improved child outcomes will depend on later classroom experiences (Magnuson et al., 2007b).

It is possible that child care can also have some negative effects on children that have to be weighed against the positive cognitive, academic, and language effects (Magnusson et al., 2007a; Baker, Gruber, & Milligan, 2008).[1]

The NICHD-ECCRN (2001, 2003) found evidence that more hours in a child care arrangement in the United States is associated, at 24 and 54 months and in kindergarten, with various behavioural problems. Specifically, more hours in child care up to age 2 years were associated with more negative interactions with peers and more behavioural problems as reported by caregivers, and less social competence as reported by mothers (NICHD-ECCRN, 2001). Measured cumulatively up to age 4.5 years, more hours in child care were associated with more negative play, lower social competence, and more externalizing behaviours. A higher number of hours in child care were associated with more teacher–child conflict in kindergarten. These effects were moderated by the quality of child care and the quality of parenting received by the

---

1 One Canadian study has found evidence of strong negative effects of Quebec's child care reforms on children's socio-emotional status and on indicators of parental well-being (Baker et al., 2008). Although the authors interpret this evidence as a measure of the general effects of child care, it is likely that many of the negative effects are the result of problems associated with the rapid phasing-in of the program, and quality problems because of the strong reliance on family-based child care provided by untrained caregivers.

child, but were still statistically significant and quantitatively important after controlling for these influences.

The effects on behaviour do not appear to be related to a threshold level of hours, but it is only children in child care for more than thirty hours per week who, on average, had more than normal behavioural problems, and only children spending over forty-five hours per week over the whole period from 3 to 54 months who displayed high levels of negative externalizing behaviours (Vandell, 2004).[2] Most Canadian children do not enter child care until the end of the one-year parental leave period, so it is unclear how these results would apply to Canadian children. It is also unclear what role modest behavioural problems play in later development. Duncan et al. (2007) analysed six longitudinal data sets to find that math, reading, and attention skills at school entry were important in explaining later school achievement, but that socio-emotional behaviours, including internalizing and externalizing problems and social skills, were generally insignificant predictors of later academic performance, even among children with relatively high levels of problem behaviours. On the other hand, Cunha, Heckman, and Schennach (2010) emphasize the importance of non-cognitive skills (i.e., personality, social, and emotional traits) in supporting cognitive skill development.

What Are the Effects of ECEC on Parental Employment?

As discussed at the beginning of this chapter, one central reason for public investment in early childhood education and care is to provide support for parental employment or to reduce the conflicts that arise between parental employment and raising a family. For instance, maternity, paternity, and parental benefits provide income support to allow parents to take time to bond with children when they are very young, while not suffering loss of employment. In the European Union, the desire of governments to increase the female labour force participation is linked to maintaining economic growth and sustaining pension and social protection systems in the face of an aging population. Other

---

2 Lefebvre, Merrigan, and Verstraete (2008) hypothesize that the flat-rate design (e.g., $7 per day per child) of the Quebec child care program encourages parents to use regulated child care for too many hours per day and per week when children are quite young, with negative effects for children in Quebec.

governments favour women's employment as an anti-poverty measure (especially for single mothers) or on the grounds of increasing gender equity in both home and employment domains.

In most societies, it is the mother's role to take the primary responsibility for both the provision of care to young children and the making of day-to-day decisions about their lives. Accordingly, it is nearly always the mother's career that is foregone if someone stays home with the children; it is the mother who works part-time when children are young, who declines opportunities for advancement, who neglects the acquisition of skills that might permit moving to a job with a higher income. Of course, young children make life forever different for fathers as well; often fathers may work harder or longer hours, and there is a considerable amount of off-shifting, where fathers and mothers adjust work schedules to avoid having to hire paid caregivers while both work. The evidence, however, seems overwhelming that changes in ECEC policy will have more dramatic direct effects on the daily lives of mothers, but on fathers more indirectly.

Studies disagree on how big an effect subsidizing ECEC services is likely to have on mothers' labour force decisions. In a recent review, two noted American economists (Blau & Currie, 2007) judged that the price of child care only has a small effect on labour force participation and hours of work. According to the studies they cite, we should expect a decline of 10 per cent in the price of child care to increase labour force participation by about 1 per cent to 2 per cent. These authors also find a small anticipated effect on the hours that mothers work each week.

However, recent Canadian evidence of the impact of the Quebec child care reforms (1997–2001) contradicts these pessimistic conclusions. The Quebec reforms produced a sort of 'natural experiment' for economists to study. Lefebvre and Merrigan (2005, 2008) reported that, in 2002, the policy change increased the participation rate of mothers with at least one child aged 1 to 5 years of age by 8 percentage points (to a new level of 69% participation; on the previous base, this is an increase of about 13%). Hours of work per year and weeks worked per year also increased; on average, hours worked increased by 231 hours (an increase of 22%). Annual weeks worked were thirty-seven, and rose on average by 5.17 weeks (or 16.2%). Annual earnings of these women rose by between $3,000 and $6,000 per year (not very precisely estimated). The authors' conclusion was that 'the substantial decrease in the price of day care in the province of Quebec caused by a policy of generous subsidization of day care providers had a substantial positive effect on labour supply and earnings' (2008, p. 545).

Lefebvre and Merrigan's study does not stand alone. Baker et al. (2008) analysed the impact of Quebec's child care policy on maternal work for mothers in two-parent families, and found results very similar to Lefebvre and Merrigan, using a different data set.[3]

For the United States, Gelbach (2002) analysed the impact of public kindergarten. His estimates indicated that access to free-of-charge part-day kindergarten increased the probability of a single mother being employed by 4 to 5 percentage points. Cascio (2009) studied the impact of increased funding of kindergartens (incorporated into the public school system) over time (1950 to 1990) on the employment rate of single mothers with a youngest child aged 5 years. She documented that the positive effects on employment range from 7.3 to 8.1 percentage points. Other natural experiments (Piketty, 2005; Schone, 2004) provide supporting evidence that labour force participation of mothers of young children is sensitive to the effective price of early childhood services.

Lefebvre, Merrigan, and Verstraete (2009) looked at the longer-term effects of the Quebec child care reforms. They examined the issue of whether mothers who were encouraged to join the labour force by the availability of subsidized child care when their children were young would stay in the labour force once their children reached school age. These results were surprisingly positive. In particular, they found long-term and growing effects of the child care subsidy program and that the strongest effects were for mothers with lower levels of education. This is a group for whom attachment to the labour force is traditionally weak. The implication would appear to be that the child care reforms have had an important effect on families most at risk of being in poverty by encouraging these mothers to join and stay in the labour force.

---

3 A further important effect of the increase in parental employment and incomes in Quebec was that government tax revenues rose and geared-to-income family benefits and social assistance benefits fell. The result, calculated by Baker et al. (2008), is that 40 per cent of the cost of the program reforms in Quebec was covered by these fiscal effects.

What Do We Know about the Costs of ECEC?

There are a small number of studies of the costs of producing early childhood education and care services. However, most of these are not very informative about the key issues of interest that relate to cost-benefit analysis: (1) What are the true costs of different types of care, and is there any substantial cost difference in different services that provide similar experiences for children? (2) What is the marginal cost of increments to quality within existing ECEC services? (3) By how much will the cost of ECEC services rise when governments fund services sufficiently to make them universally available and affordable (and, in general, what will the effect on costs be of different possible child care policy reforms)?

One useful study of centre costs was produced by the U.S. General Accounting Office (1999), which analysed the costs of producing high-quality child care in centres on U.S. Air Force bases. All Air Force centres have been accredited according to the National Association for the Education of Young Children (NAEYC) guidelines and are therefore considered to be high quality – more precisely at a rating of 4.5 and above on a 7-point process quality evaluation scale, similar to the Early Childhood Environment Rating Scale-Revised (ECERS-R; Harms, Clifford, & Cryer, 1998).

Direct labour costs (wages and benefits of caregiving staff directly involved with the children) are slightly over half of all costs (52.4%), while indirect labour (including directors and administrators, curriculum development staff, and cooks) forms nearly another quarter (23.05%). Occupancy cost is 10 per cent and supplies (classroom and administrative materials) and food are 12 per cent.

The estimated cost per child hour was U.S. $3.86 in 1997 or an annual cost per child of about $8,028 (approximately 2,080 hours for the average child). The costs vary dramatically by age of child ranging from about $5.40 per hour for infants (less than 12 months), $4.72 for children 12 to 24 months, $3.96 for children 24 to 36 months of age, to $3.23 for children 3 to 5 years of age. Using 2,080 hours as the standard, that gives annual costs of $11,231 for infants (less than 12 months), $9,817 for children 12 to 24 months, $8,236 for children 24 to 36 months of age, and $6,717 for children 3 to 5 years of age.

The large majority of the cost of providing ECEC in centres is composed of the cost of labour. As a result, any policy decisions affecting the number or skill level of workers required will necessarily have a significant impact on costs. In most countries, the ratio of staff to children for the care of infants is much higher (e.g., 1:4) than the ratio for children 3 to 5 years of age (e.g., 1:12). Assuming that staff at the same average skill and salary levels are employed with infants and pre-schoolers, this implies that direct labour costs per child hour will be close to three times as high for infants as for pre-schoolers. Thus, in the 1999 U.S. GAO study, direct labour costs for infants were about $3.75 per child hour and for 3- to 5-year-olds were about $1.38 per child hour. Direct labour costs comprised nearly 70 per cent of all costs for infants, compared with about 43 per cent of all costs for children 3 to 5 years of age. Nearly all the rest of the centre costs (indirect labour, supplies, utilities, food, equipment, and the cost of space) do not vary by child age and so are attributed equally to each child hour of service (adding about $1.70 to $1.85 to the hourly costs at each age level; U.S. GAO, 1999, pp. 48–49).

There is some evidence that the quality level of ECEC can be increased in some countries without dramatic increases in cost. An econometric analysis of centre costs based on the Cost, Quality, and Child Outcomes Study (Mocan, 1997) projected that a 25 per cent increase in quality – as measured by process outcome measures such as ECERS-R (Harms et al., 1998) – could be achieved with only a 10 per cent increase in costs. The positive aspect of this finding is the suggestion that there is a range of factors determining the quality of ECEC experiences provided to children in child care centres and that, in some countries at least, there may be some scope to improve quality without improving staff:child ratios or hiring more qualified teachers. Helburn and Howes (1996) suggest that key factors that may influence quality with minor impact on cost include 'a child care director's administrative experience and effectiveness . . . personality traits of staff, staff commitment to good quality, and effective teamwork' (p. 79). There are several studies of the key components of quality in ECEC that support the contention that many factors affect quality, not only staff:child ratios and staff education levels (Blau, 1997, 2000; Cleveland & Hyatt, 2002). However, for substantial changes in quality (e.g., a 25% increase), it seems unlikely that this would be achieved across an entire system of ECEC with only minor cost implications.

There is some evidence for economies of scale in the production of ECEC services. Mocan (1997) found evidence that average costs per child served would fall slightly as the size of a child care centre rose beyond sixty-seven full-time-equivalent children served. Other authors have found some similar evidence. Given fixed staff:child ratios by child age, it is unlikely that these savings are in direct labour costs. It is likely, however, that the services of directors, administrators, accountants, cleaning and maintenance staff, cooks, and individuals who specialize in staff training and curriculum development could be spread over a larger number of children more efficiently than over a small number of children. Looking at data from the Cost, Quality, and Child Outcomes Study, Helburn and Howes have written that 'labour cost, total cost and total revenue per child were significantly higher in centres serving fewer than 40 children on a full-time basis than in centres serving more than 40' (1996, p. 75).

The term *economies of scope* refers to reductions in the average cost of production that are enjoyed by a company that offers a range of different services (or goods) rather than concentrating on a single service (or good). There is some evidence of economies of scope in the provision of child care services. Mocan (1997) indicates that serving infants-toddlers and pre-school children (i.e., 3 to 5 years old) in the same centre leads to some cost savings, as does serving pre-school children and school-aged children together. However, there are no cost efficiencies to be gained by serving infants-toddlers and school-aged children jointly (but not pre-schoolers).

One recent study of ECEC costs in the United States suggests that there may be substantial differences in costs between care of different kinds. Besharov, Myers, and Morrow (2007) calculated the full average cost of providing Head Start, ordinary child care financed by the Child Care and Development Fund, and pre-kindergarten programs in the United States (see also Barnett & Robin, 2006, on the cost of good quality pre-school). On an hourly basis, in 2003–04, Head Start costs $8.41, centre-based child care costs $3.52, and state-funded pre-kindergarten programs cost $5.53. Given that the majority of Head Start and pre-kindergarten programs are part-day, it is somewhat odd that the authors also give annual costs based on fifty hours per week and forty-nine weeks per year. On this basis, the annual costs are $21,305 for Head Start, $8,908 for ordinary centre care, and $14,026 for pre-kindergarten programs per child. The virtue of these calculations is the confirmation that the details about service provision can affect costs dramatically, and that, despite Mocan's (1997) findings, quality increments may be quite costly.

These findings echo those from Cleveland and Krashinsky's paper (2004a) for the Canadian Council on Social Development national conference 'Child Care for a Change: Shaping the 21st Century.' The authors found that the costs of producing centre-based child care in Canada were strongly related to the assumed child:staff ratio and the wages paid to teaching staff at different qualification levels. At a ratio of 3:1 (a very good ratio for infant care) with teachers earning $26,000 per year, the annual full-time cost of care per child is $15,200, rising to $20,700 annually at a salary of $35,000. With a child:staff ratio of 5:1, the corresponding total costs become $9,500 and $13,000 per year per child. With a child:staff ratio of 10:1, the total costs are $5,100 (with the lower salary) and $7,200 with the higher salary. At a ratio of 15:1, this becomes $3,700 and $5,200 annually per child. The point is that quality choices matter to costs, and the age level of children (correlated, of course, with appropriate child:staff ratios) also matters dramatically to costs.

Who Should Receive the Benefits of the Investment in ECEC?

Should governments target assistance to the most needy, perhaps in the form of specially designed early childhood intervention programs? Or should they seek to develop universal pre-school education and integrate those children with special or extra needs? Should governments concentrate financial resources on older pre-school children? Or should they spend most on the very young?

The evidence cited above suggests that early childhood education and care services can have positive effects on children whether they are targeted to disadvantaged children (e.g., Abecedarian, Head Start programs) or whether they are made universally available (Tulsa pre-kindergarten, *bornehaven* for 3- to 6-year-olds in Norway). It is true that the ratio of benefits to costs will be greater for disadvantaged children than for children from ordinary backgrounds. However, targeted services tend to develop a stigma as 'welfare services,' which can affect their success and parents' willingness to participate. And, as many have observed (e.g., Doherty, 2007), an important fraction of those children who could most benefit from ECEC services would never be identified for targeting – they live in ordinary advantaged, rather than disadvantaged, families.

The other aspect of who should receive services concerns the age of the child. My opinion is that the priority ages for ECEC services should be older pre-schoolers (ages 2 or 3 to 5 years of age), while substantial investments for younger children should initially concentrate on improving maternity, paternity, and parental leave and benefits for children up to, perhaps, 1.5 years of age, with provisions to ensure that both parents are involved in early care. This opinion reflects the demonstrated choices of Canadian parents (who are increasingly comfortable with pre-school services, especially centre-based, as children grow towards school age). But, it also reflects the concerns of some researchers that long hours in child care, particularly centre-based care, from very early ages will have negative behavioural effects on some children. Also relevant is the very high cost of good quality care when children are very young, because the number of children per trained staff member cannot be high, and for some children the cost of services may exceed the benefits received.

How Should Governments Invest in ECEC?

Should assistance go directly to parents, or should governments finance services, reducing the cost to parents? Should governments play an important role in enhancing the quality of services, or should governments rely on consumer choice to deal with issues of service quality?

One issue is whether public intervention will occur on the demand side or on the supply side. Some governments direct funding through families, allowing parents to make decisions on what kinds of ECEC are best suited to their children. These demand-side subsidies can flow through the tax system as credits or deductions. Alternatively, they can be provided directly through vouchers, or they can be provided by allowing parents to choose types of care and then designing funding mechanisms in which the funds follow the children. The biggest problem with demand-side subsidies is that they provide inadequate mechanisms to ensure that parents purchase high-quality care that will support children's optimal development (Cleveland & Krashinsky, 2004b). Since quality is the key determinant of child care's effects on children, this is a central problem.

Some governments subsidize certain types of ECEC directly and arrange for those services to be provided to parents and children. These supply-side subsidies are usually limited to specific types of care and are designed in such a way so as to enhance the quality of the chosen types of care, so that parents who choose other types of ECEC may receive no subsidization. Approved types of care will thus be provided to parents at below-market prices (and, in some cases, for free). Supply-side subsidies can also be provided in a variety of ways. ECEC services can be provided directly through the public sector by various levels

of government or through the public education system, or ECEC services can be provided by subsidizing private sector producers who
are regulated and monitored to encourage the maintenance of certain
standards. When the government chooses the latter option – that is,
when it chooses to, in effect, contract out production to the private
sector – there still remains the question of whether for-profit firms will
be considered eligible for subsidy, or whether subsidies will be limited
to non-profit organizations (see Cleveland & Krashinsky, 2009, for a
discussion of why non-profit child care provides systematically better
quality in larger urban areas).

The biggest problem with either demand-side or supply-side subsidies (when the level of government financial assistance is high) is providing incentives to increase quality while maintaining a lid on cost
increases. A key public policy problem is determining how to ensure
that increases in costs reflect increases in quality, rather than simply
paying more for ECEC services that are inadequate for children's needs.

Finally, it is important to keep in mind that the most important component of the care of the young child will occur within the child's home
and will be provided by the child's parents or guardians. Even the most
extensive ECEC programs generally provide no more than forty to fifty
hours a week of ECEC to children, implying that the rest of the day and
night-time hours are provided by the child's parents. Most studies of
child outcomes identify parents as the most important factor in influencing children's development. Parental leave and benefits are, therefore, a key component of Canada's ECEC system. Quebec now offers
more generous funding of parental leave than the rest of Canada. The
rest of Canada should imitate Quebec's innovations, while providing
incentives and regulations to ensure that fathers take a much greater
share of total parental leave.

In sum, there is no one best funding mechanism for all circumstances.
However, successful ECEC funding mechanisms will be those that ensure that program benefits exceed costs.

Conclusion

Good quality early childhood education and care services are an important employment support for families and can provide substantial
developmental benefits for children. However, the evidence on the
benefits and costs of ECEC does not suggest that all and any expenditure of public money on ECEC will generate benefits greater than costs

(see Barnett & Ackerman, 2006). The precise design of investments in early childhood education and care matters. In particular, the ratio of benefits to costs is clearly affected by the quality of ECEC services available; benefits to children rise with quality level, but they may be higher for some children, and benefits may rise more slowly when current quality levels are already high. Costs also rise as the quality level of ECEC services rises. This suggests there may be an optimum quality level. The ratio of benefits to costs is similarly affected by the degree of employment support for mothers that ECEC programs provide. Programs should be designed to maximize the excess of benefits over costs for any child, and should, at a minimum, include all children and families for whom benefits exceed costs.

Several propositions would seem to follow logically from the research literature as it currently stands. These are:

1 *Quality of services is of primary importance for the effects on children, but it is also a major driver of costs.* Research on the effects of ECEC on the development of young children comes close to consensus that these services can have important positive effects on cognitive abilities and language. Many studies have also found positive socio-emotional effects, particularly for disadvantaged children. However, it is widely accepted that these potential benefits are conditional; ECEC services need to be of good quality, or these positive effects will be diminished or reversed (particularly for vulnerable children). Poor quality services can have negative effects on children's development. Mediocre quality services may have no positive effects on children. Much of the observed differences in research results about the effects of ECEC are due to variations in the quality of services studied. Systems that focus primarily on rapid expansion of access tend to downgrade quality (e.g., Australia until the past couple of years, the Netherlands). In these circumstances, costs may rise substantially without improvements in quality. When this is true, it is difficult to put the genie back in the bottle and difficult to enhance quality at a reasonable public cost.

2 *There are likely to be expensive and inexpensive ways to improve child care quality.* Discussions of quality improvement often centre on increasing staff:child ratios, increasing staff wages, and improving qualifications of staff across the board (e.g., all teaching staff should have a university degree). The extant literature on costs suggests that these will be expensive ways to improve quality. Other

measures – increased and improved professional development training, changes in group size, enhanced curriculum/program planning, improvements in physical facilities, improved qualifications and leadership abilities of centre directors, changes in the percentage of centres that are not-for-profit – are likely to be much less resource-intensive ways to increase quality. Unfortunately, much of the early childhood literature on quality ignores the issue of costs. Discussion should focus on determining the degree to which alternative quality improvement measures are cost-effective.

3 *However child care is delivered, policy should treat ECEC as a public service.* Intense debates over for-profit vs. not-for-profit vs. public delivery of services sometimes miss the central point, which is that ECEC is already, in essence, a public service, which may or may not be delivered by private providers. It is not a market commodity, traded in a normal market situation. In a large and increasing number of jurisdictions (including Australia, the Netherlands, the United Kingdom, Quebec, and most of the EU countries), governments pay 60 per cent to 100 per cent of the costs of providing early childhood education and care because of the substantial public benefits believed to come from ECEC. In this circumstance, normal market mechanisms do not work (in particular, normal market mechanisms do not restrain increases in costs); government policies are therefore responsible for ensuring desired outcomes even if a substantial component of services is delivered by for-profit or not-for-profit providers, rather than by the public sector.

4 It is important to ensure that good quality services reach children who are more economically and socially disadvantaged, who are more likely to be vulnerable, or to have less than adequate parenting, or other sources of stimulation. These children have a high ratio of benefits to costs, and public support for public financing depends on the system's success in equalizing opportunities. Disadvantaged children (in fact, many children have different degrees of disadvantage or vulnerability) can be accommodated and receive appropriately special treatment within the context of a universal program of services. The alternative of highly targeted services has very substantial problems (Doherty, 2007). However, there needs to be more planning for how ECEC services will foster the development of vulnerable children within the context of universally accessible programs. One issue is access to universal services. In a situation where there is likely to be an inadequate supply of services, low-income

families tend to be slower off the mark in ensuring access, and when they do find spaces, their children are often in lower-quality centres. As a result, disadvantaged children may not gain the substantial developmental benefits that ECEC can provide.

5 Those who develop ECEC policies, and particularly those planning major ECEC reforms, need to consider providing incentives and supports that will maximize the surplus of benefits over costs. For instance, flat-fee policies that are very common in regulated child care (a flat-fee per day, per week, or per month) encourage parents to leave their children in care for long hours (Lefebvre et al., 2008). This adds to the costs of providing care, but may not enhance children's development.

References

Baker, M., Gruber, J., & Milligan, K. (2008). Universal childcare, maternal labor supply and family well-being. *Journal of Political Economy, 79,* 709–745.

Barnett, W.S. (1985). Benefit-cost analysis of the Perry Preschool Program and its policy implications. *Educational Evaluation and Policy Analysis, 7,* 333–342.

Barnett, W.S. (1996). *Lives in the balance: Age 27 benefit-cost analysis of the High/ Scope Perry Preschool Program.* Ypsilanti, MI: High/Scope Foundation.

Barnett, W.S., & Ackerman, D.J. (2006). Costs, benefits and long-term effects of early care and education programs: Recommendations and cautions for community developers. *Journal of the Community Development Society, 37*(2), 86–100.

Barnett, W. S., Lamy, C., & Jung, K. (2005). *The effects of state pre-kindergarten programs on young children's school readiness in five states.* New Brunswick, NJ: National Institute for Early Education Research.

Barnett, W.S., & Robin, K.B. (2006). *How much does quality preschool cost?* Working Paper. New Brunswick, NJ: National Institute for Early Education Research.

Belfield, C.R., Nores, M., Barnett, S.W., & Schweinhart, L.J. (2006). The High/ Scope Perry Preschool Program: Cost-benefit analysis using data from the age-40 follow-up. *Journal of Human Resources, 41,* 162–190.

Besharov, D.J., Myers, J.A., & Morrow, J.S. (2007). *Costs per child for early childhood education and care: Comparing Head Start, CCDF child care and prekindergarten/preschool programs (2003/2004).* Washington, DC: American Enterprise Institute for Public Policy Research.

Blau, D.M. (1997). The production of quality in child care centers. *Journal of Human Resources, 32,* 354–387.

Blau, D.M. (2000). The production of quality in child care centres: Another look. *Applied Developmental Science, 4*, 136–148.

Blau, D.M., & Currie, J. (2006). Who's minding the kids? Preschool, day care, and after school care. In E. Hanushek & F. Welch (Eds.), *The handbook of the economics of education* (pp. 1116–1278). New York: Elsevier/North-Holland.

Cascio, E. (2009). Maternal labor supply and the introduction of kindergartens into American public schools. *Journal of Human Resources, 44*, 140–170.

Cleveland, G., & Hyatt, D. (2002). *The recipe for good quality early childhood care and education: Do we know the key ingredients?* University of Toronto, Scarborough (mimeo).

Cleveland, G., & Krashinsky, M. (1998). *The benefits and costs of good childcare: The economic rationale for public investment in young children.* Monograph Number 1. Toronto: Childcare Resource and Research Unit, University of Toronto.

Cleveland, G., & Krashinsky, M. (2003). *Fact and fantasy: Eight myths about early childhood education and care.* Toronto: Childcare Resource and Research Unit, University of Toronto.

Cleveland, G., & Krashinsky, M. (2004a). *Financing early learning and child care in Canada.* Discussion paper prepared for the Canadian Council on Social Development's National Conference 'Child Care for a Change: Shaping the 21st Century,' Winnipeg, 12–14 Nov.

Cleveland, G., & Krashinsky, M. (2004b). *Financing ECEC services in OECD countries.* Paris: OECD.

Cleveland, G., & Krashinsky, M. (2009). The non-profit advantage: Producing quality in thick and thin child care markets. *Journal of Policy Analysis and Management, 28*, 440–462.

Cunha, F., Heckman, J., & Schennach, S. (2010). Estimating the technology of cognitive and noncognitive skill formation. *National Bureau of Economic Research Working Papers* No. 15664. Cambridge, MA: National Bureau of Economic Research.

Currie, J., & Thomas, D. (1995). Does Head Start make a difference? *American Economic Review, 85*, 341–364.

Currie, J., & Thomas, D. (1999). Does Head Start help Hispanic children? *Journal of Public Economics, 74*, 235–262.

Doherty, G. (2007). Ensuring the best start in life: Targeting versus universality in early childhood development. *Choices, 13*(8), 1–50. Montreal: Institute for Research on Public Policy.

Duncan, G.J., Dowsett, C.J., Claessens, A., Magnuson, K., Huston, A.C., & Klebanov, et al. (2007). School readiness and later achievement. *Developmental Psychology, 43*, 1428–1446.

Garces, E., Thomas, D., & Currie, J. (2002). Longer term effects of Head Start. *American Economic Review, 92,* 999–1012.

Gelbach, J. (2002). Public schooling for young children and maternal labor supply. *American Economic Review, 92,* 307–322.

Gormley, W.T. Jr., Gayer, T., Phillips, D., & Dawson, B. (2005). The effects of universal pre-K on cognitive development. *Developmental Psychology, 41,* 872–884.

Grunewald, R., & Rolnick A. (2003). Early childhood development: Economic development with a high public return. *Region, 17*(4), 6–12.

Harms, T., Clifford R.M., & Cryer D. (1998). *Early Childhood Environment Rating Scale: Revised.* New York: Teachers College Press.

Havnes, T., & Mogstad, M. (2009). *No Child Left Behind: Universal childcare and children's long-run outcomes.* Discussion Papers No. 582. Oslo: Statistics Norway, Research Department.

Heckman, J.J., Moon, S.H., Pinto, R., Savelyev, P., & Yavitz, A. (2010). *A new cost-benefit and rate of return analysis for the Perry Preschool Program: A summary.* Working Paper 16180. Cambridge, MA: National Bureau of Economic Research.

Helburn, S.W., & Howes, C. (1996). Child care cost and quality. *Future of Children, 6*(2), 62–82.

Karoly, L.A., & Bigelow, J.H. (2005). *The economics of investing in universal preschool education in California.* Santa Monica, CA: RAND.

Karoly, L.A., Greenwood, P., Everingham, S., Hoube, J., Kilburn, R., Rydell, P., Sanders, M., & Chiesa, J. (1998). *Investing in our children: What we know and what we don't know about the costs and benefits of early childhood interventions.* Report no. MR-898-TCWF. Washington, DC: RAND.

Kilburn, R., & Karoly, L.A. (2008). *The economics of early childhood policy.* Santa Monica, CA: RAND.

Lefebvre, P., & Merrigan, P. (2005). *Low-fee ($5/day/child) regulated childcare policy and the labor supply of mothers with young children: A natural experiment from Canada.* Working Paper 05–08. Montreal: Inter-university Centre on Risk, Economic Policies and Employment (CIRPEE).

Lefebvre, P., & Merrigan, P. (2008). Child-care policy and the labor supply of mothers with young children: A natural experiment from Canada. *Journal of Labor Economics, 26,* 519–548.

Lefebvre, P., Merrigan P., & Verstraete, M. (2008). *Childcare policy and cognitive outcomes of children: Results from a large scale quasi-experiment on universal childcare in Canada.* Working Paper 08–23. Montreal: Inter-university Centre on Risk, Economic Policies and Employment (CIRPEE).

Lefebvre, P., Merrigan, P., & Verstraete, M. (2009). Dynamic labour supply effects of childcare subsidies: Evidence from a Canadian natural experiment on low-fee universal child care. *Labour Economics, 16*, 490–502.

Ludwig, J., & Phillips, D. A. (2007). *The benefits and costs of Head Start.* Working Paper no. 12973. Cambridge, MA: National Bureau of Economic Research.

Lynch, R. (2004). *Exceptional returns: Economic, fiscal and social benefits of investment in early child development.* Washington, DC: Economic Policy Institute.

Magnuson, K.A., Ruhm, C., & Waldfogel, J. (2007a). Does pre-kindergarten improve school preparation and performance? *Economics of Education Review, 26*, 33–51.

Magnuson, K.A., Ruhm, C., & Waldfogel, J. (2007b). The persistence of preschool effects: Do subsequent classroom experiences matter? *Early Childhood Research Quarterly, 22*, 18–38.

Masse, L.N., & Barnett, W.S. (2002). *A benefit-cost analysis of the Abecedarian Program.* New Brunswick, NJ: National Institute for Early Education Research.

Mocan, H.N. (1997). Cost functions, efficiency and quality in day care centers. *Journal of Human Resources, 32*, 861–891.

NICHD-ECCRN. (2001). Child care and children's peer interaction at 24 and 36 months: The NICHD Study of Early Child Care. *Child Development, 72*, 1498–1500.

NICHD-ECCRN. (2003). Does amount of time spent in childcare predict socioemotional adjustment during the transition to kindergarten? *Child Development, 74*, 976–1005.

NICHD-ECCRN, & Duncan, G. (2003). Modeling the impacts of child care quality on children's preschool cognitive development. *Child Development, 74*, 1454–1475.

Piketty, T. (2005). L'impact de l'allocation parentale d'éducation sur l'activité féminine et la fécondité en France, 1982–2002. *Les Cahiers de l'INED*, no. 156, 79–109.

PricewaterhouseCoopers. (2003) *Universal childcare provision in the UK: Towards a cost-benefit analysis.* Discussion paper. London: PricewaterhouseCoopers.

PricewaterhouseCoopers. (2004). *Universal early education and care in 2020: Costs, benefits and funding options.* London: Daycare Trust/Social Market Foundation.

Reynolds, A.J., Temple, A.J., Robertson, D.L., & Mann, E.A. (2002). Age 21 cost-benefit analysis of the Title 1 Chicago Child-Parent Centres. *Educational Evaluation and Policy Analysis, 24*, 267–303.

Schone, P. (2004). Labour supply effects of a cash-for-care subsidy. *Journal of Population Economics, 17*, 703–727.

108   Gordon Cleveland

United States General Accounting Office (U.S. GAO). (1999). *Child care: How do military and civilian center costs compare?* GAO/HEHS-00-7. Washington, DC: Author.
Vandell, D. (2004). Early child care: The known and the unknown. *Merrill-Palmer Quarterly, 50,* 387–411.

4 Canadian Child Care Regulations Regarding Training and Curriculum

ELLEN JACOBS AND EMMANUELLE ADRIEN

Although non-parental out-of-home child care has been a common option for families for several decades, the quality of children's daily experiences in these settings has been a topic of concern for parents, educators, researchers, and policy makers. As one response, a multitude of national and international studies have focused on factors that are strongly associated with the delivery of high-quality care. Initially, researchers conducted single-variable studies, and as individual factors were identified, they undertook the examination of multiple variables under a variety of conditions. More recently, complex statistical procedures have enabled researchers to follow the paths of influence and the relative strengths of a wide variety of variables (Goelman et al., 2006), which have been categorized in terms of their structural or process features (Lamb & Ahnert, 2006). Structural variables can be quantified and measured with ease, and typically include group size, educator:child ratios, and educator training. Process variables are more difficult to quantify and include factors such as the type and tone of educator–child interactions and, thus, determine children's daily classroom experiences. Both structural and process variables are considered to be critical components of the global child care environment, which can positively or negatively influence child developmental outcomes (Lamb & Ahnert, 2006). As such, it is important to study the means by which the structural and process variables can be influenced. Government regulation may be one way of achieving the goal of high-quality care – ensuring that children are protected from harm, guaranteeing that they are well cared for, and providing stimulating educational and social experiences that may result in optimal developmental outcomes. However, the regulatory system is complex in terms of its components (i.e., regulations, exemptions, monitoring, and enforcement), the political intent behind the regulated standards, and the political will behind the exemptions and enforcement of the regulations.

This chapter examines regulations drafted by Canadian provincial and territorial governments to address structural and process variables in child care. It also explores the intertwining of elements (e.g., educator pre-service and in-service training programs) that play a role in the development of the educator's skills, values, and beliefs that influence her or his decisions regarding programming and classroom behaviour. All of these factors impact upon children's experiences in child care (National Research Council [NRC], 2001).

The focus of the chapter is the relationship between provincial regulations regarding educator training and mandated curriculum; in addition, we examine the association between provincial regulations and the training provided by colleges in the various Canadian jurisdictions. All of these factors are designed to have an impact on educator practices. We briefly address the way educator practices are guided by the early learning frameworks recently formulated in four Canadian provinces (see chapter by Rachel Langford in this volume). We wish to underline the fact that several of these early learning frameworks are intended to be guidelines regarding practices with young children. Therefore, as in the case of British Columbia, these frameworks may fall under the auspices of a different ministry than those that have child care as their mandate. In this chapter, we focus on the regulations regarding child care that were current at the time that this chapter was written.

Regulations

Definition

Regulations are government or ministerial orders that carry the force of law. Failure to comply with these legal orders is a contravention of the law, and as such, sanctions can be meted out in accordance with the specifics of the regulation(s). For the most part, government bodies draft regulations to control the quality of a service or product. In Canada, child care regulations are mainly set by provincial or territorial governments. Specific aspects of a child care centre's functioning (e.g., food storage, playground equipment, room size) are governed by regulations drafted by different government bodies (e.g., ministries of health, public security, public affairs, and environment). These regulations establish a baseline below which it is unlawful to operate, and while ensuring minimal standards for children's health, well-being, and safety, they may not address best practices or establish a level of operation that results in high-quality child developmental outcomes. We note that while regulations require child care centres to meet a particular baseline of functioning in a variety of areas, these baselines do not necessarily set a low standard of requirements; the level of the standards set depends on what the regulations specify.

Research and Regulated Factors

Some regulations address factors related to the quality of care provided, including group size (Ruopp et al., 1979; Smith, 1999); adult:child ratios (Dunn, 1993; Howes, 1997; Phillipsen et al., 1997); educator training and experience (Barnett, Gareis, & Brennan, 1999; Howes & Olenick, 1986; Whitebook, Howes, & Phillips, 1989); and wages (Whitebook, Phillips, & Howes, 1993). These factors are structural variables and can be observed, documented, and measured, and thus, they are easy to regulate and monitor. While all provinces and territories have regulations that address the aforementioned variables, the baselines differ across jurisdictions and are a function of the history, values, culture, and geography of the particular jurisdiction (Morgan, 1984).

Process variables are important to the daily functioning of the centre and have an impact on child developmental outcomes. They are more difficult to quantify and measure, and therefore, they are more difficult to regulate (Lamb & Ahnert, 2006). These include curriculum/programming (Wiggins & McTighe, 1998), educator warmth (Arnett, 1989), and educator–child interactions (Cornell, Sénéchal, & Broda, 1988; Sénéchal et al., 1996), as well as educator support of the development of children's language (McCartney, 1984), social skills (Phillips, McCartney, & Scarr, 1987), and judgment and reasoning skills (Frede, Austin, & Lindhauer, 1993; Weikart, 1972).

While process variables determine the nature of the child's daily environment, the type and content of the educators' training programs (Isenberg, 1999; Snider & Fu, 1990) and their professional development activities (Epstein, 1993; Whitebook, Hnatiuk, & Bellm, 1994) are positively linked to effective curriculum planning, warm and supportive interactions, and children's language, social, judgment, and reasoning skills.

Monitoring and Enforcement

Monitoring regulations is the first of two procedures necessary to make regulations effective, and this involves the overseeing of compliance or adherence to regulations. In jurisdictions with infrequent monitoring, adherence to the regulations may be uneven. Centres that experience difficulty meeting some aspects of the regulations may disregard those features, but meet requirements that are easier to fulfil (e.g., not hiring a sufficient number of fully qualified educators, but posting daily schedules). Thus, in the same jurisdiction, some children may be in centres that do not meet the baseline for regulated functioning, whereas other children may be in centres offering care that is commensurate with or better than required by the regulations.

Enforcement involves the arm of the law that addresses breaches of the regulations; enforcement procedures allow government agents to bring centres into compliance with the regulations (Ward, 1994). Enforcement can take many forms such as a provisional licence to operate for a specific time during which the breaches must be rectified. The government agent may work closely with the centre to reach a solution in a timely manner; it is in the agent's purview to establish the required steps, the order in which they should occur, and the time for completion. There are situations in which it is truly impossible for centres to meet specific regulations and, at the discretion of the government agent and the director of services, an exemption may be allowed.

Exemptions

Morgan suggests that the enforcement of regulations should not be 'arbitrary' as the 'regulations are laws that should be applied fairly and uniformly to all' (1979, p. 23). Her solution to the arbitrary application of regulations is having carefully worded regulations. However, while Morgan advocates strict adherence to the regulations if they are in the best interests of the children, she recommends that regulations should not be strictly applied if they are likely to cause hardship. Thus, an exemption means that a child care centre may continue to offer its services even though it has not met the stated requirements for a licence to operate.

Most of the regulations drafted in Canadian jurisdictions include the possibility of exemptions when considered necessary. Yet local conditions can influence the granting of exemptions for every existing regulation. For instance, in some cases, it is impossible for a centre to meet the regulations regarding training qualifications, and the provincial agents must determine what is in the best interests of their population. In some remote areas, educator training programs may not be easily accessible; consequently, it may be difficult for centres to hire the requisite number of individuals with educational qualifications to meet provincial regulations. However, in rural areas where children living on farms may encounter dangerous situations, a child care program may be an important option for families. Thus, the licensing agent must determine whether it is better to allow a centre to operate with a proportion of unqualified educators, or to deny the centre a licence until there are a sufficient number of educators who meet the training requirements.

In sum, regulations are legal directives that govern the functioning of a child care facility; contravention of these directives, as identified by monitoring, can lead to sanctions as serious as closure (rarely applied). However, exemptions are usually integrated into the regulatory system to meet community needs for a specific period of time during which the facility must make adjustments to comply with the regulations.

What Is Regulated?

In Canadian jurisdictions, most aspects of child care facilities are regulated including the structural features and process variables indicated above. Given that research demonstrates that such factors are associated with child care quality, it would seem wise to include regulations for each of them. However, there may be valid reasons for not regulating all factors (e.g., curriculum should reflect the interests of the specific population, as discussed in the chapter by Alan Pence and Veronica Pacini-Ketchabaw in this volume).

This section of the chapter addresses the contents of the regulations in terms of the items addressed and the rigour of the expectations. Keeping in mind that regulations are legal directives, the potential effectiveness of the regulations will be critiqued in terms of their ability to achieve the goal of high-quality child care and optimal child developmental outcomes. We focus on regulations limited to (1) the type of training requirements for educators, (2) the professional development specified, and (3) the curriculum or programming requirements for children. The rationale for selecting these variables is that educator preparation is an important factor influencing children's daily experiences (Goelman et al., 2006). The curriculum, designed by the educators, determines the children's activities and the substance of what they do on a daily, weekly, monthly, and yearly basis (Bennett, 2005). Thus, it is essential to examine the content of the regulations that address training, professional development, and curriculum.

Regulations Regarding Qualifications
for Employment as an Educator

EDUCATOR TRAINING
The training of child care staff, hereafter called educators, is a complex factor in both form and content. Research indicates that an educator's knowledge of child development and his or her skills have a larger impact on what children learn than other factors do (Darling-Hammond, Wise, & Klein, 1999), specifically, training in early childhood education (ECE) is positively correlated with better quality care (Epstein, 1999; Kontos & Wilcox-Herzog, 1997). Thus, children's developmental outcomes are enhanced when the educator has an understanding of child development and learning theories, as well as the requisite skills for observing children's understanding and their construction of knowledge, and when the educator is equipped to reflect upon children's current knowledge and then plan for further learning (NRC, 2001).

Educators' abilities that improve the quality of care and child developmental outcomes are guidance and support skills, verbal responsiveness, sensitivity to children's needs, and ability to encourage pro-social behaviour (Howes, 1983, 1997). To develop this skill set, training programs should offer courses that focus on child development and learning theories, program design, observation and evaluation techniques, decision making regarding materials, equipment and the learning environment, program planning and implementation, and field placements (Snider & Fu, 1990).

TRAINING OPTIONS
Educator training takes many forms. In Canada, it may be delivered at the college or university level, and the length of the program may range from less than a year (e.g., 9-month *Attestation* in Quebec) to more than three years (e.g., diploma program in Quebec). In most jurisdictions, educators also have the opportunity to qualify as trained individuals by having their prior field experience assessed through a formal process evaluated by the jurisdiction's director of child care. This process

contributes to their qualifications in combination with formal courses and additional supervised fieldwork. Where this option is offered, it is referred to as prior learning assessment recognition (PLAR), competency-based assessment, or a prior learning assessment program.

Canadian Jurisdictional Regulations

The 2010 regulations for each jurisdiction were examined for (1) qualifications for employment as an educator, (2) proportion of staff required to be qualified, and (3) specifics of training required to meet qualifications. Information was obtained from government websites.

Regulations Concerning Educator Training

TRAINING QUALIFICATIONS
Of the ten Canadian provinces and three territories, 84.6 per cent (n = 11/13) require child care centre staff to have formal training qualifications. Levels of training required for an educator to be considered qualified were identified in 76.9 per cent (n = 10/13) of jurisdictions.

LEVELS OF TRAINING TO BE CONSIDERED QUALIFIED
For our purposes, training qualifications were grouped into four levels (i.e., entry = one or more courses but less than a year; basic = one year; intermediate = 2 years; and advanced = more than 2 years). In jurisdictions that identified the maximum level of training, 30 per cent (n = 3/10) of regulations described an intermediate level and 70 per cent (n = 7/10) an advanced level.

Nunavut and the Northwest Territories are the two jurisdictions in which the regulations do not address formal training. Alberta is one jurisdiction with an intermediate level of qualifications with three possible classifications: (1) a child development assistant must have completed an orientation course for child care approved by the minister; (2) a child development worker must have a one-year certificate in early childhood development; (3) a child development supervisor is required to have a two-year diploma in early childhood development. Additionally, one can meet the requirements of the three categories by completing course work that the minister considers to be equivalent to the course work required for each of the levels.

Manitoba is an example of a jurisdiction offering an advanced level of qualification, specifically a degree in child care from an approved educational institution, or a diploma from an approved child care program, or a certificate in an area of specialization in child care from an approved institution. At least 60 per cent ($n = 6/10$) of jurisdictions had explicit information regarding prior learning assessment recognition as an optional route for training qualifications.

Exemptions. In 72.7 per cent of the jurisdictions ($n = 8/11$), the regulations address exemptions to formal training, and they typically deal with course equivalencies that are determined by the director of child care services. In two jurisdictions, exemptions are made only when all attempts to hire a qualified individual have failed; in both cases, the individual is required to work towards achieving the qualifications within a particular time frame (e.g., Prince Edward Island allows three years to completion).

PROPORTION OF STAFF REQUIRED TO BE QUALIFIED

While one set of regulations for training gives possible options for the individual worker, there are a second set of regulations about the required proportion of qualified workers in a centre. These regulations were examined in the documentation for the eleven jurisdictions that have training qualification requirements, and 90.9 per cent ($n = 10/11$) stated the proportion of staff required to meet training qualifications. British Columbia is the exception. In 45.5 per cent ($n = 5/11$) of the jurisdictions, the proportions are linked to levels of training. For example, in Alberta one-quarter of the educators must hold a child development worker qualification, while three-quarters must hold a minimum of child development assistant certification. It was noted that 72.7 per cent ($n = 8/11$) of jurisdictions specified the proportion of trained individuals required for the facility during hours of operation. In 50 per cent ($n = 4/8$) of these jurisdictions a proportion of the staff without training may be employed (e.g., in Nova Scotia 'effective May 1, 2012, at least two-thirds of the staff working directly with children in a full-day program or a part-day program must have a level 1, level 2 or level 3 classification' (Nova Scotia, Regulation 36(4a), Day Care Regulations, 2011).

Exemptions. In 60 per cent ($n = 6/10$) of the jurisdictions that regulate the proportion of qualified staff, exemptions are included. In Manitoba, the exemption concerns the level of qualification and is not an exemption from qualifications altogether. In two provinces, the exemption allows for a deferral, at the discretion of the director of child care services, when it is not possible to hire qualified educators. In Saskatchewan, the director can provide authorization to hire an unqualified individual if his or her qualifications are deemed to be appropriate at the time and an education plan has been submitted to remedy the 'deficiencies' within a reasonable period of time.

SPECIFICS OF TRAINING REQUIRED TO MEET QUALIFICATIONS
In the majority of jurisdictions, the type of training required is listed in broad terms, but usually with reference to early childhood education (e.g., a one-semester university course in early childhood development; a diploma of college studies in ECE). However, 27.3 per cent ($n = 3/11$) of jurisdictions include detailed descriptions of the specifics of the training in the body of the regulations. Two jurisdictions list the specific training institutions and programs; one-third specify the course content areas to be completed (e.g., child development, children's hygiene and health).

Exemptions. Only British Columbia includes information that exempts an educator from taking a course that the director of the Early Childhood Education Registry deems equivalent to a course completed when qualifying for another profession.

Regulations Concerning Professional Development

Definition

Professional development is defined as training that may continue after the initial certification has been acquired and varies widely in form, content, and length. There are the typical single topic workshops, a series of workshops on a related topic, or the professional conference (two or three days) where the attendees select topics of special interest. Responsibility for enrolment in a professional development program may rest with the educators, and sometimes they must pay for the program themselves and/or lose a day's wages due to absence from work. Regulations addressing pre-service and in-service training differ significantly across jurisdictions and depend on many factors including values, beliefs, availability of training programs, and geographical location.

Professional development programs are more effective if they are well designed (Katz, 1993), coherent, focused (Epstein, 1993), and address relevant topics (Kontos et al., 1992). It is difficult to enhance practice or change values and beliefs via the single workshop model (Fullan & Stiegelbrauer, 1991; Jacobs et al., 2002), thus some researchers propose a move towards a mentoring or consultant model (Blank & Kershaw, 2009; Hawkey, 1997; Jacobs et al., 2002; Odell, 1990; White-book et al., 1994; Whitebook & Bellm, 1996). Both the mentoring and consultation models can provide educators with 'on-site mentoring, individualized attention, immediate feedback, and a continuous program of study' (NRC, 2001, p. 274; see Nina Howe and Ellen Jacobs' chapter on mentoring in this volume).

Regulations

There are requirements for professional development in 53.8 per cent ($n = 7/13$) of the jurisdictions (e.g., seminars, conferences, workshops, and continuing education courses). More than half of these jurisdictions ($n = 4/7$) identify the length of time between professional development opportunities; every three years in Newfoundland, Nova Scotia and Prince Edward Island to every five years in British Columbia. These jurisdictions specify professional development as a requirement for educators to maintain their certification. No jurisdiction mandates specific content nor are there exemptions in the seven jurisdictions regulating professional development.

Regulations Concerning Program of Activities or Curriculum

Definition

The program or curriculum is broadly defined as the children's daily activities, along with the methods used to teach concepts, and the social environment in which the learning takes place – all of which are important issues in children's learning (NRC, 2001). The nature of children's experiences in their child care centres can affect their developmental outcomes (Lamb & Ahnert, 2006). These points have been underscored in a report by the U.S. National Research Council (1999), which argued that three important principles of learning are significant in the pre-school years: (1) children develop ideas and concepts through experiences in the real world, and interactions with peers and adults help them build on their existing knowledge; (2) children need factual knowledge, skills, and comprehension as a basis on which to build further knowledge; and (3) they need to develop learning strategies that are supportive and meaningful. Additionally, children need experiences to enhance their learning in the foundational areas of literacy, math, and science and with the creative arts (i.e., music, dance, art), gross motor activities, and opportunities for social and emotional experiences (e.g., dramatic play; NRC, 2001).

The regulations regarding staff training are important for the children's program. Educators have the most influence over the centre's program of activities, and as stated earlier, training in early childhood education and child development is positively correlated with the quality of the global environment in classrooms. Given that researchers have specifically identified curriculum content, methods of imparting information, and the development of children's learning strategies to be essential, it is important to examine regulations regarding these factors.

Regulations Regarding Curriculum Content

Regulations

All Canadian jurisdictions define curriculum requirements. Some jurisdictions regulate an extensive number of elements to be included in the program of activities, whereas other jurisdictions allow the program of activities to be open-ended and, therefore, the description of requirements is limited.

ELEMENTS OF REGULATIONS
We identified specific factors for possible inclusion in jurisdictional regulations and included the frequency of occurrence of ten factors; developmental appropriateness; behavioural guidance; schedule of program activities; holistic nature of the curriculum; cultural sensitivity; inclusivity and acknowledgment of differences; community as a resource; indoor/outdoor activities; creativity (i.e., as part of activities, drama, music); and large/small group and group/individual collaborations. This list was derived from factors included in several of the early learning frameworks recently drafted in four Canadian jurisdictions, as well as from the content of regulations in force from other jurisdictions for quite some time (see chapter by Rachel Langford in this volume).

The regulations are not prescriptive; they avoid specifying the way in which these elements are to be addressed. Rather, they offer educators an armature on which to shape the curriculum while taking into consideration the required elements (e.g., a holistic approach, cultural sensitivity).

DEVELOPMENTAL APPROPRIATENESS

The program/curriculum is regulated in 92.3 per cent (n = 12/13) of provinces/territories by specifying that activities and/or materials must be developmentally appropriate. The wording is similar in all jurisdictions: for example, programming should be 'appropriate to the developmental levels of the children enrolled' (i.e., Regulation 53(1), Day Nurseries Act, 2007, Ontario) or 'indoor and outdoor furnishing and equipment, including play materials are developmentally appropriate for the ages of the children cared for' (i.e., Schedule 1, Regulation 20a(ii), Child Care Licensing Regulation, 2008, Alberta).

BEHAVIOURAL GUIDANCE

In 84.6 per cent (n = 11/13) of the jurisdictions, mention is made of how children's behaviours should be monitored and acted upon by the educators. The terminology used to refer to this issue varies: *child discipline* in Alberta, Northwest Territories, and Nunavut; *behavioural guidance* in British Columbia, Newfoundland, and Nova Scotia; and *behaviour management* in Manitoba, Ontario, Prince Edward Island, Saskatchewan, and Yukon. Each term has a different connotation that may reflect the jurisdictional attitude towards handling children's (mis)behaviour. The regulations dictate which methods are unacceptable when managing children's behaviours; 72.7 per cent (n = 8/11) of the jurisdictions clearly prohibit the use of physical punishment and verbal or emotional abuse by any staff member. Quebec and New Brunswick do not address the issue of behavioural guidance or management in their regulations.

SCHEDULE OF ACTIVITIES

While all provinces and territories have program of activities or curriculum requirements in their regulations, 69.2 per cent (n = 9/13) refer to the frequency with which a program of activities is to be provided and specify a daily basis (e.g., 'the daily schedule must provide . . .' Regulation 16(2), Child Care Centre Program Regulations, 1995, Yukon; 'a licensee must adhere to the daily program standards established . . .' (Regulation 18(1), Day Care Regulations, 2011, Nova Scotia). Alberta,

Newfoundland, New Brunswick, and Quebec do not refer to a daily program or schedule of activities in their regulations.

HOLISTIC NATURE OF THE PROGRAM

Children's holistic development including specific domains (e.g., intellectual, social, emotional, physical) is included in 69.2 per cent ($n = 9/13$) of the jurisdictions, but only 66.7 per cent ($n = 6/9$) include language development (i.e., British Columbia, Northwest Territories, Nova Scotia, Nunavut, Ontario, and Yukon).

INDOOR/OUTDOOR ACTIVITIES

In 61.5 per cent ($n = 8/13$) of the jurisdictions, provision of indoor and outdoor activities is regulated. In British Columbia, the regulations state that 'a program of activities is provided that encourages the physical development of children including providing indoor and outdoor activities that encourage the development of large and small muscle skills appropriate to each child's level of development' (Schedule G; Section 44(1), Child Care Licensing Regulation, 2007). Regulations in Manitoba regarding outdoor play refer to weather conditions that restrict outdoor play.

INDIVIDUAL DIFFERENCES AND INCLUSIVITY

In 53.8 per cent ($n = 7/13$) of the jurisdictional regulations, reference is made to the individual differences of children (British Columbia), ensuring that children with special needs are integrated into the program of activities (Northwest Territories, Nunavut, and Nova Scotia), and/or ensuring that the program is inclusive of children with special needs (Ontario) or of requiring additional supports (Manitoba).

COMMUNITY AS A RESOURCE

In 38.5 per cent ($n = 5/13$) of the jurisdictions, the regulations refer to the use of the community as a resource. In British Columbia, this is stated as 'providing experiences that facilitate a child's feeling of belonging to a family, community and the world at large' (Schedule G, Section 44(5e), Child Care Licensing Regulation, 2007). In Nunavut, the Northwest Territories, and New Brunswick, it appears in a reference to 'local community services that may be used to enhance the quality of programs and services in the facility/day care centre' (Regulation 25, Child Day Care Standards Regulations, 1990, Nunavut and Northwest Territories; Regulation 3(2)(f/iv), New Brunswick Regulation 83–85,

1983). The Yukon details the balance that should be achieved in the daily program including 'activities that promote cultural awareness, social responsibility, and community involvement' (Regulation 16(3)(k), Child Care Centre Program Regulation, 1995, Yukon).

CULTURAL SENSITIVITY

The inclusion of cultural sensitivity in program activities is mentioned in only 30.8 per cent ($n = 4/13$) of the jurisdictions: British Columbia, Northwest Territories, Nunavut, and the Yukon. Cultural sensitivity is reflected in regulations that stress the need for 'a daily program of activities that is sensitive to each child's cultural heritage' (Regulation 16(1), Child Care Centre Program Regulation, 1995, Yukon) and 'the provision of a comfortable atmosphere in which children feel proud of their cultural heritage and cultural sharing is encouraged' (Schedule G, Section 44(4c), Child Care Licensing Regulation, 2007, British Columbia).

CREATIVITY

Reference to creativity is included in 38.5 per cent ($n = 5/13$) of the jurisdictional regulations, specifically for providing art, drama, and music activities. In Alberta and Manitoba, creativity is identified in a list of important provisions: 'physical, social, intellectual, creative and emotional needs of children' (Schedule 1, Regulation 2(1), Child Care Licensing Regulation, 2008, Alberta). In the Yukon, this regulation refers to 'activities that promote creative expression through the fine arts of music and drama' (Regulation 16(3)(i), Child Care Centre Program Regulation, 1995, Yukon). In British Columbia, the regulations are more explicit and refer to the requirement for 'activities and materials that encourage creative endeavours such as art, music, movement, imaginative play, storytelling and construction' (Schedule G, Section 44(2d), Child Care Licensing Regulation, 2007, British Columbia).

LARGE–SMALL GROUP AND GROUP–INDIVIDUAL COLLABORATIONS

The inclusion of large and small group activities is regulated in 38.5 per cent ($n = 5/13$) of the jurisdictions. In British Columbia, the regulation reads as 'providing an environment for children to work independently and to share and work cooperatively in small groups' (Schedule G, Section 44(5a), Child Care Licensing Regulation, 2007, British Columbia). In Manitoba, the regulation requires 'play activity in groups as per ratio

requirements and includes daily individual and small group . . . activities' (Regulation 10(3)(a) Child Care Regulation, 1986, Manitoba). In
the Yukon, 'small and large group activities which provide for social
and emotional development' are required (Regulation 16(3)(h), Child
Care Centre Program Regulation, 1995, Yukon). In Prince Edward Island, the first requirement mentioned regarding the daily program of
activities is the inclusion of 'group and individual activities' (Regulation 27(a), Child Care Facilities Act Regulations, 2005, Prince Edward
Island). In Nova Scotia, the regulations require 'a licensee [to] adhere
to the daily program standards established by the Minister' (Regulation 18(1), Day Care Regulations, 2011, Nova Scotia). The province's
daily program standards document mentions that children should be
provided with materials and equipment that support 'individual and
group play' (Standards for the Daily Program in Licensed Child Care
Facilities, 6.3(a), 2011, Nova Scotia).

Conclusion

The regulations regarding curriculum presented above are the product
of several iterations for most of the jurisdictions. More recently, four
provinces have addressed curriculum and best practices by generating
comprehensive documents referred to as *frameworks* that are intended
to guide child care practices: New Brunswick, Ontario, Saskatchewan,
and British Columbia. Manitoba is currently in the process of developing a framework document but it is not yet available. These frameworks
are tools educators in child care centres can use in their daily practice
to foster children's development. Whereas curriculum regulations describe what each child care centre is required to provide, the provincial
frameworks include best practices, address how to create a rich learning environment, and guide educators in their reflective practice, but
adherence to the frameworks is not made mandatory by the regulations. New Brunswick has passed the Early Learning and Child Care
Act in 2010, however, which stipulates that 'the operator of a licensed
facility shall use, in its or their entirety, one or both of the curriculum
frameworks provided by the Minister' (Act 18(1), Early Learning and
Child Care Act, 2010, New Brunswick). Ministries working in collaboration with representatives from universities, colleges, and the early
childhood field in each province developed these frameworks (see
chapter by Rachel Langford in this volume).

Training Programs in Colleges

The majority of the early childhood education training programs are located in the Canadian college system, which offers post-secondary education and training for individuals who wish to pursue a vocation. Students can earn a two- or three-year diploma (e.g., British Columbia, Diplôme d'Études Collégiales/DEC in Quebec, respectively) or a one-year certificate. College programs are usually the responsibility of the ministry accountable for post-secondary education. Typically, the content of these training programs is the result of 'best practice' information as interpreted by college instructors, and in some cases, the content is driven by provincial learning outcome mandates. Some colleges have specialized programs in ECE and a variety of programs (e.g., certificates or diplomas in pre-school education, special education, school-aged care). Once a student has completed the required courses in an early childhood program, he or she is usually considered qualified to work as an educator in the jurisdiction.

We examined a sample of the certificate and diploma programs available to determine whether they enable an individual to meet the qualifications required by the jurisdiction. In order to discuss the relationship between the regulations regarding educator qualifications and the ECE program courses, we reviewed academic calendars from a sample of colleges across Canada. As of 2010, an ECE training program was not available in the Northwest Territories. One diploma and one certificate program was examined for each jurisdiction offering both types of programs. In some cases, the certificate program was not offered in the same institution as the diploma program, thus two different colleges were reviewed. The program details (i.e., course lists and course content) were retrieved from each college website. Many, but not all Canadian colleges offered both certificate (one year) and diploma (two years) options in their ECE programs. The programs are structured so that the first year generally counts as the certificate year and after completing the second year, a diploma is granted. Thus, diploma programs are built on the foundation of the certificate program; consequently, diploma programs consist of twice as many courses and, in some jurisdictions, diploma students can also specialize in children with special needs, Aboriginal studies, or school-aged care. Colleges in some of the jurisdictions offer only diploma programs (i.e., Manitoba, Newfoundland, Nova Scotia, and Ontario).

Ten aspects of the ECE programs were examined including: (1) child development courses, (2) behavioural guidance, (3) observation courses, (4) curriculum or program planning courses, (5) field placements or practica, (6) cultural diversity, (7) special needs, (8) creative activities, (9) play, and (10) developmentally appropriate practice. Data are reviewed for all jurisdictions except the Northwest Territories ($n = 12/13$).

Child Development

Child development courses are listed in all certificate ($n = 6$) and diploma programs ($n = 11$) and range from one to two required in the certificate programs to a total of two to six courses in diploma programs. At the lower range in the certificate programs, New Brunswick and Saskatchewan require only one child development course whereas, 66.7 per cent ($n = 4/6$) of the certificate programs reviewed require two courses. For the diploma programs reviewed, Manitoba requires six courses, 45.5 per cent ($n = 5/11$) of jurisdictions require three child development courses, 27.3 per cent ($n = 3/11$) require two, and 18.2 per cent ($n = 2/11$) list just one course in child development.

Behavioural Guidance

All educators require knowledge about effective behavioural guidance strategies, although not all programs have a specific course on this topic. In 66.7 per cent ($n = 4/6$) of the certificate programs and 72.7 per cent ($n = 8/11$) of the diploma courses reviewed, at least one course dealing specifically with child discipline and/or behavioural guidance or management is included. This information may be included in other courses in the programs; however, in two certificate and three diploma programs this was not obvious from website descriptions.

Observation and Assessment

Observational skills have been recognized in the ECE field as a valuable tool for assessment as well as a means of gathering information for program planning and curriculum design. A specific course in learning how to observe young children is a skill that is taught in 50 per cent ($n = 3/6$) of the certificate programs and 45.5 per cent ($n = 5/11$) of the diploma programs reviewed.

Curriculum or Program Planning

Learning how to design and plan a curriculum for young children is important for daily classroom activities. Curriculum courses inform educators about learning theories relevant for teaching young children and usually provide information about the curriculum design process. Some courses focus on single topics such as art or music, while others combine related topics such as language and literacy, science and math, or music and movement. Since the quality of daily activities impact child developmental outcomes, courses on curriculum design and planning should be a major component of ECE programs (NRC, 2001).

In the six certificate programs examined, five have curriculum development as a requirement, 40 per cent ($n = 2/5$) specify two courses, 40 per cent ($n = 2/5$) list three, and one program requires four courses. In the diploma programs, the requirements range from one to two courses in the Yukon and Prince Edward Island, respectively, to eight courses in Saskatchewan. Four colleges (36.4%) require three courses, 18.2 per cent ($n = 2/11$) list four curriculum courses, and another 18.2 per cent ($n = 2/11$) specify five curriculum design courses as required in the program.

Across the jurisdictions, each program seems to have a different philosophical bent influencing how these courses are presented as a part of the college curriculum. For instance, the diploma program in Manitoba lists five curriculum courses and four other courses that focus on play as the means of delivering the curriculum for that topic area (e.g., *Plan for play-based programs*).

Field Placements or Practica

Field placements, which are common to most professions (e.g., teaching, nursing, accounting), provide students with real life experiences that may ultimately influence their decision to pursue the career or not. Field placements are akin to apprenticeships, and in child care settings students learn about all aspects of the work involved in becoming an educator. Most colleges aim to place their students in model classrooms with an experienced and accomplished educator, who is interested in helping students develop the skills required to be a successful educator. One Canadian college (diploma program) has students spend time working in the kitchen of child care centres to learn about nutrition, children's food preferences, and allergies (e.g., Kitchen placement, Prince Edward Island). The number of placements for each program ranges from one to three in certificate programs to three to six in diploma programs. Only a few diploma programs, 18.2 per cent ($n = 2/11$) have seminars linked to these placements, along with one certificate program. In the seminars, the instructor discusses the students' positive experiences and challenges in their placements, in order to facilitate problem solving in all aspects of the students' training. While it is customary for students to speak with their supervisor on an individual basis immediately following the supervisor's visit to the field placement, the seminars would involve all students in a review and discussion of their settings and the issues that arise. As such, the co-construction of knowledge that occurs in seminars through the exchange of ideas among students offers a relevant and meaningful experience that builds on individual discussions with a supervisor. The seminar helps students to experience the interactions that occur in a community of learners, although, as we note, it is a part of the field placement experience in only a few cases.

Cultural Diversity

Although cultural diversity is listed as an important curriculum issue in the regulations of four jurisdictions, only Manitoba has a specific course that addresses cultural issues, but it is not one of the four jurisdictions requiring a focus on cultural diversity. However, Alberta has a program that includes an option for a specialization in Aboriginal Studies. The program in Nunavut includes a course entitled Traditional Child Rearing that focuses on culturally relevant learning such as elder teaching, storytelling, and the preservation of cultural language, values, and beliefs. We discuss the lack of courses addressing cultural diversity per se in other jurisdictions in a later section.

Special Needs

In all jurisdictions, the diploma programs include one or two courses on children with special needs. The course titles range from Children with Diverse Abilities (Saskatchewan) to Children with Special Needs (Ontario) and Principles of Inclusion (Prince Edward Island). In British Columbia, the colleges offer a three-course package that forms a Special Needs Citation within the diploma program.

Creative Activities

Five of the diploma programs require students to complete courses that address the development of creativity through music, movement, drama, and art. In both Quebec (three courses) and Newfoundland (four courses), the course titles reflect course philosophy and content (e.g., Quebec – Literature and Creative Drama, The Creative Educator; Newfoundland – Creative Activities 1-Art; Creative Activities III-Music). Creativity is also reflected in course descriptions in Ontario, Manitoba, and the Yukon.

Play

Play, which is a very important aspect of early childhood programs, is mentioned in the program courses in Manitoba, Nova Scotia, Prince Edward Island, Saskatchewan, and Yukon. Clearly, some programs deliver the messages about the importance of play through courses that have play as a main focus, whereas other programs may embed the message into other courses. For example, in the courses listed for the Manitoba college, five clearly focus on play as a medium for learning in the early childhood classroom (i.e., Interact with Children through Play; Prepare for Play; Facilitate Symbolic Play; Foster Discovery and Creative Play; Extend Children's Play).

Developmentally Appropriate Practice

While developmentally appropriate practice is mentioned in the regulations for a number of jurisdictions, only two (Nova Scotia and Prince Edward Island) have college courses specifically titled Developmentally Appropriate Practice. The lack of specific courses with this title in other programs does not mean that the developmentally appropriate practice is not a component of other courses. It would typically be addressed in courses such as Principles and Practices (British Columbia), Basic Methods I (Nunavut), and Introduction to Early Childhood Education (Saskatchewan).

Summary

In this review of a sampling of college certificate and diploma programs in Canadian jurisdictions, it is evident that some courses are more commonly included in the curricula than others. A ranking of courses by topic indicates that field placements would head the list followed by curriculum and child development courses. Most training programs that include behavioural guidance in their curriculum offer one or two courses. Working with children with special needs seems to be addressed in one or two courses in every program, as are creative activities for children.

Discussion

Regulations

Regulations provide rules of functioning for individuals engaged in a specific profession and also protection for consumers of the service. As stated earlier, the regulatory body for a particular profession may establish qualification standards that vary in degree of demands. If the standards are so high that they are unattainable by most individuals, the outcome is likely to be stress and professional demoralization (NRC, 2001), which may limit the willingness of individuals to work in that field. Depending on the profession's public importance, this may create hardship within the general population. Alternatively, very basic and lenient standards may lead to the provision of a poor quality service if individuals only aim to meet the low level of criteria established by the regulations. Of course, in the field of child care, it is expected that the goal of educators will be the provision of care that enhances children's developmental outcomes.

Child care is a service offered to families for children from birth through elementary school age. Children do not themselves have the opportunity to express an opinion about the service or to petition for improvements, if warranted. In addition, parents, those who do have a voice, frequently have few alternative care options or do not have extensive knowledge about quality care. Thus, the users are a vulnerable clientele, who require protection afforded by strong and meaningful regulations. However, providers of the service, the educators, also deserve respect and trust from the regulators regarding their ability, willingness, and desire to offer high-quality care that translates into positive child developmental outcomes.

Forty years of child care research has generated extensive knowledge about the impact of different types of care on various populations on a variety of variables (see Lamb & Ahnert, 2006, for an extensive review).

As stated earlier, several factors are well known to have an impact on the quality of child care and on children's developmental outcomes; this knowledge should inform members of regulatory bodies and form the basis for the regulations.

The results of our research indicate that most of the jurisdictional regulations are based on research that has established the importance of these elements of care for enhanced child developmental outcomes. Given our focus on curriculum, only related factors such as educator training were included in the review of regulations. We now discuss each factor and comment on the contents and details of the regulations.

Qualifications for Employment as an Educator

TRAINING QUALIFICATIONS

Given that research indicates the importance of training in early childhood education, it is surprising that only eleven of thirteen provinces and territories included this in their regulations with nine specifying required levels of training. Three provinces required an intermediate level, while six identified an advanced level. The descriptions of the basic levels indicated that very little training was expected. Provinces with an intermediate level of qualifications had multilevel requirements for educators with the requirements becoming more demanding with the increase in levels. Those requiring an advanced level of qualifications met the research recommendations, namely, education and training in ECE were most likely to result in high-quality classroom experiences for pre-school-aged children. Training programs that are specific to ECE are likely to provide the educator with opportunities to develop an understanding of theories of learning and child development, acquire observation skills, have field experiences that support experimentation with the application of theories (e.g., literacy, numeracy, learning through play), develop applied skills (e.g., creative activities), and to work effectively with the children with special needs. All of this is essential for the creation of a child care environment that supports active learning.

EXEMPTIONS

More than half of the jurisdictions included exemptions in their regulations regarding formal training. Upon first glance, this might be surprising given the importance of formal training; however, the willingness of regulators to permit exemptions may underline the fact that formal training might sometimes be difficult to obtain. The problem might be a function of geography (e.g., remote location of centre), inaccessibility (e.g., lack of training facilities in the district), inconvenience (e.g., hours of centre's operation conflict with training program), or financial issues (e.g., expense of program or cost of transportation to the training facility). Additionally, when an individual without qualifications begins working, balancing the needs of the job and a training program can be challenging. Thus, the provision of a realistic time frame for completing training (i.e., average of three years) may be required. That the ECE profession allows individuals to obtain the necessary training while employed attests to the need for staff and the commitment of the regulatory bodies to staff training.

Proportion of Staff Required to Be Qualified

Several jurisdictions allow different levels of staff training in child care centres and different proportions of educators with different levels of training to work at certain times of the day. Monetary compensation (i.e., wages) typically differs in accordance with an educator's training; the more advanced the level of training, the higher the hourly wage. Yet, many settings cannot afford to pay the requisite wages when 100 per cent of the staff are fully qualified. Thus, regulators have made it possible for centres to operate with a proportion of fully qualified staff, or qualified to a certain level (e.g., ECE I, II, or III). The regulations regarding proportions vary across jurisdictions and may be a function of the number of children, time of day (e.g., before 8 a.m. and after 4 p.m.), location of the facility (e.g., on school site), number of hours that a person with a particular type of training is working, and/or the children's ages. We must assume that the drafters of the regulations have local knowledge and expertise about the needs in child care centres to include special proportional conditions. What might be acceptable and/or necessary in one jurisdiction may not be in another (e.g., rural settings versus urban environments).

Additionally, when two-thirds of a centre's staff must be qualified and one-third are not, this may result in situations in which some children are guided by a fully trained individual, whereas others are not. This is an inequity that is unacceptable as it can have an impact on children's daily experiences and ultimately on their development.

EXEMPTIONS

The varied needs of different communities within a jurisdiction may necessitate exemptions to the regulations that enable centres to hire different proportions of trained educators than are specified in the regulations. Once again, the remoteness of the centre's location and/or the inaccessibility of training programs may necessitate flexibility in the regulations. So, while the intentions of the regulations may be noble, the reality of the situation and the needs of the community must be given due consideration. The hardship created by inflexible or unrealistic regulations may be more detrimental than exempting standards set by particular regulations for a predetermined period of time.

Specifics of Training Required to Meet Qualifications

Given that training in early childhood education is significantly correlated with enhanced child developmental outcomes, it is not surprising that jurisdictions have specified the type of training required. In the majority of the jurisdictions, the type of training required is listed in broad terms. In these regulations, reference is usually made to ECEC as a program or a set of courses within a program. Some jurisdictions specify the qualifying training institutions, list the required courses, or provide descriptions of the course content. This level of detail may be unnecessary as the ECE college programs have been designed by faculty members who utilize the research in designing their programs to address the specific training needs of educators. New research findings can point the way for change in some child care practices or approaches, and colleges can respond by altering their programs or course content within a twelve-month period. On the other hand, regulations take longer to be altered; in many jurisdictions, regulations are reviewed and changed only at specified intervals (e.g., once every three years). Additionally, regulatory committees must consider the impact of new regulations on the functioning of all child care programs in their jurisdiction, whereas colleges as self-contained units may consider the impact of changes only on their own program.

Professional Development

In most professions, in-service professional development is one of the most salient requirements for the maintenance of certification. Thus, the lack of attention to professional development within the regulations by 46.2 per cent ($n = 6/13$) of the jurisdictions is notable. This raises the question of whether this is an oversight by the regulatory bodies or whether educators are not perceived as professionals who can benefit from in-service programs. Certainly, as the literature demonstrates, there are many benefits for providing quality child care that are derived from regular professional development (Borko, 2004; Epstein, 1993, 1999; Klein & Sheehan, 1987; Venn & Wolery, 1992). We believe it is appropriate that the seven jurisdictions that regulate professional development have specified neither the type nor the topics to be addressed. Participants should choose the topics for professional development, and the format (e.g., seminars, conferences, workshops, continuing education courses) should be related to the topic. The typical one-session workshop is rather ineffective in changing attitudes, beliefs, and practices, whereas mentoring or consultant models are the most effective forms of professional development (Fantuzzo et al., 1997; Galinsky et al., 1994; Whitebook et al., 1994). Although no jurisdiction mentioned differentiated professional development, it is important for organizers to consider the different needs and interests of individual educators based on their level of training and experience.

Program or Curriculum Requirements and College Course Content

Regulations for all provinces and territories were examined regarding program or curriculum design. A detailed analysis of the specific contents of the requirements revealed that as many as seventeen aspects of programming were addressed and those discussed in this chapter (i.e., 10) existed in at least one-quarter of the jurisdictions. The courses offered in a sample of college programs in each jurisdiction were reviewed to enable an examination of the relationship between regulations for curriculum requirements and the college courses. This exercise was undertaken to ascertain whether students who completed the college programs would be properly prepared to meet the regulations regarding curriculum or programming.

SCHEDULE OF ACTIVITIES
The high percentage of jurisdictions with regulations that specify that planning and programming must be a daily occurrence is an acknowledgment of the relevance of daily planning. Planning usually involves at least some level of reflection, and if legislation stipulates daily planning, this should increase the likelihood that while the routine may be

consistent, a variety of activities will be offered. If educators plan daily rather than weekly, there is the distinct possibility that the activities will be related and will respond to the growth in the children's knowledge through their daily experiences. Curriculum courses usually address program content and the nature of daily activities, and all jurisdictions with training programs had curriculum courses that were part of the core program.

BEHAVIOURAL GUIDANCE

There was not a definitive correspondence between jurisdictional regulations regarding behavioural guidance and relevant college courses. We noted that many colleges required students to complete at least one course in the monitoring of children's behaviour, labelled the courses as *guidance*. This reflects the current attitude regarding the educator's role wherein they have been taught to *guide* rather than *manage* or *discipline* children's inappropriate behaviour. Given that children may spend the majority of their waking hours in child care, it was mystifying that some jurisdictions did not refer to behavioural guidance in their regulations, and several college programs did not have courses that focused specifically on behavioural guidance. Certainly, one of the most difficult aspects of working with children involves dealing with challenging behaviours, and most educators, especially novices, find this to be the case (Kaiser & Rasminsky, 2007).

DEVELOPMENTAL APPROPRIATENESS

The use of this terminology is purposeful and reflects one of the philosophical directions in the field (Bredekamp, 1987). Additionally, by using this terminology, the regulations convey a sense of trust and respect for the educator's ability to do what is appropriate and right for the group of children in his or her care. While the term *developmental appropriateness* appears in some course descriptions in the college calendars, Nova Scotia and Ontario have courses devoted to the topic of developmental appropriateness per se.

HOLISTIC NATURE OF THE PROGRAM

More than half of the jurisdictions include an extraordinary level of description in regulations addressing the holistic development of children. Evidently, these jurisdictions view the regulations as an appropriate place to insert this level of description. Perhaps these jurisdictional regulatory bodies are making certain that all aspects of a child's development are addressed; however, regulations carry the force of law and failure to comply constitutes an offence for which sanctions can be applied. Therefore, the question may arise as to whether regulations with extensive descriptions are due to a concern about the educator's ability to interpret developmental appropriateness and/or knowledge about goals for different areas of children's development. Perhaps policy developers view holistic development as such an important aspect of child care programming and curriculum design that they decided to enshrine it in the regulations. All jurisdictions with an ECE college-level training program have at least one child development course and one curriculum course; however, most have two or more. Curriculum and child development courses customarily address the holistic development of the child in their content.

CULTURAL DIVERSITY

Interestingly, this factor is included in the regulations for only four jurisdictions (British Columbia, Northwest Territories, Nunavut, Yukon), and it may be a function of the large Indigenous population of the latter three jurisdictions. They may be more sensitive to cultural issues and place a great deal of value on the recognition of heritage and the sharing of traditions. In the fourth jurisdiction – British Columbia – Indigenous Peoples have a strong voice and a concern about culture, ethnicity, and identity (see chapter by Alan Pence and Veronica Pacini-Ketchabaw in this volume). As well, in British Columbia, a significant proportion of the population is composed of first-generation immigrants whose concerns about traditions and cultural values are also recognized by the provincial regulatory body. Other jurisdictions have experienced a significant influx of immigrants, which increases the diversity of their populations (e.g., Ontario, Quebec). Perhaps, there was no reference in the regulations to cultural diversity in these jurisdictions because their regulations were written prior to the significant increase in diverse populations and subsequent revisions will address this issue.

As far as college courses are concerned, only two jurisdictions (Manitoba, Nunavut) have courses on cultural diversity in general; however, Alberta has a course that focuses specifically on Aboriginal children and families. Given the rich cultural diversity of the Canadian population, the authors expected that colleges would have specialized courses rather than integrating the issue of diversity into other courses.

INDIVIDUAL DIFFERENCES AND INCLUSIVITY

More than half of the jurisdictions have pointed to the need to attend to individual differences in their regulations, which highlights the importance of this factor. However, it does not mean that the other jurisdictions do not perceive children's individual differences and inclusivity as being important. The jurisdictions that refer to individual differences use phrasing that provides for flexibility in program planning and activities to recognize and meet the needs and interests of individual children. In examining the college course offerings, we noted that four of the six jurisdictions that specify inclusivity in their curriculum regulations also have college courses that address inclusivity. It is important to note that in 91.7 per cent ($n = 11/12$) of the jurisdictions where training is offered, courses for special needs are included in the college programs. In British Columbia, a special needs citation (i.e., three courses with a focus on special needs) is offered in the diploma program. Given the inclusion of special needs courses in all but one college program, clearly educators are receiving training on working with children with special needs.

COMMUNITY AS A RESOURCE

Five jurisdictions make clear reference to the use of the community as a resource for children in their regulations. Four of the five jurisdictions also refer to cultural sensitivity and individual differences. In jurisdictions with large Aboriginal populations, there may be a respectful response to the desires of some Aboriginal communities to develop curricula that reflect their culture and heritage. To do so, one must rely on the community as a resource for curriculum development. Community members serve as a source of information, and their involvement can make the concepts come alive in a more effective manner than textbooks can.

Even without regulations about the use of the community as a resource, educators in most jurisdictions tend to seek interesting places to take their children and interesting people for the children to meet (e.g., local markets, community parks, libraries, museums, pools, skating rinks). These outings provide children with a sense of local geography and community resources and introduce them to facilities and individuals (e.g., librarian, museum docent) with which/whom their parents might not be familiar. All college programs included at least one course with a focus on families and the community.

INDOOR/OUTDOOR ACTIVITIES

Given that children tend to be in a child care setting for the majority of their waking hours, educators must ensure that they are outdoors for a portion of the day. Six of the eight jurisdictions that refer to indoor/outdoor play are in colder climates, and the winter weather may be the motivating factor regarding the drafting of regulations for outdoor play. All eight specify weather conditions in which children should not be taken outside. Getting children ready to play outside during the winter months can be a difficult endeavour (e.g., many layers of clothing), but having specific regulations is more likely to result in children having outdoor play experiences. No reference to outdoor activities is evident in the course content of the college programs but may exist in the health, safety, and play courses.

CREATIVITY

Creativity is an important concept in program planning for young children. Music, drama, art, dance, and literature/storytelling allow children to have experiences if an educator values and supports children's development in these areas. Given the long hours most children spend in child care, their only access to the creative arts might be through the activities included in the daily program; thus, regulations regarding creative activities will ensure that children will have such experiences. Seven of the eleven diploma programs reviewed require a range of one to three creative arts courses. In the jurisdictions with both regulations and college courses, educators should be sufficiently skilled to include the creative arts in children's daily programs.

LARGE–SMALL GROUP AND GROUP–INDIVIDUAL COLLABORATIONS

Although few jurisdictions ($n = 5/13$) refer to providing children with large and small group experiences, it is an important factor in their daily experiences. Spending a full day in a child care centre translates into always being with a group of children and fewer opportunities for solitary or dyadic play. Many young children need time alone or in very small groups in order to practise skill development. For instance, some children are reluctant to speak in a large group situation and having the opportunity to interact with only a few peers may be more comfortable for the shy or reluctant child. Including this concept in regulations may reflect the fact that government agents are aware of educators' propensity to see the group rather than the individual as their focus.

Children's language skills develop more effectively when children have the opportunity to converse with adults rather than just peers (McCartney, 1984). When an educator has small group discussions, the focus can be transferred to the individual child rather than the whole group. While no college had a course specifically addressing work with large and small groups, it may be included in the courses on planning.

Summary

All provinces and territories have regulations that address curriculum in child care centres. Yukon, British Columbia, Manitoba, Northwest Territories, Nunavut, Nova Scotia, and Ontario included half or more of the ten curriculum items examined. For some of the jurisdictions, the list is particularly extensive (e.g., Yukon, 14 elements; British Columbia, 12 elements), and as regulations are enforceable, centres in these jurisdictions are required to address these curriculum elements on a daily basis. The diploma programs in Manitoba and Ontario require several curriculum courses that appear to support the curriculum components of the regulations. However, several other jurisdictions have diploma programs with a large number of required courses in curriculum development (e.g., Newfoundland, Saskatchewan, Quebec) and thus, do not appear to be driven by jurisdictional regulations. Classroom activities comprise a large proportion of the time that children spend in child care; thus, it is not surprising that colleges require several courses devoted specifically to program planning and curriculum development. More unusual is the extensive number of elements described in the regulations for two jurisdictions, as these must be acted upon regularly if the child care programs are to be in compliance with the regulations.

Conclusion

The regulations drafted by jurisdictions in Canada generally address the most important issues that influence the quality of child care programs. Most jurisdictions regulate a wide variety of factors, some of which are expected (e.g., educator training), while others are surprising (e.g., program or curriculum requirements). Since regulations carry the force of law, one would expect regulated factors to be those that (1) ensure the health and safety of children, (2) have been shown through research to be associated with quality care, (3) can be measured and monitored for compliance, and (4) can be enforced.

There are many factors that meet this set of conditions and they are within the purview of several ministries within each jurisdiction (e.g., equipment in indoor and outdoor play areas, and sanitary conditions by departments of health; adult:child ratios by child care licensing offices). These factors are structural variables and, while they support or influence what happens in the classroom, process variables are vitally important, but hard to regulate (e.g., daily activities, educator warmth, communication with parents). However, this review of regulations reveals that almost all jurisdictions regulate process variables (e.g., program or curriculum). This is an admirable effort on the part of regulatory bodies to ensure quality care for Canadian children. However, while regulating process variables may be beneficial if the regulations are adhered to, one can ask whether it is reasonable to regulate everything including what the educators decide to do with the children on a daily basis (i.e., program or curriculum).

Perhaps rather than regulating educators' daily practice with the children, what is really needed are regulations that enable, empower, and support the educator. We argue that regulations that require educators to have specialized training in ECE should address this need. An educator who has completed a two- or three-year specialized training program should be able to apply the information she or he has learned to the classroom setting. Empowered with the ability to observe, reflect, and plan appropriately, the educator should be able to design activities that guide children in the construction of meaningful knowledge. She or he ought to be able to take into account individual and cultural differences and enhance all aspects of children's development. Regulations specifying specialized training should ensure that graduates of ECE programs have the skills to perform these tasks, and then it should not be necessary to regulate everything they do. Society should be able to trust the judgment of skilled educators to act in the children's best interest, therefore regulatory bodies should not feel compelled to make laws about classroom processes.

Many of the jurisdictions include exemptions regarding some of the most important aspects of quality child care. We advocate for the need for flexibility and responsiveness in the design of regulations, because there are many factors that influence the decisions taken by regulatory bodies to include specific elements and allow for exemptions. The most salient of these factors are culture, history, values, and geography. There is no federal regulatory agency that drafts regulations for all Canadian jurisdictions. Rather provincial/territorial regulatory bodies are composed of individuals who are aware of the unique features of the particular jurisdiction. In this review, we have noted that some jurisdictions included regulations that address certain issues that others did not include. These differences are explained in terms of the different cultural composition of the various jurisdictions. Clearly, diverse cultures include many different sets of values and the regulations must address those that are specific to the jurisdiction. Respect and regard for the local values and traditions are essential if the various populations are to use and benefit from child care programs. In jurisdictions composed of diverse cultures, it is essential to address cultural sensitivity in the regulations. Those that do so ensure attention to diversity and the wording sets a tone of awareness and acceptance. Regulations that address diversity tend to expand upon the concept of traditions and values in the jurisdiction and pave the way for experiences in the child care classroom that will broaden children's horizons.

Jurisdictions that are composed of many remote communities might take into consideration issues such as extensive training requirements. The regulatory body in such a jurisdiction must make a choice between allowing centres to hire less qualified educators than in communities where there are many, easily accessible training institutions. The alternative of requiring trained staff may limit the number of educators available and keep centres from offering services needed by the families. If safety and security are the main issues of concern for the jurisdiction, then hiring untrained but responsible adults may be a viable option in a remote community; however, if one values good child developmental outcomes, then it would be essential to hire well-trained educators. Given the ability of colleges to use technology to reach remote areas, it would be socially responsible to design online courses that could facilitate the completion of a pre-service educator's studies. Internships might be more of a challenge; however, offering on-line theoretical courses would go a long way to meeting the needs of families living in remote communities who require child care from qualified educators.

The provincial frameworks recently developed in several provinces offer educators ways to create quality learning environments for children and tools for them to engage in reflective practice. These detailed documents indicate the best practices in child care education, and their content is not prescriptive, contrary to the content of the regulations, except in the case of New Brunswick where the Early Learning and Child Care Act passed in 2010 stipulates that the frameworks must be used in all child care facilities. As far as programming is concerned, a limited level of detail is evident in the regulations, perhaps because regulations are not meant to serve as tools for educators to use in their daily practice, but as indicators of minimal requirements. To date, regulations have not been as effective as one would have hoped, perhaps because the regulations are not worded in a manner that is easily understood and user friendly. Thus, we presume that most educators do not make reference to the regulations once completing their education. Perhaps the new framework documents that are purposefully written for educators will be more effective in influencing them in their daily practice.

The frameworks were developed in partnership with ministries and early childhood education college programs. This collaboration may ensure that the content of the frameworks will reflect what future educators are being taught in their courses and that these students will be given the tools that will allow them to deliver quality child care, as described in the frameworks. The framework documents are lengthy, and we presume that not all educators will truly make full use of them in their daily practice. Although the different provinces have organized some workshops to introduce these frameworks to early childhood educators, we ask if there can be a lasting influence from these limited workshop opportunities (see professional development section), and if this will result in a generalized use of the frameworks by all educators. The provinces that have developed frameworks seem to have been inspired by efforts that can be observed in other parts of the world, and also by each other, since the documents were produced contemporaneously. It remains to be seen whether other jurisdictions will follow their lead and develop their own curriculum frameworks. The use of these documents could result in educators having some continuous guidance in their practice, and ultimately increase the quality of child care education in Canada.

References

Alberta. Legislative Assembly. (2008). *Alberta Child Care Licensing Regulation*, 143/2008. Retrieved from http://www.qp.alberta.ca/574. cfm?page=2008_143.cfm&leg_type=Regs&isbncln=9780779735570.

Arnett, J. (1989). Caregivers in day care centres: Does training matter? *Journal of Applied Development Psychology, 10*, 541–552.

Barnett, R.C., Gareis, K.C., & Brennan, R.T. (1999). Fit as a mediator of the relationship between work hours and burnout. *Journal of Occupational Health Psychology, 4,* 307–317.

Bennett, J. (2005). Curriculum issues in national policy-making. *European Early Childhood Education Research Journal, 13*(2), 5–23.

Blank, M.A., & Kershaw, C.A. (2009). *Mentoring as collaboration: Lessons from the field for classroom, school, and district leaders.* Thousand Oaks, CA: Corwin.

Borko, H. (2004). Professional development and teacher learning: Mapping the terrain. *Educational Researcher, 33*(8), 3–15.

Bredekamp, S. (Ed.). (1987). *Developmentally appropriate practice in early childhood programs serving children from birth through age 8.* Washington, DC: National Association for the Education of Young Children.

British Columbia. Legislative Assembly. (2007). *Child Care Licensing Regulation.* B.C. Reg. 332/2007. Retrieved from http://www.canlii.org/en/bc/laws/regu/bc-reg-332-2007/latest/bc-reg-332-2007.html.

Cornell, E.H., Sénéchal, M., & Broda, L.S. (1988). Recall of picture books by 3-year-old children: Testing and repetition effects in joint reading activities. *Journal of Educational Psychology, 80,* 537–542.

Darling-Hammond, L., Wise, A.E., & Klein, S.P. (1999). *A license to teach: Raising standards for teaching.* San Francisco, CA: Jossey-Bass.

Dunn, L. (1993). Proximal and distal features of day care quality and children's development. *Early Childhood Research Quarterly, 8,* 167–192.

Epstein, A.S. (1993). *Training for quality: Improving early childhood programs through systematic inservice training.* Ypsilanti, MI: High/Scope Press.

Epstein, A.S. (1999). Pathways to quality in Head Start, public school, and private non-profit early childhood programs. *Journal of Research in Childhood Education, 13,* 101–119.

Fantuzzo, J., Childs, S., Hampton, V., Ginsburg-Block, M., Coolahan, K.C., & Debnam, D. (1997). Enhancing the quality of early childhood education: A follow-up evaluation of an experiential collaborative training model for Head Start. *Early Childhood Research Quarterly, 12,* 425–437.

Frede, E.C., Austin, A., & Lindhauer, S. (1993). The relationship of specific developmentally appropriate teaching practices in preschool to children's skills in first grade. *Perspectives in Developmentally Appropriate Practice: Advances in Early Education and Day Care, 5,* 95–111.

Fullan, M., & Stiegelbrauer, S. (1991). *The new meaning of educational change.* New York: Teachers College Press.

Galinsky, E., Howes, C., Kontos, S., & Shinn, M. (1994). *The study of children in family child care and relative care: Highlights of findings.* New York: Families and Work Institute.

Goelman, H., Forer, B., Kershaw, P., Doherty, G., Lero, D., & LaGrange, A. (2006). Towards a predictive model of quality in Canadian child care centres. *Early Childhood Research Quarterly, 21,* 280–295.

Hawkey, K. (1997). Roles, responsibilities, and relationships in mentoring: A literature review and agenda for research. *Journal of Teacher Education, 5,* 325–335.

Howes, C. (1983). Caregiver's behaviour in centre and family day care. *Journal of Applied Developmental Psychology, 4,* 99–107.

Howes, C. (1997). Children's experiences in center-based child care as a function of teacher background and adult:child ratios. *Merrill-Palmer Quarterly, 43,* 404–425.

Howes, C., & Olenick, M. (1986). Family and child care influences on toddler compliance. *Child Development, 65,* 264–273.

Isenberg, J.P. (1999). *The state of art in early childhood professional preparation.* Washington, DC: National Institute on Early Childhood Development and Education.

Jacobs, E.V., Mill, D., Jennings, M., & Fiorentino, L.M. (2002). *Licensing, monitoring, and enforcement procedures in the Canadian school-age context.* Final report of the National School-Age Child Care Research Project. Montreal: Concordia University.

Kaiser, B., & Rasminsky, J. (2007). *Challenging behavior in young children: Understanding, preventing, and responding effectively.* Boston, MA: Pearson Education.

Katz, L.G. (1993). *Training for quality: Improving early childhood programs through systematic inservice training.* (Foreword). Ypsilanti, MI: High/Scope Press.

Klein, N., & Sheehan, R. (1987). Staff development: A key issue in meeting the needs of young children in day care settings. *Topics in Early Childhood Special Education, 7,* 1–12.

Kontos, S., Machida, S., Griffin, S., & Read, M. (1992). Training and professionalism in family day care. In D.L. Peters & A.R. Pence (Eds.), *Family day care: Current research for informed public policy.* New York: Teachers College Press.

Kontos, S., & Wilcox-Herzog, A. (1997). Influences on children's competence in early childhood classrooms. *Early Childhood Research Quarterly, 12,* 247–262.

Lamb, M.E., & Ahnert, L. (2006). Nonparental child care: Context, concepts, correlates, and consequences. In W. Damon & R.M. Lerner (Eds.). *Handbook of Child Psychology,* vol. 4 (pp. 950–1016). New York: Wiley.

Manitoba. Legislative Assembly. (1986). *Manitoba Child Care Regulations,* M.R. 62/86. Retrieved from http://web2.gov.mb.ca/laws/regs/pdf/c158–062.86.pdf.

McCartney, K. (1984). The effect of quality day care environment upon children's language development. *Developmental Psychology, 20,* 244–260.

Morgan, G. (1979). Regulations: One approach to child care quality. *Young Children, 34,* 22–27.

Morgan, G. (1984). Change through regulation. In J. Greenman & R. Fuqua (Eds.), *Making day care better* (pp. 163–184). New York: Teachers College Press.

National Research Council (NRC). (1999). *How people learn: Brain, mind, experience, and school.* Committee on Developments in the Science of Learning. Washington, DC: National Academy Press.

National Research Council (NRC). (2001). *Eager to learn: Educating our preschoolers.* Committee on Early Childhood Pedagogy. Washington, DC: National Academy Press.

New Brunswick. Legislative Assembly. (1983). *Family Services Act and Day Care Regulations, 83–85,* as amended. Retrieved from http://www.gnb.ca/0062/regs/83–85.htm.

New Brunswick. Legislative Assembly. (2010). *Early Learning and Child Care Act, Chapter E-0.5.* Retrieved from http://laws.gnb.ca/en/showfulldoc/cs/E-0.5//20120219

Newfoundland and Labrador. House of Assembly. (2007). *Child Care Services Regulations 37/99.* Retrieved from http://www.canlii.org/en/nl/laws/regu/nlr-89–05/latest/nlr-89–05.html.

Northwest Territories. Legislative Assembly. (1988). *Child Day Care Standards and Regulations.* Retrieved from http://www.justice.gov.nt.ca/PDF/REGS/CHILD_DAY_CARE/Child%20Day%20Care%20Standards.pdf.

Nova Scotia. Legislative Assembly. (2011). *Day Care Regulations* made under Section 15 of the *Day Care Act,* amended to N.S. Reg. 155/2011. Retrieved from http://www.gov.ns.ca/just/regulations/regs/dayregs.htm.

Nova Scotia. (2011). *Standards for the Daily Program in Licensed Child Care Facilities.* Retrieved from http://gov.ns.ca/coms/families/provider/documents/day_care_regs/Standards_Daily_PROGRAM.pdf

Nunavut. Legislative Assembly. (1994). *Child Day Care Standards and Regulations.* Retrieved from http://www.canlii.org/en/nu/laws/regu/rrnwt-nu-1990-c-c-3/latest/rrnwt-nu-1990-c-c-3.html.

Odell, S.J. (1990). *Mentor teacher programs: What research says to the teacher.* Washington, DC: National Education Association.

Ontario. Legislative Assembly. (1990). *Ontario Regulation 262* (Amemded 1998, 1999, 2006). Retrieved from http://www.search.e-laws.gov.on.ca/en/isysquery/01ab9402–1107–483f-9bc7-a3303f406ea9/1/doc/?search=browse Statutes&context=#hit1.

Phillips, D.A., McCartney, K., & Scarr, S. (1987). Child care quality and children's social development. *Developmental Psychology, 23,* 537–543.

Phillipsen, L.C., Birchinal, M.R., Howes, C., & Cryer, D. (1997). The prediction of process quality from structural features of child care. *Early Childhood Research Quarterly, 12,* 281–303.

Prince Edward Island. Legislative Assembly. (1988). *Child Care Facilities Regulations.* Retrieved from http://www.gov.pe.ca/law/regulations/pdf/C&05G.pdf.

Quebec, Government of. (2009). *Educational Childcare Regulation.* Retrieved from http://www.canlii.org/en/qc/laws/regu/2006-goq-2-2161/latest/2006-goq-2-2161.html.

Ruopp, R., Travers, J., Glantz, F., & Coelen, G. (1979). *Children at the center.* Cambridge, MA: Abt Associates.

Saskatchewan. Legislative Assembly. (2001). *The Child Care Regulations.* Retrieved from http://www.canlii.org/en/sk/laws/regu/rrs-c-c-7.3-reg-2/latest/rrs-c-c-7.3-reg-2.html.

Sénéchal, M., LeFevre, J., Hudson, E., & Lawson, E.P. (1996). Knowledge of storybooks as predictor of young children's vocabulary. *Journal of Educational Psychology, 88,* 520–536.

Smith, A.B. (1999). Quality child care and joint attention. *International Journal of Early Years Education, 7,* 85–93.

Snider, M.H., & Fu, V.R. (1990). The effects of specialized education and job experience on early childhood teachers' knowledge of developmentally appropriate practice. *Early Childhood Research Quarterly, 5,* 69–78.

Venn, M.L., & Wolery, M. (1992). Increasing day care staff members' interactions during caregiving routines. *Journal of Early Intervention, 16,* 304–319.

Ward, R.M. (1994). The role of licensing in ensuring quality child care. In C.A. Baglin & M. Bender (Eds.), *Handbook on quality child care for young children: Settings, standards, and resources* (pp. 65–86). San Diego, CA: Singular Publishing Group.

Weikart, D.P. (1972). A traditional nursery program revisited. In R.K. Parker (Ed.), *The preschool program in action: Exploring early childhood programs.* Boston, MA: Allyn & Bacon.

Whitebook, M., & Bellm, D. (1996). Mentoring for early childhood teachers and providers: Building upon and extending tradition. *Young Children, 52*(1), 59–64.

Whitebook, M., Hnatiuk, P., & Bellm, D. (1994). *Mentoring in early care and education: Refining an emerging career path.* Washington, DC: National Centre for the Early Childhood Work Force.

Whitebook, M., Howes, C., & Phillips, D. (1989). *Who cares? Child care teachers and the quality of care in America.* Final Report of the National Child Care Staffing Study. Oakland, CA: Child Care Employee Project.

Whitebook, M., Phillips, D., & Howes, C. (1993). *National child care staffing study revisited*. Oakland, CA: Child Care Employee Project.

Wiggins, G., & McTighe, J. (1998). *Understanding by design*. Alexandria, VA: Association for Supervision and Curriculum Development.

Yukon Territory. Legislative Assembly. (1995). *Child Care Centre Program Regulation*. Retrieved from http://www.gov.yk.ca/legislation/regs/oic1995_087.pdf.

Part I Commentary: Towards a Geology of Early Childhood Education and Care in Canada

HILLEL GOELMAN

These four chapters provide four layers of understanding of the complex interaction of factors that contribute to a geology of early childhood education and care (ECEC) in Canada. These four conceptual layers help to describe the ways in which history, policy, economics, and curriculum issues account for the unique configurations, the possibilities, and the limitations currently faced in ECEC in Canada today. Prochner and Robertson provide a valuable 'deep structure' of the current situation by identifying the historical factors and developments that have done so much to shape the current reality. Friendly and Prentice have written a detailed analysis of the current 'surface structure' of ECEC in Canada and have shown how the shifting tectonic plates of funding, social policy, and policy factors have contributed to Canada's low international ranking in the provision of ECEC services. Cleveland's chapter draws our attention to the economic landscape that constrains the expansion of ECEC services, identifies ways in which economic costs and benefits of expanded service might be calculated, and suggests ways of determining economic and program priorities to alter the current landscape. Jacobs and Adrien focus on the ways in which the regulatory environments of ECEC services shape the contours and lived reality of ECEC programs across different ecological jurisdictions in Canada. Taken together, the four chapters contribute to a rich and nuanced, multidimensional portrayal of key factors that define and determine ECEC in Canada. In this commentary, I review the individual contributions of the chapters and suggest some ways of integrating and synthesizing these contributions. The four chapters help us understand the current state of ECEC in Canada and both implicitly and explicitly identify areas for further research and program development in the future.

Prochner and Robertson provide a very helpful and detailed examination of ECEC programs and services in the period after the Second World War. They point out how social and economic changes framed transformations in family life and the development of early childhood programs in the public, private, and non-profit sectors. They discuss the ways in which previous paradigms encountered the current realities of that era and laid the groundwork for subsequent growth in early childhood education and care in Canada. The immediate postwar era, for example, dealt with conflicting legacies, including the nursery education movement, the influence of the Institute of Child Study at the University of Toronto, the prominence of Gesell-inspired maturational theories of child development, the child welfare orientation of most child care programs, and the expansion (and then closure) of wartime child care programs. Added to this mix was the growing impact of John Bowlby's work on attachment and separation, which was further buttressed by Mary Ainsworth's strange situation research paradigm, both of which were seen to provide scientific evidence against non-parental

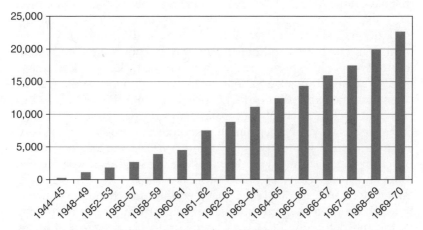

Figure C1.1. Number of children enrolled in kindergarten classes in British Columbia, selected years, 1944–1969. Data compiled from British Columbia, Royal Commission on Education, *Report of the Royal Commission on Education* (Victoria, BC: Queen's Printer, 1960); Canada, Dominion Bureau of Statistics, *Survey of Education in the Western Provinces, 1969–1970* (Ottawa: Information Canada, 1971).

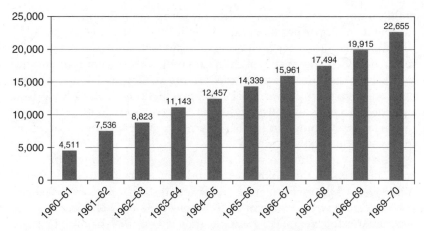

Figure C1.2. Number of children enrolled in public kindergarten classes in British Columbia, 1960–61 to 1969–70. Data compiled from British Columbia, Royal Commission on Education, *Report of the Royal Commission on Education* (Victoria, BC: Queen's Printer, 1960); Canada, Dominion Bureau of Statistics, *Survey of Education in the Western Provinces, 1969–1970* (Ottawa: Information Canada, 1971).

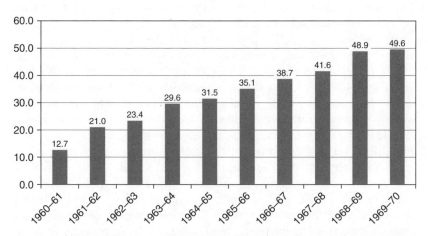

Figure C1.3. Percentage of 5-year-old children enrolled in public kindergarten classes in British Columbia, 1960–61 to 1968–69. Data compiled from British Columbia, Royal Commission on Education, *Report of the Royal Commission on Education* (Victoria, BC: Queen's Printer, 1960); Canada, Dominion Bureau of Statistics, *Survey of Education in the Western Provinces, 1969–1970* (Ottawa: Information Canada, 1971).

child care in the early years for fear of disrupting the mother–child attachment bond. The popular and academic literature of the day strongly discouraged mothers from entering the paid labour force and generally took a dim view of pre-school child care programs (except those for the poor). Half-day nursery programs for pre-school- and kindergarten-aged children were deemed to be acceptable. Prochner and Robertson provide especially helpful analyses of the ways in which these developments also contributed to teacher education programs and curriculum innovation during this time.

It was towards the end of this baby boom era that growth in ECEC programs in both the United States and Canada began to take off in a major way. Children born at the tail end of these boom years (1960–65) encountered a wider range of ECEC choices than did children born in the previous five years. For example, data from British Columbia in the postwar era (see Figures C1.1 to C1.3) show the exponential increase in the numbers and percentages of children attending public kindergarten programs. The increase is especially noteworthy since these statistics were compiled *before* publicly funded kindergarten was mandated by provincial legislation in 1973.

Thus, the period discussed by Prochner and Robertson was characterized by subtle but important shifts in ECEC thinking and practice. The launch of Sputnik in 1957 inaugurated the space race and American government-sponsored education programs felt they had to invest in education – and in ECEC in particular – in order to catch up in the technological race for space. The U.S. War on Poverty, with its emphasis on early education and Head Start programs, did much to bridge the historic chasms between the child study centre movement towards enrichment programs for middle-class children and child care and/or child welfare programs for poor children. These developments caused much reflection and rethinking among early childhood educators, academics, and others. The maturational approach of providing safe environments where children's natural development would unfold at the right time was in the process of being replaced by approaches that encouraged practices that challenged and engaged children in more active learning and developmental processes. While programs and services might have looked similar on the surface in 1946 and in 1964, big changes were already underway at a deeper level.

Prochner and Robertson's analyses of a period of growth and change appear to parallel the current paradigm shifts underway in Canada.

Provincial and municipal jurisdictions across Canada are moving towards full-day kindergartens and publicly funded pre-school programs, and it will be interesting to see if, first, the ripple effects of this growth will continue during a period of economic recession and, second, whether there will be a similar ripple effect in teacher education, curriculum, and the philosophy of ECEC programs that Prochner and Robertson describe occurred during the baby boom era.

In many ways, the Friendly and Prentice chapter continues the narrative begun by Prochner and Robertson by providing a detailed analysis of the current policy landscape of ECEC programs and services in Canada. In doing so, they contextualize this landscape within both the relevant international literature as well as in the dominant neo-liberal/conservative discourse that characterizes social policy today at different levels of government. Friendly and Prentice do an admirable job of summarizing the diversity of ECEC programs, policies, services, and regulations across federal, provincial, and territorial jurisdictions. Indeed, they point to the absence of a coherent, national strategy with national standards as a major problem with ECEC in Canada today. Their work raises the question whether it is even possible to refer to 'ECEC in Canada today,' because of the extreme variations in service provision, regulation, and administration of ECEC services and programs across the jurisdictions.

Their chapter reminds us that both the OECD and the UNICEF Innocenti Reports identified major criticisms of early childhood programs and policies in Canada on almost every relevant benchmark: the low numbers and percentages of children served by existing programs; the lack of importance assigned to early childhood matters by jurisdictions across Canada; the small percentage of GDP used to fund early childhood programs; and the patchwork of programs, policies, and administrative vehicles used to provide early ECE and/or child care programs. They justifiably critique the federal government for not providing leadership, direction, and priorities that would result in needed affordable, accessible, and quality services. The persisting view that dominates ECEC policy in Canada continues to emphasize the importance of free-market ideology over a sense of entitlements to children and families as citizens. In short, Friendly and Prentice provide a very good picture of a very bad situation.

While the chapter is long on descriptive material and offers some analytical insight into the reasons for the current situation in Canada, it is not clear how the authors see a way out of the current political and economic impasse. For example, will there have to be major political and economic reform before a more universal, affordable, and accessible suite of ECEC services is offered or can there be some form of incremental, long-term change within existing frameworks? Will future federal governments promote or produce the possibility of strong leadership for national reform?

There is growing interest in a number of recent initiatives taken by two of Canada's most neo-liberal regimes, Ontario (Pascal, 2009) and British Columbia (Government of British Columbia, 2010), both of which are investing in new programs during an era of restraint. And both of which are occurring in social welfare regimes that fall into the neo-liberal, market-oriented approach to social, health care, and education services. Something has shifted to affect these changes, but what exactly? Perhaps it is the increasing emphasis on 'school readiness,' which may be driving both full-day kindergartens and publicly funded pre-school programs. Much of the literature on an expanded public role and increased funding in ECEC seems to be driven by the school readiness argument that children need ECEC programs in order to be more 'ready' for school, to subsequently perform better in school, to have higher graduation rates from high school, and subsequently to go on to more economically productive lives by contributing to societal and economic expansion. Thus, the school readiness and human capital investment approaches appear to be prioritizing ECEC programs and services as a means of generating more wealth for the common good. When ECEC programs were considered part of the U.S. War on Poverty, the primary economic argument was to assist American families in rising out of poverty. The current discourse is generalized to all children, regardless of social or economic class with major payoffs expected for children from all economic strata. Whether one agrees with this stance or not, it is important to recognize this as a relatively new and increasingly popular development in the ECEC discourse. Thus, the expansion of ECEC services during a time of spending restraint and cutbacks to other public services in the name of 'school readiness' is worthy of close observation and analysis in the coming years.

Cleveland's chapter examines ECEC in Canada through an economic lens. He delves into questions of (current and future) costs and benefits of programs and services and considers the impact (and costs) of high-quality programs. He discusses the particular difficulties involved in conducting economic analyses of ECEC and the ways in which ECEC differs from other activities subjected to economic analyses. As such, Cleveland draws on a wide range of research to conclude that ECEC can provide economic benefits over and above the costs needed to fund these programs, but that these benefits are highly dependent on other factors, primarily, the quality of the ECEC programs whose effects are being studied. Cleveland quite accurately points to the importance of quality in ECEC services; quality programs will generate greater benefits and will be worth greater investment. One missing piece to the calculation of cost for quality programs is the increased cost of ECEC training programs. Research has consistently found that better trained staff – with more years of both general and ECEC education – provide higher levels of quality care. Yet, as far as I have seen, neither Cleveland nor other economic analysts have calculated the costs of, for example, doubling the ECEC training programs from one to two years. The costs, as far as I can tell, never include training costs, neither pre-service nor in-service. It would be fascinating – and an important contribution to the quality literature – to establish some way of comparing the economic costs of preparing different professionals (e.g., physicians, nurses, massage therapists, etc.) with the costs of preparing qualified early childhood educators.

Cleveland's analyses offer a logical extension to the arguments put forward by the Prochner and Robertson and the Friendly and Prentice chapters. All three of these chapters highlight the interaction of historical, educational, social, political, and economic factors, which together have an impact on ECEC programs, costs, and benefits. The corollary of this position is that none of these factors operates in isolation. It is interesting to note that some of these bodies of literature cited by these authors did not even exist during the baby-boom era examined by Prochner and Robertson. While educators and psychologists were discussing early childhood education and child welfare in the postwar era, I am not aware of any policy or economic analyses that were conducted during this time frame. In the past twenty-five years, however, not only have the data and the answers changed, but there has been a marked shift as well in the nature of the questions that are being asked. These include questions about societal needs for ECEC services, the obligations of states to provide these services, equity issues regarding women and work, idealized and practical realities about the nature and function of family life, and the major questions Cleveland asks about the costs and benefits of ECEC services and programs. Like shifting tectonic plates, which can result in the realignments of surface realities, the interaction of these various strata in the geology of early childhood education and care also account for complex and diverse landscapes in the lived reality of children and families.

All three of these chapters, and the fourth, which will be discussed presently, focus almost exclusively on one form of programming: licensed group child care programs. Yet, the lived reality of ECEC programs and services includes a wide range of environments, including, most prominently, licensed child care centres, licensed and unlicensed family child care, early intervention services for children with developmental challenges, Aboriginal ECEC programs, and cultural and linguistically diverse ECEC programs. Conducting research on children enrolled in full-time group child care programs is relatively straightforward, yet this group of children arguably forms the minority of all children who participate in ECEC services in Canada. Continued research in this area must broaden its scope to include the harder-to-define, harder-to-find, and harder-to-study forms of ECEC, which contribute to the complex ecology of early childhood education and care in Canada.

The Jacobs and Adrien chapter brings us directly to the doorways of early childhood classrooms as they explore the regulatory contexts that frame the licensing of early childhood settings and the training of early childhood professionals. If the three prior chapters provide excellent context to ECEC in Canada, Jacobs and Adrien succeed in providing an excellent window on the kinds of learning and developmental experiences – the content – of what goes on in centres and classrooms across the country. Their near-encyclopedic analysis of different policy jurisdictions will provide researchers and professionals with a valuable body of work.

The work they produce is a profile in diversity. Regulations and regulatory frameworks vary widely across jurisdictions as do requirements for entry to practise by ECEC professionals. It would be fascinating to drill down into these different jurisdictions in an attempt to uncover the various historical, social, political, and perhaps economic factors that have resulted in this diverse patchwork of regulation. Looking ahead, as jurisdictions begin to implement publicly funded pre-school programs, it is expected that conflicts will emerge between, for example, regulations that govern public education and regulations that govern ECEC programs. These conflicts will manifest themselves in many different ways including, but not limited to, understanding the nature of the young learner, the purpose of education, the appropriateness of different learning materials and approaches, forms of assessment and observation, and the requirements for pre-service and in-service professional development.

As mentioned above, this discussion of regulations brings us to the doorway of the ECEC classroom, but not quite inside. There are challenges with any discussion of regulations, and these involve the extent to which regulations are, in fact, implemented and what else goes on in the lived curriculum of everyday life in these settings. These are factors in the quality of ECEC programs that defy easy definition and measurement. They include, for example, responsive and contingent interactions with children, understanding and empathizing with children, acknowledging and affirming children's feelings, expanding on children's questions and insights, multitasking in the classroom, remembering what a child painted yesterday and how that affects what she is drawing today. In other words, there are aspects of life with young children that go far beyond regulation and training. Perhaps we can define the important regulatory and training frameworks as the 'science' of ECEC, and the day-to-day, moment-to-moment interactions as the 'art' of ECEC.

All four chapters in Part I of this book provide readers with important contextual information on ECEC in Canada today. The authors have assembled a powerful collection of data, observations, reflections, and perspectives which, taken together, describe the most important contours of early education and care in Canada, and for this we thank and acknowledge them. Ultimately, however, it is the task of the readers to weave these different perspectives together into a meaningful whole based on their own professional and disciplinary orientation. For some, the policy and economic analyses will be most important in terms of providing guidance for future policy decisions; for others, it may be the historical analyses that will help to explain how we got to where we are today. And for others, the information in these chapters may help further discussions and planning around regulatory and ECEC training programs. All readers of these chapters, I am certain, will gain a firm understanding of the interconnectedness of all of these different perspectives.

References

Government of British Columbia. (2010). *Early Years Initiatives.* Retrieved from http://www.bced.gov.bc.ca/early_learning/fdk/.

Pascal, C. (2009). *With our best future in mind: Implementing early learning in Ontario.* Toronto: Queen's Printer.

PART II

Children, Curriculum, and Teachers

5 Revisioning Multiculturalism in Early Childhood Education

VERONICA PACINI-KETCHABAW
AND JUDITH K. BERNHARD

During the past few decades, issues related to newcomer populations have received considerable attention in the media and political debates in Canada and in other immigrant-receiving countries. Immigration has also become a key issue for the advancement of early childhood education and care (ECEC) in Canada, well known as a multicultural, pluricultural society (OECD, 2003). Newcomers constitute two-thirds of Canada's population.[1]

The country accepts an average of 250,000 immigrants a year (Statistics Canada, 2005) including over 40,000 refugees. In addition, thousands of families who come under temporary work programs remain in the country long term or return year after year. Many people also cross the border into Canada on student visas, tourist visas, or as refugee claimants and then overstay their visas, go underground after failed refugee claims, fail to show up at deportation hearings, and so forth.

The increase in the immigrant population has been more than three times the increase in the Canadian-born population (OECD, 2003; Statistics Canada, 2005). In fact, it is estimated that by 2030, immigration will become the only source of population growth for Canada (Ley, 2005; Mahoney, 2007). Immigration allows Canada to avoid the stark economic implications of an aging population and a birth rate that is insufficient to sustain the system. Immigration is also important for meeting the needs of particular industries. For example, in 2007, enough

---

1 Throughout the chapter we use the overall term *newcomers* to refer to not only those with official status as landed immigrants but also those who are in the process of obtaining refugee status and those who live with less than full legal status.

temporary workers were admitted to work 1,800 farms. An additional 4,000 women came into the country under the live-in caregivers program. As population growth is affected through immigration, newcomer children will become (if they are not already, in metropolitan, multicultural centres such as Toronto and Vancouver) the majority of children attending child care centres (OECD, 2003).

Although migration to Canada is continually increasing, updates to immigration laws have caused a dramatic shift in the place of origin of Canada's immigrants. Previously predominant source countries (i.e., Anglo-European countries) have been replaced by those in East and South Asia, the Middle East, Africa, and Latin America. As a result, Canadian cities that were once populated by white middle-class families are now diverse. Current data indicate that over three-quarters of immigrants now entering Canada are from non-European countries (Ambert, 2006; George & Young, 2006). Furthermore, the children of new immigrants are likely to be affected by the change in status that comes with the underemployment their parents typically face in Canada. Approximately 16 per cent of 'visible minorities' in Canada are children between the ages of 0 and 14 years (Statistics Canada, 2005).[2] Even though these groups will be a numerical majority, they are by no means likely to become true functioning majorities with the power that accrues to the present majority, in part because, unlike previous immigrant groups, recent immigrants are racialized minorities. Various studies have shown that 'non-white origin creates a penalty for visible minorities in the labour market' (Li, 1998, p. 126). Racialized groups are more highly represented among the poor than are white Canadians (Galabuzzi, 2005).

Given the statistics mentioned earlier, the OECD report on the situation of early childhood education in Canada calls for appropriate services 'to assist young immigrant children from different cultures to adjust to Canada and learn English and French' (2003, p. 20).

---

2 The Canadian use of the term *visible minority* has recently been questioned in a U.N. report released by the Committee on the Elimination of Racial Discrimination because it is considered by some to be a discriminatory term (CBC, 2007). Therefore, in the rest of this chapter we refer to *racialized minorities* (see text below for an explanation of this term).

Governments and advocates also have recognized the need to create policies that respect and are sensitive to the needs of immigrant families with young children (OECD, 2003). These responses are indicative of the official multiculturalism of Canada and show its weaknesses in rather stark terms. First, adjustment to English or French Canada is clearly stated as a goal, and no corresponding adjustment is pictured for the English or French long-time citizens of Canada. Second, the creed of respect, sensitivity, and tolerance, while admirable as far as it goes, risks being condescending or, in any case, ineffective in addressing the serious problems of the newcomers who require a great deal more than sensitivity (e.g., schooling, jobs). We discuss these and other shortcomings later in this chapter.

This chapter illuminates some of the complexities and possibilities for the field of early childhood education as it responds to the influx of newcomers. It uses anti-racist and transnational feminist theoretical underpinnings to explore the possibilities of moving beyond a multicultural approach in ECEC. This chapter broadly explores the following questions: How can early childhood education and care better respond to the challenges and opportunities of migrations? How does the centring of discussions around multicultural education and culture close the door for other meaningful discussions and other voices? What does an anti-racist and transnational feminist ECEC promise? Our two main objectives are as follows: First, we will look critically at the discourses that are employed in the contexts of multicultural early childhood education. Second, having examined the problems, we will look at proposed solutions, especially alternative theoretical stances that have been developed to understand this situation.

In particular, we will examine how anti-racist and transnational feminist perspectives can be applied to support newcomer children and families in early childhood in more effective and meaningful ways. We begin by providing a brief description of the challenges that newcomer children and families, as well as those providing services to them, face on a daily basis in the Canadian ECEC context. Then, we present a detailed analysis of multiculturalism – specifically a critique to the discourses embedded in multicultural ECEC. Third, we outline some of the main ideas embedded in anti-racist, and transnational feminist conceptual frameworks. Finally, we conclude with examples of studies that have attempted to apply anti-racist and transnational feminist perspectives to the field of early childhood education.

Challenges of Diversity in ECEC Settings

A number of published reports provide evidence of the challenges faced by newcomer children and families as they engage with the Canadian education system (e.g., Abada & Tenkorang, 2009; Ali, 2008; Bernhard et al., 2007; Borzykowski, 2009; Magalhaes, Carrasco, & Gastaldo, 2010; Pacini-Ketchabaw & McIvor, 2005; Xu et al., 2007). The first issue is related to cultural capital and valued types of skills and knowledge. A mainstream valorization that is implicit is an attributed deficit to the newcomers. These categorizations are relevant for white middle-class children, and they can be expected to obtain the right forms of knowledge and do well. The newcomers, said to be behind, will not do so well (on dropouts, see Anisef et al., 2008; People for Education, 2008; on overrepresentation in special education, see Klingner et al., 2005). The second issue, resulting from the first, is the cutting off of newcomer families from the education system. Often parents find their interventions are not welcome, and sometimes their own respect for experts keeps them from complaining or strongly advocating on behalf of their children.

Service providers, including caregivers in the field of early childhood, have training and experiences that make it almost inevitable that they subscribe to the views we have mentioned, namely, that the cultural capital that newcomer families bring is not worthy and that the parents, in any case, are not all that interested in participating in their children's education. These service providers are often unacquainted with the extensive published research about the realities of family life of diverse groups of immigrants newly arrived in Canada. Families react in a number of ways to their situation and treatment regardless of how sensitive and enlightened it is officially said to be. Many are not, for example, able to access basic services (e.g., psychological testing). They are also unwilling to turn to child protection agencies or the police to deal with neglectful or even dangerous situations (Alaggia & Maiter, 2006; Berk & Schur, 2001; Fix & Zimmerman, 1999).

Further, caregivers tend to be unaware of the phenomenon of stepwise migration and what has been labelled transnational family living. It is a complex phenomenon to which we will return later in the chapter but, for now, we include some basic points. For example, children are often separated from their parents for significant periods of time. Caregivers may only be dimly aware, if at all, that no parent is present and that a number of transnational family structures are possible. Another common phenomenon is that parents often emigrate first and their children only join them much later, creating situations where children feel completely alienated from their parents when reunited. Diffusion of family authority is also common and this greatly affects the ability to parent and relate to service providers. Caregivers face a number of complexities, mostly below the horizon of awareness in trying to help such families regardless of their good intentions. Research is needed so that service providers can effectively respond to the day-to-day challenges experienced by families from a range of migration pathways. Decision making could be facilitated if service providers made use of the existing literature on the experiences and needs of recent newcomer families.

Multicultural policies and training are generally blind to the issues we have mentioned, and this is not an incidental omission. We will argue that the blind spots are intrinsic to this view of society. In summary, the field of early childhood education, particularly as it applies to newcomers, is intrinsically limited if not destructive. We need to consider other approaches, especially those recognizing the realities of power, authority, and cultural capital. Before outlining these approaches, we take a critical look at the concept of multiculturalism in Canada.

Discourses of Multiculturalism in Canada

The 1985 Multicultural Act (Government of Canada, Ministry of Justice, 1985) is designed to 'promote the understanding that multiculturalism reflects the cultural and racial diversity of Canadian society' and to recognize the rights of ethnocultural groups and communities to preserve their heritage. Canada's multicultural trends have become institutionalized after long histories of entrenched racism (Ley, 2007). Multiculturalism was first included in the 1982 Constitution Act, followed by the Multiculturalism Act in 1985 and the 1995 Employment Equity Act. Multiculturalism and cultural pluralism, as used by the Department of Canadian Heritage, have become the major identifiers for Canadian governments (Ley, 2005, 2007). The official face of multiculturalism is framed in the terms just described, and according to an official statement, multiculturalism is recognized in order to 'encourage racial and ethnic harmony' (Government of Canada, Department of Canadian Heritage, 2007).

The discourse about multiculturalism has not gone without careful scrutiny, and critiques have been put forward by various scholars (e.g., Corson, 1998; Gordon & Newfield, 1996; Lee & Lutz, 2005; Parekh, 2000; San Juan Jr, 2002). The critics, including the present authors, are not suggesting that multiculturalism is not useful and, therefore, needs to be dismissed. Rather, the argument is that there is a need for a critical approach and better theorizing about newcomer children and families as they adjust (or fail to adjust) to Canadian society. The Multiculturalism Act and its derivative policies and implications are simply not enough to adequately make a real difference to newcomer families, especially the more recent ones. The desirability of further changes to the reception of newcomers that really do show respect has been noted by Friendly and Prabhu (2010).

The official face of multiculturalism is deeply embedded in many Canadian institutions (Ley, 2007), including ECEC policies and services (Pacini-Ketchabaw, White, & Armstrong de Almeida, 2006). Let us consider the present day application of the official multicultural approach embedded in the renowned work by Louise Derman-Sparks and her *Anti-Bias Curriculum* (Derman-Sparks & A.B.C. Task Force, 1989; Derman-Sparks, Gutierrez, &, Phillips, 1992; York & Derman-Sparks, 1995). We find much to admire in her approach, especially at the time in which she was a pioneer in the field. Further, she is by no means blind to systemic problems of the sort we are discussing. That said, the guidelines proposed for educators tend to be somewhat individually focused. In other words, the children's attitudes are the main focus of intervention. For instance, she mentions as the first two goals: (1) nurture each child's construction of a knowledgeable, confident self-concept and group identity, and (2) promote each child's comfortable, empathetic interaction with people from diverse backgrounds. In these, and the other goals, the focus seems to be on conflict avoidance or resolution. Although we doubt it was Derman-Sparks' intention, providers can easily take from such broad goal statements that polite children and conflict avoidance are at the top of the agenda.

We now turn to some of the detailed critiques of mainstream approaches that have been published in the past ten years. First, multiculturalism is inherently based on the assimilation and change of 'different' populations to better fit the image of the desirable Canadian citizen (Lee & Lutz, 2005; Pacini-Ketchabaw et al., 2006). Although multiculturalism may well have been introduced to preserve the integrity of the diverse cultures in Canada, the actual effect of the policies and interventions leads in the direction of assimilation. The critiques of assimilation are well known and date back over several decades (see Abu-Laban, 1999; Ghosh & Abdi, 2004; Giroux, 1993, 2001; Mac Naughton & Davis, 2009). A common thread of all these critiques is that multiculturalism tends to group all immigrant populations into a single category and ignores the unequal location of different groups in society (Fass, 2005). These critiques also 'interrogate the structural and subjective workings of normative whiteness as universal, homogenized and essential' (Robinson & Jones-Diaz, 2006, p. 66) that are embedded in multicultural practices. Robinson and Jones-Diaz argue that the normativity of whiteness is largely anchored in universalistic child development discourses, a topic we elaborate on below.

Multiculturalism, as approached in early childhood education, is often framed in essentialist and universalist views of culture and development. These erase complexity and heterogeneity within, across, and among children; create newcomers as 'others'; and pathologize newcomer children and families through vulnerability discourses (Pacini-Ketchabaw et al., 2006; Robinson & Jones-Diaz, 2006). Such approaches have been critiqued by a number of investigators over the past decades (e.g., Geertz & Sanchez Dura, 1996; Pacini-Ketchabaw et al., 2006; Super & Harkness, 1998). The present situation of newcomers makes the re-examination of these theories even more crucial.

A second line of critique has been that multicultural approaches ignore constitutive social relations of power (Becher, 2004; Mac Naughton, 2005; Robinson & Jones-Diaz, 2006; Vandenbroeck, 2004, 2007). The anti-bias approach (Derman-Sparks & A.B.C. Task Force, 1989; Derman-Sparks, Ramsey, & Edwards, 2006) has been recognized for its consideration of power relations. The analysis of power relations, however, requires further elaboration and later researchers have focused on micro-interactions, complexities, and contradictions of power dynamics in the newcomers' adopted country (Robinson & Jones-Diaz, 2006; Vandenbroeck, 2004, 2007; Vandenbroeck, Roets, & Snoeck, 2009).

The third line of critique focuses on stereotypical views of other cultures. These explanations are framed around the notion that different cultural groups have different cultural values (e.g., Chinese culture values scientific thinking). Lee (2007) questions essentialistic explanations that construct spaces of social exclusion for newcomer groups. She says: 'Culturally essentialistic explanations draw upon and feed stereotypes about certain groups by simplifying complex issues into simple logics of one-dimensional cause and effect . . . In unquestioningly accepting essentialistic explanations . . . individuals are in danger of reinscribing outdated assimilationism as normative' (Lee, 2007, p. 81).

Several dangers lie in the approach to using culture as the analytical tool of interpretation. If we interpret the reference to other ways of doing and thinking about children and their education as simply a matter of cultural difference, then we might run the risk that the 'other' would be seen as a threat to the cohesion of Canada as a nation (Inda, 2000; Lee, 2007; Worley, 2005). The risk lies in that the others might be seen as asserting their views to shift away from normative ideas of ECEC in Canada. Then, practices and policies would concentrate on adjusting and preparing children and families to become aligned with normative ideas of child care. Cohesion or uniformity of views becomes what is desirable (Mac Naughton, 2005). However, what is left unquestioned are the normative discourses embedded in ideas of cohesion and uniformity.

Several alternative theoretical models have been proposed to deal with these limitations of multiculturalism. In the following section, we focus on two promising theoretical perspectives: anti-racist perspectives and transnational feminist perspectives.

Anti-racist and Transnational Feminist Perspectives

In this section, we provide a brief review of the main ideas embedded within anti-racist and transnational feminist perspectives. The section that follows reviews specific examples of how these theories have been applied in the field of early childhood education and care.

Anti-racist perspectives provide ways to analyse differences in new and innovative ways and depart from the assumption that racism can be understood merely in relation to race. Rather, race is viewed as intersecting or interlocking with other systems of inequality such as gender, nationality, migration, class, sexuality, ability, language, and so on (Anthias & Lloyd, 2002; Grewal & Kaplan, 1994, 2006; hooks, 1984; Razack, 2002). Furthermore, anti-racist scholars use the terms *racialization* and *racialized* as a way of moving away from reinforcing problematic concepts such as race and ethnicity. The term *racialization* requires us to move from an unexamined conception of race as an essential category towards an analytical view of assumptions about race and how these are fundamental to our understanding of people and their cultures (Ali, 2006). Anti-racist perspectives also pay specific attention to the racial normalization and categorization that is part of society (Lee & Lutz, 2005). Goldberg argued as follows: 'Racialized discourse does not consist simply in descriptive representations of other. It includes a set of hypothetical premises about human kinds . . . and about the differences between them (both mental and physical). It involves a class of ethical choices . . . And it incorporates a set of institutional regulations, directions, and pedagogical models' (1993, p. 47).

Anti-racist approaches re-envision the issue of identity and simultaneously question the often-assumed construction of newcomers as 'vulnerable' and 'uncivilized' when compared with the categories of the white civilized and superior Euro-American citizen (Grewal & Kaplan, 2006). Instead of being understood as natural and fixed, newcomers' identities are seen as active, productive, ongoing, and complex. Identity is seen as socially constructed, mobile, multiple, and always in a process of formation in relation to the social context and to others in the lived environment; identity emerges through discourse and representation (Bhabha, 1994; Hall, 1990, 1997). As such, newcomer children are viewed as crafting mixed identities within the cultural boundaries of their communities and nation (Back, 1996; Mahtani, 2001; Rattansi, 2005).

A transnational approach shares many of the ideas proposed by anti-racist theories and adds new dimensions to discussions of newcomers. Transnational theories question the idea of interpreting migrants' lives within the context of a nation state. Raising children across geographical nation states implies rethinking the idea of national boundaries, which are often taken for granted in migration scholarship (Bernhard, Landolt, & Goldring, 2009; Landolt & Da, 2005; Levitt & Schiller, 2004; Pareñas, 2001; Schiller, Basch, & Blanc, 1995).

This perspective challenges us to deconstruct national boundaries by using early childhood education as its context. The approach of transnationality is used to analyse how newcomers construct their identities in interaction with a multitude of, sometimes conflicting, social locations.

Transnational feminism, in particular, provides important insights into issues of citizenship, and by doing so departs from multicultural understandings of who is the desired citizen. Transnational feminism approaches citizenship through culture, as opposed to philosophy, ethics, or law (e.g., Delanty, 2000; Gibbs, 1996; Isin & Wood, 1999; Kymlicka, 1995; Stevenson, 2001). It engages with identity formation in newcomers' relationships to citizenship (Alexander & Mohanty, 1997; Anthias & Yuval-Davis, 1991; Friedman, 1998; Grewal & Kaplan, 1994; Ong, 1999; Yuval-Davis, 2000). Citizenship identities – understood as 'flexible,' 'in transition,' and 'negotiated' – are a relational process and not a status (Ong, 1999). Citizenship identities are forged in everyday interactions and lived environments that are hierarchically organized and mediated by dominant white and other ethnic minority cultural formations. Thus, identity formation is not seen only as a matter of gender, age, and stage of development, but also in terms of children's community histories, dominant and resistant discourses, material practices, local community contexts and structures, and individual and groups' own social positioning and sense of self-making.

Transnational feminist frameworks also bring into perspective the ways in which gender, class, race, and nationality (among other social factors) articulate with globalization (Caragata, 2003; Ehrenreich & Hochschild, 2002; Pareñas, 2001; Sudbury, 2005): 'A transnational approach pays attention to the inequalities and differences that arise from new forms of globalization as well as from older histories of colonialism and racism. [It] emphasizes the world of connections of all kinds that do not necessarily create similarities' (Ong, 2003, p. xix). This literature also shows how globalization tends to increase the already existing inequalities based on genderization, racialization, and economic opportunities (Caragata, 2003).

Anti-racist and Transnational Feminist Perspectives in ECE

We explored the limitations of multicultural approaches in ECEC and proposed the use of anti-racist and transnational perspectives to read the narratives of newcomer children and families in ECEC. We end this chapter by highlighting four studies that draw on one or both of these promising approaches.

Scholars in Australia, examining the social construction of whiteness and considering the critique of multiculturalism, have done extensive work with young children by exposing the racial power games as well as the reconfiguration of these games in early childhood classrooms (see Mac Naughton & Davis, 2009). In a study entitled *Preschool Children's Constructions of Racial and Cultural Diversity*, Mac Naughton, Davis, and Smith (2009) explored how young children use race in the processes of actively constructing their complex, multiple, shifting identities. To do so, they employed a wide range of methodologies that allowed them to uncover the subtle ways in which children engage in producing their own subjectivities. For example, through the process of asking children to draw a self-portrait and then interviewing them about their own portraits as well as other children's self-portraits, the researchers were able 'to connect with the dynamics of children's lived experiences and their negotiations of subjectivities as connected to theirs and others' "race" identities' (Mac Naughton et al., 2009, p. 43). They were able to use a common activity in the child care centre such as drawing to understand how children view and negotiate race. (See below for an example of how the authors analysed the findings of the study.) They also used observation in order to explore the hierarchies of race and the dynamics of race relations that are common in early childhood classrooms. Specifically, they observed how children grouped themselves during playtimes, the characters they chose to play during free-time play, the roles that different children chose to take during play, and the dynamics of inclusion/exclusion evident during play. Another interesting method employed was ethnographic feedback – actively seeking feedback from children on the data gathered by the researchers. Through this process, the children were able to elaborate, correct, or fill in how they negotiate race in their daily activities (Mac Naughton et al., 2009).

Finally, the researchers used storytelling with persona dolls. They developed stories containing instances of inclusion/exclusion based on the data they gathered through other methods and used persona dolls to tell the story back to the children. Then, they interviewed the children and asked them what they thought about what had happened in the story, whether they had seen something like this happen before, how the doll character could attempt to respond to the situation, and what they themselves could do about it (Mac Naughton et al., 2009).

The processes of data analysis and findings of the *Preschool Children's Constructions of Racial and Cultural Diversity* study were as complex and multilayered as the data gathering strategies. One example, however, will suffice for the purposes of this chapter. To analyse some of their data, Davis, Mac Naughton, and Smith (2009) used rhizoanalysis, which allowed them to uncover how the politics of whiteness worked in the construction of children's identities. 'Rhizoanalysis aims to produce new meanings by using a tactically chosen text to "cast a shadow" over another text, and, by doing so, to disrupt and challenge the politics of the initial text' (p. 50). Using this process they analysed a discussion that one of the researchers had with Spot, an Anglo-Australian girl.

In this discussion, Spot noted that whiteness was something desirable and likeable – specifically, in response to one of the researcher's question: 'What about Franca makes her look pretty?' Spot said: 'because . . . she has white skin and I like white skin. And I like her hair' (p. 52). The researchers then selected other texts with political intent to help them to disrupt discourses of privilege they assumed in Spot's words. The texts selected by the researchers included two autobiographical accounts of Indigenous women (one of a woman growing up in the 1920s and 1930s in Australia, and the other of an Indigenous academic woman who wrote biographical stories of Indigenous Peoples in Australia), and an additional account of an Australian-Chinese woman. Although they did not show these other accounts to Spot, they helped the authors to unpack the ways in which white privilege functions in early childhood classrooms as well as how young children 'can and do make strategic choices in relation to their "racing"' (Mac Naughton et al., 2009, p. 36). These identity choices are not merely developmental but also have a political element.

Pacini-Ketchabaw and her colleagues in British Columbia have begun to experiment with the possibilities of the methods proposed by Mac Naughton and Davis (2009) in Australia. The focus has been on how early childhood educators in British Columbia can employ these strategies to uncover the dynamics of racialization in their own classrooms and actively challenge racism. In the Investigating Quality Project (see Alan Pence and Veronica Pacini-Ketchabaw in this volume), early childhood educators are engaged in developing new languages to understand their practices and to actively challenge dominant discourses related to newcomer children and families (Pacini-Ketchabaw & Berikoff, 2008; Pacini-Ketchabaw & Nxumalo, 2010). For example, the fifty-eight educators in the study engaged in multiple readings of the observations they collected from their classrooms (Pacini-Ketchabaw & Berikoff, 2008). Through multiple readings, they read events from developmental and multicultural perspectives as well as other alternative frameworks, including anti-racist and transnational feminist perspectives.

In one case, an educator shared the story of a group of newcomer children talking about the effects of racialization in language that is often unacceptable in many early childhood settings. When the educators read the transcripts from a multicultural perspective, they emphasized the violence exhibited by the children in the discussion and noted that in the group there were problem children, as well as victims. The solution, from a multicultural perspective, was to address the behaviour of the individual children who were cursing and being aggressive in the dialogue. The educators suggested, for example, that they would have talked individually to the children who were aggressive to ensure that the children did not exhibit the same behaviour again in the classroom. This approach would involve letting the children know that curse words and violence were not allowed in the classroom. This interpretation reflects the application of multicultural education and anti-bias perspectives that assume children's understanding of racism as a matter of maturation and higher levels of developmental understanding. The educators, however, also recognized that their actions were not making a difference in their classrooms – as the children continued to engage in similar conversations. They recognized that the multicultural approach they had been using until then did not go far enough to tackle the issues that had emerged in their classrooms. Therefore, together, the researchers and the educators looked for alternative frameworks to understand the situation differently. Anti-racist and feminist approaches were found to be useful.

When the educators read the dialogue from an anti-racist perspective, they noted that they had to challenge the violence inherent in colonialism and the operation of power through discourse of whiteness that created racialized hierarchies (Pacini-Ketchabaw & Berikoff, 2008). By shifting the way in which they read the dialogue, they realized that racism was, in fact, part of their everyday classrooms and, therefore, required further action and vigilance in the ways in which they interpreted their observations. This meant that the educators did not hide instances of racism in their classrooms anymore, but instead, realized that everyone was implicated in racism, and hiding it was not going to eliminate it. Of course, this did not mean that they had all the answers when racism appeared, but rather, that they were opening the dialogue and, therefore, looking for ways to resist it when racism appeared. This resistance involved engaging in conversations with children about how racism might be taking place in their classrooms and what they might be able to do about it. The educators are now actively seeking situations in which racism might be masking itself in some other guise. Now they collect their observations of free play, for example, and share and reflect on them with the larger group of educators when they suspect that racism might be exercised. Then, the educators go back to their child care centres and address the issues with the children and also engage the families in the dialogue. What the group has done is open up the dialogue about racism, allowing for more opportunities to learn how to counter it.

Taking a similar approach in a different research context, Vandenbroeck, Roets, and Snoeck (2009) conducted a study in Belgium, employing a transnational framework to the reading of transcripts of three newcomer mothers with babies. They sought to identify the 'dynamics of citizenship and identity trans/formations, stimulated through their participation in child care' (p. 205). Specifically, the researchers used child care as a context for understanding the processes in which newcomer mothers become citizens and how they negotiate their own position as citizens in daily encounters and relationships with educators. Conducting a transnational citizenship study meant that when the researchers analysed/read the mothers' narratives, they did not just report on the mothers' perceptions on child care. But rather, the focus was to make visible the ways in which democracy and citizenship took place in the everyday interactions between the mothers and the child care providers. The child care providers were participating in a larger project on how to create respectful encounters with diversity in their centres. The researchers highlighted the agency of the mothers in creating multiple social belongings through several micro-events such as sleeping and eating habits. The mothers attended to the child care providers' suggestions, but also created their own spaces within the centre – both for themselves and for the children. By conceptualizing the mothers as belonging to multiple social contexts, the researchers did not see differences in eating habits at home and at the centre as being in conflict, but rather as something that the mothers constantly negotiated in the creation of their own citizenship identities as newcomers.

For example, Fatima, one of the mothers in the study, reported that she wanted to learn more about the future educational possibilities for her baby daughter. Although the caregiver was initially reluctant to provide this information, she researched local schools and shared the findings with Fatima. The researchers noted that this was an example of how this mother was reshaping the public sphere of child care and, consequently, was actively creating new citizenship identities for newcomer families. This was a dyadic, dynamic process in which both the educator and the mother were open to change. The researchers paid attention to the agency of the mothers in the processes of subject formation. Needless to say, the child care context with which these mothers were interacting understood these mothers' actions from a perspective that valued active citizenship.

In the fourth set of studies highlighted in this chapter, Bernhard, Landolt, and Goldring (2009) investigated the difficulties experienced by forty Latin American mothers who experienced geographical separation from their children as a result of migration to Canada. Latin American mothers in this setting generally lacked the social networks, normative frameworks, and institutional resources for coping with the separation. The service providers they encountered were highly re-spected by the families and, therefore, in an ideal position to make a difference for these families. In one case, a child had been biting other children at the child care centre. The educator interpreted these actions as the child having poor social skills and suggested that he join an after-school play group. In fact, the educator was mistaken about both her interpretation of the child's behaviour and thus, her recommendation. As the mother revealed to one of the researchers, the child had been separated from her for two years, and they had recently experienced a rocky reunification process. The child was missing his grandmother to whom he had become securely attached in the home country. The re-searchers encouraged the mother to talk to the educator about this, and she was then able to make better decisions regarding possible referrals and interventions. Had we not been aware of transnational studies, we would not have been able to deal effectively with the situation. Insti-tutions concerned with children's health and welfare are of particular importance and can create serious problems for a transnational family, especially if the institutions are not able to make an accurate assess-ment of the family structure and patterns of authority.

Bernhard and her team also used a transnational theoretical approach in their Parenting Circles Program, a dialogue group set up to help em-power Latina immigrant mothers to reach out to educators and, there-fore, become meaningfully involved in the education of their children (Bernhard, 2010; Garcia, 2008; Pinkus, 2008). The mothers had picked up on teachers' implicit and not so implicit cues about speaking Span-ish in the home, and they began to speak to their children in English in-stead of their native language. In fact, prior to the start of the Parenting Circles intervention, the parents were asked to rate their goals and de-sires for their children for the next five years. Fluency in English, adap-tation to the new environment, and academic success were the top three goals identified by the group members, with adaptation and academic success seen as dependent on English fluency. Had we taken a multicul-tural approach, we would have responded to the parents by providing instruction in English. Our theoretical commitment to a transnational framework, however, led us to find ways to tap into the knowledge and cultural capital that the mothers brought with them including the fund of knowledge provided by continued contact with extended family in the home country and in other countries around the world.

The Parenting Circles Program involved parents writing self-authored books or identity texts about themselves, their families, and their goals. Scanned photographs and word processing were used to create the books, which allowed parents to communicate and share their personal experiences. The process of involving immigrant parents in self-authoring books was geared towards the acquisition of a strong sense of self-worth and pride in cultural identity. The focus of the texts written by the parents was on affirming the linguistic and cultural identity of their children and covered such themes as, *This Is Who I Am, The Story of My Name, A Special Person in My Life,* and *Hopes and Dreams for My Child.* By setting up groups where the mothers' cultural capital was recognized, the message that the mothers received was that they had much to contribute to their children's education.

The last three studies show that newcomer families and their children have the potential to influence the education of their children in the new country. In many ways, they have exceptional strengths; in favourable circumstances, they can draw upon assets stemming from their continuing transnational connections. If service providers were aware of the effects of migration pathways on family functioning, they would see that the usual goals and assumptions do not always apply. By gaining the family's trust and drawing on their fund of knowledge, the likelihood would be greater that the full potential of these families and their children would be realized.

Conclusion

In this chapter, we have argued that given the complexities and nuances of current migration patterns in Canada alternatives to multicultural approaches are needed to support newcomer children and families in order to use early childhood institutions in more effective ways. We analysed some of the limitations of multiculturalism, that is, practices as they currently exist, and provided a brief overview of the promise of frameworks such as anti-racism and transnational feminism for early childhood education. Through a review of four sets of studies, we demonstrated new and alternative practices.

These studies not only exemplify the need to employ alternative theoretical frameworks, but they also highlight the use of methodological approaches that allow for in-depth investigations and are open to fresh findings and perspectives. The studies reviewed employ narrative, interpretative, and ethnographic approaches to data gathering and analysis and, therefore were able through the use of anti-racism and transnational frameworks to capture the nuances and dynamics of the situations under study. Large-scale surveys that attempt to account for the perspectives of newcomer children, families, or service providers often tend to obscure the deeper issues as well as the micro-analysis of day-to-day processes.

In conclusion, Canada should honour its newcomers and their children, especially at a time when the composition of its society is drastically changing, and it is just beginning to face the challenges that an aging population and a non-immigrant declining birth rate entail to sustain the country.

References

Abada, T., & Tenkorang, E.Y. (2009). Gender differences in educational attainment among the children of Canadian immigrants. *International Sociology, 24*, 580–608.

Abu-Laban, Y. (1999). The politics of race, ethnicity and immigration: The contested area of multiculturalism. In J. Bickerton & A.G. Ganon (Eds.), *Canadian Politics* (pp. 463–483). Peterborough, ON: Broadview.

Alaggia, R., & Maiter, S. (2006). Domestic violence and child abuse: Issues for immigrant and refugee families. In R. Alaggia & C. Vine (Eds.), *Cruel but not unusual: Violence in Canadian families.* Waterloo, ON: Wilfrid Laurier University Press.

Alexander, M.J., & Mohanty, C.T. (Eds.). (1997). *Feminist genealogies, colonial legacies, democratic futures.* New York: Routledge.

Ali, M. (2008). Loss of parenting self-efficacy among immigrant parents. *Contemporary Issues in Early Childhood, 9*(2), 148–160.

Ali, S. (2006). Racializing research: Managing power and politics? *Ethnic and Racial Studies, 29*, 471–486.

Ambert, A. (2006). *Changing families: Relationships in context.* Toronto: Pearson.

Anisef, P., Brown, R.S., Phythian K., Sweet, D., & Walters, D. (2008). *Early school leaving among immigrants in Toronto secondary schools.* CERIS Working Paper No. 67. Retrieved from http://ceris.metropolis.net/Virtual%20Library/WKPP%20List/WKPP2008/CWP67.pdf.

Anthias, F., & Lloyd, C. (Eds.). (2002). *Rethinking anti-racisms: From theory to practice.* London: Routledge.

Anthias, F., & Yuval-Davis, N. (1991). Connecting race and gender. In F. Anthias & N. Yuval-Davis (Eds.), *Racialized boundaries: Race, nation, gender, colour, and class and the anti-racist struggle* (pp. 96–131). London: Routledge.

Back, L. (1996). *New ethnicities and urban culture.* New York: St Martin's Press.

Becher, A.A. (2004). Research considerations concerning cultural differences. *Contemporary Issues in Early Childhood, 5*, 81–94.

Berk, M.L., & Schur, C.L. 2001. The effect of fear on access to care among undocumented Latino immigrants. *Journal of Immigrant Health, 3*, 151–156.

Bernhard, J.K. (2010). From theory to practice: Engaging immigrant parents in their children's education. *Alberta Journal of Educational Research, 56*(3), 391–334.

Bernhard, J.K., Goldring, L., Young, J., Berinstein, C., & Wilson, B. (2007). Living with uncertain legal status in Canada: Implications for the wellbeing of children and families. *Refuge, 24*, 101–113.

Bernhard, J.K., Landolt, P., & Goldring, L. (2009). The institutional production and social reproduction of transnational families: The case of Latin American immigrants in Toronto. *International Migration, 46*(2), 3–31.

Bhabha, H.K. (1994). *The location of culture.* New York: Routledge.

Borzykowski, B. (2009). The kids who fall between the cracks. *Canadian Business, 82*(18), 107–108.

Caragata, L. (2003). Neoconservative realities: The social and economic marginalization of Canadian women. *International Sociology, 18*, 559–580.

CBC News. (2007, 8 March). Term 'visible minorities' may be discriminatory, UN body warns Canada. Retrieved from http://www.cbc.ca/canada/story/2007/03/08/canada-minorities.html.

Corson, D. (1998). *Changing education for diversity.* Philadelphia, PA: Open University Press.

Davis, K., Mac Naughton, G., & Smith, K. (2009). The dynamics of whiteness: Children locating within/without. In G. Mac Naughton & K. Davis (Eds.), *'Race' and early childhood education: An international approach to identity, politics, and pedagogy* (pp. 49–65). New York: Palgrave Macmillan.

Delanty, G. (2000). *Citizenship in a global age: Society, culture and politics.* Buckingham, UK: Open University Press.

Derman-Sparks, L., & A.B.C. Task Force (1989). *Anti-bias curriculum: Tools for empowering young children.* Washington, DC: National Association for the Education of Young Children.

Derman-Sparks, L., Gutierrez, M., & Phillips, C. (1992). *Teaching young children to resist bias: What parents can do.* Washington, DC: National Association for the Education of Young Children.

Derman-Sparks, L., Ramsey, P.G., & Edwards, J.O. (2006). *What if all the kids are white? Anti-bias multicultural education with young children and families.* New York: Teachers College Press.

Ehrenreich, B., & Hochschild, A.R. (Eds.). (2002). *Global woman: Nannies, maids, and sex workers in the new economy.* New York: Metropolitan/Owl.

Fass, P. (2005). Children in global migrations. *Journal of Social History, 38,* 937–953.

Fix, M.E., & Zimmermann, W. (1999). *All under one roof: Mixed-status families in an era of reform.* Washington, DC: Urban Institute.

Friedman, S.S. (1998). *Mappings: Feminism and the cultural geographies of encounter.* Princeton, NJ: Princeton University Press.

Friendly, M., & Prabhu, N. (2010). *Can early childhood education and care help keep Canada's promise of respect for diversity?* CCRU, Occasional Paper no. 23. Retrieved from http://action.web.ca/home/crru/rsrcs_crru_full.shtml?x=128572.

Galabuzzi, G.-E. (2005). Factors affecting the social economic status of Canadian immigrants in the new millennium. *Canadian Issues,* (Spring), 53–57.

Garcia, C.B. (2008). Parenting Circles Program: The key elements for the meaningful engagement of Spanish-speaking parents to support their children's school success. *Theses and dissertations: Ryerson University.* Paper 110. Retrieved from http://digitalcommons.ryerson.ca/dissertations/110.

Geertz, C., & Sanchez Dura, N. (1996). *Los usos de la diversidad.* Buenos Aires: Paidos.

George, U., & Young, J. (2006*). Immigration to Canada: The case of Mexicans.* Unpublished report. Toronto: Metropolis Network and the Foundation of Population, Migration and Environment.

Ghosh, R., & Abdi, A.A. (2004). *Education and the politics of difference: Canadian perspectives.* Toronto: Canadian Scholars' Press.

Gibbs, J.T. (1996). Triple marginality: The case of young African-Caribbean women in Toronto (Canada) and London (England). *Canadian Social Work Review, 13,* 143–157.

Giroux, H.A. (1993). *Living dangerously: Multiculturalism and the politics of difference.* New York: Peter Lang.

Giroux, H.A. (2001). *Living dangerously: Public spaces private lives – Beyond the culture of cynicism.* Lanham, MD: Rowman & Littlefield.

Goldberg, D.T. (1993). *Racist culture: Philosophy and the politics of meaning.* Cambridge, MA: Blackwell.

Gordon, A., & Newfield, C. (Eds.). (1996). *Mapping multiculturalism.* Minneapolis, MN: University of Minnesota Press.

Government of Canada. Department of Canadian Heritage (2007) *What Is Multiculturalism?* Ottawa: Author. Retrieved from http://www.canadianheritage.gc.ca/pc-ch/sujets-subjects/divers-multi/index_e.cfm.

Government of Canada. Ministry of Justice. (1985). *Canadian Multiculturalism Act.* Retrieved from http://laws-lois.justice.gc.ca.

Grewal, I., & Kaplan, C. (Eds.). (1994). *Scattered hegemonies: Postmodernity and transnational feminist practices.* Minneapolis, MN: University of Minnesota Press.

Grewal, I., & Kaplan, C. (Eds.). (2006). *An introduction to women's studies: Gender in a transnational world.* Boston, MA: McGraw-Hill.

Hall, S. (1990). Cultural identity and diaspora. In J. Rutherford (Ed.), *Identity: Community, culture, difference* (pp. 222–237). London: Lawrence & Wishart.

Hall, S. (1997). Introduction. In S. Hall (Ed.), *Representation: Cultural representations and signifying practices* (pp. 1–12). London: Open University Press and Sage.

hooks, b. (1984). *Feminist theory from margin to center.* Boston, MA: South End Press.

Inda, J.X. (2000). Foreign bodies: Migrants, parasites, and the pathological nation. *Discourse: Journal for Theoretical Studies in Media and Culture, 22*(3), 46–62.

Isin, E.F., & Wood, P.K. (1999). Cultural citizenship: Consuming identities. In E.F. Isin & P.K. Wood (Eds.), *Citizenship and identity* (pp. 123–152). London: Sage.

Klingner, J.K., Artiles, A.J., Kozleski, E., Harry, B., Zion, S., Tate, W., Durán, G.Z., & Riley, D. (2005). Addressing the disproportionate representation of culturally and linguistically diverse students in special education through culturally responsive educational systems. *Education Policy Analysis Archives, 13*(38). Retrieved from http://epaa.asu.edu/ojs/article/view/143.

Kymlicka, W. (1995). *Multicultural citizenship: A liberal model of minority rights.* Oxford: Clarendon.

Landolt, P., & Da, W.W. (2005). The spatially ruptured practices of transnational migrant families: Lessons from the case of El Salvador and the People's Republic of China. *Current Sociology, 53,* 625–653.

Lee, J. (2007). Localities and cultural citizenship: Narratives of racialized girls living in, through, and against whiteness. In P. Gurstein & L. Angeles (Eds.), *Learning civil societies: Shifting contexts in democratic planning and governance* (pp. 59–88). Toronto: University of Toronto Press.

Lee, J., & Lutz, J. (Eds.). (2005). *Situating 'race' and racisms in time, space, and theory: Critical essays for activists and scholars.* Montreal and Kingston: McGill-Queen's University Press.

Levitt, P., & Schiller, N.G. (2004). Conceptualizing simultaneity: A transnational social field perspective on society. *International Migration Review, 38,* 1002–1039.

Ley, D. (2005). *Post-multiculturalism?* RIIM Working Paper Series, No. 05–18. Vancouver, BC: RIIM. Retrieved from http://www.riim.metropolis.net/Virtual%20Library/2005/WP05–18.pdf.

Ley, D. (2007). *Multiculturalism: A Canadian defence.* RIIM Working Paper Series, No. 07–04. Vancouver, BC: RIIM. Retrieved from http://www.riim. metropolis.net/Virtual%20Library/2007/WP07–04.pdf.

Li, P. (1998). The market value and social value of race. In V. Satzewich (Ed.), Racism and social inequity in Canada (pp. 115–130). Toronto: Thompson Educational.

Mac Naughton, G. (2005). *Doing Foucault in early childhood: Applying poststructural ideas to early childhood.* London: Routledge Falmer.

Mac Naughton, G., & Davis, K. (Eds.). (2009). *'Race' and early childhood education: An international approach to identity, politics, and pedagogy.* New York: Palgrave Macmillan.

Mac Naughton, G., Davis, K., & Smith, K. (2009). Exploring 'race-identities' with young children: Making politics visible. In G. Mac Naughton & K. Davis (Eds.), *'Race' and early childhood education: An international approach to identity, politics, and pedagogy* (pp. 31–47). New York: Palgrave Macmillan.

Magalhaes, L., Carrasco, C., & Gastaldo, D. (2010). Undocumented migrants in Canada: A scope literature review on health, access to services, and working conditions. *Journal of Immigrant & Minority Health, 12,* 132–151.

Mahoney, J. (2007, 14 March). All immigrants by 2030. *Globe and Mail,* pp. A1, A8.

Mahtani, M. (2001). 'I'm a blonde-haired, blue-eyed Black girl': Mapping mobile paradoxical spaces among multiethnic women in Toronto, Canada. In D. Parker & M. Song (Eds.), *Rethinking 'mixed race'* (pp. 173–190). London: Pluto.

Ong, A. (1999). *Flexible citizenship: The cultural logics of transnationality.* London: Duke University Press.

Ong, A. (2003). *Buddha is hiding: Refugees, citizenship, the new America.* Berkeley, CA: University of California Press.

Organization for Economic Co-operation and Development (OECD). (2003). *Early childhood education and care policy: Canada country note.* OECD Directorate for Education. Retrieved from http://www.oecd.org/dataoecd/42/34/33850725.pdf.

Pacini-Ketchabaw, V., & Berikoff, A. (2008). The politics of difference and diversity: From young children's violence to creative power expressions. *Contemporary Issues in Early Childhood, 9,* 256–264.

Pacini-Ketchabaw, V., & McIvor, O. (2005). Negotiating bilingualism in early childhood: A study of migrant families and early childhood practitioners. In V. Pacini-Ketchabaw & A. Pence (Eds.), *Canadian early childhood education: Broadening and deepening discussions of quality* (pp. 109–126). Ottawa: Canadian Child Care Federation.

Pacini-Ketchabaw, V., & Nxumalo, F. (2010). A curriculum for social change: Experimenting with politics of action or imperceptibility. In V. Pacini-Ketchabaw

(Ed.), *Flows, rhythms and intensities of early childhood education curriculum* (pp. 133–154). New York: Peter Lang.

Pacini-Ketchabaw, V., White, J., & Armstrong de Almeida, A.E. (2006). Racialization in early childhood: A critical analysis of discourses in policies. *International Journal of Educational Policy, Research, & Practice: Reconceptualizing Childhood Studies, 7*, 95–113.

Parekh, B.C. (2000). *Rethinking multiculturalism. Cultural diversity and political theory.* Cambridge, MA: Harvard University Press.

Pareñas, R.S. (2001). *Servants of globalization: Women, migration and domestic work.* Stanford, CA: Stanford University Press.

People for Education. (2008). *Urban and suburban schools 2008: A discussion paper on the schools we need in the 21st century.* Toronto: Author. Retrieved from http://www.peopleforeducation.com/urban-suburban-schools.

Pinkus, S. (2008). The effect of the Parenting Circles Program on home language retention and parental engagement: The case of a Spanish-speaking parent group in Toronto. *Theses and dissertations: Ryerson University.* Paper 111. Retrieved from http://digitalcommons.ryerson.ca/dissertations/111.

Rattansi, A. (2005). *The dream of the decade.* North Charleston, SC: BookSurge.

Razack, S. (2002). *Race, space, and the law: Unmapping a white settler society.* Toronto: Between the Lines.

Robinson, K.H., & Jones-Diaz, C. (2005). *Diversity and difference in early childhood education: Issues for theory and practice.* Maidenhead, UK: Open University Press.

San Juan Jr, E. (2002). *Racism and cultural studies. Critiques of multiculturalist ideology and the politics of difference.* Durham, NC: Duke University Press.

Schiller, N.G., Basch, L., & Blanc, C.S. (1995). From immigrant to transmigrant: Theorizing transnational migration. *Anthropological Quarterly, 68,* 48–63.

Statistics Canada. (2005). *Visible minority population, by age group* (2001 Census). Retrieved from http://www40.statcan.ca/l01/cst01/demo50a.htm.

Stevenson, E. (Ed.). (2001). *Culture and citizenship.* London: Sage.

Sudbury, J. (Ed.). (2005). *Global lockdown: Race, gender, and the prison-industrial complex.* New York: Routledge.

Super, C.M., & Harkness, S. (1998). The development of affect in infancy and early childhood. In M. Woodhead, D. Faulkner, & K. Littleton (Eds.), *Cultural worlds of early childhood* (pp. 34–47). London: Routledge.

Vandenbroeck, M. (2004). Diverse aspects of diversity: A European perspective. *International Journal of Equity and Innovation in Early Childhood, 1*(2), 27–44.

Vandenbroeck, M. (2007). Beyond anti-bias education: Changing conceptions of diversity and equity in European early childhood education *European Early Childhood Education Research Journal, 15,* 21–35.

Vandenbroeck, M., Roets, G., & Snoeck, A. (2009). Immigrant mothers crossing borders: Nomadic identities and multiple belongings in early childhood education *European Early Childhood Education Research Journal, 17,* 203–216.

Worley, C. (2005). 'It's not about race. It's about the community': New Labour and 'community cohesion.' *Critical Social Policy, 25,* 483–496.

Xu, S., Connelly, F.M., He, M.F., & Phillion, J. (2007). Immigrant students' experience of schooling: A narrative inquiry theoretical framework. *Journal of Curriculum Studies, 39,* 399–422.

York, S., & Derman-Sparks, L. (1995) *Multicultural practical strategies for developing cultural awareness and appreciation.* New York: Scholastic.

Yuval-Davis, N. (2000). Citizenship, territoriality and the gendered construction of difference. In E.F. Isin (Ed.), *Democracy, citizenship and the global city* (pp. 172–188). London: Routledge.

6 Intergenerational Learning Programming from a Curriculum Studies Perspective: New Directions, New Possibilities

RACHEL M. HEYDON

Recently, I was giving a talk about intergenerational (IG) singing programs – programs that bring people of different generations together to create learning and interactional opportunities through song. The audience was a committed group of early childhood educators (ECEs) who specialized in music. In part of my talk, I shared the following observation I had made in an IG art class at Blessed Mother, a unique 'shared site' IG program located in the United States, where elder and child care share space and programming:[1]

> I'm standing with the video camera trying to decide how to capture everything that's going on in this room. Three large tables are populated by children, elders, and younger adults [with disabilities], and all are working hard to solve the problem the [IG] art teacher has set out for them: choose an item from a clear bucket of mystery objects then use it as a catalyst to create a drawing. As I look about the room I see Susan, the art teacher, move towards a table of four. She is holding large, bright photographs of various forms of art, including some interesting examples of post-modern architecture. Susan gently touches Bonnie (age 82) who is asleep in her wheelchair. Rebecca (age 80), who is across from them, laughs and says loudly while pointing at Bonnie, 'She wakes me up at 4:00 o'clock, so wake her up!' I smile at the casual ribbing of one room-mate to another. Bonnie indeed wakes up to view the photographs just as Carl (age 5), who

---

1 All names are changed with the exception of Wendy Crocker, who was a project director on the 'Picasso' IG program study.

is sitting next to her, looks up from contemplating his strange, wooden object and pronounces, 'Let me see!' Katie (age 4) gets in on the viewing, and then everyone begins to discuss his or her object. Rebecca has a neon orange piece of plastic that looks like the letter 'E.' She holds it up for the others and announces, 'I don't know what this is.' Katie says it looks like a comb, or if you turn it this way, an 'E'! Carl nods, then tries to turn his wooden object into a spinning top. He can't quite get the spin right. Rebecca offers that maybe this isn't a top at all, as the proportions are wrong. Katie suggests that the object looks like a local building. Carl makes a face like he supposes so, but then goes on to say it reminds him of a candle. Susan says she likes how Carl uses his imagination to 'see' the solid wood as a flame. Rebecca, who has now indicated on the sly to Susan that she's figured out that the object is an archaic juicer, decides to follow the metaphoric route. She therefore interjects with the idea that maybe it's a beach umbrella. While Bonnie sits silently but watches everything and Katie uses the E/comb to trace patterns on a large piece of paper, Rebecca and Carl continue to wrestle with the wooden object, now using drawing to explore its contours. Every single person in this room will continue in this focused, thoughtful manner for an hour-and-a-half until the lunch crew arrives and forces them to disperse. Later, when I'm out of the field and tell this story to my former early-years teacher colleagues, they will gasp in disbelief. No 4- and 5-year-olds, they will claim, can stay on one task this long. And it is then that I am again reminded of the limits so many of us well-meaning educators place on the possibilities for children and their learning. (Heydon, 2007, pp. 35–36)

As with my past experience in sharing this story, a member of the early childhood education and care (ECEC) music group who was pursing graduate studies in the area but had limited teaching experience seemed somewhat incredulous yet also wanted to know more: 'How did the teacher get the children to attend for so long?' he asked and then shared stories of his own 'failed attempts' to engage his students in activities that he thought would be attractive to them. What was the 'secret' of the IG art class?

Educators are perennially looking for 'best practices.' For reasons that are explained later, this chapter will likely not satisfy this thirst for the best way to educate and care for young children. What it can provide, however, are some understandings about IG learning programs and people's experiences within them that can hopefully be used by readers to make informed judgments about the transferability and sig-nificance of the research to their own situations (Donmoyer, 2001). This chapter provides an introduction to IG learning programs and their curricula as a new direction in ECEC. It begins with a general contex-tualizing of IG programs by describing the benefits the literature has identified for participants, the various forms programs can take, the advice the literature gives about how to create learning programs with optimal benefits, and a look at the theoretical proclivities of the IG field. Next, I narrow the lens from this macro-perspective of the field to the particularities of my own IG research and what it might teach about curriculum and young children.

Introduction to Intergenerational Learning Programs

Benefits of IG Programs

Formal IG programs (under which IG learning and shared-site pro-grams fall) have been on the continent for decades. The U.S. Foster Grandparent Program of 1963, where older adults worked with chil-dren and youth deemed 'at risk,' was one of the first 'systematically planned' IG programs in North America (Larkin & Newman, 1997). Since then, IG programs have grown considerably (Kuehne & Collins, 1997), yet are still not commonplace. That they are not more wide-spread is surprising given that IG programs hold many documented benefits for participants. For child participants, benefits include a sense of continuity in lives where there might otherwise be little IG contact, the understanding that learning is lifelong (Brummel, 1989), the chance to better understand older adults, which can minimize fears children might have of them, a fostering of children's acceptance that aging is a normal and natural part of the life cycle (Kaplan et al., 2003), increased appreciation for diversity (Jarrott & Bruno, 2007), and increased em-pathy towards older adults (Schwalbach & Kiernan, 2002). For older adults, IG programs can minimize fears they might have of children (Kaplan et al., 2003) and create a calming effect in those with dementia (Ward, Kamp, & Newman, 1996). For both generations, programs can create IG understanding, provide opportunities for lifelong learning (Brummel, 1989), help generations locate commonalities across age and culture (Elders Share the Arts, n.d.), and provide opportunities to build IG relationships (Jarrott & Bruno, 2007).

Structure of Intergenerational Learning Programs

Intergenerational learning programs can take many forms under four basic models: older adults providing service to children (e.g., elders rocking HIV-positive infants in hospital settings), young people serving older people (e.g., reading to people in elder care settings), IG groups performing community service (e.g., environmental projects), and shared-site programs (Intergenerational Programming, n.d.). While each model has its benefits and place, shared-site IG programs (also known as co-located programs), where participants come together in formal and informal ways for learning and relationship building, have many strengths including the following:

- More frequent interaction can lead to stronger relationships and better understanding between the generations.
- Transportation between the programs is not an issue due to the co-location or close proximity of the programs.
- Informal interactions are possible through routine elements such as shared indoor and outdoor spaces, a common entrance for both generations, and ease of movement between the adult programs and children programs.
- Scheduling activities is easier since space is shared, staff are cross-trained, and many sites have an intergenerational coordinator to facilitate activities. (Generations United, 2006, pp. 3–4)

Shared-site programs are not add-ons to existing programs but, rather, the very form and physical structure of the programs creates opportunities for IG interaction and relationships.

Regardless of whether a site is shared or not, there are other structural concerns that must be addressed for participants to garner benefits from any IG program. These include the need for formal, institutionalized administrative agreements regarding a commitment to IG programming, participant choice over whether to participate, and the provision of 'cross-training' for practitioners so they are not solely focused on the populations with whom they typically work (e.g., educators being educated about working with older adults and recreation therapists being educated about working with children). Cross-training can also include educating participants before programs begin about the generation they are about to encounter (Jarrott, 2007).

Creating Optimal Opportunities for Learning

Although program models are important to consider, simply bringing different generations together may not create positive effects (e.g., Aday, McDuffie, & Sims, 1993). Strong prospects for learning and IG interaction come from contexts that support IG 'programming' rather than mere 'activities.' The difference between these approaches is that programming 'provide[s] a way for experiences and interactions to take on meaning relevant to one's life' whereas activities 'do not allow the level of meaning to exist because they lack depth and long term significance' (Friedman, 1997, p. 105). IG activities are usually one-meeting occasions where people are parachuted together (e.g., panel of visiting elders in a classroom). Activities like this can have some 'positive outcomes,' yet more generally, programming that is longer term is more meaningful and tends to 'reduce ambiguities about . . . relationship[s], lessen social distance, and support intergenerational solidarity' (Jarrott, 2007, p. 6). Some of the structural issues introduced above can help foster IG programs, but the literature has also identified important, more curricular-oriented issues that should be addressed.

Jarrott (2007) found that a particular notion of 'equal group status' should be sought in programs where 'each participant has something to contribute and something to gain from the contact setting' (p. 5). Equal group status can, at least in part, be accomplished through programs that help participants cooperate and work towards 'common goals' (p. 5). Further, some 'essential criteria' (Friedman, 1997) for IG programming, have been identified as: 'programs should be beneficial to all [participants]; programs should be on-going, lasting for a significant length of time to establish relationships; programs should serve the community; programs should include a curricular . . . component' (p. 105). This last point begs for the inclusion of curriculum studies in any IG learning program conversation.

Theoretical Approaches to Intergenerational Learning

Accompanying the birth of IG programs is a growing interdisciplinary IG research tradition. In general, IG research is made up of perspectives and methods from gerontology, psychology, education, and other human development specialties (Larkin & Newman, 1997). Regarding trends in the research, the benefits of IG programs generally and learning programs specifically are thought to be well known. Consequently, more recent research is considering 'best practices,' such as asking how programs can 'build on [the] respective strengths' (Kaplan et al., 2003, p. 7) of participants and create opportunities for them to foster 'meaningful relationships' (Griff et al., 1996, p. 5). There is also attention paid to the evaluation of programs (e.g., Cox, Croxford, & Edmonds, 2006).

Theoretically, the bulk of IG research draws on developmental theories, especially those of Erik Erikson (VanderVen, 1999) and supports evaluation of programs based on instrumentalist theories (Hayes, 2003; Kuehne & Kaplan, 2001) with the goal of achieving a degree of prediction and control (Habermas, 1972). The focus on a fairly monolithic notion of what is best bespeaks these theoretical orientations. Undoubtedly, this type of IG learning research has greatly contributed to the knowledge of IG learning phenomena, which is significant to the development and maintenance of IG learning programs. At the same time, knowledge and understanding of IG learning can only increase through the inclusion of a diversity of methodologies and theories. Consequently, my own research relies on the foundation laid by the dominant research of IG learning, yet employs theories and methodologies that come from research traditions that make sense to me as a former teacher and now educational researcher.

My IG studies are located in the field of curriculum studies and work through a critical theoretical framework. Curriculum studies is an established field within educational studies that queries the various orientations to and levels of curriculum and seeks to answer teaching and learning questions that fall into three main 'orders' of questions: (1) the 'nature of curriculum' (questions relating to issues concerning the 'essence' and 'properties' of curriculum); (2) the 'elements of curriculum' (questions relating to issues concerning the 'teacher, students, subject, milieu, aim, activity,' and 'result'), and (3) the 'practice of curriculum' (questions relating to issues concerning action and thought; Dillon, 2009, pp. 344–348). While curriculum studies researchers might call upon methods and frameworks from distinct fields such as sociology, anthropology, psychology, philosophy, and the like to answer these questions, they do so from a uniquely curriculum studies vantage and approach. Curriculum studies 'may draw on any external discipline for methodological help but does not allow the methodology to determine inquiry' (Egan, 1978, p. 16). This allows researchers to tailor methodologies to suit the specific circumstances under investigation and ground their studies in specific *teaching* and *learning* contexts. Thus, my studies of IG curriculum draw on ethnographic tools from anthropology, yet my use of them is 'looser' (p. 16) than in a classically anthropological sense. This is the consequence of curriculum researchers' need to tailor methodologies to suit the specific circumstance under investigation. Given that IG programs and research are in a nascent stage, this flexibility is particularly necessary.

When coupled with a critical theoretical orientation, curriculum studies decries the ability of any curriculum to be best, for this perspective sees curriculum as multiple and dynamic and not as something that can be predicted and controlled. While 'the curriculum' is sometimes reduced to what is 'intended' to be taught (Eisner, 2005) and equated with a 'document' (e.g., a paper copy of a provincial curriculum guide), educators like Routman council that curriculum is a 'dialogue' (2000, p. xxxviii). Schwab's (1973) curricular 'commonplaces': teachers, learners, subject matter, and milieu clarify what might be included in this dialogue. Together, the commonplaces create the 'operational curriculum' (i.e., how the curriculum is actually 'played out'; Eisner, 2005, p. 147). Curriculum can also be considered at the levels of the 'null' curriculum (Eisner, 2002) where the very absence of teaching something has an effect, and the 'hidden' curriculum (e.g., Apple, 1971), which accounts for the unstated goals of curriculum. There are also many types of curricular orientations that affect the degree to which the commonplaces, especially teachers and learners, are provided opportunities to be 'curricular informants' (Harste, 2003). These orientations run from rigid, 'prescriptive' forms to more flexible 'emergent forms' (Heydon & Wang, 2006).

The specific critical component of my studies comes through the goal of emancipation, which refers to the desire to 'free human-kind of what presents itself as "natural" or given by making apparent the points of view from which such a version of "reality" are constructed' (Habermas, 1972, p. 311). Considering phenomena critically means asking questions such as: What is taken for granted? What are other ways of seeing this? What socio-political issues are at play? What actions might forward the goal of social justice (e.g., Lewison, Flint, & Van Sluys, 2002)? For instance, one might question the notion of a universal best in ECEC, asking, 'Best for whom? What are the different iterations of best? How do they relate to a person's social positioning? Who does this notion of best serve?'

A Curriculum Researcher Discovers Intergenerational Programs

I began studying IG learning programs after visiting an IG art class at Blessed Mother. Created by the Catholic Church, at the time of the visit, Blessed Mother was a long-term care facility that included retirement apartments and ran what it called a Generations Together Learning Center (GTLC), a child care program for children ages 6 weeks to 6 years that was part of a shared-site program. The mission of the GTLC was to create opportunities for IG learning and interaction; thus, many measures were taken to ensure shared facilities and programming. Foremost was that the entire 300,000 square feet of Blessed Mother was licensed for child care, making the facility a space that literally and symbolically invited children to be present. Next, the architecture of Blessed Mother supported its IG mandate. The GTLC was prominently housed in a main part of Blessed Mother and had large windows to the hallway so that adults and children could see each other and adults would be more apt to stop in and visit. An outside play area was located close to the adults' living areas, and an observation area was included allowing more chances for IG interaction. Moreover, there was a satellite GTLC area for toddlers located in the heart of two 'neighbourhoods' (i.e., where the adults had their bedrooms, lounge, and eating areas). This room was said to be a shared space between adults and children and maximized IG contact. Apart from the architecture, Blessed Mother also offered many formal IG programs (e.g., art classes, IG music, and exercise). Thus, Blessed Mother was a prime example of a mature IG organization that met many of the essential criteria the literature lists for IG programs.

Trajectory of the Intergenerational Studies

My first inquiry into IG shared-site learning was a naturalistic study of the IG art class as part of the IG shared-site program at Blessed Mother. The research questions were: What are the constituents of learning opportunity-rich IG learning programs, and how are they organized? What (if any) learning opportunities are created by the IG art class? What forms of collaboration occur among participants? How does this collaboration build individual and communal capacities? I recorded through video and field notes what was occurring in two IG art classes and one adult art class (which I used as a counterpoint to the IG classes). I interviewed participants, faculty, staff, administration, and Susan, the art teacher who functioned as a collaborator. In my analysis of the class, I found many learning opportunities created by an 'asset oriented' (Heydon & Iannacci, 2008) form of curriculum: a curriculum that focused on participants' strengths and recognized their need to communicate in a wide variety of ways. Thanks to a multimodal literacy framework (e.g., Jewitt & Kress, 2003), the notion that literacy is not just reading and writing print text, but includes a range of ways people communicate (e.g., print, image, and gesture), I identified that many of the learning opportunities were literacy-related. Participants were provided opportunities, for example, to learn how to work through fundamental communication decisions: consider their interests that drive what they want to communicate, learn a number of different ways of communicating their message, and decide given the context the most apt way to structure their message (Kress & Jewitt, 2003). These learning opportunities were created through the class structure, which was organized around five components: (1) strategies to (re)acquaint participants with each other and foster community and a sense of safety (e.g., games to remind each other of participants' names); (2) a catalyst for that day's project that could induce conversation and activate schema related to the subject matter and/or media to be used (e.g., an image of a Faith Ringgold story quilt for a print project concerning humorous stories); (3) explicit instruction, modelling, and support to use the media in the project (e.g., print making); (4) sustained opportunities to work on the project and to draw on fellow participants for support; and (5) opportunities to share the work with an audience (e.g., in class, displays in the hallways, at a yearly public art show; Heydon, 2007).

Following the initial studies at the Mount, I wondered how other IG shared-site learning programs might provide similarly rich learning opportunities (in particular as they related to communication) and create productive forms of collaboration and relationship building. Thus, I visited a number of IG shared sites in southwestern Ontario and undertook a similar study to the one at Blessed Mother at a site called Watersberg. I chose Watersberg because it seemed representative of the other IG sites in the southwestern Ontario area that I had visited as it was run by the same child and elder care organizations and employed the same type of IG structure, elder care philosophy, and curricular orientation in the child care portion of the program (i.e., an emergent curriculum). Located in a suburban to rural area, Watersberg was a secular, privately run, for-profit, assisted living facility for the elderly that rented space to a private, non-denominational Christian, non-profit child care organization. The shared site was less than five years old at the time of the research, and the building was planned and built to house a child care facility on its main floor. Although a Watersberg administrator told me that per square foot elder care was more profitable than child care, they chose to include child care because their guiding philosophy was to provide their residents with opportunities to engage with nature, animals, and children.

Adults and children at Watersberg participated in pre-planned IG learning activities, and there were some opportunities for adults to visit the child care centre unannounced. In general, although I identified some opportunities for interaction and learning at Watersberg, they did not seem as rich as at Blessed Mother. This observation was substantiated by the practitioners who, while they all said how much the IG component brought to the program, admitted they had difficulty 'coming up' with what to do with the participants, or when they did decide on an activity it sometimes 'wasn't so great.' Watersberg struggled to turn activities into programs and to have a true curricular component; thus, there were few identifiable learning opportunities. For instance, a number of practitioners pointed to a teddy bear social as a ubiquitous yet 'failed' activity. One educator explained, 'We sat in a circle and each person sat there with their bear on their lap.' Other frequent activities that were slightly more successful but still did not challenge or create much meaning for participants were 'beauty parlour,' where participants did each other's hair and nails; 'ice cream social,' where participants watched as practitioners made and served sundaes; and 'free play,' where bins of children's toys were placed on tables for IG participants.

While the educators expressed ease in programming for young children and the recreation therapists were comfortable programming for older adults, neither group had much experience or training in working with IG groups. Thus, wanting to support practitioners such as the ones at Watersberg, I wondered if I could create a resource from a curriculum studies perspective to allow them to offer IG programming that created rich learning and interactional opportunities, in particular in the area of communication. Over a three-year period, I built and field tested an IG curriculum support guide that had the goal of capitalizing on art making and viewing as a way of expanding participants' communication options and as being a medium for relationship building. I adapted many of the projects from Blessed Mother's art program and authored others to be used by non-artists. Practitioners took these projects and, with support, implemented them at 'Picasso.'

Picasso was a retirement and nursing home in urban southwestern Ontario that was secular and for-profit. At the time of the research, it was approximately twenty years old and rented space to Picasso Child, an independent, secular, not-for-profit child care centre. Prior to the research there was no shared programming and there was a stark delineation between children's and adults' spaces. Picasso consented to have my research team work with them to create an IG art program and, in turn, develop the curriculum resource guide. The team worked with Picasso's own resources and existing structures to build an IG art program as an entrée into IG programming. The practitioners used the guide as a starting point for teaching in the program and provided feedback so we could revise the guide. We documented this process and collected data that related to the participants' responses to the projects and the program as a whole.

For data analysis, I used a modified version of the constant comparison method (Handsfield, 2006). Data were coded according to predictive themes and pattern-matched. To retain their complexity, data that fit between themes did not automatically discredit themes but were included and the discontinuities presented. In the remainder of the chapter, I flesh out the previous literature review and add a voice from curriculum studies through a synopsis of findings from my IG studies (e.g., Heydon, 2005, 2007, 2008, 2009; Heydon & Daly, 2008).

Adding to the IG Literature from the Perspective of Critical Curriculum Studies

The findings of my intergenerational studies are organized according to the pertinent headings from the literature review portion of this chapter, then subdivided according to any curricular commonplaces that might apply. In general, the findings substantiate and illustrate the literature review while the critical analysis adds a further dimension. In deciding which findings to include, in addition to the literature review, I let the spirit of the question of the educator from the beginning of this chapter be my guide: What are some of the curricular and structural features of IG programs that can help to create rich learning opportunities for participants?

Benefits of IG Programs

LEARNERS

Intergenerational programs should seek to foster 'equal group status' (Jarrott, 2007) whereby programs and participant relationships are planned for and viewed as reciprocal and meaningful to all generations. Taking this further, a critical reading of IG curricula requires a focus on socio-political issues; this required me to study the positioning of the social categories of the participants in the programs: childhood and old age. In so doing, I identified the ubiquity of human capital theory in ECEC policy and curriculum. This theory emphasizes the 'development of skills as an important factor in production activities' (Olaniyan & Okemakinde, 2008, p. 157) and only (or primarily) because of this is education taken to be important. The significance, then, of education is never in the present and does not belong to children themselves but is rather always delayed to the future and belongs primarily to the economy.

As I describe in detail elsewhere (e.g., Heydon, 2005), human capital theory has been adopted in ECEC policy and curriculum as a response to the rapid social changes of the new millennium. There have been far-reaching technological (Kress, 2010) and economic changes that have caused concern and anxiety on the part of governments and their citizenry. In turn, discourses that set out an 'efficient' (Stein, 2001) plan for ECEC that focuses on raising young children into able workers have become very popular. Even before the global economic crisis of 2008, David and her colleagues (2000) observed that the 'adult manipulation of the childhood experience has come to the fore with a severity not seen since children's direct involvement in industry in the eighteenth century' (p. 21). It is my contention that human capital theory and its ensuing education practices and policies deny children's full personhood and belie the many reasons why engaging in learning can bring significance, meaning, and pleasure to people's lives in the here and now. Relatedly, the social category of old age holds much in common with the social category of childhood. Most notably, the similarities between the categories exist in that members are judged against the 'normate' (Thomson, 1997): 'the constructed identity of those who, by way of the bodily configurations and cultural capital they assume, can step into a position of authority and wield the power it grants them' (p. 8). Here, the normate is the able 'adult' who contributes directly to the economy. In a society that defines itself primarily in post-capitalist economic terms, young children and older adults are not generally considered to be contributing members of the citizenry. Thus, they are seen as in need of control with the dominant means for control being segregation and scientific technology (e.g., Thomson, 1997). One can see this in the way that older adults and young children are generally segregated by age and, for young children, curriculum (e.g., Ontario Ministry of Education, 2006) tends to be scientific and instrumental (e.g., Bobbitt, 1971; Tyler, 1949) in that it constructs knowledge as a product that can be predicted and controlled (Heydon & Wang, 2006).

When IG participants are understood in critical terms, they bring the generations together to engage in learning and interactions that defy instrumental ends can be seen as radical. While the IG benefits literature is often couched in terms that are commensurate with human capital theory (e.g., Jarrott's 2007 speech to the United Nations was at a conference whose title concerned strengthening 'economic' ties), the value of IG programs need not be defined through outcomes. Instead, a critical approach calls for an appraisal of what one recognizes as benefits, why, and on whose terms. This entails an attempt to respect participants' personhood by allowing their perspectives of what is valuable to, at the very least, take priority in the discussion.

In my IG studies, participants expressed explicitly and through their behaviour that being with people of another generation and forming relationships with them was gratifying. This substantiates the literature's identification of the creation of IG relationships as a major feature of IG programs (e.g., Jarrott & Bruno, 2007). I have documented hundreds of interactions between participants that suggest that relationships were established and important in their own right. I saw children asking for older adults and being disappointed when an adult was absent from class, physical displays of affection (hugging and kissing) and smiling between participants, and participants saving seats for each other in class (Heydon, 2009). I also recorded adults saying things such as, 'These children are so inspiring' (Rebecca, age 90); 'Oh yes, I like it when the children come!' (Pete, age 83); '[The children] are getting a good education. They're not afraid of old people or wheelchairs . . . They add life to the building' (Ida, age 77); 'This is my day! I love these children' (Frieda, age 96). More than this, however, I saw long-term relationships established. The case of 'Keith' is an example of this.

At Picasso, where one group spent two years together and had evidently bonded, Keith, an adult participant, had been ill and missed a number of classes. Then, on a cold February day, he returned and took his seat before the children arrived. All that the other adults could talk about was how much the children had missed Keith: 'Lisa asked for you, Robbie asked for you . . .' Keith replied, 'I seem to have adopted another six or seven grandchildren. I'm not sure that I needed them, but I have them!' Keith's joke referred to the previous spring's art show when he proudly introduced his biological grandchildren to his 'adopted' grandchildren hugging each and ensuring everyone shook hands. Shortly after this joke, the children came in the room and lit up to see Keith. Roger (age 5), ran to sit beside him and the buddies caught up with each other (e.g., Keith answered many curious queries about his new oxygen tank). For this class, the participants made 'heart maps,' visual renderings of what was important to them. In discussing

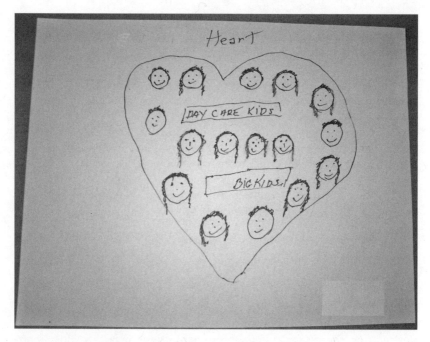

Figure 6.1. Keith's heart map.

with Nona, another adult participant, what he might put in his map, Keith laughed, 'I have four daughters and twelve grandchildren so that pretty much fills (my heart) up. All girls.' Nona widened her eyes and said, 'All girls then, no grandson.' Keith looked down at Roger drawing beside him and answered, 'Just Roger.' When the maps were done, Keith's contained sixteen smiling faces within a heart shape (see Figure 6.1). The faces were explained by the captions 'Day Care Kids' and 'Picasso Big Kids.' Roger smiled at Keith and showed him his map saying, 'I've got you on my map.' 'You like me,' responded the honorary grandfather. As this example shows, IG learning programs are radical educational sites given that they emphasize coming together for learning for reasons other than economic prosperity. Participants construct and maintain positive relationships that can last over time, and by the simple fact that half the participants of such programs are literally at the ends of their lives, the adults teach by example that learning is not about preparation for the future but about what it can add to today (see Figure 6.1).

TEACHERS

Finally, in relation to the benefits of IG programs, it bears noting that participating adults and children are not the only potential beneficiaries: IG programs can be powerful professional development tools for practitioners. As my opening narrative shows, IG learning programs taught me to readdress taken-for-granted ideas about young children and their attention spans, and practitioners at all my research sites told me that mixing the populations they typically worked with helped them see children, older adults, themselves, and their work in new ways. Stunningly, I have documented how one educator reoriented his world view when he began working in an IG context (e.g., Heydon, 2005): It forced him to come to terms with his fears of aging and death and made him determined to help the children in his care avoid similar fears.

Structure of Intergenerational Learning Programs

MILIEU

The literature itemizes the strengths of the shared-site structure. Ideally such programs are not add-ons to existing programs, but rather by their very nature the programs create opportunities for IG learning, interaction, and relationship building. Picasso, as an emerging IG shared-site program, is a prime illustration of the challenges of establishing a shared site. As mentioned, Picasso, an over twenty-year-old elder care facility rented space to Picasso Child, a child care centre. Picasso Child was located in a remote part of the building, and no shared programming had ever taken place until our research team suggested there was potential for development. After negotiating with Picasso Child and Picasso, the team established an IG art program, first acting as the teacher leaders and then gradually handing control to the site's practitioners. Three years after its inception, using the support materials we developed (e.g., a book of project lesson plans, samples of projects to use as models, art supplies, modelling of teaching, workshops), practitioners were organizing and teaching art classes, and the program had begun to lead to other IG opportunities. For instance, noticing the bonds that had developed between participants and wondering what would happen once art classes went on hiatus for the summer, practitioners arranged for children to visit the adults in their rooms. Adults were then observed dropping by the children's play area, and formal gatherings were held around holidays.

Despite these gains, three years after the program had begun, the door leading into Picasso Child from Picasso still had a prominent sign posted on it saying 'Private' and staff, faculty, and administration still saw the IG component as an add-on; for example, Picasso administration counted the purchasing of art supplies for the IG art class as extraneous to the core budget for craft supplies for adults-only classes. Picasso Child administration counted preparation time for IG art class as outside the educator's regular preparation time (thus, they saw it as an additional expense), and despite two years of successful art shows, under their control, practitioners chose not to hold another one (citing the work involved as the rationale). These examples demonstrate how IG activities were perceived as outside of the normal course of practice and had not become integrated, regularized parts of practice or policy. This case evidently lies on a different part of the IG spectrum from Blessed Mother's program. The Picasso example speaks to the need for time, leadership, and a critical questioning of the social positioning of elder and child care and the people who work within them. In the following I rationalize this last statement.

LEARNERS

The studies add to the literature related to the need for IG programs to be structured so that participants can make decisions especially about whether or not to participate. More broadly, however, the studies teach that generational diversity brings with it a diversity of needs and respecting participants' personhoods demands a flexible, responsive program structure. For instance, some older adults at Blessed Mother expressed that they needed to know they could leave art class with no notice to tend to toileting, etc. To maintain dignity, they did not want to have to explain or be excused. As well, children in class remained engaged with a particular project for differing amounts of time. Although I never observed a child want to leave an art class before the one-hour mark (the typical length of a class), I found occasions where children did not feel finished by the end of class and wanted to stay to complete their own project or assist an adult with theirs. Art class was able to accommodate most of these needs: Susan, the art teacher, stayed with the children and adults who wanted to remain in class, children returned with an educator or volunteer to the GTLC, and volunteers helped any adult who wanted to leave early. Further, the art classes that were held in the neighbourhoods where the elders lived also addressed the adults' needs, most notably related to mobility.

Blessed Mother's flexibility was largely dependent on volunteers as there was not enough staff to provide the demanded level of support. For example, Doris, a regular art class adult participant who had mobility issues, was absent from class one day, and I found her crying in her neighbourhood. She told me she was crying because she could not find anyone to take her to class. Usually volunteers helped in situations like this but on this day Doris had missed the volunteer, and although there were support staff (e.g., nursing assistants) that might be recruited for the task, my interviews indicated such staff generally prioritized more standard caregiving tasks (e.g., changing a soiled bed) above tasks such as helping someone to a class. The data suggest that the institutional definition of the roles and tasks of workers needed to be addressed before programs could have optimum flexibility. Picasso and Watersberg, however, had nowhere near the level of flexibility as Blessed Mother. The child-to-educator ratio in U.S. and Canadian sites was strict but in the Canadian sites there was no flexible staff, few volunteers, and Blessed Mother employed Susan as an IG educator, whereas there was no IG staff in the Canadian sites. This prevented many participants from making decisions around participation.

TEACHERS

The literature suggests the need for cross-training of faculty and staff (Jarrott, 2007). In my studies, educators and recreation therapists in all sites complained about the lack of IG professional development opportunities. In fact, one educator who recognized her limitations in IG programming, stated that she had no one to learn from and was the main presenter at a national ECEC conference under the IG theme. I also witnessed an administrator at a Canadian site who had worked for years in the IG area try unsuccessfully to get an IG curriculum component adopted in a college-level ECEC program. Importantly, I witnessed a high attrition rate for all practitioners. With the exception of the GTLC educators, practitioners in all sites mentioned low pay, difficulty of obtaining full-time employment, lack of benefits, undesirable hours, and the desire to upgrade; these reasons why people left their jobs are all commensurate with the literature as it pertains to ECEC workers (e.g., Doherty, Friendly, & Beach, 2003). Therefore, on-the-job IG professional development was difficult. This returns the focus to the earlier discussion of the social positioning of IG participants and raises questions about the valuing of people who work with young and old. Evidently, these issues, which are structural, affect learning and relationship-building opportunities.

Creating Optimal Opportunities for Learning

Despite the challenges, intergenerational programs undoubtedly can provide excellent learning opportunities, lead to meaningful relationships, and enhance people's lives. Some of the lessons that have been captured in the studies and that could be of use to people like the music educator who attended my talk are as follows. First, as mentioned, IG relationships figure prominently in the literature and the studies' data. Relationships that are built within a community of learners are important in their own right, and they can also help to create learning opportunities, particularly pertaining to the development of receptive and expressive communication (Heydon, 2007). The studies have documented a number of ways that curriculum and programs as a whole can establish a sense of community in which relationships can grow. Of note is the practice of rituals for beginning and ending program sessions and for modelling communication. The art classes at Blessed Mother, for instance, always began with a sharing of names with Susan modelling in a big, clear voice to ensure everyone could hear and make sense of names that might be unfamiliar to them. At Picasso, a slightly more ad hoc strategy was used where artefacts related to that day's project were set out (e.g., travel brochures for a collage project), and with the support of an educator, participants explored and discussed them. For instance, in one class, participants eagerly looked through brochures with project manager Wendy Crocker asking, 'Are you curious about what all of these pictures might be for?' 'Yes!' exclaimed the children while many of the adults giggled and smiled. 'Well,' began Wendy, 'last week we travelled inside ourselves to think about maps of our heart. This week we're going to be travelling in our imagination anywhere you would like to go [in the world]. So I would like you, right now, to turn and look at the big [and little] partner you'll be working with today. Who is it?' This kind of questioning prompted responses like 'I'm with Gertrude!' and when participants could not recall each other's names Wendy prompted them: 'Crystal [age 5], who are you going to be with today?' Crystal pointed to Monica. 'What's her name?' asked Wendy giving a hint: 'Starts with an /m/.' 'Monica!' interjected Roger. 'Perfect!' Wendy said turning to the duo and helping to add a connection, 'You're going to make a good pair because you both like to draw and are very imaginative.' Closings occurred always with a standard song at Watersberg. At Picasso and Blessed Mother, closings involved the sharing of artwork and the end of a season of art classes closed with a public art show.

Seating plans facilitated interaction with the goal of building relationships. Blessed Mother favoured an adult/child, child/adult plan around a large table so children could easily interact with adults but not feel segregated. Programs in neighbourhoods often attracted a number of adults who simply liked to watch the IG class: they had the option of positioning themselves behind the main table to do this. Picasso and Watersberg experimented with a variety of seating arrangements aimed at accommodating the specific projects and participants. For instance, Gregory was 3 years old when he began art class at Picasso. He cried and said he did not want to sit with anyone. Gregory was interested, however, in making art. Thus, we sat him on his own but where he could see people and gradually he moved closer and closer to the other participants. Eventually, Gregory became one of the most enthusiastic participants in class. Regardless of the specific seating arrangement what was always of importance was to provide for the comfort and safety of participants (e.g., ensure children could reach the table top, adults had arms on their chairs to prevent falling) and to arrange people so that they could easily interact and assist each other with their projects.

SUBJECT MATTER

Finally, and importantly, the literature indicates the need for a curricular component in the programs (Friedman, 1997), which is likely a recommendation for the inclusion of subject matter learning opportunities. The studies found art to offer numerous and high-quality learning and interactional opportunities and to be very well suited to the IG situation. Besides having the chance to learn about art and artists, participants, as mentioned, gained chances to broaden and improve their communication: They were invited to consider the content of their communication, to learn and practice expressing themselves in a variety of ways, and to view or read other's ideas in visual form. Thus, art provided a vehicle for participants to get to know each other. Also, because class insisted on production and on participants assisting each other with idea formation and technical tasks (e.g., cutting), participants explored their own and each other's strengths and worked for a common purpose. The projects were also inherently differentiated as people with differing levels of skill and knowledge could participate and be challenged by the technical and subject matter aspects of the creation of art. Last, the public display of products in the building and in art shows gave purpose and audience to participants' work and solidified relationships by providing opportunities for family and friends to bear witness to the participants' bonds (e.g., Keith introducing his biological family to his 'adopted' family).

Conclusion

It has been a privilege to witness intergenerational learning programs in action. Bringing young and old together for friendship and learning has forced me to stop and savour the beauty that is, in the words of one IG educator, 'the circle of life.' IG programs have much to teach about curricular commonplaces in and out of IG settings. Thus, to the music educator who asked for the magic ingredients of the IG art class this chapter says: While there are certain issues that must be addressed at a societal level (e.g., the valuing of childhood, old age, and those who educate and care for them) within the specific teaching and learning context the following may help to create learning opportunities: respecting people's personhood (e.g., considering what meaning learning holds for the individual and group); establishing a community where people find pleasure and support in each other's company and can develop meaningful relationships; ensuring participants' safety and comfort and remembering the significance of ritual and routine; providing a purpose for learning tasks and venues for sharing products; allowing for participant decision making; and focusing on learning that is challenging and meaningful to everyone through differentiated projects.

Acknowledgments

I would like to acknowledge the support of the Social Sciences and Humanities Research Council (Standard Research Grant, Rachel Heydon, principal investigator; Major Collaborative Research Initiative Grant, Annabel Cohen, principal investigator, Rachel Heydon, co-investigator); the University of Western Ontario Academic Development Fund; and the Petro Canada Young Innovators Award. I would like to thank IG art teacher Bridget Daly, and all of the research assistants on the various projects, especially Wendy Crocker and Zheng Zhang. Finally, I would like to express my gratitude to the research participants.

References

Aday, R.H., McDuffie, W., & Sims, C.R. (1993). Impact of intergenerational program on black adolescents' attitudes toward the elderly. *Educational Gerontology, 19*, 663–673.

Apple, M. (1971). The hidden curriculum and the nature of conflict. *Interchange, 2*(4), 27–40.

Bobbitt, J.F. (1971). *The curriculum.* New York: Arno Press.

Brummel, S.W. (1989). Developing an intergenerational program. *Journal of Children in Contemporary Society, 20*(3–4), 119–133.

Cox, R., Croxford, A., & Edmonds, D. (2006). *Connecting generations tool kit: Best practices in intergenerational programming.* Toronto: United Generations Ontario.

David, T., Raban, B., Ure, C., Goouch, K., Jago, M., & Barriere, I. (2000). *Making sense of early literacy: A practitioner's perspective.* Stoke on Trent: Trentham.

Dillon, J.T. (2009). The questions of curriculum. *Journal of Curriculum Studies, 41*(3), 343–359.

Doherty, G., Friendly, M., & Beach, J. (2003). *OECD thematic review of early childhood education and care: Canadian background report.* Ottawa: Her Majesty the Queen in Right of Canada.

Donmoyer, R. (2001). Paradigm talk reconsidered. In V. Richardson (Ed.), *Handbook of Research on Teaching* (pp. 174–197). Washington, DC: American Educational Research Association.

Egan, K. (1978). What is curriculum? *Curriculum Inquiry, 8*(1), 65–72.

Eisner, E.W. (2002). *The educational imagination: On the design and evaluation of school programs.* Upper Saddle River, NJ: Prentice-Hall.

Eisner, E.W. (2005). *Reimagining schools: The selected works of Elliot Eisner.* London: Routledge Falmer.

Elders Share the Arts. (n.d.). *Intergenerational Arts.* Retrieved from http://www.elderssharethearts.org/.

Friedman, B. (1997). The integration of pro-active aging education into exciting educational curricula. In K. Brabazon & R. Disch (Eds.), *Intergenerational approaches in aging: Implications for education, policy and practice* (pp. 103–110). Binghamton, NY: Haworth.

Generations United. (n.d.). About us. Retrieved from http://www.gu.org/about.asp.

Griff, M.D., Lambert, D., Fruit, D., & Dellman-Jenkins, M. (1996). *Link-Ages: Planning an intergenerational program for preschool.* Menlo Park, CA: Addison-Wesley.

Habermas, J. (1972). *Knowledge and human interests* (J.J. Shapiro, Trans.). Boston, MA: Beacon Press.

Handsfield, L. (2006). Being and becoming American: Triangulating habitus, field, and literacy instruction in a multilingual classroom. *Language & Literacy, 8*(2). Retrieved from http://www.langandlit.ualberta.ca/current.html.

Harste, J. (2003). What do we mean by literacy now? *Voices from the Middle, 10*(3), 8–12.

Hayes, C.L. (2003). An observational study in developing an intergenerational shared site program: Challenges and insights. *Journal of Intergenerational Relationships, 1*(1), 113–131.

Heydon, R. (2005). The de-pathologization of childhood, disability and aging in an intergenerational art class: Implications for educators. *Journal of Early Childhood Research, 3,* 243–268.

Heydon, R. (2007). Making meaning together: Multimodal literacy learning opportunities in an intergenerational art program. *Journal of Curriculum Studies, 39*(1), 35–62.

Heydon, R. (2008). Communicating with a little help from friends: Intergenerational art class as radical, asset-oriented curriculum. In R. Heydon & L. Iannacci, *Early childhood curricula and the de-pathologizing of childhood* (pp. 100–129). Toronto: University of Toronto Press.

Heydon, R. (2009). We are here for just a brief time: Death, dying, and constructions of children in intergenerational learning programs. In L. Iannacci & P. Whitty (Eds.), *Early childhood curricula: Reconceptualist perspectives* (pp. 217–241). Toronto: Detselig.

Heydon, R., & Daly, B. (2008). What should I draw? I'll draw you! Facilitating interaction and learning opportunities in intergenerational programs. *Young Children, 63*(3), 80–85.

Heydon, R. & Iannacci, L. (2008). *Early childhood curricula and the de-pathologizing of childhood.* Toronto: University of Toronto Press.

Heydon, R., & Wang, P. (2006). Curricular ethics in early childhood education programming: A challenge to the Ontario kindergarten program. *McGill Journal of Education, 41*(1), 29–46.

Intergenerational Programming – Rationale – why Now? (n.d.). In *Marriage and Family Encyclopedia.* Retrieved from http://family.jrank.org/pages/902/Intergenerational-Programming-Rationale-Why-Now.html.

Jarrott, S.E. (2007). Programs that affect intergenerational solidarity. *Proceedings of the United Nations Expert Group Meeting 'Intergenerational Solidarity:*

Strengthening Economic and Social Ties.' Retrieved from http://www.un.org/esa/socdev/uNew Yorkin/documents/egm_unhq_oct_07_jarrott.pdf.

Jarrott, S.E., & Bruno, K. (2007). Shared site intergenerational programs: A case study. *Journal of Applied Gerontology, 26*(3), 239–257.

Jewitt, C., & Kress, G. (2003). *Multimodal literacy.* New York: Peter Lang.

Kaplan, M., Duerr, L., Whitesell, W., Merchant, L., Davis, D. & Larkin, E. (2003). *Developing an intergenerational program in your early childhood care and education center: A guidebook for early childhood practitioners.* University Park, PA: Pennsylvania State University Press.

Kress, G. (2010). *Multimodality: A social semiotic approach to contemporary communication.* London: Routledge.

Kress, G., & Jewitt, C. (2003). Introduction. In C. Jewitt & G. Kress (Eds.), *Multimodal literacy* (pp. 1–18). New York: Peter Lang.

Kuehne, V.S., & Collins, C.L. (1997). Observational research in intergenerational programming: Need and opportunity. In K. Brabazon & R. Disch (Eds.), *Intergenerational approaches in aging: Implications for education, policy and practice* (pp. 183–193). New York: Haworth.

Kuehne, V.S., & Kaplan, M.S. (2001). *Evaluation and research on intergenerational shared site facilities and programs: What we know and what we need to learn.* Washington, DC: Generations United.

Larkin, E., & Newman, S. (1997). Intergenerational studies: A multidisciplinary field. In K. Brabazon & R. Disch (Eds.), *Intergenerational approaches in aging: Implications for education, policy and practice* (pp. 5–16). Binghamton, NY: Haworth.

Lewison, M., Flint, A.S., & Van Sluys, K. (2002). Taking on critical literacy: The journey of newcomers and novices. *Language Arts, 79*(5), 382–392.

Olaniyan, D.A., & Okemakinde, T. (2008). Human capital theory: Implications for educational development. *European Journal of Scientific Research, 24*(2), 157–162.

Ontario Ministry of Education. (2006). *Kindergarten program* (revised). Toronto: Author.

Routman, R. (2000). *Conversations: Strategies for teaching, learning and evaluating.* Portsmouth, NH: Heinemann.

Schwab, J.J. (1973). The practical 3: Translation into curriculum. *School Review, 81*, 501–522.

Schwalbach, E., & Kiernan, S. (2002). Effects of an intergenerational friendly visit program on the attitudes of fourth graders toward elders. *Educational Gerontology, 28*, 175–187.

Stein, J.G. (2001). *The cult of efficiency.* Toronto: Anansi.

Thomson, G.R. (1997). *Extraordinary bodies: Figuring physical disability in American culture and literature.* New York: Columbia University Press.

Tyler, R.W. (1949). *Basic principles of curriculum and instruction.* Chicago, IL: University of Chicago Press.

VanderVen, K. (1999). Intergenerational theory: The missing element in today's intergenerational programs. In V.S. Kuehne (Ed.), *Intergenerational programs: Understanding what we have created* (pp. 33–47). Binghamton, NY: Haworth.

Ward, C.R., Kamp, L.L., & Newman, S. (1996). The effects of participation in an intergenerational program on the behavior of residents with dementia. *Activities, Adaptation and Aging, 20*(4), 61–75.

7 Innovations in Provincial Early Learning Curriculum Frameworks

RACHEL LANGFORD

Since 1997, an unprecedented number of provinces have addressed the absence of early learning pedagogical guidelines and developed new curriculum frameworks. This development set innovative directions in what is now expected in early childhood programs.[1] Quebec's Ministry of Family and Children was the first, in 1997, to develop *Meeting Early Childhood Needs: Quebec's Educational Program for Childcare Service*,[2] which drew upon and adapted the American High/Scope curriculum approach. The *Educational Program* was revised in 2007 to help child care personnel and home child care providers 'update their role in a context that has undergone several changes in recent years' (Government of Quebec, 2007, p. 5). In December 2006, Ontario's Ministry of Children and Youth Services completed *Early Learning for Every Child Today*, a curriculum and pedagogical framework for children from birth to age 8 years.[3] In 2008, three frameworks were released. New Brunswick's Department of Social Development produced an English *Early Learning and Child Care Curriculum* and a *Curriculum éducatif*, which stressed the importance of cultural belonging and integration that was designed for francophones by francophones (Government

---

1 At the time of writing, the Government of Manitoba, Ministry of Family Services and Consumer Affairs early learning curriculum framework was in development.

2 An English translation is used for this chapter. The educational guide is based on the program, *Jouer, c'est magique!* (Playtime is magical!), which is a Quebec version of the American High/Scope Educational Approach initially used as an intervention framework for disadvantaged children (Tougas, 2002).

3 In Ontario, *The Full-Day Early Learning Kindergarten Program* (Draft Version) is a specific curriculum with learning outcomes for full-day early learning programs for 4- and 5-year-old children.

of New Brunswick, 2008a, 2008b).[4] In Saskatchewan, the Ministry of Education launched *Play and Exploration: Early Learning Program Guide* (Government of Saskatchewan, 2008a) for the early learning and child care sector at a professional association conference. British Columbia's Ministry of Education, in partnership with the Ministry of Health and the Ministry of Children and Family Development, released an *Early Learning Framework,* 'intended to guide and support early childhood educators, StrongStart facilitators, early years' professionals, service providers, communities and governments' as well as inform families, kindergarten, primary school teachers/educators, and administrators (Government of British Columbia, 2008, p. 2).

This chapter describes and analyses the development, purposes, and content of these provincial curriculum frameworks as well as highlights the tools for practice they offer. Attention is given to particular theoretical perspectives articulated in the frameworks and to examining how the frameworks address the critical issue of diversity within provincial contexts (Pacini-Ketchabaw & Pence, 2006). An account of the implementation and evaluation of the curriculum frameworks in early childhood settings within each province is provided as well as a discussion on the requirements for sustaining the use of the frameworks by early childhood educators (ECEs; Bennett, 2004).

Framework Development

It is not easy to discern the reasons why a significant number of provinces have recently produced early learning curriculum frameworks, the majority which focus on services for young children, birth to age 4 years. What has made it possible to produce frameworks that function either as a policy or as a regulation in these particular provinces at this point in time? In general, it appears that development of the frameworks has not been clearly coordinated with other major policy changes to a province's delivery of early childhood education and care (ECEC). An exception is Quebec, where their ninety-four-page educational program guide for child care centres was revised ten years later as part of its publicly funded, coherent, and regulated ECEC system.[5]

---

4 Personal Communication, Diane Lutes, Program Consultant, Early Childhood and School-Based Services, Program Development and Monitoring, Social Development, Government of New Brunswick.
5 Personal Communication, Kathleen Flanagan, Montague, Prince Edward Island.

Certainly, Canadian provinces had a benchmark: by 2004, most member countries in the Organization of Economic Co-operation and Development (OECD) had developed either pedagogical frameworks or curricula for children aged 3 to 6 years at a national level or, in the case of Australia, at a federated state level (Bennett, 2004; Dickinson, 2006). Provinces had, as Bertrand (2007) noted, 'a substantial and growing research base [which] points to the importance of a clear purpose, goals and approaches in establishing the what (curriculum) and how (pedagogy or educational strategies) in early learning and child care programs for preschool children' (p. 3). The OECD, in its evaluation of early childhood programming in Canada, recommended a national quality framework for early childhood services across all sectors, which would include:[6] 'A statement of the values and goals that should guide early childhood centres . . . to facilitate development and learning, an outline of the knowledge, skills, dispositions, and values that children at different ages can be expected to master across broad developmental areas; and . . . pedagogical guidelines outlining the processes through which children achieve these goals, and how educators should support them' (OECD, 2004, p. 11).

In 2004, Canada's Liberal minority federal government sought provincial agreement on a national Foundations Program to build a universal and regulated early learning and child care (ELCC) system with a quality framework (Friendly & Prentice, 2009). By 2005, all the provinces had agreed to move forward, and in New Brunswick, Saskatchewan, and Ontario, provincial framework development had begun, tied to federal funding targeted for early childhood services. However, in January 2006, the new Conservative federal government ended the Foundations Program, and dashed advocates' hopes for a quality framework at a national level (Friendly & Prentice, 2009). But New Brunswick, Saskatchewan, and Ontario chose to continue with their framework development despite a reduction in federal funding. In Saskatchewan, for example, the development of a common early learning program guide was a major feature of the province's ELCC five-year plan developed in response to the federal 2005 ELCC Initiative. The plan was not released publicly when the federal government changed

---

6 New Brunswick did not participate in the OECD evaluation in Canada.

in 2006 and anticipated funding was discontinued. However, the program guide was one of a number of policy initiatives the province of Saskatchewan continued to work towards. One component of the 2004 Ontario Best Start strategy – a plan funded in part with federal dollars and designed to establish a coherent system for young children – was a Ministry of Children and Youth Services (MCYS) Best Start Expert Panel on Early Learning. Ontario's 110-page curriculum framework emerged out of the panel's work but the ministry did not publicly announce it as a new early childhood policy direction or mandate its use. However, the curriculum framework later became a central feature of the 2009 premier's policy report on implementing early learning in Ontario.

In British Columbia, curriculum framework development emerged out of changes to the mandate of a ministry. In 2005, the Ministry of Education's mandate was expanded to include early learning (i.e., children younger than kindergarten age). One of the first policy actions the ministry undertook in collaboration with the Ministry of Children and Family Development (MCFD), which was responsible for child care programs, was to articulate a common understanding and vision for early learning in a curriculum framework.

What is quite clear is that the work of committed individuals drove the development of frameworks. At the request of the B.C. Ministry of Education, an Early Learning Advisory Group was established, and, as in Ontario and Saskatchewan, the involvement of both the ECEC and formal education sectors was intended to foster the integration of the traditional divide between care and education. The Government of New Brunswick's Department of Social Development contracted a twenty-five-member early childhood research and development team led by Pam Whitty and Pam Nason at the Early Childhood Centre, University of New Brunswick, to carry out the development of the province's early learning framework. Empirical research on various aspects of ELCC curriculum informed the development of the framework and further changes were made to the 220-page framework based on feedback from expert readers. In Saskatchewan, Caroline Krentz was the primary author of the province's seventy-five-page program guide with contributions from early childhood educators (ECEs), content experts, and field reviewers (Government of Saskatchewan, 2008b).[7]

---

7 Caroline Krentz is a professor emerita, University of Regina.

A Curriculum Framework Rather
than a Prescribed Curriculum

The meaning assigned to the terms *curriculum* and *curriculum framework* clarifies, as the New South Wales (NSW) Early Learning Framework states, how 'a curriculum framework is not the same thing as a curriculum' (Office of Childcare, 2004, p. 20). According to Friendly, Doherty, and Beach (2006), curriculum is how programs are organized to support goals and philosophy. Drawing on the New Zealand *Te Whā riki* framework, the Saskatchewan document defines curriculum as 'the whole array of experiences, planned and unplanned, that takes place in a young child's learning environment' (Government of Saskatchewan, 2008b, p. 66). The NSW Early Learning Framework document goes on to describe a framework: 'A possible metaphor for a framework is that it is a sieve through which the professional "sifts" thinking as a means of reflecting critically on practice' or in other words, on the practice of curriculum (Office of Childcare, 2004, p. 20). The 'thinking' that the NSW framework refers to is the vision, beliefs, values, and principles related to early learning and pedagogy.

The OECD recommends that a curriculum framework should be flexible so that well-trained early childhood educators can adapt it to the level of the individual program while still being consistent with the broad vision, beliefs, values and principles (Bennett, 2004). Ontario's document articulates this flexibility: '*Early Learning for Every Child Today* complements, rather than replaces, specific curricular and pedagogical approaches, early identification protocols, and regulated requirements now in place in Ontario early childhood settings' (Government of Ontario, 2006a, p. 4). At the same time, the framework 'provides direction for programs that do not have an explicit curriculum or consistent pedagogical approach' (p. 4). Whitty, one of the lead authors in the development of the New Brunswick framework, indicated that a framework can serve to encourage ECEs 'to shift from prescribed, preprogrammed curriculum to co-constructed curriculum' based on negotiated beliefs, values and principles related to early learning (2009, p. 50).

As thinking tools, the provincial curriculum frameworks are not theoretically neutral documents. Rather, each one adopts an implicit or explicit theoretical orientation. Australia's recent national early years learning framework, *Belonging, Being and Becoming* identifies the range and combination of possible theoretical orientations that shape explanations of adults' identities as educators and children's identities as learners in the provincial frameworks:

- Developmental theories that focus on describing and understanding the processes of change in children's learning and development over time
- Socio-cultural theories that emphasize the central role that families and cultural groups play in children's learning and the importance of respectful relationships to provide insight into social and cultural contexts of learning and development
- Socio-behaviourist theories that focus on the role of experiences in shaping children's behaviour
- Critical theories that invite early childhood educators to challenge assumptions about curriculum and consider how their decisions may affect children differently
- Post-structural theories that offer insights into issues of power, equity, and social justice in early childhood settings. (Commonwealth of Australia, 2009, p. 11)

In Ontario, the panel undertaking the development of a framework favoured 'approaches that espoused developmental approaches' while recognizing the 'specific needs of diverse groups including newcomers, refugees, special needs, additional language and Indigenous populations' (Government of Ontario, 2006a, p. 5). The theoretical foundations of Quebec's educational program are explicitly stated as an 'ecological approach' and as 'attachment theory' (Government of Quebec, 2007). The British Columbia, Saskatchewan, and New Brunswick development teams were influenced by New Zealand's early childhood curriculum, *Te Whāriki*, which takes a socio-cultural approach, and by Reggio Emilia's critical and post-structural image of the powerful, competent child. Saskatchewan's *Early Learning Program Guide* clearly states that it 'offers a new perspective on how educators are evolving in their view of children' (2008, p. 13).

In addition, interprovincial influences were apparent; for example, British Columbia recognized New Brunswick and Saskatchewan as contributors to their framework development. The Ontario and New Brunswick frameworks offer descriptions of the distinctions made by Bennett (2004) between pre-primary (focus on prescriptive and detailed goals and outcomes) and social pedagogical (focus on broad developmental goals that can be locally interpreted) approaches to early learning. Both frameworks are clearly aligned with the latter approach. This supports Dickinson's comment in an appendix to Ontario's document that 'while Canada demonstrates aspects of the pre-primary tradition, this was balanced by relative freedom from province to province with regard to curriculum' (2006, p. 81). In discussing the design of a post-foundational (a term often used interchangeably with post-structural) curriculum document, Whitty described how the development team worked against the dominance of 'developmentism' to create a document 'that emphasizes a social-cultural approach to children's learning and care; one that recognizes children's and educator's interests, passions and strengths' (2009, p. 36).

Framework Content

The key purpose of a curriculum framework is, of course, for early childhood educators to use it on a daily basis. The frameworks (as well as their supporting documents[8]) offer content that can be used in two key ways: (1) to stimulate discussion and dialogue among ECEs, family members, and allied professionals about their values, theories, and beliefs concerning early learning, and (2) to offer ECEs the pedagogical tools for providing rich early learning experiences for young children, which reflect the framework's vision and principles.

Discussions on Values, Theories, and Beliefs

While most sections in the frameworks lend themselves to discussion, some are explicitly designed to provoke debate. All frameworks offer a clear statement of values or principles that are open to 'negotiation, critique and change' (Government of New Brunswick, 2008a, p. 6). Despite the different ways values or principles are expressed and/or weighted within a particular theoretical orientation, the frameworks taken together share common values and principles. For example, all

---

8 British Columbia: *Understanding the British Columbia early learning framework: From theory to practice* (2009); Saskatchewan: *Assessment and evaluation in Pre-K: A planning guide for school divisions and their partners, leading for change, creating early learning environments* (2008b); New Brunswick: *Well-being professional support document* (2008b).

frameworks focus on children as 'competent learners' (Government of Saskatchewan, 2008b, p. 5) and 'primary agents of their development' (Government of Quebec, 2007, p. 18). However, the British Columbia, Saskatchewan, and New Brunswick documents highlight the importance of an early childhood educator examining his or her image of the child as well as children's rights as 'citizens to reach their fullest potential' (Government of British Columbia, 2008, p. 7).

All frameworks also focus on the following: relationships with families 'who have the most important role in promoting their children's well-being, learning and development in the context of supportive communities' (Government of British Columbia, 2008, p. 15); 'respect for diversity, equity and inclusion' (Government of Ontario, 2006a, p. 6); and 'open and flexible environments where playful exploration, problem-solving and creativity are encouraged and purposefully planned' (Government of New Brunswick, 2008a, p. 15). Interestingly, one Ontario framework principle stands out as different – 'Knowledgeable, responsive early childhood professionals are essential' (Government of Ontario, 2006a, p. 6) – certainly, a principle unlikely to be disputed by others.

In their value statements, all the frameworks reaffirm the importance of play as central to childhood and early learning and as a source of great 'pleasure' for children (Government of Quebec, 2007, p. 20). The Ontario framework (2008, p. 15) draws upon the Ontario Elementary Teachers Federation's document on kindergarten to describe how 'early childhood settings that value children's play create a "climate of delight" that honours childhood.' The Saskatchewan document (2008, p. 20) urges ECEs to reclaim their passion and delight in valuing children's play. The New Brunswick document (2008, p. 36) describes 'dizzy play,' which is loud and boisterous (e.g., rough and tumble play), and asks early childhood educators 'to recognize and accept this kind of play valuing it for what it provides for the children; a release of physical energy, a sense of power, and often an expression of pure joy.'

Tools for Practice

Four tools for practice are evident in the frameworks: (1) learning goals, (2) reflection questions, (3) educator–child interactions, and (4) assessment and documentation of learning. This content in the frameworks relates to two of the three broad sets of quality criteria for early childhood settings (Bennett, 2004): specifically (1) orientation quality, which refers to the values and understanding of the educators, and (2) interaction or procedural quality, which refers to the quality of relationships and the socio-pedagogical interactions between educators and children. Accompanying some curriculum frameworks are supporting documents that provide more detailed explanations of the tools. For example, the document *Understanding the British Columbia Early Learning Framework: From Theory to Practice* describes the steps in pedagogical narration using a particular 'ordinary moment,' namely, an example of water and sand play.[9]

Learning Goals

As Whitty (2009, p. 42) indicates, each development team made conscious and deliberate choices to describe their framework's early learning goals in a particular way and to outline how these goals were linked to the provision of enriched learning experiences that support young children's optimal well-being. Bennett (2004) identified two broad types or choices of curricular emphasis: broad developmental goals and focused cognitive goals. The Ontario framework also notes how framework developers might consider their choices: 'the idea of including broad developmental domains and pathways to organize a curriculum framework has been questioned by some recent initiatives (e.g., New Zealand's innovative *Te Whāriki* approach)' (Government of Ontario, 2006a, p. 21; 2006b). Each provincial framework then responded to this 'questioning' in their particular articulation of learning goals.

The New Brunswick and British Columbia frameworks can be characterized as using 'broad developmental goals.' The New Brunswick framework has four goals – well-being, play and playfulness, communication and multiple literacies, diversity, and social responsibility – which Whitty states, 'moved away from foregrounding developmental outcomes and deficit-based assessment to much broader-based learning goals and narrative assessment' (2009, p. 43). Aspects or facets of each goal are identified (e.g., one facet of well-being is physical health in which children explore body and movement). Sample narratives of children's learning drawn from early childhood sites in which the

---

9 *Pedagogical narration* is the process of observing, recording, and individually and collectively interpreting a series of related ordinary moments in practice. Similar tools are pedagogical documentation and learning stories.

New Brunswick framework was piloted illustrate each facet of a goal. Similarly, the British Columbia framework employs four broad areas of early learning based on its vision and principles: well-being and belonging; exploration and creativity; languages and multiple literacies; and social responsibility and diversity. Key goals are identified in each area of learning; for example, to promote a sense of well-being and belonging; adults provide a learning environment where young children can feel safe and respected; understand and follow routines; and adapt to and enjoy the experiences of change, surprise, and uncertainty. The Quebec, Saskatchewan, and Ontario frameworks draw on developmental theories to identify developmental domains and patterns of development, although certainly, their choice of learning goals cannot be characterized as cognitively focused. The Saskatchewan *Play and Exploration* document briefly discusses areas of young children's holistic development – social-emotional, physical, intellectual, spiritual, and language and literacy – noting that the guide 'assumes that early childhood educators have an understanding of the developmental changes that typically occur in children during the preschool years' (p. 28). The framework further states that knowledge of this holistic development guides ECEs in providing 'interesting and meaningful opportunities that support children in developing skills' (p. 28). A central component of the Ontario framework is a Continuum of Development that reflects a particular understanding about human development based on brain research and the science of early development (McCain & Mustard, 1999) rather than age-related expectations. The Continuum, which consists of domains, skills, and indicators of skills, is designed to assist early childhood educators in their observations and documentation of children's emerging abilities so as to inform curriculum planning and implementation. The Quebec education guide offers the most content on child development and outlines for information purposes (in an appendix) the acquisitions made by children in each area of their development, according to their age.

Reflection Questions

A second tool for practice offered by four of the frameworks, Quebec, New Brunswick, Saskatchewan, and British Columbia, is a series of questions that require early childhood educators to reflect individually or collaboratively on their understanding of the learning goals or developmental skills. Some frameworks make a distinction between questions to consider for infants, toddlers, and pre-school-aged children, whereas others focus on pre-schoolers exclusively. For example, in the British Columbia framework, questions such as the following are posed to readers about pre-school language, communication, and creative expression: 'How are children encouraged to use a wide variety of materials and expressive mediums to represent and communicate their ideas (e.g. languages, music, drama, dance, art)?'(p. 30). In the Saskatchewan document, educators are asked to engage in reflection, decision making, and evaluation through the following questions: 'How do children in my program have the opportunity to experience social, emotional, physical, intellectual and spiritual development? What might I add to support holistic learning in my program? How will I know if my program demonstrates holistic learning?' (p. 34).

Educator–Child Interactions

All curriculum frameworks highlight the importance of the educator's role in building strong, responsive, and respectful relationships in which purposeful interactions with young children support optimal learning. Central to the Quebec document are the 'solid attachment relationships that are formed between each child and adult in a child care setting' (2007, p. 15). This emphasis supports Bennett's (2004) observation that early childhood educators are being 're-positioned' so that it is no longer sufficient for ECEs 'to provide a secure and stimulating environment for young children who would then ensure their *own* development' (p. 16). Rather, Bennett states that it is understood that 'human development and learning is an exercise in co-construction, in which children, parents and educators have all a role to play' (p. 16). This shift in thinking about the roles of early childhood educators is nicely summarized in the British Columbia framework: 'Adult's responses to children's activities – whether they respond, and the creativity of their responses – affect young children's early learning capacities and their growing sense of themselves as members of their communities. Adults who are skilled at supporting early learning and development are careful observers of children and encourage them to go beyond their current level of understanding or skill' (2008, p. 10).

The New Brunswick framework offers 'a supportive structure for educators as they co-construct curriculum with children, families and communities at the local level' (2008, p. 3), which is in the form of suggested provisions and practices (illustrated with photographs) related to aspects of the learning goals. These provisions and practices begin with educator behaviours such as 'document,' 'model,' 'listen,' 'respect,' 'join in,' 'invite,' and 'ask questions.' The Saskatchewan document (2008) provides a separate section on the changing and evolving role of the educator linked to a new understanding of the child as a competent learner. This educator is an observer, documenter, listener, researcher, creator of stimulating environments, co-constructor of knowledge, negotiator, supporter of children's participation in decision making, facilitator of small group learning, supporter of social relationships, partner with parents, and supporter of diversity. Throughout the Saskatchewan document, highlighted sections entitled 'Quality in Action' identify what educators can do within their expanded roles to support and encourage optimal development. To expand educator practices, the Ontario framework (2006) provides descriptions of 'interactions,' which are examples of 'adult-child communications, contacts and joint activity that support the child's accomplishment of what he/she knows or does to show that a skill is emerging, being practiced or being elaborated' (p. 23).

Assessment and Documentation of Learning

All frameworks (and in some cases, their supporting documents) provide educators with the tools 'to assess and document children's early learning in effective, innovative ways' (Government of British Columbia, 2009, p. 2). According to Bennett (2005, p. 3), 'approaches to curriculum strongly influence modes of assessment' described in a pedagogical or curriculum framework. Table 7.1 indicates that all five provincial frameworks favour a social-pedagogical and formative approach to assessment in which the processes of learning for each child 'are set by negotiation (educator-parent-child) and informally evaluated unless screening is necessary' (Bennett, 2005, p. 8). Consistent with others, the Ontario framework describes the primary purpose of assessment: 'to support curriculum planning based on where the child is at and what interests the child has . . . and to ensure that the child is benefiting from the early childhood setting' (2006, p. 60). All frameworks ask educators to link 'where the child is at' to the framework's learning goals or developmental skills and to regard them as child strengths rather than deficits. The New Brunswick and British Columbia frameworks offer a more extensive focus on narratives and learning stories as valuable forms of pedagogical documentation.

Table 7.1. Assessment Processes Described in Provincial Early Learning Curriculum
Frameworks and Support Documents

Province	Assessment Processes Related to Curriculum	Support Documents
British Columbia	Pedagogical narration: Anecdotal observations Children's work Photographs Audio or video tape recordings	*Understanding the British Columbia Early Learning Framework: From theory to practice (2009)*
Saskatchewan	Anecdotal records Checklists Learning stories Videotape recordings Photographs Portfolios Documentation posters, panels, and books	*Assessment and Evaluation in Pre-K: A Planning Guide for School Divisions and their Partners (2008b)*
Ontario	Based on Continuum of Learning: Observations Learning stories Portfolios of children's creations and work Developmental screening tools (i.e., Nipissing District Developmental Screen)	None
New Brunswick	Observations Recording children's questions and theories and conversations Displaying and annotating children's artwork Annotating photos of children in learning processes Learning story portfolios Albums of learning events Project webs Daily invitational family information boards Samples of children's work	*Well-Being Professional Support Document (2008b)*
Quebec	Observations: anecdotal, charts, logs Work or photos of children carrying out activities they have planned	None

Recognizing Diversity

Pacini-Ketchabaw and Pence (2006, p. 14) have remarked that broadening and deepening cross-cultural understandings 'is a very *Canadian* area of interest' since the mix of cultures, particularly in our cities, is a defining feature of Canada (see chapter by Pacini-Ketchabaw & Bernhard in this volume). The Quebec, British Columbia, Ontario, and New Brunswick frameworks note this diversity in relation to provincial uniqueness. For example, one of the objectives of educational child care services outlined in the Quebec document is to introduce young children 'to values that [their] society cherishes: self-respect, respect for others and the environment, peaceful resolution of conflicts, equality between sexes and individuals, acceptance of differences, sharing and solidarity' (2007, p. 6). A framework section is devoted to British Columbia's 'great geographic, social, culture, linguistic and economic diversity' (2008, p. 5). The section concludes with the following statement: 'Children, with their boundless imagination and sense of adventure, along with the different ways of living and learning that are part of their individual, social and cultural heritages, will be the leaders and innovators who shape British Columbia in the future' (p. 6). Finally, the New Brunswick framework, adopting the language of a post-structural orientation states:[10] 'The diversity of cultures in New Brunswick is rendered more complex by its socio-demographic diversity. With an almost equal split between rural and urban populations, a curriculum designed specifically for New Brunswick must embrace rural and urban lifeways by creating spaces for the inclusion of local knowledge, a sense of place and the discussion of differences' (2008, p. 9).

Frameworks from New Brunswick, Ontario, and British Columbia have a 'focus on cultural identity that is so essential for Aboriginal children' (Government of British Columbia, 2008, p. 8). The British Columbia framework, in particular, emphasizes throughout the document the importance of cultural and linguistic revitalization and a First Nations cosmology and world view in all early learning contexts. British

---

10 The Ontario framework refers readers to the document *Aménagement linguistique* (2006b) a language planning policy for Ontario's early childhood settings and francophone communities. Saskatchewan's program guide was translated into French in 2008.

Columbia's document recognizes that the early learning curriculum framework is a starting point for discussion and that Aboriginal communities may develop 'their own culturally specific early learning framework' (p. 2).

One of the underlying principles in the New Brunswick, Ontario, and British Columbia frameworks specifically addresses diversity; for example, the Ontario framework states: 'Demonstration of respect for diversity, equity and inclusion are prerequisites for optimal development and learning' (2006, p. 11). Frameworks reference 'culturally appropriate curriculum' (Government of Saskatchewan, 2008b, p. 18), children's 'additional languages' (p. 32), and also integrate examples of these in sections on questions to consider (British Columbia), provisions and practices (New Brunswick), quality in action (Saskatchewan), and adult–child interactions (Ontario). The current analysis indicates a consistent focus on cultural and linguistic diversity across four of the provincial frameworks and, thus, raises the question as to whether this emphasis is more reflective of provincial uniqueness or a pan-Canadian mosaic.

The focus on children with special needs in the provincial frameworks appears to be less integrated throughout the documents. Certainly, all the frameworks recognize the specific needs of diverse groups including children with special needs. Reflecting its origins as an intervention framework (*Jouer, c'est magique!*) for disadvantaged American children, the Quebec guide is more explicit about the role of child care services in detecting children with disabilities and in promoting 'the quality of chances' for all children. The Ontario framework situates all children's skills within the context of a developmental continuum rather than evaluating their performance against age-related expectations. The British Columbia framework states: 'In putting forward an image of a capable child, full of potential, it is recognized that children differ in their strengths and capabilities, and that not all children have the same opportunities to develop their potential' (2008, p. 4).

However, this recognition of differences and the need for educators 'to provide additional support as required to ensure each child's right to full participation' (Government of New Brunswick, 2008a, p. 5) is, in contrast, to the focus on cultural and linguistic diversity, not always carried through to practise examples in the frameworks. Examples do not typically include naturalistic descriptions of children using specific materials such as 'Braille, Sign Language, or pictographs' (evident in the New Brunswick document) to communicate to readers that the learning environment is designed for, and includes, all children. It is noteworthy that the New Brunswick document, which takes a post-foundational/post-structural theoretical orientation states 'in order to practice inclusivity, there is a call for a critical re-thinking of the language and practices of curricula' (2008, p. 190). The document successfully includes the multiple ways in which children can communicate and engage in reciprocal communication with peers.

Implementation and Evaluation

Outlining the content of the provincial early learning curriculum framework in the last section naturally leads to the key questions for this section: Are early childhood educators in the provinces under discussion aware of the frameworks? Are they actually using them?

Analysis indicates that the five curriculum frameworks fall within several categories in relation to the scope of their implementation and evaluations. Implementation can be broadly characterized as province-wide or targeted, and professional training/development activities involved in the implementation may be described as comprehensive or limited. Informal or formal evaluations of implementation approaches have been conducted in British Columbia, Saskatchewan, Ontario, and New Brunswick, with a published report available in the British Columbia case.

In Quebec, framework implementation can be described as province-wide, but professional development focused on the framework is limited. Every educator who operates a home child care centre received a copy of the *Educational Program for Childcare Centres,* and all directors of Quebec child care centres attended a meeting and were introduced to the document,[11] with the expectation that the directors would introduce it to their staff.[12] Ontario's implementation and evaluation led by the Ministry of Children and Youth Services involved seven targeted Best Start urban and rural demonstration sites that included a multi-service

---

11 Personal communication, France Deschênes, Coordonnatrice aux opérations, Ministère de la Famille et des Aînés, Direction des services à la famille Nord-Ouest.
12 Quebec's early childhood educator professional association offers workshops on the Educational Program for Child Centres.

agency, Aboriginal, and francophone venues.[13] An evaluation began with an assessment of staff training and their familiarity and use of *Early Learning for Every Child Today.* Evaluators conducted an on-site visit to assess adult–child interactions and the learning environment. One of the observations that emerged out of the Ontario evaluation was that ECEs can be situated at one of four levels of change leading to full implementation of the framework. At the first level, an educator has a basic knowledge of the curriculum framework and is followed by a second level in which an educator is able through self-assessment and observation to determine how well her or his practices are aligned with the vision and principles of the framework. To assist ECEs at the second level in going beyond a superficial understanding of the document, workshops with materials that visually illustrate principles and practices were valuable. As well, reflective practice skills led to greater utilization of the framework although inconsistencies were still evident. At the third level, an educator utilizes the framework as a key resource for observations, intentional program planning, and documentation. Finally, at the fourth level, an educator fuses together principles and practices, and consistently uses the framework. At this level, ECEs display greater confidence and are able to articulate and affirm what they know and their beliefs. Implementation evaluators of the Ontario framework identified several factors that appear to be important in an educator reaching the fourth level: being part of a broader learning community, which may involve schools, other community programs, and post-secondary ECEC programs; active coaching by a mentor (see chapter by Nina Howe and Ellen Jacobs in this volume); regular staff meetings for discussing the framework; and staff training. Overall, evaluators found that the sustainability of framework implementation was enhanced when the professional culture in a program promoted staff learning and change.

The targeted implementation of the Saskatchewan *Early Learning Program Guide* involved a first phase that introduced participants interested in the guide to its vision and principles.[14] In the second implementation

13 Personal communication, Wanda St Francois and Lois Saunders, Affiliated Services for Children and Youth, Hamilton, Ontario, who led the evaluation of the implementation of Ontario's framework. While the framework was formally implemented and evaluated at seven demonstration sites, it has been used extensively in George Brown College's lab school programs.

14 Personal communication, Twyla Mensch and Laurie Hudyma, Senior Policy and Program Analysts, Early Childhood Education Unit, Early Learning and Child Care Branch, Ministry of Education.

phase, workshops on the value of play, holistic learning, observation, and documentation were offered as well as opportunities for an ECE staff team to visit one of ten program sites that exemplified play and exploration practices. The Saskatchewan Ministry of Education provided grant support to sites to develop tours and materials and to cover staff replacement costs. Informal feedback from participants has indicated that educators need time to make conceptual shifts in their understanding of the value of play and the role of ECEs and to put into practice this new knowledge and understanding. Phase three is currently being developed in light of these results.

In British Columbia, an implementation project led by three faculty members from the University of Victoria, Northern Lights College, and Camosun College, consisted of a province-wide and comprehensive three-strand, train-the-trainer approach:[15] Strand One concentrated on developing trainers called field leaders, who delivered training about the framework and its implementation at the local level; Strand Two brought field leaders (from Strand One) together with ECEC college instructors; and in Strand Three, the field leaders in collaboration with ECEC college instructors delivered workshops to ECEC practitioners throughout the province. British Columbia's professional development 'focused on the processes and skills involved in critical reflection and offered a tool, called pedagogical narrations, to give educators skills and techniques to deepen their understanding of the ordinary moments of children and to provide enriched learning opportunities' (2008, p. 7).

Based on a review of participant feedback from Strands One and Three, British Columbia's formal evaluation report indicated that the professional training and curriculum approach adopted by the implementation team and supported by the Ministry of Education led to a 'successful introduction of the Early Learning Framework, its theory and practice, into the ECEC community across the province' (2008, p. 37). Nevertheless, the report recommended that further work needed to be done with educators to solidify and reinforce the ideas and tools to become part of their daily practice. Other recommendations included the following: field leaders need to continue to deliver the Early Learning Framework Implementation workshops with substitution time support in order to organize and regionalize and/or localize the workshops; options should be explored to create and maintain a database

15 Information from June 2009, *The BC Early Learning Framework Implementation Project Report, March 2007 to March 2009*.

of exemplars that reflect the cultural diversity of young children and ECEC practitioners, as well as the diversity of care arrangements in the province; and college instructors must incorporate the framework and the tool of pedagogical narrations into their curriculum to ensure that new entrants to ECE are familiar with these provincial initiatives.

The New Brunswick curriculum framework project team created specific documents to support province-wide implementation and professional development at a comprehensive level. Over three implementation phases, a government-supported program of professional learning for all ECEs in the province and consisting of direct program support, institutes, training sessions, and consultation services, was undertaken. A formal evaluation is planned but Whitty (2009), one of the curriculum developers comments that 'many educators find the broad-based goals more open and relaxing and more related to the what and how of children's learning; moreover, educators report that these goals inform and expand their own pedagogical practice' (p. 44).

Bennett identified three conditions for the successful implementation of a curriculum framework: '(1) the presence of well-qualified, motivated staff who are trained to understand and implement the curriculum; (2) the requisite structural features such as adequate investment in buildings and outdoor environments, in human resources and staffing, varied learning materials, adequate ratios of qualified educators to children; and (3) appropriate monitoring and support systems to provide information and improve quality and accountability across the field, including in private provision' (2004, p. 18).

Based on the implementation of the provincial frameworks described above, it would be fair to say that to a certain extent they meet Bennett's conditions. The pre-service educational qualifications for early childhood educators range across the provinces from untrained to a minimum of a one- or two-year early childhood education diploma. Nevertheless, in New Brunswick, which has the lowest qualifications for ECE staff, implementation of the early learning curriculum framework was most comprehensive. Whereas Ontario, which has the highest level of qualifications for ECE staff, delivered only targeted to limited professional training (see chapter by Ellen Jacobs and Emmanuelle Adrien in this volume for information on regulations for staff training).

Finally, in some provinces, funding for in-service professional development activities and evaluations has ended, which will make it difficult to sustain staff commitment to put the framework's vision and principles into practice. Overall, it can be concluded that while early childhood educators across Canada may be aware of their provincial early learning curriculum frameworks, the extent to which they are using them is uncertain.

Conclusion

This chapter has provided an introduction to recent provincial early learning curriculum frameworks, their dissemination and implementation to front-line early childhood educators and in some provinces, the evaluation of this implementation. An analysis of the content of the curriculum frameworks indicates that there is much to inspire and motivate ECEs to think about their philosophies of early learning and to provide rich learning environments for young children.

Yet, the evaluations have only provided limited insights into what the implementation of these curriculum frameworks means for broadening and deepening ECEs' understandings of children, child development, family involvement, early childhood educator roles, and program quality. In Quebec, where there has been a mandated educational guide for all ECEs since 1997, several years later only 'one-quarter of its child care settings offered a level of quality that was considered good, very good or excellent' (Friendly & Prentice, 2009, p. 60). While this finding may be a 'result of shifts in government policy, significant quality differences between for-profit and non-for-profit centres, and limited quality improvement activities' (p. 60), it signals to all provinces that Bennett's call for appropriate monitoring and support systems needs to be seriously addressed. As a result of their assessment of the quality of child care services in Quebec, Japel, Tremblay, and Côté (2005) concluded that a high-quality educational program 'can be successful only' if educators thoroughly understand and apply the principles underlying the program and articulated in an education guide (see chapter by Christa Japel in this volume).

Professional development seems particularly important when curriculum frameworks rely on tools of reflective and critical practice that are designed to challenge and shift educator values, beliefs, and theories about teaching and learning. These frameworks require educators to be more than technicians who simply apply standardized technical skills prescribed by experts (Moss, 2006). Rather, the frameworks require educators who are thinkers and interpreters of early childhood philosophies and principles, and who can thoughtfully and critically translate them into practice. These different kinds of understanding of ECEs can become more apparent and sharper when a framework is used as a guideline or a regulation for practice. The ambitious New Brunswick framework, for example, is set to be codified in law (Bill 49) as the province's mandated early learning curriculum, and this codification may influence how the framework is translated into practice by early childhood educators.

In several provinces, the implementation of an early learning curriculum framework has come at a time when full-day kindergarten programs for 4- and 5-year-olds are being introduced. The continuities and differences between curriculum frameworks and guides that focus on children from birth to age 4 years and those for kindergarten children require further investigation. An analysis of provincial frameworks that offer a more comprehensive focus from birth to school age such as the Ontario framework could provide a better understanding of how a framework 'can act as a unifying influence across services for different age groups' (Centre for Community Child Health, 2008) and address the persistent divide between care and education. This chapter began with a vision of a national, universal, and regulated system of early childhood education and care with a quality framework, but has described the increasing number of provinces with their own early learning curriculum framework. Moss (2007) comments that while uniformity is not necessary across the provinces and each curriculum framework can be interpreted locally, it is also desirable for provinces to work towards identifying, at a national level, a body of agreed upon values, principles, and objectives for early learning. In introducing an innovation – an early learning curriculum framework – the governments of British Columbia, Saskatchewan, Ontario, New Brunswick, and Quebec have opened up new directions in early childhood care and education in Canada. To sustain the promise of these directions much is required in terms of supports, evaluations, and analyses by governments in collaboration and consultation with those most affected: early childhood educators, children, and families.

References

Bennett, J. (2004). *Curriculum issues in national policy-making*. Keynote address. Paris: Organization for Economic and Co-operation and Development at the European Early Childcare Education Research Association (EECERA) Conference, Malta, 2 Sept.

Bennett, J. (2005). Democracy and autonomy get an early start. *Children in Europe, 9,* 2–3.

Bertrand, J. (2007) Preschool programs: effective curriculum. Comments on Kagan and Kauerz and on Schweihart. In R.E. Tremblay, R.G. Barr, & R deV. Peters (Eds.). *Encyclopedia on Early Childhood Development* [online]. Montreal: Centre of Excellence for Early Childhood Development. Retrieved from http://www.excellence-earlychildhood.ca/documents/BertrandANGxp. pdf.

Centre for Community Child Health. (2008). Towards an Early Years Learning Framework. Melbourne, Australia: Centre for Community Child Health. Retrieved from http://www.rch.org.au/emplibrary/. . ./PB12_Towards_EY_Learn_Fwork.pdf.

Commonwealth of Australia. (2009). *Belonging, being & becoming: The early years learning framework for Australia.* Canberra: Department of Education, Employment and Workplace.

Dickinson, P. (2006). *International curriculum framework literature survey: Prepared for the Best Start Expert Panel on early learning.* Toronto: Government of Ontario.

Friendly, M., Doherty, G., & Beach, J. (2006*). Quality by design.* Toronto: Childcare Resource and Research Unit, University of Toronto.

Friendly, M., & Prentice, S. (2009). *About Canada: Childcare.* Halifax: Fernwood.

Government of British Columbia. (2008). *British Columbia early learning framework.* Victoria: Ministry of Health and Ministry of Children and Family Development.

Government of British Columbia. (2009). *Understanding the British Columbia early learning framework: From theory to practice.* Victoria: Ministry of Health & Ministry of Children and Family Development.

Government of New Brunswick. (2008a). *Early learning and child care curriculum.* Fredericton: Department of Social Development.

Government of New Brunswick. (2008b). *Well-being professional support document.* Fredericton: Department of Social Development.

Government of Ontario. (2006a). *Early learning for every child today.* Toronto: Best Start Panel on an Early Learning Program.

Government of Ontario. (2006b). *Aménagement linguistique: A language planning policy for Ontario's early childhood setting and francophone communities.* Toronto: Author.

Government of Quebec. (2007). *Meeting early childhood needs: Quebec's educational program for childcare services.* Quebec City: Ministry of Family and Children.

Government of Saskatchewan. (2008a). *Play and exploration: Early learning program guide.* Regina: Ministry of Education.

Government of Saskatchewan. (2008b). *Assessment and evaluation in Pre-K: A planning guide for school divisions and their partners, leading for change, creating early learning environments.* Regina: Ministry of Education.

Japel, C., Tremblay, R., & Côté, S. (2005). *Quality Counts! Assessing the quality of daycare services: Based on the Quebec longitudinal study of child development. IRPP Choices, 4*(5), 1–42. Montreal: Institute for Research on Public Policy.

McCain, M., & Mustard, F. (1999*). Early years study.* Toronto: Government of Ontario.

Moss, P. (2006). Structures, understandings and discourses: Possibilities for re-envisioning the early childhood worker. *Contemporary Issues in Early Childhood, 7*(1), 30–41.

Moss, P. (2007). Bringing politics into the nursery: Early childhood education as a democratic practice. *European Early Childhood Education Research Journal, 15*(1), 5–20.

New Zealand. Ministry of Education. (1996). *Te Whāriki: Early childhood curriculum.* Wellington, NZ: Author.

Office of Childcare. (2004). *New South Wales curriculum framework for children's services: The practice of relationships, essential provisions for children's services.* New South Wales, Australia: Department of Community Services.

Organization for Economic Co-Operation and Development, Directorate for Education. (2004). *Early childhood care and education policy: Canada country note.* Paris: Author. Retrieved from http://www.oecd.org/dataoecd/42/34/33850725.pdf.

Pacini-Ketchabaw, V., & Pence, A. (2006). Introduction: The reconceptualizing movement in Canadian early childhood education, care and development. In V. Pacini-Ketchabaw & A. Pence (Eds.), *Canadian early childhood education: Broadening and deepening discussions of quality* (pp. 5–20). Ottawa: Canadian Child Care Federation.

Tougas, J. (2002). *Reforming Quebec's early childhood care and education: The first five years.* Toronto: Childcare Resource and Research Unit, University of Toronto.

Whitty, P. (2009). Towards designing a postfoundational curriculum document. In L. Iannacci & P. Whitty (Eds.), *Early childhood curricula: Reconceptualist perspectives.* Calgary, AB: Detselig.

8 The Investigating Quality Project: Innovative Approaches in Early Childhood Education

ALAN PENCE AND VERONICA PACINI-KETCHABAW

This chapter is an overview of the Investigating Quality Project (IQP) five years into its history. It has numerous starting points. One was the work of Dahlberg, Moss, and Pence (1999; 2nd ed. 2007), *Beyond Quality in Early Childhood Education and Care*, which, although first published in 1999, was initially discussed in the early 1990s – and those discussions also had their antecedents. Another starting point was the second author's exposure to post-structuralist thought as a doctoral student in the mid-1990s. These experiences and others ultimately led to a collaborative effort entitled the Investigating Quality Project (Pence & Pacini-Ketchabaw, 2009), the intent of which was to explore what might lie beyond British Columbia's and, more broadly Canada's, contemporary worlds of early childhood practice, training, research, policies, and governance. The intent, from the beginning, was to engage these various sectors/worlds of early childhood education and care (ECEC) in the investigation itself. Another intent was to identify where, internationally, some of the most innovative and rigorous work was taking place, to bring those innovators to British Columbia and Canada to discuss their work, and to explore those possibilities in a B.C. context.

Principal sources of inspiration included Sweden, northern Italy, and Aotearoa/New Zealand, but there were other international guests as well who brought into the IQP forums held in Victoria, British Columbia, additional issues of culture and context, social equity, pedagogical innovation, democratic engagement, documentation, assessment, participatory development, and more. The intent throughout was not replication, but inspiration, and to bring ideas into engagement with action in a Canadian environment.

The chapter commences with a brief review of the Canadian context as seen through the lens of the IQP, then considers points of inspiration from principal sources; this is followed by a discussion of the IQP with early childhood educators (ECEs), an overview of IQP engagement with other sectors of early childhood education and care, and finally, our evolving thoughts and theories regarding professional learning and the role and possibilities of government.

Canadian Early Childhood Care and Development: Research and Practice

Child care and early childhood education in Canada closely follow on dynamics in the United States (Pence & Benner, 2000; Pence & Pacini-Ketchabaw, 2009). For example, in both countries, similar types of child care research emerged at nearly the same time: community-need surveys in the mid- to late 1960s; somewhat simplistic 'is child care good or bad' studies throughout the 1970s; the emergence of more complex ecologically oriented studies in the 1980s; major national survey work in the late 1980s; an increasing number of cost-benefit analyses in the 1990s; and, more recently, a number of statements suggesting associations between the brain development of individual children and broader state-level, socio-economic developments. Political and policy dynamics of 'mother *versus* other care' have a long-standing history in both countries – continuing until the present; program and professional issues are often framed similarly in both countries (in part, owing to the cross-border influence of the very large U.S.-based National Association for the Education of Young Children). Both countries, for the most part, have taken a minimum standards approach to regulation, and both have been heavily influenced by marketplace orientations to service provision (see chapter by Gordon Cleveland in this volume). This history shares similarities with other anglophone countries (the United Kingdom, Australia, and New Zealand up until the late 1980s), but it is most similar to the United States. It is a history that is substantially different and substantially weaker than is the case for most developed countries – rating last of ten countries studied on UNICEF's recent report card (2007), and drawing criticism in an international report by the Organization of Economic Co-operation and Development (OECD, 2003).

Despite the gap between ECEC in North America and many other industrialized countries in Europe, both Canada and the United States became quite interested, in the latter part of the 1990s, in various continental European approaches to early childhood programs. Scandinavian countries, France, and in particular Reggio Emilia, Italy, became popular at that time, and study tours abounded. This interest, however, was framed through long-established North American perspectives that tended to focus more on outward manifestations of programs without adequate appreciation of, or background in, the deeper, philosophical bases of the programs. For example, the fact that Reggio Emilia's pedagogical and philosophical foundations were, to a significant degree, born out of a 'never again' reaction to acquiescence regarding the rise of Fascism in Italy, lies well outside North American orientations and consciousness. Too often the veneer of European programs found their way into North American ECEC, but not the substance that lay beneath them which gave them their unique vitality and quality.

The superficial quality of a great deal of programming in North America relates, in part, to the long-established use of checklist orientations towards monitoring quality care found throughout North American state and provincial jurisdictions. Early childhood education and care (ECEC) in North America has failed to evolve as a truly professional service with self-regulation based on a substantial number of years of professional training, adequate compensation, and societal respect (see chapter by Ellen Jacobs and Emmanuelle Adrien in this volume). Such professional respectability, with a basis in substantial educational training (typically a Bachelor of Arts degree), is found in Scandinavian countries and in some other parts of continental Europe, as well as in Aotearoa/New Zealand; these developments have opened the door to a far more sophisticated and complex understanding of children and children's programs.

The initial steps in the Investigating Quality Project involved looking more closely at those programs and international program approaches that were based on a more sophisticated understanding of children and children's programs.

Points of Inspiration

As the quote below reveals, the experimental aspects of work in Reggio Emilia, the Stockholm Project, and Aotearoa/New Zealand provided us with a multitude of ideas and possible actions. Of central interest for the IQP were the *questions* from these locations, rather than the answers: 'How to achieve another construction of the child, knowledge, learning and the conditions needed for learning? How to reconstruct an early childhood pedagogy which has its starting point in the child's theories, hypotheses, dreams and fantasies and in a view of knowledge and learning as co-construction? How to border-cross the project of modernity, holding out the prospect of a continuous and linear progress, certainty and universality, by recognizing uncertainty, diversity, non-linearity, multiple perspectives, temporal and spatial specificities?' (Dahlberg et al., 2007, p. 133).

We value key principles of the projects examined, principles that, as we see them, are practice-oriented but not detached from theory. For example, the Stockholm Project, a professional development initiative in Sweden (see Dahlberg et al., 2007), reminds us that 'theory does not express, translate, or serve to apply practice: it is practice. It is therefore not a totalizing instrument, but one that multiplies potentialities' (Hand, 1988, p. vii). The Stockholm Project embraces key elements of postmodernism: the loss of certainty, control, and predictability; openness to the presence of many voices and views; and the need to engage with those other views and explore a world of profound diversity. These elements of postmodernism figure prominently in the preface to the second edition of *Beyond Quality,* by Carlina Rinaldi (president of Reggio Children and director of the Loris Malaguzzi International Centre), published in 2007: 'We feel the book to be an expression of our [Reggio Children's] identity too' (Dahlberg et al., 2007, p. xix). In the postmodern era, process, engagement, dialogue, and co-construction take precedence over routines, non-contextualized best practices, exclusivity, and the safe haven of predetermined outcomes.

Aotearoa/New Zealand, in activities undertaken since the mid-1980s, has also been a source of inspiration. Aotearoa/New Zealand was valuable for many reasons, not least of which is that it alone among the industrialized anglophone countries has taken a distinct and innovative way forward that has challenged dominant assumptions, structures, and approaches regarding policy directions and regulations (Meade, 1988), culturally generated programs (Te Kohanga Reo National Trust, 1982), national curricula (Carr & May, 1992; New Zealand, Ministry of Education, 1996), assessment (Carr, 2001), strategic long-term planning (New Zealand, Ministry of Education, 2002), and more. Anne Meade, in her landmark report to government, *Education to Be More* (1988), opened the door to possibilities beyond 'governance as usual' that called for a system that recognized 'the diversity of programmes, philosophies and cultures within New Zealand while balancing support for that diversity with certain national values and objectives' (Smith & Farquhar, 1994, p. 123). Meade's approach brought regulation within the grasp of local programs, empowering them to engage actively and meaningfully with questions of quality – a process long established in places like Reggio Emilia. In part, Meade's work was a recognition of local decision making already evident by that time in several Maori communities, and particularly so with the Te Kohanga Reo early childhood programs (Te Kohanga Reo National Trust, 1982). The Te Kohanga Reo movement and Meade's innovative and liberating report made possible further innovation. As noted, in 1992 Carr and May, working in cooperation with Maori Elders, published *Te Whāriki: National Early Childhood Curriculum Guidelines in New Zealand* that incorporated concepts of culture, identity, knowledge, skills, and dispositions in ways and levels never before seen in national curricula published in English; this was followed by *Assessment in Early Childhood Settings: Learning Stories* (Carr, 2001), an approach to evidence-based assessment quite removed from the instrument-based approaches so familiar in Canada and the United States.[1] These and other creative activities call out for Canadian innovation as well.

The Stockholm Project, Reggio Emilia, and Aotearoa/New Zealand have been able to challenge modernity's reliance on positivism and standardization by disrupting key elements of early childhood practice. In particular, these international approaches took issue with a modernity approach, typical of North American programs, because they included a narrow articulation of developmentally appropriate practice, restrictive and prescriptive definitions of quality, and theories of child development that assume universal laws and norms. By engaging in this process, these international projects have questioned the existence of a singular truth and universality (Cannella, 1997; Dahlberg et al., 2007). They have problematized early childhood education's construction of a *true* child, which allows us to make sense of what children are, what children should be, and what children need in order to fit into a specific ideal (Burman, 2008; Grieshaber & Cannella, 2001; Hultqvist & Dahlberg, 2001; Moss & Petrie, 2002). These innovative projects can be seen as movements that do not treat reality as independent of the knower and the process of knowing. They acknowledge the importance

---

1 For a series of examples of learning stories, see http://www.educate.ece. govt.nz/learning/curriculumAndLearning/Assessmentforlearning/ KeiTuaotePae.aspx.

of context and values; see Dahlberg et al. (2007) for a review of modernist and postmodernist perspectives.

Our readings and engagement with these projects and their leaders have allowed us to challenge common North American understanding of the Reggio Emilia Project. Reggio Emilia has been interpreted by some in the Canadian context as an addition to the growing body of ECEC knowledge, as an incremental step forward. The prevailing metaphor in parts of Canadian early childhood history has been an evolutionary spiral. Early childhood educators are too often seen as having developed, since the days of the infant schools in the 1820s, ever more sophisticated understandings of children and their development and appropriate care. The evolutionary spiral is consistent with the modernist view of progress. We, however, see Reggio Emilia as revolutionary, and not evolutionary (Pence, 2000). Consistent with this view, the Stockholm network has seen Reggio Emilia as a practice that can stimulate the rethinking of practices and the examination of the assumptions underlying practices. Indeed, Reggio Emilia has been used as a tool to stimulate a discussion of early childhood education and care in the postmodern era. Reggio Emilia has been seen as enabling the deconstruction of ECEC discussions of quality centres defined from managerial perspectives that are closely tied to developmentally appropriate discourses. Unfortunately, the Reggio Emilia Project has seldom been used in this way in Canada.

The Investigating Quality Project: A Relational Learning Project

Following insights from Reggio Emilia, the Stockholm Project, and Aotearoa/New Zealand, we understood that to begin a discussion of the values embedded in current practices in the field and, more importantly, to challenge the dominant discourses that underpin everyday practices, we needed to engage in dialogue with early childhood educators. We felt that to engage in the discourse of meaning making and challenge the taken-for-granted assumptions of the discourse of quality, it was important to engage in discussions *with* front-line practitioners (*educators* is the term used in British Columbia) directly involved in pedagogical work. From the perspective of the discourse of meaning making, change emerges from dialogue: 'To change a pedagogical practice, it is necessary to start by problematizing and deconstructing [dominant] discourses and to understand and demonstrate how they are related to what is going on in pedagogical practice' (Dahlberg et al., 2007, p. 131).

Work with twenty-six ECEs was launched in 2006, and currently we are working with over a hundred educators. Since the start of the project, we have experimented with different configurations and formats, which have often been driven by funding availability. Overall, we engage in dialogue in different ways: a series of smaller learning circles, larger sharing circles, online discussions, and site visits. Monthly *learning circles* provided opportunities for small groups of ECEs to share and dialogue about established and emerging practices as well as to become familiar with, reflect upon, discuss, struggle with, and challenge postmodern critical approaches to practice. Educators collected moments of practice using journal writing, photography, and video and audio recording in their centres, which were then shared with the group, following the process of pedagogical documentation (Dahlberg & Moss, 2005; Dahlberg et al., 2007; Project Zero, 2004). During our learning circles, we critically reflected together on each educator's documentation and made visible how we might work with postmodern theories to extend their practices. *Sharing circles* were organized to bring together all of the ECEs from the different learning circles to interact and share the work produced as a result of their involvement in the learning circles, and to revitalize our discussions by engaging in dialogue with individuals from other locations (international guests). Many Swedish colleagues have visited us at the University of Victoria and provided valuable insights into this work. The *online space* (listserv) was created and used by ECEs and researchers to communicate between learning and sharing circles and to circulate materials of interest. In addition to facilitating the workshops, members of the research team provided individual support to each educator through visits to ECE centres, providing opportunities for one-on-one conversations between the educators and the researchers.

Through our critical dialogue we intend to move beyond definitions of quality that embrace prescriptive and universal measurements that detach quality from the everyday practices of early childhood institutions and from those who are involved in those institutions (Dahlberg et al., 2007). We believe we are experimenting with what it means to work from a postmodern perspective with the discourse of meaning making:

> In the field of early childhood, the discourse of meaning making speaks first and foremost about constructing and deepening *understanding* of the early childhood institution and its projects, in particular the pedagogical work – to make meaning of what is going on . . . The discourse of meaning making calls for explicitly ethical and philosophical choices, judgments

of value, made in relation to the wider questions of what we want for our children here and now and in the future . . . The discourse of meaning making therefore not only adopts a social constructionist perspective, but relates to an understanding of learning as a process of co-construction, by which in relationship with others we make meaning of the world. (Dahlberg et al., 2007, pp. 106–107)

In response to our current context and our interest in postmodern approaches, we worked towards creating opportunities with early childhood educators to network and critically reflect on their own practices through the use of pedagogical documentation. Pedagogies characterized by depth, meaning, purpose, engagement, discussions, and dialogue were used to explore meaningful understanding of practices.

Our work with ECEs is ongoing, tentative, transformative, and a process of experimentation. We are interested in working together with educators to build capacity in, and bring innovation, to the field. This is of particular interest to us given the situation in which child care is positioned in British Columbia (e.g., low pay, high rates of staff turnover, difficulties recruiting new ECEs to the field, and retaining those who are currently in the field). The idea of working together is not a simple one, particularly if, as Dahlberg et al. (2007) note, we are to move beyond empowerment. We have used, as has the Stockholm Project, questions that have helped us to think through our work: 'How then can researchers position themselves less as "masters of truth and justice" and more as creators of a space where those directly involved can act and speak on their own behalf? How can researchers be other than the origin and legitimization of what can be known and done? Who are we to know better than the pedagogues? How can we conduct research about the child and his everyday life that recognizes and values complexity and context?' (Dahlberg et al., 2007, p. 141). Through taking a co-construction approach in the project, we found that ECEs and researchers began to value their work more and, more importantly, began to expand their horizons in relation to the possibilities of their participatory work and the knowledge bases within the field.

Critical reflection, as noted above, is a key component in the discourse of meaning making and, therefore, in our work with educators. Mac Naughton (2003) argues that reflecting critically on our own practices opens up opportunities for learning and motivates us to make changes when necessary, and also to be creative. In their work on effective professional development, Mitchell and Cubey argue that 'if early childhood education centers are to be learning communities for teachers as well as children, parents and others, there need to be opportunities within the work environment for reflection, experimentation and planning' (2003, p. xv). In the Investigating Quality Project, we have introduced pedagogical documentation as a tool for reflection, deconstruction, planning, experimentation, and action within the discourse of meaning making. Our use of pedagogical documentation embraces the values of the early childhood project of Reggio Emilia, which regards the child as an active learner, values the role of the community and relationships in learning, and views learning and life as ongoing experimentation and research.

Overall, the IQP has provided a space for professional revitalization of educators by challenging each other to think differently about ECEC issues. The opportunity to connect, participate, collaborate and grow with colleagues has been an invaluable component noted by many of the participants. They spoke about the importance of having the opportunity to network and make ongoing and meaningful connections with others working in the field. They indicated that they appreciated the various ideas that were discussed as well as the critical edge that the discussions involved. In the words of one of the educators: 'These critical discussions enabled all of us to view our work in alternative ways. The ongoing nature of the program, as well as the time provided for thinking and reflecting outside of the time with children, made us feel valued as professionals.'

Beyond the Project–Practice Nexus

In addition to engaging front-line early childhood educators in approaches based on *Beyond Quality* concepts and critical reflections on the field and its dominant discourses, the IQP has also sought to engage college and university-college instructors, government staff and officials, professional association members, and interested members of the broader public in these ideas. To that end, most of the ten forums offered between February 2006 and January 2010 included opportunities for engagement with each of these audiences as part of their basic structure (a list of the forums is found in the Appendix at the end of the chapter). On two occasions, the forums were scheduled to coincide with the annual meetings of the Provincial Day Care Directors, in order that Investigating Quality Project discussions could reach across Canada. In addition to the forums, the IQP also hosted the 16th Reconceptualizing

Early Childhood Education Conference – the first time it has been held in Canada. That conference and two symposia organized as part of the forums each attracted over 120 participants.

The forum (Forum Ten), held in January 2010, was designed to stimulate greater interprovincial and international discussion by bringing together a number of key participants for a week including the following: Charles Pascal, Ontario's Special Advisor to the Premier on Early Learning; Peter Moss, international authority regarding early learning and child care in the European Union countries; Margaret Carr, co-author of the *Te Whāriki: National Early Childhood Curriculum Guidelines in New Zealand;* and the IQP principal investigators. Activities included discussions on government structures and policies vis-à-vis early learning and child care in various jurisdictions; engagements with senior staff and with elected officials from key B.C. ministries regarding aspects of those discussions; a well-attended evening event for the broader public and the early years' community; and two days of workshops with practitioners led by Margaret Carr and Veronica Pacini-Ketchabaw.

While the IQP has considered a great number of conceptual as well as structural issues related to practice, policy, training, and research in early childhood education and care over the past five years, in many respects the work is still under development, with multiple avenues requiring further work for these approaches to reach their full potential, as they have in their countries of origin. Two of those avenues for further consideration are examined below, with the first, professional learning, represented by an summary of a chapter by Pacini-Ketchabaw, Kocher, and Sanchez (2009), and the second, which addresses issues of structural and policy challenges for government, representing tentative thoughts emerging from Forum Ten.

Continuing Our Thinking about Professional Learning

Our thoughts about professional learning continue to shift as we learn from our experiences and try to push ourselves to imagine other worlds and other possibilities for early childhood education and care. We are currently thinking about the idea of professional development, and interrogating it using a postmodern style of thinking (as proposed in Dahlberg et al., 2007). Professional development programs in North American ECEC typically engage educators in changing their knowledge, beliefs, skills, and practices (see chapter by Nina Howe and Ellen

Jacobs in this volume). The emphasis is on the outcomes of the changes produced within the ECEs themselves and their practices in response to the implementation of specific sources of change (e.g., Smith & Gillespie, 2007). Our interrogation involves problematizing assumptions embedded in the idea of professional development, following the work of post-foundational theorists (see Bogue, 2004; Chia, 1995, 1999; Tsoukas & Chia, 2002). For a detailed review of this work, see Pacini-Ketchabaw et al. (2009).

Reimaging Policy and Regulation

While professional change is critical for the field of early childhood education and care to move into a place of enhanced possibilities, key elements of that change are contingent upon counterpart transformations in government policies, structures, and regulations. The two are interdependent and synergistic – change in one facilitates change in the other.

Aotearoa/New Zealand provides Canada with a good example of how a government with a similar British colonial background, similar parliamentary and governance structures, and a similar history of a weak and fragmented early childhood sector can, through transformations at governmental, professional, educational, and program levels, move towards international recognition as a leader in creating truly innovative systems supportive of children and families in a context of social diversity.

Steps towards such a place of innovation *have* taken place in British Columbia. Most notable was the Ministry of Education's support for the development of an Early Learning Framework (Government of British Columbia, 2008) based to a significant degree on innovations in Aotearoa/New Zealand (see chapter by Rachel Langford in this volume). Through the work of an advisory committee with broad theoretical and practice representation (including members who were knowledgeable regarding postmodern international work), and a government committed to becoming an international leader regarding children's well-being, an innovative step was taken.

The fact, however, that the Framework is seen as applying only to those programs administered through the B.C. Ministry of Education (Early Learning), and not necessarily those of the Ministry of Child and Family Development (Child Care), underscores the importance of large-scale government transformation, to accompany professional transformations as pursued by the Investigating Quality Project.

Such government transformations, moving away from fragmented responsibilities and services towards more coherent and coordinated systems that still understand, appreciate, and support the importance of diversity and flexibility at the local level have become a hallmark of positive changes for early years in a wide range of jurisdictions internationally (Bennett, 2003; Moss, 2010). Such coordination with respect for diversity was a key part of change in Aotearoa/New Zealand, as it was in Sweden. The idea of governmental transformations in British Columbia in relation to early learning and child care is now becoming part of the Canadian landscape as well. The approach proposed in Ontario (Government of Ontario, 2009a, 2009b) bears closer investigation (see chapters by Rachel Langford and Janette Pelletier in this volume).

In November 2007, Charles Pascal was appointed Special Advisor to the Premier of Ontario on Early Learning. His first report was issued in June of 2009: *With Our Best Future in Mind* (Government of Ontario, 2009a). The report is an ambitious examination of how early learning and child care can be more effectively coordinated, integrated, and extended. Pascal notes in the report the complex fragmentation (*chaos* is the term used in the report) that currently characterizes programs for young children in Ontario (a scene very similar in other parts of the country, including British Columbia). Pascal boldly calls for changes that seek to transform chaos into integration, calling for key efforts on the part of school systems to create 'Community Schools for children 4–12 years' and a system of 'Best Start Child and Family Centres for children 0–3 years' (p. 21).

While Pascal's main report, *With Our Best Future in Mind*, is ambitious, the follow-up report focusing on curriculum and pedagogy, *Every Child, Every Opportunity* (Government of Ontario, 2009b), is (from the perspective of the IQP) much less innovative. The report is grounded in long-established North American discourses of program routines, top-down monitoring, and restrictive, universalist outcomes, based largely on the Developmentally Appropriate Practice (DAP) orientation of the National Association for the Education of Young Children (NAEYC). Missing in the follow-up document is the call by Loris Malaguzzi, one of the leaders of the Reggio Emilia movement, for a multitude of languages of children, Aotearoa/New Zealand's myriad woven mats facilitative of diversity and unknown possibilities (*Te Whāriki*), or Sweden's explorations of places 'beyond,' which routinely allow Sweden's children to out-perform Canadian and U.S. children even on conventional, international measures of development and school success.

Conclusion

It is perhaps ironic to end this chapter on a note of international measures – the counter-point of much that has driven the Investigating Quality Project over its five-year history. Ironic, perhaps, but not irrelevant, for the approaches explored and pursued by the IQP (and those locations and leaders it has learned from) that have demonstrated that children and their caregivers thrive within postmodernist structures such as those explored and implemented by the IQP. Such efforts to move beyond checklist-driven understandings of quality, inappropriately derived norms, narrow truths, and the structures and regulations that have for far too long poorly served North America, represent not threats – but opportunities. The first author is reminded of an experience from over twenty years ago when he first began to explore 'the other side,' doing so in partnership with Indigenous communities in northern Canada (Pence, with Meadow Lake Tribal Council, 1989; see commentary by Pence in this volume). While the approach to tertiary education that was co-constructed was well outside the norm, Pence could see very little down side to such evaluation-based experimentation as the history of tertiary education had been so dismal for Indigenous Peoples in Canada for so long; we really had nothing to lose. We feel the same way about the current state of early learning and child care in Canada today: we have little to lose and much to gain.

Appendix: Forums

Indigenous Knowledges in Early Childhood Education. 24 Feb. – 2 March 2006. Victoria, BC. Presenters: Elizabeth Pakai, Lesley Rameka, Karen Martin, Marcelle Townsend-Cross, Claude S. Endfield, Mike Niles, Noelani Iokepa-Guerrero, Margo Greenwood, Nadine Rousselot, and Carmen Rodriguez.
Investigating 'Quality' Early Learning Spaces. 23–28 April 2006. Victoria, BC. Presenters: Sandra Griffin, Judith L. Evans, Peter Moss, Margaret Carr, and Robert Myers.
Rethinking Pedagogy in ECCD: International Perspectives. 6–11 Aug. 2006. Victoria, BC. Presenters: Glenda MacNaughton, Beth Blue Swadener, Hillevi Lenz Taguchi, Patrick Hughes, and Wendy Lee.

Innovative Approaches to Assessment in ECCE: The Use of Learning Stories. 10–12 June 2007. Victoria, BC. Margaret Carr and Wendy Lee.

Early Childhood Care and Development: Perspectives from the Majority World. 16–17 Nov. 2007. Victoria, BC. Presenters: Radhika Viruru, Lourdes Diaz Soto, Michael Niles, Bame Nsamenang, Jennie Ritchie, and Gail Yuen.

A Time of Change in ECE: Challenging Our Ways of Thinking about Our Identity. 28 Feb. 2008. Presenters: Karin and Per Alernvik, Stockholm Project.

IQP Consultation and Early Childhood Educators of British Columbia Conference. 29–31 May 2008. Presenters: Gunilla Dahlberg, Helen May, Radhika Viruru, and Kylie Smith.

Strengthening Africa's Contributions to Child Development Research (with SRCD). 31 Jan. – 7 Feb. 2009. Victoria, BC. Presenters: Robert Levine, Sara Harkness, Peter Mwaura, Robert Myers, Bame Nsamenang, Robert Serpell, and Charles Super.

University of Victoria Early Years Institute. 25–26 May 2009. University of Victoria. Victoria, BC. Presenters: Glenda MacNaughton, Cheryl Rau, and Helen Penn.

Moving Beyond Minimum Standards: A Vision of Early Learning and Childcare. 17–20 Jan. 2010. University of Victoria. Victoria, BC. Presenters: Margaret Carr, Peter Moss, and Charles Pascal.

References

Bennett, J. (2003). Starting strong. *Journal of Early Childhood Research, 1*(1), 21–48.

Bogue, R. (2004). Search, swim and see: Deleuze's apprenticeship in signs and pedagogy of images. *Educational Philosophy and Theory, 36*, 327–342.

Burman, E. (2008). Deconstructing developmental psychology. New York: Routledge.

Cannella, G. (1997). Deconstructing early childhood education: Social justice and revolution. New York: Peter Lang.

Carr, M. (2001). Assessment in early childhood settings: Learning stories. Thousand Oaks, CA: Sage.

Carr, M., & May, H. (1992). *Te Whāriki: National early childhood curriculum guidelines in New Zealand*. Hamilton, NZ: Waikato University.

Chia, R. (1995). From modern to postmodern organizational analysis. *Organization Studies, 16*, 579–604.

Chia, R. (1999). A 'rhizomic' model of organizational change and transformation: Perspective from a metaphysics of change. *British Journal of Management, 10*, 209–227.

Dahlberg, G., & Moss, P. (2005). *Ethics and politics in early childhood education.* London/New York: Routledge/Falmer.

Dahlberg, G., Moss, P., & Pence, A.R. (1999). *Beyond quality in early childhood education and care: Postmodern perspectives.* London: Falmer.

Dahlberg, G., Moss, P., & Pence, A.R. (2007). *Beyond quality in early childhood education and care: Languages of evaluation.* 2nd ed. London: Routledge.

Government of British Columbia. (2008). *British Columbia early learning framework.* Victoria: Ministry of Education, Ministry of Health, Ministry of Children and Family Development, & Early Learning Advisory Group.

Government of Ontario. (2009a). *With our best future in mind.* Toronto: Author.

Government of Ontario. (2009b). *Every child, every opportunity: A compendium report to 'With our best future in mind.'* Toronto: Author.

Grieshaber, S., & Cannella, G.S. (2001). From identity to identities: Increasing possibilities in early childhood education. In S. Grieshaber & G.S. Cannella (Eds.), *Embracing identities in early childhood education diversity and possibilities* (pp. 3–21). New York: Teachers College Press.

Hand, S. (1988). Translating theory, or the difference between Deleuze and Foucault. (Translator's Introduction). In G. Deleuze (Ed.), *Foucault* (pp. vi–ix). New York: Continuum.

Hultqvist, K., & Dahlberg, G. (2001). *Governing the child in the new millennium.* New York: Routledge/Falmer.

Mac Naughton, G. (2003). *Shaping early childhood: Learners, curriculum and contexts.* Maidenhead, UK: Open University Press.

Meade, A. (1988). *Education to be more: Report of the early childhood care and education working group.* Wellington, NZ: Government Printer.

Mitchell, L., & Cubey, P. (2003). Best evidence synthesis: Characteristics of professional development linked to enhanced pedagogy and children's learning in early childhood settings. Wellington, NZ: Ministry of Education Te Tahuhu o te Matauranga.

Moss, P. (2010). *Experiences in moving beyond minimum standards: A vision for early learning and child care.* Keynote address at Early Years Conference, Unit of Child Care Research and Development, University of Victoria, Victoria, BC.

New Zealand. Ministry of Education. (1996). *Te Whāriki: Early childhood curriculum.* Auckland, NZ: Author. Retrieved from http://www.educate.ece.govt.nz/learning/curriculumAndLearning/TeWhariki.aspx.

New Zealand. Ministry of Education. (2002). *Pathways to the future: Nga Huarahi Arataki.* Auckland, NZ: Author.

OECD. (2003). *Early childhood education and care policy: Canada country note.* OECD Directorate for Education. Retrieved from http://www.oecd.org/dataoecd/42/34/33850725.pdf.

Pacini-Ketchabaw, V., Kocher, L., & Sanchez, A. (2009). Rhizomatic stories of immanent becoming and intra-activity: Professional development reconceptualized. In L. Iannacci & P. Whitty (Eds.), *Early childhood curricula: Reconceptualist perspectives* (pp. 87–119). Calgary, AB: Destilig.

Pence, A. (2000). Invited introduction, in S. Fraser, *Authentic childhood: Experiencing the Reggio Emilia approach in the classroom*. Toronto: Nelson Thomson Learning.

Pence, A., with Meadow Lake Tribal Council. (1989). *Proposal to develop a community-sensitive ECE tertiary education program*. Unpublished proposal. University of Victoria.

Pence, A., & Benner, A. (2000). Child care research in Canada, 1965–99. In L. Prochner & N. Howe (Eds.), *Early childhood care and education in Canada* (pp. 133–160). Vancouver: UBC Press.

Pence, A., & Pacini-Ketchabaw, V. (2009). *Investigating quality: Early learning environments project*. Victoria: Unit for Childcare Research, University of Victoria.

Project Zero. (2004). *Making learning visible: Children as individual and group learners*. Reggio Emilia, Italy: Reggio Children.

Smith, A.B., & Farquhar, S. (1994). The New Zealand experience of charter development in early childhood services, In P. Moss & A. Pence, *Valuing quality in early childhood services*. New York: Teachers College Press.

Smith, C., & Gillespie, M. (2007). Research on professional development and teacher change: Implications for adult basic education. In J. Comings, B. Garner, & C. Smith (Eds.), *Review of adult learning and literacy: Connecting research, policy, and practice* (pp. 205–244). New York: Routledge.

Te Kohanga Reo National Trust. (1982). *Description of the Te Kohanga Reo National Trust*. Retrieved from http://www.kohanga.ac.nz/.

Tsoukas, H., & Chia, R. (2002). On organizational becoming: Rethinking organizational change. *Organization Science, 13*, 567–582.

UNICEF. (2007). Child poverty in perspective: An overview of child wellbeing in rich countries (Report Card 7). New York: Author.

9 Elements of Mentoring: Two Case Studies of In-service Professional Development for Early Childhood Educators

NINA HOWE AND ELLEN JACOBS

Professional development for early childhood educators (ECEs; e.g., child care) can either constitute pre-service training (e.g., community college programs) or be delivered via in-service programs once educators are employed. The goals of in-service professional development vary from providing basic training for unqualified staff to continuing education for teachers with formal qualifications (Ackerman, 2006; Epstein, 1993; Fantuzzo et al., 1997; Horm-Wingerd et al., 1997). The focus of this chapter is on in-service professional development for educators with pre-service training.

In-service professional development allows educators to keep abreast of new directions in the field and enhance their knowledge and practice. There are various definitions and forms of in-service professional development (Buysse, Winton, & Rous, 2009), but it generally encompasses short-term workshops or seminars (two to three hours), intensive short-term training (one to five days), or long-term courses (three to twelve months) provided by an agency or community college (Burchinal et al., 2002). There is limited literature on the effectiveness of in-service professional development on educator knowledge, practice, and beliefs, and Ackerman (2004) notes that most programs have not been assessed. The few studies evaluating the efficacy of in-service professional development have generally assessed short-term (e.g., Fantuzzo et al., 1997) rather than long-term programs (Burchinal et al., 2002; Cassidy et al., 1995). However, longer, more intensive models of training appear more effective in promoting parental involvement, positive classroom interactions, and enhancing educators' observation skills (e.g., Catapano, 2005; Epstein, 1993; Fantuzzo et al., 1997).

Nevertheless, workshops remain the most frequently used approach for delivering in-service professional development.

The Value of In-service Professional Development: A Critique

A number of criticisms have been raised about the workshop approach. The typical two- to three- hour workshop offers a snapshot of fragmented and episodic information on a topic that may or may not be of interest for the participants (Borko, 2004). The content may be superficial, disconnected from the educator's prior knowledge and practice, and ineffective in addressing how adults learn (Helterbran & Fennimore, 2004). Further, the workshop approach rarely provides an in-depth examination of relevant topics such as curriculum or assessment of children's development. Continuing feedback is typically not included following the workshop which would help educators integrate new knowledge into their classroom practice in developmentally appropriate ways. In contrast, Borko (2004) argues that the delivery of in-service training may require a situated learning framework that uses the educator's classroom as a meaningful context for facilitating professional growth. To address some of these problems, we employed a consultant model of in-service professional development in our study.

Finally, most studies on in-service professional development have focused on educator or child outcomes and have not examined the processes involved in affecting change in the educator's behaviour, particularly regarding curriculum. Little attention has been devoted to the notion of mentoring or coaching of in-service educators, although there is some literature on the mentoring of pre-service students or novice educators (e.g., Clifford, 1999; Whitebrook & Bellm, 1996). Even the few studies that examine mentoring as a means of promoting positive change in educator behaviour have not addressed the specific strategies employed by the mentor or the processes of change (e.g., Assel et al., 2007; Fuligni et al., 2009).

Mentoring: Effecting Change in Educator Behaviour and Classroom Environments

Mentoring is one avenue for helping educators develop their professional and personal skills necessary for working with young children. It is a 'catch-all expression that describes the relationship between a learned, skilled person and a novice' (Whitebrook & Bellm, 1996, p. 59). In our case, *mentoring* refers to the process of how educators can become more skilled at working with children. Mentors must establish a close, trusting relationship with their protégés in order to help them effect change in their understanding of child development, the classroom environment, and their own ways of thinking (Blank & Kershaw, 2009). Mentors act as guides and problem solvers, engage in scaffolding and modelling, and provide encouragement and support in assisting educators through the process of learning, while recognizing that learning is a dyadic process (Whitebrook & Bellm, 1996). Clearly, there are positive benefits for mentors, such as enhanced professional self-concept, sharing expertise, or developing reflective practices (Blank et al., 2006; Kershaw et al., 2006).

Whitebrook and Bellm (1996) outlined five underlying assumptions of mentoring programs and advocated using a social constructivist (Vygotskian) approach: (1) child and adult growth in child care settings are inextricably linked; (2) both children and adults learn effectively via hands-on, concrete experiences that lead to opportunities to apply new knowledge; (3) mentoring creates a community of learners that facilitates the optimal development of both children and educators; (4) mentoring is effective for keeping educators abreast of new developments; and (5) mentoring facilitates educators' abilities to meet new challenges in the workplace. Effective mentoring programs require release time from regular classroom duties for mentors and educators to discuss, analyse, and observe the children and their environment, and to assess the educator's behaviour and thinking, while solving issues that arise (Blank & Kershaw, 2009).

A number of key elements that define mentoring have been identified (Whitebrook & Bellm, 1996). Specifically, mentoring should include a discussion of the concept of professional development, reflective practice strategies, teaching skills, assessing change, and professional advocacy. Blank and Kershaw (2009) identified specific coaching strategies for mentors, namely, communication, reflective practice, problem solving, 'coachable' moments, scaffolding, modelling, collaborative planning, observing, analysing data, giving feedback, and making data-based instructional decisions. As discussed by Whitebrook and Bellm (1996), there are also personal qualities required for an effective mentor: a strong background in early childhood education and experience, positive interpersonal skills, and a commitment to the process of mentoring. As Ryan and Hornbeck (2004) point out, mentors act as agents of change by providing expertise and guidance to less skilled educators. Yet, the process whereby mentors effect change is rarely described in studies (e.g., Assel et al., 2007; Ryan & Hornbeck, 2004). Thus, the purpose of the present study was to analyse the process of mentoring to help educators implement a constructivist approach to curriculum in their classrooms.

Mentoring a Constructivist Approach to Curriculum

Constructivism is a 'theory of knowing that emphasizes the role that each person plays in the construction of their own knowledge and is based upon the premise that children learn through their interaction with the environment' (Branscombe et al., 2003, p. 10). The focus of constructivist theory is on learning and not on teaching (Fosnot, 2005), since both educators and children actively learn by interacting with one another and with the content of the learning (Duckworth, 1987; Perkins, 1999). Educators act as guides and facilitators as their own knowledge expands during interactions with children; educators also create environments to help children construct new knowledge and/or modify existing concepts (New, 1991). From this perspective, the social community is a source of information; thus, children's learning is enhanced through discussions (e.g., clarification of ideas), group work, and problem solving (e.g., social conflicts). The educator observes children's learning styles; looks for evidence of current knowledge; interacts with them to understand their thinking, reasoning, and judgment processes; and reflects on the most effective ways to enhance their learning by organizing materials and presenting provocations (i.e., challenges to thinking).

Constructivism is the basis of a number of programs such as High/Scope, Developmentally Appropriate Practice (DAP), Reggio Emilia, and the Project Approach (DeVries & Kohlberg, 1987, 1990; Edwards, Gandini, & Forman, 1993; Forman & Kaden, 1992; Kamii & DeVries, 1980; Katz & Chard, 2000). However, even with pre-service training, many educators appear to have difficulty implementing a constructivist curriculum, based on the poor ratings for the sub-scale on classroom activities on the Early Childhood Environment Rating Scale-Revised (ECERS-R; Cryer & Phillipsen, 1997; Japal, Tremblay, & Côté, 2005). Since curriculum is at the heart of the child's daily activities, it formed the basis for our larger investigation described below.

The Present Study

The present study is part of a larger investigation called the Canadian Child Care Curriculum Study (Howe et al., 2012). The purpose of this study was to assess the effectiveness of three approaches of delivering in-service professional development regarding constructivist curriculum during a fifteen-week program to ninety-four educators (all with pre-service education) in forty-four not-for-profit centres in three cities (Montreal, Halifax, and Winnipeg). Educators in Group 1 received the consultant model (five centres/site); Group 2 had the workshop method (five centres/site); and Group 3 participated in readings only (four to five centres/site). In the present study, we focused only on the consultant group. The consultant worked individually with each educator to give guidance and feedback on classroom activities and educator practices during weekly visits. In keeping with a constructivist philosophy, she employed a developmentally appropriate focus with hands-on activities. The consultant kept a detailed journal of her interactions with the educators, her reflections on the intervention program, and her experiences using the research project's training manual on constructivist curriculum. We present here an analysis of the consultant's (Mary) journal and her experiences with two educators (Carrie and Pat) from two different centres, who were part of the consultant group in one city; all names for the consultant, educators, and children are pseudonyms. Our goal was to identify the specific strategies and processes that Mary employed with the two educators to improve their understanding of a constructivist curriculum and implement change in their classrooms.

Method

Participants

The consultant was a 28-year-old Caucasian woman with a Bachelor of Human Ecology degree and eight years of experience in the early childhood field. Specifically, Mary had worked as a consultant on curriculum for a multiple-site day care centre, taught early childhood development at the local community college, mentored child care staff on inclusion, and had been active in the provincial professional association. Based on this background, Mary was hired to work as the consultant with the participating day care centres in one city.

The first educator, Carrie, was a Caucasian woman with nine years of experience working in child care (four years at one centre) and two afterschool care programs (two years each); she had been in her current job for nine months, working in a centre affiliated with a program for children with both normal and impaired hearing. She received her early childhood education degree at the local community college. Carrie's employer paid for the first year of the training program (1991), and she enrolled in the evening continuing education section. In Carrie's second year of training, she changed to the prior learning assessment section and eventually completed the program as a full-time student in 2001.

The second educator, Pat, was a Caucasian woman with approximately four years of experience working in seven child care centres; in five centres, she had been employed for only one to two months at a time. She had been in her current place of employment for three years; initially, she was hired as a substitute, then as a part-time educator before becoming a full-time employee. She received her preservice training in early childhood education at the local community college where she studied part-time over a number of years, graduating in 1993.

Consultant Group Intervention

In collaboration with the authors, three external curriculum experts developed a training manual (Jacobs, Vukelich, & Howe, 2007) on constructivist education based on the extant literature (e.g., Curtis & Carter, 2000; Fosnot, 2005). The manual included the following five pathways to constructivism::

1 *Values and beliefs:* information regarding how values and beliefs are the foundation of teaching philosophy and impact on practice, exploration of personal beliefs
2 *Constructivism and the early childhood curriculum:* constructivist views of children and education, principles of the constructivist classroom (organization, programming, communication with children)
3 *Observation:* key to understanding child learning and development, preparation and methods of observation (narrative, sampling), interpreting observations, applying observation to classroom practice
4 *Documentation:* examples (drawings, portfolios, documentation panels), strategies for classroom documentation, communication tool
5 *Reflection:* self-reflection and analysis regarding philosophy, classroom practice, interactions with children and parents.

Each pathway included activities and training tools to facilitate exploration of the pathways. The consultant visited each centre weekly (for at least four to five hours) and engaged in classroom observations and feedback sessions, modelled during ongoing classroom activities, and discussed issues in the manual, handouts, and articles. The content of these sessions varied according to the needs and issues raised by educators as well as issues as observed by Mary. She kept detailed journals about each visit with the educators, and these form the basis of the current case studies.

Methodological Approach

A case study approach was employed (Stake, 1995), and a grounded theory approach to handling the data was implemented (Strauss & Corbin, 1998). First, the authors randomly selected two of five journals that Mary kept about the educators in the consultant model group. Using the two journals allowed for data source triangulation (Stake, 1995), namely, to determine if Mary's journals could be interpreted in similar ways by both researchers. Then, the two authors independently read one of the two journals and identified behaviours indicative of mentoring. To meet the criteria for theory triangulation (Stake, 1995), the authors met to compare their lists and examples of each mentoring behaviour. Overlapping themes were identified, and following discussion, the extensive list of twenty-two sub-themes was reduced by aggregating them into a set of general themes. Following this step, the authors read both journals to verify that the general themes were appropriate for identifying the elements of mentoring. The authors then compared their examples and discussed problems of interpretation. After this discussion, the cross-referenced behaviours and examples were used in the following analysis. Member checking was conducted by Mary, who provided feedback on the analysis and interpretation of the findings.

Findings

Overview of the Two Educators

After completing our analysis of the journals, we developed some overall conclusions about the skills of the two educators. These general conclusions are based on the more detailed analysis that follows and are presented first so as to provide a context for the findings.

Carrie appeared to have more advanced teaching skills than Pat and was particularly interested in the topics of implementing a constructivist curriculum, learning to document children's development, designing curriculum webs, and engaging in more in-depth interactions with parents. Carrie had a longer and more stable history of employment in child care than Pat, although she (Carrie) was a more recent graduate of the early childhood education program. Pat appeared to be functioning at a more basic level as evidenced by the issues that were of concern to her, namely, a focus on classroom management (e.g., transitions) and arranging the physical setting to ensure a more orderly and peaceful environment. Interestingly, Mary skilfully adjusted her use of mentoring strategies and resources according to the individual needs, abilities, knowledge, and level of understanding of the two educators.

Key Elements of Mentoring

Our analysis illuminated five major elements that Mary employed consistently while mentoring during each visit: (1) observation, (2) participation, (3) discussion, (4) planning, and (5) assessing the educator's progress. Mary's journals contained numerous examples that illustrated the importance of these key elements in the mentoring process; in fact, we considered these to be the foundation from which Mary selectively employed more specific strategies that individualized the mentoring. Here we describe the five key elements and provide a short analysis of each.

OBSERVATION

We defined *observation* as the times when Mary specifically watched the classroom activities and recorded notes about the children's and educator's behaviours and the classroom environment. Each week, Mary observed extensively for a significant portion of the day. Initially, the observations were more general and focused on understanding the classroom dynamics, such as the nature and quality of the child interactions, room organization, daily schedule, routines (e.g., lunch, transitions), and educator behaviour (e.g., response to conflicts). Examples from Mary's first visit to Carrie's classroom included:

> Educator behaviour: In the short time I spent with C., I observed that she was able to use language to help the children problem solve many times.

Environment: I noticed several webs written on the windows with window writers. The windows are adult height with benches for the children to stand on so they too can enjoy the view. The space is aesthetically pleasing, with soft, soothing colors throughout. (Week 1)

Over the weeks, Mary's observations in Carrie's classroom became more focused. For example, in Week 5, during an experiment with steam (ice melting on a griddle), Mary observed that one child said, 'Water was made out of bubbles.' In the following week, Carrie introduced a water table activity to help clarify the child's understanding that soap makes bubbles. She provided different soaps, vegetable peelers to shave the soap, and toilet paper and water to make 'clean mud.'

When I arrived, C. was allowing the children to pick hidden items out of a basket. These items included different types of soap (Ivory and Dove bar soap, Palmolive dish soap, speciality soap for the bath, Ivory laundry soap, etc.). They discussed that soap makes bubbles, then made clean mud out of soap shavings, water and toilet paper. (Week 6)

Over the ensuing weeks, Mary's attention continued to focus on behaviours and issues that Carrie had identified as some of her goals during Week 1 (i.e., allowing the children greater opportunities for problem solving and learning to act as a support rather than telling children what to do). In Week 13, Mary observed Carrie's behaviour at the water table:

She had added bubble solution to the table and had put the bottle directly into the table so the children could manipulate it. I thought that this was a step for her as I had not observed her do this before.

These observations were the basis for discussion, assessment, and identification of issues for follow-up analysis, future planning, and scaffolding or guiding the educator to reflect on particular behaviours or incidents. In the last example, the observation also allowed Mary to assess Carrie's progress in meeting her own goals. We return to these more specific strategies below.

PARTICIPATION
Participation was defined as instances when Mary joined the ongoing classroom activity and interacted with the children, which happened weekly. For example, in Pat's classroom, Mary joined the children

during classroom free play and for lunch (Week 1) or outside play (Week 2). At times, participating with the children allowed Mary to model behaviour that she was encouraging Carrie and Pat to adopt. We return to modelling below, because it was specific to the needs of each educator.

DISCUSSIONS

Every week, Mary scheduled private (release) time away from the children to meet with the educator for at least an hour to talk about her observations, listen to the issues raised by the educator, provide and review resources, and discuss other issues pertinent to the intervention.

> The best part of the visit today for me was a discussion about transitions. I asked P. why she felt it was so 'crazy' when the children were getting ready for outside today. (Week 9)

In a second example, Mary wrote:

> P. and I met after circle and she showed me what she had recorded so far (in her journal) . . . P. talked to me about observing the children in the art area. She has seen the children create things and carry them with them around the room. She said she has not quite figured out why they are doing this or what it means, but is determined to do so. She discussed with me the internal struggle for her that the children are creating something even if they use a ton of glue and all of the scrap pieces of paper. (Week 10)

As these examples indicate, discussions allowed Pat to analyse and understand the children's behaviour and reflect on her responses to the students' actions. In the second example, Pat struggled because the children had created art work by gluing pieces of paper together in a way that she thought was a waste of materials.

Discussions were also devoted to the training manual and how the principles of constructivism and other pathways were pertinent to each classroom.

> During C.'s lunch break, I went over the principles of constructivism from the manual with her . . . She began to discuss that she would like to create a website for the parents to see the work the children have done in relation to science. She is the staff person responsible for science (Week 4). [After analysing C's documentation panel], we ended up in a discussion about

open-ended questions and constructivism. I was saying that children needed the opportunity to explore in order to construct their knowledge. This could be done with open-ended materials and open-ended questions. (Week 14)

In sum, discussions had a number of purposes such as helping the educators to understand their own behaviour and that of the children, linking the information in the training manual and readings to an analysis of the impact of the classroom environment, and also as providing a context for planning of the program.

PLANNING

During the discussion sessions, Mary and the educators engaged in various aspects of planning regarding their next course of action. Planning might be as simple as arranging meeting times (Pat: Week 1) or agreeing on an issue to discuss in the following week ('We did come up with a plan to begin a documentation panel around the mixing and pouring the children are doing'; Carrie: Week 7). In a very focused and individualized way, Mary used her observations and discussions as the basis for planning and goal setting with each educator. Interestingly, by returning to the issues identified over the course of the intervention program, Mary ensured continuity in the discussions. One recurrent theme for Carrie was how to link her planning to her observations of the children's behaviour and then how to construct a documentation panel based on her observations. Here is an example of Mary's observation of an experiment of ice melting on a griddle (Week 5) and her plan to use it in a discussion with Carrie:

Cally (a child) repeatedly told C. that the ice was made of bubbles and bubbles were made of soap. At one time C. said 'the ice which is made out of . . . ' and Cally answered, 'bubbles!' From across the room, Sharon (a child) said 'water!' Sharon seemed annoyed that Cally didn't 'get it.' It was obvious that the concept of ice to water to steam, although being shown to Cally, was not within her schema yet. I would like to speak to C. about this in more detail.

Next, in Week 6, Mary observed the activity with soap and clean mud described above (section on Observation). Later that morning, Carrie added new equipment to the water table such as spoons, whisks, and funnels with windmills (see Figure 9.1). Embedded in the ensuing

Figure 9.1. Water table.

discussion was Carrie's desire to create a documentation panel and to record some of the children's language, as Mary had done during her observations.

During Week 7, Mary brought Carrie a reading on documentation panels, which became the basis of a thoughtful analysis on the use of questions when interacting with children. Week 9 included an activity on planting in which the children were interested in mixing the dirt (see Figure 9.2), but Carrie took over the planting because one child left some roots uncovered. Mary identified this as a lost opportunity to conduct an experiment (i.e., What happens if some of the roots are left exposed?) and wrote, 'I would like to discuss this at our next meeting.'

In Week 10, Mary said,

> Next week we are going to go over her [Carrie's] observations of the children to focus on what is driving the interest and maybe begin a panel.

During Week 13, Carrie added sponges to the water table, and the children stuck them into the funnels to plug them up to recreate a prior

Figure 9.2. Planting.

incident with a plugged toilet at the day care. During their weekly discussion, Carrie said that she would inform Mary where she might take
the activity of the plugged funnel/toilet. Here there is evidence that
Carrie was taking responsibility for identifying critical issues to consider and address in the following weeks. Eventually, Carrie achieved
her goal and produced two documentation panels, including one on
the sensory table (Week 14; see Figures 9.3 and 9.4). As is evident from
this analysis, Mary also planned when to introduce pertinent resources,
such as the training manual and readings. We return to this strategy
below.

Assessing the Educator's Progress

The final key element that Mary employed weekly was assessing the
educator's progress (e.g., achieving goals, reflecting on practice):

> I can see that P. is focusing on specific tasks she would like to accomplish
> for the program . . . Every week, I see her reflecting on her practice and the

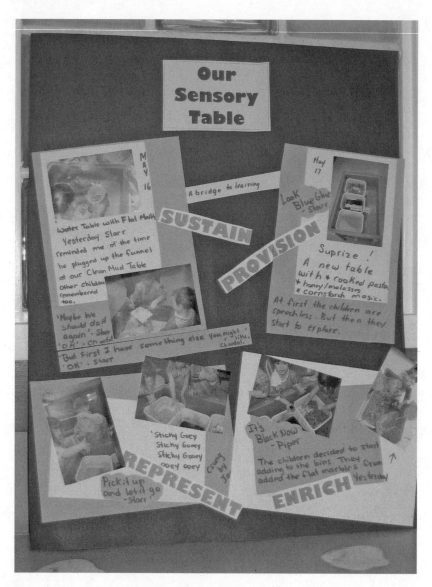

Figure 9.3. Carrie's documentation panel.

Figure 9.4. Carrie's documentation panel.

program itself, and it is amazing to watch the growth that occurs due to her thoughtfulness. (Week 10)

Pat was concerned about the length of time allowed for free play. Here Mary notes Pat's reflections about the issue and her progress in changing the schedule:

> P. then brought up that she is trying to give the children more time for free play because when she thought about it, the children were never really in the room for very much of the day. For example, in the morning, they go to the gym, go outside, and then have lunch . . . So they have been staying inside in the morning for free play in the room and going outside a bit later in the afternoon so that the children have time for free play. (Week 6)

Pat's concerns also prompted a subsequent discussion of the issue with her co-educators:

P. shared with the other staff that if there is a time of day that seems over-whelming or stressful that if they sat back and observed what was hap-pening during and prior to this time, they could figure out what is really happening and change it. It is not happening because the children are crazy at this time, it is because something should be changed. (Week 10)

As a result of this discussion, the educators reduced the number of af-ternoon transitions between naptime and outdoor play, and almost im-mediately the children became calmer and more focused.

Mary also took pictures of the children participating in various class-room activities to document the changes that she wrote about in the journal. For example, as an aid to reinforce her analysis of Carrie's progress in planning the sensory activities at the water table (e.g., clean mud, bubbles), she embedded many pictures of the activities into her journal. She also used the pictures during discussions with Carrie.

Individualizing Mentoring Strategies: Meeting the Needs of Each Educator

Using the five main elements as a springboard for change, Mary also employed five other strategies in varying degrees or in context-specific ways depending on the needs of the educator and children. First, we discuss teaching strategies, which include a number of specific meth-ods of coaching. Two teaching strategies (asking probing questions and modelling) were significant enough to warrant separate analysis. Fi-nally, we address resources and motivational behaviour.

TEACHING STRATEGIES

Mary employed a range of direct instruction strategies such as provid-ing examples, explanations, information, suggestions, or instruction in observation rubrics. The purpose of these strategies was to help both educators develop their skills in areas such as recording and document-ing children's behaviour, using the camera and printer, encouraging re-flection, and using explanation and knowledge to make links between aspects of development and children's behaviour.

For example, in helping Carrie create a documentation panel, Mary showed Carrie her own observation notes and demonstrated how the use of key words allowed her to recall the observation in fuller detail at a later time (Week 6). The following week, Carrie and Mary dis-cussed a reading on documentation panels, and when Carrie asked for examples, Mary encouraged her to 'use the points in the article to decide how to display the information' on the panel. Carrie then asked if she was documenting the children's interactions properly. Mary offered:

a couple of tips on what she could include in her written statements. I noted how she is interpreting the play during her documentation. She decided that she would include the details of what is happening and then add the interpretations later, perhaps using a different-coloured pen so she could decipher later where to go from here. I encouraged her to jot down information while the play was occurring and to use her journal time later for adding to what she had. (Week 6)

By Week 8, Mary noted Carrie's progress in recording the children's behaviour and adding more detail afterwards about the questions she had asked the children during the morning's activities and their responses. However, Mary believes that Carrie did not understand the concept of representation (i.e., having the children record their learning through drawing):

We continued to talk about her recording and we talked about how to extend further what the children wanted to know about as well as how to allow the children to represent their learning. It was clear that C. was not understanding about what I meant by *representation,* so I left it and said I would bring more information next time. (Week 8)

The following week (9), Mary brought a reading on representation, but it was not until Week 11 that Carrie integrated the concept into her planning (i.e., having children draw pictures of planting activities; see Figure 9.5).

Mary and Carrie also collaborated on the construction of the first documentation panel on planting; Mary provided guidance but also some direct instruction:

We printed pictures we wanted to use and began our documentation panel as promised last week . . . C. asked many questions when we got to describing the photos and learning that had been taking place for the children during that time. For example, she asked, 'What should I say about this photo?' I would give an example of what she could write, and she would put it in her own words on paper. (Week 9)

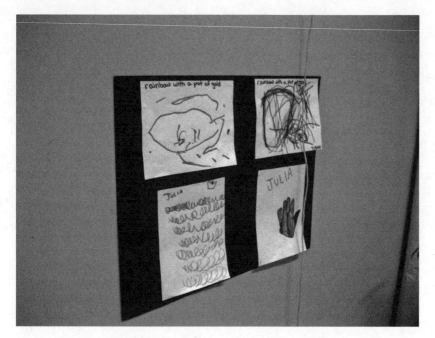

Figure 9.5. Representing learning.

During Week 10, Mary and Carrie analysed the elements of the documentation panel using a checklist from one of the readings, and Carrie decided to use more direct quotes from the children in her next panel. During the analysis, Carrie asked Mary for her opinion three times. Mary reflected in her journal that perhaps she (Mary) was too 'educator directed' in her approach, but that her answers were always redirected back to Carrie, 'What do *you* think?' Thus, Mary monitored her own teaching strategies and was sensitive to being a guide rather than 'the expert.'

PROBING QUESTIONS

Mary was skilled at asking probing questions that encouraged the educators to think at a deeper level and to analyse the children's behaviour and the effect of the environment on the children: e.g., 'Why do you think that is happening?' At one point, the children were poking at some large pieces of Styrofoam, and Mary provoked Pat to analyse their behaviour by asking, 'What do you think this is all about?' (Week 5). Mary also helped Pat analyse her own behaviour with the children ('I asked her what she was doing while this happened': Week 11). Also, Mary asked Pat a probing question to address in her own journal to stimulate further thinking and action. After Pat wrote in her journal about the children's interest in monsters, Mary asked why the children were fascinated with monsters and then:

> 'How can you allow the children to represent their play?' I have a concern that although she is observing, reflecting and recording, she is not plan- ning activities. I think that she will get there eventually, and I just have to be patient, but I don't want to miss the opportunity either. (Week 8)

Clearly, the use of probing questions acted as provocations to stimu- late the educator's reflection of her own behaviour. Interestingly, both educators began to integrate the use of open-ended, probing questions into their own work with the children. By Week 14, Carrie asked a child, 'What else could you do?' to solve a problem independently rather than taking over the task herself (of replacing the cap on a marker).

MODELLING

Modelling is considered a key coaching strategy (Blank & Kershaw, 2009). In fact, when Mary interacted with the children, she often mod- elled appropriate behaviours by demonstrating them during ongoing activities, so the educators could directly observe her actions and lan- guage. This modelling encouraged the educators to integrate these be- haviours into their own teaching, which fostered a more constructivist approach. During Week 2, Mary joined a painting activity in Carrie's classroom and modelled questions to help children make predictions about and describe the outcome of their actions. One child wondered what would happen if she mixed purple and yellow, and Mary re- sponded, 'I don't know, what do you think will happen?' After mix- ing the colours, the child responded, 'Orange! I made orange with the paint!' Later the child dictated a description of her painting for Mary to record. Mary wrote in her journal:

> I wrote this on the bottom of the picture, along with her name, hoping this would be noticed by the staff and copied in future.

Mary was not passive in hoping that Carrie would notice this strategy but also actively ensured that she raised it during her weekly discussion with Carrie.

Another example of modelling occurred when Carrie discussed the aggressiveness of a child with a hearing impairment, particularly when his aide was absent. Although another staff member was present at these times, the change upset the child. Mary told Carrie she also observed this behaviour, especially during transition times. During the next transition, when the children were coming inside after time in the playground, Mary modelled appropriate behaviour:

> I tried to model what I thought would be appropriate for this child to get through transitions. I stayed close to him and signed as best as I could what he needed to do next. He was undressed and ready quickly, without lashing out at any of the children. I hope this was noticed by the other staff. (Week 11)

These examples demonstrate Mary's use of modelling to illustrate the power of changing one's behaviour to achieve a positive child outcome. Thus, modelling appropriate practices highlights an effective strategy for change.

RESOURCES

Mary was given a number of resources by the authors for implementing the intervention program, namely, the training manual, readings, and a digital camera and printer for each educator to document children's activities. Mary made extensive weekly use of these resources to support and guide Carrie's developing knowledge and understanding of specific issues (i.e., curriculum webs, open-ended materials, and open-ended questions). For example, in Week 5, to reinforce Carrie's desire to learn more about documentation and reflection, they analysed pertinent sections in the training manual. In Week 6, Carrie and Mary discussed recording and writing 'important things down with key words to help recall later' to assist her in creating a documentation panel. In Week 7, Mary provided a reading on documentation and asked skilful probing questions to further Carrie's understanding (Week 9). Carrie eventually produced a second documentation panel on the sensory table activities and used the digital camera to take pictures to illustrate the children's learning; she also incorporated four important concepts (sustain, provision, represent, and enrich) based on one of the readings (Curtis & Carter, 2002).

In contrast, Mary used somewhat fewer resources with Pat, although she was equally selective in conveying appropriate information. Given Pat's focus on the classroom environment, during one discussion Pat expressed a belief that she should be the person in the classroom to provide 'interesting equipment for the children' (Week 6). Mary then directed Pat to the training manual where this issue was covered, 'As I [Mary] thought it was interesting that she had come to that conclusion on her own, without any provocation from me.' Only as the intervention program was ending did Mary and Pat begin to focus on documentation and webbing, at which point Mary introduced relevant readings. Clearly, Mary had a fine sense about how to pace the intervention. She knew when and how to introduce information relevant to constructivist curriculum and when to introduce and focus on specific issues. In Pat's case, Mary addressed issues concerned with classroom organization raised by Pat before discussing curriculum issues.

MOTIVATIONAL BEHAVIOUR

The purpose of motivational behaviour (e.g., praise, positive responses to educator's reflection, discussion of behaviour) was to assist the educators in continuing with the project and to assess their own professional growth. Mary had a clear understanding that the use of judicious and specific praise could motivate the educators in the process of professional growth and changing their behaviour. For example, during a discussion about asking skilful questions, Mary wrote that she had observed Carrie using more skilful questions during her interactions with the children (Week 7). In addition, Mary gave Pat a guide for recording observations in her journal, because 'she was such a reflective person, she may find this helpful to her.' Over the next week, Pat used the observation guide and added to previous observations about how to enrich and sustain play; Mary told Pat, 'Look at all of the stuff you have done.' There were many other examples of motivational praise and behaviour in Mary's journal. Interestingly, the weekly continuity of the intervention program was sustaining in itself for the educators:

> She [Carrie] mentioned that she is glad that I am coming every week because it keeps her motivated and on track to continue documenting the children's play. (Week 7)

Ripple Effects

Mary took great delight in noting what she called 'ripple effects' in her journal, which were observations of changes in the two centres that were influenced by her work with Carrie and Pat. For example, Pat told Mary (Week 10) that now the staff was contributing jointly to the program rather than relying on one educator. In addition, she discussed ways to change the day care program by reducing the number of transitions with her colleagues so as to decrease stressful times in the day (see section on Assessing Progress). Later, Mary observed that another staff member at Pat's centre introduced an art activity with more open-ended materials than had been used previously (Week 13). Similar ripple effects were apparent in Carrie's centre, too: Another staff member brought in an activity on worms for the children to explore (Week 8). A space centre was set up, and the educator provided informational books and paper for the children to create a mural to represent their learning (Week 11). Finally, another educator created a documentation panel on baby chicks (Week 15; see Figure 9.6). Evidently, Mary's mentoring of Carrie and Pat was noticed by the other educators; for example, Carrie asked for information on observation to share with her colleagues so they would have a better understanding of the purpose of observing children (Week 8). It was clear that Pat and Carrie were establishing a community of learners in their centres (Blank & Kershaw, 2009), which served to continue the process of professional development after the end of the intervention program. One of Carrie's goals was to co-facilitate a workshop with Mary for the other educators in her centre on the principles of constructivist curriculum, journal guides, webbing, observation, and documentation. The workshop was given after the intervention program was completed.

As Mary told Pat in Week 2, 'We would work together as a team of learners.' In fact, this occurred in both centres over time. In the words of Ryan and Hornbeck (2004), Mary was an outstanding 'agent of change.'

In sum, the specific strategies of mentoring described in the literature were evident in our analysis of the two case studies (Blank & Kershaw, 2009; Kershaw et al., 2006; Whitebrook & Bellm, 1996). Our work makes an important contribution to the literature in its detailed description and analysis of the process of implementing mentoring strategies. Although we have employed a case study approach to understanding the processes involved in mentoring, our work can easily be generalized to other contexts. The five key elements that we identified in the case

Figure 9.6. Ripple effects.

studies (i.e., observation, participation, discussion, planning, and assessment) form the foundation of implementing a mentoring program and complement the existing literature. These key elements are flexible and can easily be adapted to meet the needs of particular contexts and situations, but in themselves they may not be sufficient for effective mentoring. Our case studies demonstrate that mentoring must be individualized to meet the needs of the people involved in the mentoring process. The five individualized mentoring strategies (i.e., teaching strategies, probing questions, modelling, use of resources, and motivational behaviour) can be employed in a variety of contexts and in different ways. Thus, our findings have direct relevance and implications for professional development that focuses on the use of mentoring. Certainly, careful planning, appropriate use of available resources, insightful mentors, and willing participants will help to contribute to its success. However, careful reflection about the key processes identified in our case studies should highlight effective means to generalize and adapt this information to a wide variety of contexts.

Conclusion

We believe that Mary's educational background, early childhood experience, and skilful use of the mentoring strategies significantly and positively encouraged Carrie's and Pat's professional development. In addition, Mary's personality was well suited to the role of mentor, because she was insightful, reflective, and analytical (Whitebrook & Bellm, 1996). Moreover, she demonstrated a deep understanding of child development and its links with adult behaviour, the physical environment, the classroom climate, and children's behaviour. These are all characteristics that Blank and Kershaw (2009) identified as critical for mentors. Furthermore, Mary quickly understood the needs of each educator and was able to provide the appropriate guidance in a sensitive, responsive, and warm manner by listening carefully, engaging in open discussions, analysing behaviours, and providing resources. In this way, the educators came to respect and trust her judgment; as Blank and Kershaw (2009) state, trust is the basis for establishing 'constructive and supportive one-on-one relationships' (p. 89). Mary also had a sense of humour, was flexible, and confident about her own skills.

Finally, Mary was eager to learn along with the educators and children as is evident in her reflection about what it meant to mentor. This insight indicates how Mary was also co-constructing her understanding of the mentoring process along with the educators:

> P. made a comment in passing to me about her practice. She said, 'I want to be more like you, you know, relaxed.' This took me by surprise as I wasn't expecting to be used as an example. Later as I thought about it more, I realized that this is what a mentor does, inspires people to become something they strive to be without the mentor *purposely* showing how or what to do. Yes, you are modelling behaviour, however, modelling is conscious and unconscious on the part of the mentor. The *educator* is the person who chooses what qualities to model after, not the mentor. (Week 4)

Acknowledgments

We thank the Social Development Partnerships Program, Human Development Resources Canada for funding this project. We also thank the project coordinator, Goranka Vukelich, the research assistants, consultants, and the educators and families who participated in the project, and Allyson Funamoto for editorial assistance.

References

Ackerman, D.J. (2004). States' efforts in improving the qualifications of early care and education teachers. *Educational Policy, 18,* 311–337.

Ackerman, D.J. (2006). The costs of being a child care teacher: Revisiting the problem of low wages. *Educational Policy, 20,* 85–112.

Assel, M.A., Landry, S.H., Swank, P.R., & Gunnewig, S. (2007). An evaluation of curriculum, setting, and mentoring on the performance of children enrolled in pre-kindergarten. *Reading and Writing, 20,* 463–494.

Blank, M.A., & Kershaw, C.A. (2009). *Mentoring as collaboration.* Thousand Oaks, CA: Corwin.

Blank, M.A., Kershaw, C.A., Russell, R., & Wright, D. (2006). *The impact of systemic induction on teacher retention and student achievement: Lessons learned from highly effective mentor-protégé pairs in schools with high implementing mentor teams in one metropolitan district.* Paper presented at the Annual Convention of the American Educational Research Association, 7–11 April, San Francisco, CA.

Borko, H. (2004). Professional development and teacher learning: Mapping the terrain. *Educational Researcher, 33,* 3–15.

Branscombe, N.A., Castle, K., Dorsey, A.G., Surbeck, E., & Taylor, J.B. (2003). *Early childhood curriculum: A constructivist perspective.* Boston, MA: Houghton Mifflin.

Burchinal, M.R., Cryer, D., Clifford, R.M., & Howes, C. (2002). Caregiver training and classroom quality in child care centers. *Applied Developmental Science, 6,* 2–11.

Buysse, V., Winton, P.J., & Rous, B. (2009). Reaching consensus on a definition of professional development for the early childhood field. *Topics in Early Childhood Special Education, 28,* 235–243.

Cassidy, D.J., Buell, M.J., Pugh-Hoese, S., & Russell, S. (1995). The effect of education on child care teachers' beliefs and classroom quality: Year one evaluation of the TEACH early childhood associate degree scholarship program. *Early Childhood Research Quarterly, 10,* 171–183.

Catapano, S. (2005). Teacher professional development through children's project work. *Early Childhood Education Journal, 32,* 261–267.

Clifford, E.F. (1999). Mentors and protégés: Establishing systems of assisted performance in preservice teacher education. *Early Child Development and Care, 156,* 35–52.

Cryer, D., & Phillipsen, L. (1997). Quality details: A close-up look at child care program strengths and weaknesses. *Young Children, 52*, 51–64.

Curtis, D., & Carter, M. (2000). *The art of awareness: How observation can transform your teaching.* St Paul, MN: Redleaf.

Curtis, D., & Carter, M. (2002). *Reflecting children's lives: A handbook for planning child-centered curriculum.* St Paul, MN: Redleaf.

DeVries, R., & Kohlberg, L. (1987). *Programs of early education: The constructivist view.* New York: Longman.

DeVries, R., & Kohlberg, L. (1990). *Constructivist early education: Overview and comparison with other programs.* Washington, DC: National Association for the Education of Young Children.

Duckworth, E. (1987). *'The having of wonderful ideas' and other essays on teaching and learning.* New York: Teachers College Press.

Edwards, C., Gandini, L., & Forman, G. (1993). *The hundred languages of children: The Reggio Emilia approach to early childhood education.* Norwood, NJ: Ablex.

Epstein, A.S. (1993). *Training for quality: Improving early childhood programs through systematic inservice training.* Ypsilanti, MI: High/Scope Press.

Fantuzzo, J., Childs, S., Hampton, V., Ginsburg-Block, M., Coolahan, K.C., & Debnam, D. (1997). Enhancing the quality of early childhood education: A follow-up evaluation of an experiential, collaborative training model for Head Start. *Early Childhood Research Quarterly, 12*, 425–437.

Forman, G., & Kaden, M. (1992). Research on science education for young children. In C. Seefeldt (Ed.), *The early childhood curriculum: A review of current research* (pp. 175–192). New York: Teachers College Press.

Fosnot, C.T. (Ed.). (2005). *Constructivism: Theory, perspectives and practice* (2nd ed.). New York: Teachers College Press.

Fuligni, A.S., Howes, C., Lara-Cinisomo, S., & Karoly, L. (2009). Diverse pathways in early childhood professional development: An exploration of early educators in public preschools, private preschools, and family child care homes. *Early Education and Development, 20*, 507–526.

Helterbran, V.R., & Fennimore, B.S. (2004). Collaborative early childhood professional development: Building from a base of teacher investigation. *Early Childhood Education Journal, 31*, 267–271.

Horm-Wingerd, D.M., Caruso, D.A., Gomes-Atwood, S., & Golas, J. (1997). Head Start teaching center: Evaluation of a new approach to head start staff development. *Early Childhood Research Quarterly, 12*, 407–424.

Howe, N., Jacobs, E., Vukelich, G., & Recchia, H. (2012). In-service professional development and constructivist curriculum: Effects on quality of child care, teacher beliefs and interactions. *Alberta Journal of Educational Research, 57*, 353–378.

Jacobs, E., Vukelich, G., & Howe, N. (2007). *Pathways to constructivism: An educator's guide.* Ottawa: Human Resources Development Canada.

Japal, E., Tremblay, R., & Côté, S. (2005). *Quality counts! Assessing the quality of day care services based on the Quebec longitudinal study of child development.* Montreal: Institute for Research on Public Policy.

Kamii, C., & DeVries, R. (1980). *Group games in early education: Implications of Piaget's theory.* Washington, DC: National Association for the Education of Young Children.

Katz, L., & Chard, S. (2000). *Engaging children's minds: The project approach.* Stamford, CT: Ablex.

Kershaw, C.A., Blank, M.A., Benner, S., Russell, R., Wright, D., Jackson, S., et al. (2006). *Building capacity in urban schools through teacher leadership: The Urban Specialist Certificate Program.* Paper presented at the Annual Convention of the American Educational Research Association, April, San Francisco, CA.

New, R.S. (1991). *Bello, buono, bravo: Italian early childhood.* New York: Guilford.

Perkins, D. (1999). The many faces of constructivism. *Educational Leadership, 57*, 6–11.

Ryan, S., & Hornbeck, A. (2004). Mentoring for quality improvement: A case study of a mentor teacher in the reform process. *Journal of Research in Childhood Education, 19*, 79–96.

Stake, R. (1995). *The art of case research.* Thousand Oaks, CA: Sage.

Strauss, A., & Corbin, J. (1998). *Basics of qualitative research: Techniques and procedures for developing grounded theory.* 2nd ed. Thousand Oaks, CA: Sage.

Whitebrook, M., & Bellm, D. (1996). Mentoring and early childhood teachers and providers: Building upon and extending tradition. *Young Children, 52*, 59–64.

Part II Commentary: Reflections on Children, Curriculum, and Teachers

ALAN PENCE

The Early Years

Having established with the editors that a personal reflection on the above three components of early childhood education and care (ECEC) would be suitable for this contribution to the book, I will situate myself for the reader.

My work in ECEC began over forty years ago, in 1971. I was hired as part of a soon-to-be-opened early childhood centre located on a university campus and serving the children of university students. Eight of us were hired, five women and three men (I have not seen such ratios since that time). My memory is that only two or three of those hired had worked in early childhood, and perhaps only one had ECEC training credentials. The rest of us had degrees from various disciplines: history, political science, sociology, education, and more. We were united not by our ECEC backgrounds but by our membership in the '60s generation.' For that generation, education was seen by many as a radical activity – and our ECEC staff fit that description.

For myself, as one of the few with an education degree, I was attracted to the field in large part due to the radical and reformist thinking that could be found there and the possibilities of education as a site to initiate reform. Jonathan Kozol (1967), Neil Postman (1969), John Holt (1964), A.S. Neill (1962), to name a few, seemed to be pushing back the boundaries of 'established' educational practice. Initially, in 1970, I went into high school teaching, working for a year in a new experimental, inner city high school that soon attracted national attention in the United States (see John Adams High School, *Newsweek*). While the experience was stimulating, that year convinced me that if I was to have a significant impact on children's lives, I must begin much earlier.

Although the university student union had employed a director (of similar age and background), we saw ourselves as an educational 'co-operative' – planning and decision making were shared, and the parent board took part in major decisions. Whenever we felt power was becoming too centralized, challenges were forthcoming. The centre accepted children from 6 months to 6 years of age. Initially, there were discussions regarding the degree to which the ages should be separated. Most, for reasons of health concerns, felt the infants should have their own room. Over time, rough age groupings were formed, and the remaining children were separated into an additional two rooms. There were some 'routines,' primarily around snacks and meals, but for the most part, the schedules were fairly flexible with a desire to have one of the three groups away or outside at any given play/activity period. The goal was to reduce the general volume of noise and activity as all three rooms were immediately adjacent to each other and there was only one main entrance to the outside play area and into the centre itself.

The flexible nature of the program meant that staff meetings (both within and across the groups) were a regular feature of our week. For the most part, the programs were relatively 'fluid.' I worked primarily with the 3-year-olds – my curriculum was largely determined by what would be exciting to do today, and how might that activity lead into others? Berry picking up on the surrounding hills led to the adventure of getting to and through the bushes, returning with pails of berries (and a berry trail back to the slope), rolling out the dough for pies, baking them, and inviting the others in for afternoon snacks; tobogganing down grass slopes in cardboard boxes required days of getting the racers designed, prepared, and painted in advance of the event itself; hanging out in the gym between university classes evidenced changes in skills over the weeks. My kids amazed me – they were my mates in adventure, each with certain idiosyncrasies, but no more than most adults I knew.

The director felt we could do with more ECEC education and contacted an 'expert' from one of the local colleges to observe and provide feedback. Fortunately, she felt 'different' wasn't so bad, but for the first time, I began to understand that there were 'prescriptions' and routines for this work and that not all (actually very few!) programs worked or looked like ours, being forever in a process of reinvention.

Our pay was low, minimum wage, but a side benefit was that we could take university classes for free. I entered a Master's program and began to read the child development literature. It was incredibly off-putting as the micro-facets of those children's development bore little resemblance to the flesh and bone, capable and challenging, context-situated children that I knew. Finally, in 1974, I found a psychologist I could read and appreciate: Urie Bronfenbrenner (1974) was proposing in *Child Development* an 'ecology of childhood' and with that ecology the context (of parents, siblings, friends, neighbourhoods), which was central to my understanding of 'my kids,' found a place in an otherwise largely unsatisfying literature.

Unlike most of my fellow staff, I continued in early childhood work after leaving the university centre. I was hired (as one of the few people with both high school and, now, early childhood credentials) to create a high school–based, combination ECEC training and neighbourhood service program – I taught the high school students, directed the program, and took the closing shift in the ECEC program. By this time, I was fully engaged with the ECEC literature and understood its proclivity towards specific, fairly repetitive program models. Those models reflected, in part, a marketplace approach to ECEC services, with 'brand names' such as Montessori, Waldorf, and others appealing to certain parts of the 'market,' with a large 'grey zone' of generic child care and early childhood care, education, and development programs not attached to any specific approach but diverging in their claims to provide 'pre-school' as opposed to 'child care.' By the early 1970s, Head Start programs were also major figures in ECEC, but with funding restricted to certain income groups. Within Head Start, different approaches to curriculum and pedagogy were being developed resulting in various major, national evaluations being undertaken. The field in North America at that time, and continuing to the present, was a hodge-podge of approaches and possibilities.

By the early to mid-1970s, in most states and provinces, training for employment in the ECEC sector was focused within what were often termed junior colleges or community colleges, which offered a variety of short-term (six-week to two-year) vocational training programs, and they often offered two years of university transfer courses in a separate stream. ECEC was typically within the vocational stream and had little if any transferability to four-year university institutions. Within the one- and two-year training colleges for ECEC, a fairly standard list of courses emerged that students were required to take in order to be qualified to work with pre-school-aged children (a variety of employment terms were used then, as now: child care worker, pre-school teacher, early childhood educator, and others). These courses typically fell within certain strands: child development theories, program design and implementation, communications, and practica. Additional courses and strands might address special needs children, administration, working with parents, etc.

Despite considerable growth in the numbers of children receiving ECEC services and in the number of ECEC programs across North America, the core 'types' of ECEC available and the basic approaches taken to ECEC curriculum and programming were largely in place by the mid- to late 1970s. A key to the 'shape' ECEC took was the limited amount of training required to be a practitioner (typically less than one year, and rarely more than two). Those time constraints in training limited the scope and depth of what could be addressed to qualify individuals as early childhood educators (ECEs) and prescriptive approaches continued as the mainstay of ECEC, rarely opening up to alternative and innovative 'other' approaches. Early childhood care and education as part of a revolutionary social reform movement was rapidly disappearing in the rear-view mirror.

Throughout the mid- to late 1970s, I taught in various programs as a college instructor, a rural field trainer, and a Head Start instructor. All three focused on various forms of 'best practice,' seeking to move from vocational and para-professional status to the ranks of 'professional' largely through linking child developmental theories with practice. To a certain degree, these efforts to support a transition from para- to full-professional had a counter-effect as the number of years of training required did not progress towards a professional Bachelor's degree, and the decision-making power to determine what constituted 'best practice' was increasingly vested outside the individual practitioner in a plethora of state and provincial rules and regulations and in finely diced competency documents developed by professional associations and educational institutions. Increasingly, effective ECEC services were defined in technical terms, leaving less and less space for creativity, innovation, and in my eyes, truly 'professional' and individually responsible work – a direction increasingly found in parts of Europe. By the end of the 1970s, the type of creative, alternative care that I and my fellow overeducated, academically diverse, and free-thinking child care workers were able to provide in the early 1970s was, legislatively, not possible as our 'band of reformers' did not have what was judged to be the appropriate training nor had our micro-competencies been verified.

From Field to Academy – to Field

My 1970s decade in the field culminated with combined work as an ECEC program director and completion of a doctoral program, and a position as faculty member at a university. My doctoral dissertation focused on ECEC in nineteenth-century North America, revealing other approaches to curriculum and understandings of children – two of the earliest ones being also inspired by social reform movements. The Infant Schools (circa 1816), devised by social reformer and future utopian innovator Robert Owen, were understood by him, as their names suggests, as 'Institutions for the Formation of Character' through which his *New View of Society* could be realized. Friedrich Froebel (1882), founder of the kindergarten, was also a visionary, seeing the kindergarten as a progressive tool for the reformation of German society at the time.

A close examination of programs and curriculum described by individuals like Owen and Froebel in Europe, as well as Elizabeth Peabody and Mary Mann (1863), Susan Blow (1894), and others in the United States and Canada reveals a level of sophistication seldom attained by education and training programs in 1970s North America. Those who envision ECEC as steadily progressing from less developed understandings to ever higher levels will be disappointed by the historical record. The history is more one of peaks (associated with a few creative leaders) and valleys, with long-running plateaus. For the most part, ECEC in North America has experienced such a long plateau for the past thirty to forty years due in large part to its lack of socio-political support and its concomitant failure to progress from a technically and prescriptively focused, vocational training activity of limited duration to degree and post-degree levels that could open up to individual, professional possibilities.

During the 1980s, my academic focus was primarily on research related to questions of quality care and policy development. For the first time, I had funds to operationalize Bronfenbrenner's ecological approach in undertaking early childhood research, and colleagues and I also addressed national policy issues through mounting a major national survey of early childhood (Lero et al., 1992). However, in 1989 I was provided with an opportunity to re-engage in questions of curriculum, and those engagements continue to the present.

The opportunity came in the form of a call from the Meadow Lake Tribal Council (MLTC) in northern Saskatchewan. The Council wished to submit a proposal to the federal government's Child Care Initiatives Fund (CCIF) to cooperatively develop an education and training program that would support the development of on-reserve services for their nine communities. The history of that initiative, and how it led to the creation of many other partnerships and the First Nations Partnerships Program (FNPP) at the University of Victoria, has been well documented over the years (see www.fnpp.org). From a more personal perspective, the initiative brought me back into closer contact with children, curriculum, and teachers – *and* with communities.

The desire of the Council that their community members would receive education that prepared them to work effectively both on- and off-reserve guided the development of the program suggesting a bi- or multi-cultural model. The approach envisioned an open framework for each of the courses that would not only allow, but require, that both Western *and* community perspectives were included in the educational process as equally important sources of knowledge. Students, hearing diverse perspectives, would then be in a position to engage with both, and through adding in their own experiences 'generate' new knowledge and new perspectives that could be tried out, evaluated, shared, and refined. At the time, such an egalitarian, co-constructed, co-instructed, and contextualized approach had not, to the best of my knowledge, been advocated or implemented by major universities internationally. The tenets of the approach challenged the Western, modernist assumptions of academia – that there is one 'best way,' one 'truth,' and that it is the role of the academy to identify that 'best' and teach it to students. Such a determinist orientation stood in contrast to the indeterminacy of the generative activity approach. The latter approach was potentially controversial, but when the program yielded student completion rates two to four times higher than established programs with Canadian First Nations students (over 80% completion of the first year), the basis for moving forward was in place.

Strong program engagement and high completion rates continued as the program progressed, but what was less immediately apparent were changes that were taking place in the communities themselves through the generative processes. At the conclusion of the first two-year delivery, the Council hired an Elder from outside their communities but who knew the Council and the communities well. In her impact evaluation, she acknowledged the high student engagement and completion rates, but indicated that what she felt was much more important were changes in the communities themselves, particularly in regards to the enhanced involvement of Elders in virtually all facets of community life and in Council governance. From that point on, seeing the potential for curricular processes to reach beyond children and teachers and to move beyond the micro-systems of education and programming to impact the broader community, one constant in my work has been to extend the reach of curricular activities.

That work continues to embrace engagement with Indigenous communities internationally, but through a program called the Early Childhood Development Virtual University (ECDVU, see www.ecdvu.org) it has sought to extend the generative principles to broader country-level development through targeted capacity building with senior sector leaders in African countries. Many of the curricular and philosophical aspects of the ECDVU grew out of the FNPP and the generative approach. The ECDVU believes that there are many, relevant knowledges in any socio-cultural context and that these diverse perspectives must be supported to come forward in order to achieve meaningful and effective social, health, and educational outcomes.

A very useful theoretical and philosophical adjunct to the culture and community work noted above has been engagement with postmodern, post-structural, and various critical perspectives regarding children, curriculum, and teachers. That story, commencing in the early 1990s and, for me, growing out of the MLTC and FNPP work, is described in the Pacini-Ketchabaw and Pence chapter in this part of the book. Such critical perspectives, sharing some similarities with the period of critical thought and action that took place in the 1960s, emerge in a number of the chapters contained in this volume and in particular those included in this part. Such critical perspectives are, I believe, essential for a renaissance of progressive early childhood education and care in North America.

The Chapters in Part II

Each of the chapters in this part has its own journey to describe. None is strictly linear, and all held surprises for their authors. Collectively, they help define a moment in Canada where images of children, curriculum, and teachers are increasingly in flux, although the forces for standardization, technical routinization, and homogenization remain strong. One hears in the chapters of a time when long-established mooring lines have loosened, somewhat, and new possibilities may continue to emerge.

Rachel Langford provides the reader with a macro-view of this change, noting the emergence of several, provincial early years' frameworks that do not seek to minutely script early childhood curriculum in the province but rather to provide general guidelines that can help ensure space for diversity and innovation. It is noteworthy that three of the provinces: British Columbia, Saskatchewan, and New Brunswick, all came to include recent work in Aotearoa/New Zealand and Europe, particularly northern Italy, as sources of inspiration for their own frameworks. Those sources have gone far beyond the strictures and assumptions so common in North America, to open up truly exciting possibilities.

Rachel Heydon takes the reader into a 'micro-world' of curriculum and programming captivatingly describing the possibilities that emerge in the interaction of the very young with the very old. Tossing scripts and routines aside, Heydon's intergenerational programs tread into the unknown and somewhat fearful environments of aging and dying, to find there a world of connections and care that enhance the lives of young *and* old. Heydon's descriptions truly call out for the creation of places beyond repetitive, technical models, and restrictive programming to take on all of human experience as the stuff of childhood developmental and curriculum interest.

Nina Howe and Ellen Jacobs explore another dimension of education for early years work, moving beyond pre-service training to an exploration of in-service mentoring. Again, the creation of a space that is not predetermined and pre-scripted (as is much pre-service education) opens up possibilities that are not achievable where the process and presumed dynamics are already set. In the context of mentor and early childhood educator working together in the same environment, possibilities emerge (like in Heydon's intergenerational work) that are not anticipated, that can up-end the assumed power dynamics, and in doing so create spaces for learning outside the expected.

Veronica Pacini-Ketchabaw and Judith Bernhard provide lenses that allow the reader to look beyond the assumptions of multicultural education programs to explore more deeply the lived experiences of immigrant populations in Canada and the relationship of those experiences to ECEC. Consistent with other chapters in Part II, the reader is invited to accept the challenges of complexity, critique the homogenizing impact of prescriptive programming, and engage in interactions with children and families that are neither normative nor repetitive.

Pence and Pacini-Ketchabaw complete the set with consideration of the various systems and system levels that must be involved for comprehensive change to take place within a province. Using provincial funding support to bring many of the most creative and innovative voices in ECEC globally to provide workshops in British Columbia, those innovators have engaged with front-line educators, college instructors, university academics, government staff, and elected officials to consider what possibilities lie beyond current realities.

Collectively, these chapters suggest that change is underway in Canada. It may be significant that when the opportunity to develop new approaches to children, curriculum, and teachers emerged (see Langford chapter in this volume), that a western, a prairie, and an eastern province looked beyond North America, and that each one selected places of innovation that represent the potential for profound breaks with the past. Such breaks are necessary if Canada is to move from its abysmally low standing internationally among 'developed countries' (as noted both in the OECD Report and in the UNICEF Report Card), to a place of respect and of innovation befitting a country that prides itself on support for healthy diversity.

In providing these reflections from the past forty years, it is of great concern that ECEC has advanced so little in Canada and North America over this period. While provinces and states have moved to implement policies and regulations, and considerable funds have gone into researching children's programs and child development topics, the field remains a patchwork of underfunded care that hemorrhages poorly paid, disheartened, and inadequately trained staff, while parents search desperately for programs that will, at the very least, do no harm.

In reflecting back, and considering our situation today, the time has come for a new generation of professionals to emerge who are excited by progressive possibilities and the place of early learning and care as the 'pedestal to the pyramid' (a term used by Governor DeWitt Clinton of New York state in 1826, and seldom uttered by North American politicians since!; Fitzpatrick, 1911, p. 107) to achieve not only healthy individual development, but healthy social development as well. Such developments will not be found in narrow scripting of a pre-packaged curriculum, in inadequately short education and training experiences, in assessment tools that dramatically bracket children's possibilities, nor in images of children that see them only as 'pre-': schoolers, workers, and thinkers, while ignoring the powerful beings they are *now*. As I round the marker of my fortieth year in the field of ECEC, I increasingly think back to that time in 1971 where educated, motivated, but 'untrained' dreamers were allowed to engage with an image of the child that was powerful, and a society that had lost its bearings, to consider how both might be engaged to create a future full of possibilities. We need those possibilities today.

References

Blow, S. (1894). *Symbolic education: A commentary on Froebel's mother play*. New York: D. Appleton.

Bronfenbrenner, U. (1974). Developmental research, public policy, and the ecology of childhood. *Child Development, 45*, 1–5.

Bronfenbrenner, U. (1979). *The ecology of human development: Experiments by nature and design*. Cambridge MA: Harvard University Press.

Fitzpatrick, E.A. (1911). *Educational views and influence of DeWitt Clinton*. New York: Teachers College Press.

Froebel, F.W.A. (1882). *Education of man*. Translated and annotated by William N. Hailmann. New York: D. Appleton.

Holt, J. (1964). *How children fail*. New York: Pitman.

Kozol, J. (1967). *Death and an early age*. New York: Houghton Mifflin.

Lero, D.S., Pence, A., Brockman, L., & Goelman, H. (1992). *Canadian national child care study: Introductory report*. Ottawa: National Health and Welfare and Statistics Canada.

Neill, A.S. (1962). *Summerhill: A radical approach to child rearing*. London: Gollancz.

Newsweek. (1970, 16 Feb.). John Adams High School.

Owen, R. (1816). *A new view of society*. London: J.M. Dent.

Peabody, E.P., & Mann, M. (1863). *Moral culture of infancy and kindergarten guide*. Boston, MA: T.O.H.P. Burnham.

Postman, N., & Weingartner, C. (1969). *Teaching as a subversive activity*. New York: Dell.

PART III

Government Involvement

10 The Quebec Child Care System: Lessons from Research

CHRISTA JAPEL

In most industrialized countries there has been a growing recognition of the importance of early childhood and the need to support children and their families through the provision of learning environments for all young children. Canada, however, lags behind many of its counterparts in the Organisation for Economic Co-operation and Development (OECD) with regard to early childhood development programs. In fact, a recent evaluation and comparison of early childhood services in twenty-five OECD countries placed Canada second to last because it met only one of the ten important benchmarks for early childhood education and care (ECEC) – a set of minimum standards for protecting the rights of children in their most vulnerable and formative years (UNICEF, 2008).

In Canada, education and child care fall primarily under provincial jurisdiction, and the federal government's role is limited largely to the transfer of funds to provincial and territorial governments for early childhood programs and services. Given significant disparities between the provinces and the need for a national child care agenda, the Government of Canada announced in 2004 that it would work with the provinces and territories to establish a national system of early learning and child care based on four key principles: quality, universality, accessibility, and developmental programming. These four principles are referred to by the acronym QUAD. The subsequent budget committed $5 billion over five years to enhance and expand early learning and child care and also clarified the QUAD principals, defining them as follows:

- *Quality:* evidence-based, high-quality practices relating to programs for children, training, and support for early childhood educators (ECEs) and child care providers, and provincial/territorial regulation and monitoring
- *Universally inclusive:* open to all children without discrimination
- *Accessible:* available and affordable to those who choose to use it
- *Developmental:* focused on enhancing early childhood learning opportunities and the developmental component of early childhood education and care programs and services

In 2005, the federal government began negotiations with nine provinces, but only Ontario and Manitoba entered into final funding agreements with the Government of Canada. Quebec did not sign an initial bilateral agreement-in-principle but negotiated, in October 2005, and signed a funding agreement to support its existing early learning and child care system. In January 2006, however, the new Conservative federal government gave one year's notice that it would cancel the bilateral child care agreements with the provinces and allocate funds directly to families for child care instead of favouring the development of a national child care agenda through direct funding of services.

Canada's initial goals were very similar to those already pursued by Quebec in its system of educational child care. Child care services in Quebec had, in fact, undergone a major transformation since 1997, when the government first adopted its new family policy. One of the linchpins of this innovative policy was the setting up of a network of fixed-fee services for all children aged 5 years and under, irrespective of family income. The network was intended to address the issue of work–family balance and to provide children, no matter what the financial status of their parents, with a pre-school environment fostering their social, emotional, and cognitive development and preparing them for entry into the school system (Ministère de la Famille et de l'Enfance, 1997). Previously, financial aid for child care had come through two sources: the refundable tax credit for child care expenses, and the Office des services de garde à l'enfance (child care services office), established in 1980 by the Government of Quebec, which issued operating and construction grants directly to non-profit day care centres and had a program for the provision of financial assistance with child care fees to eligible low-income families. The new policy called for the gradual implementation, beginning on 1 September 1997, of $5-a-day per child child care services; parents would pay a fixed rate of $5 per day per child for subsidized child care, with the government assuming the remaining cost. The day care spaces were initially made available to children who had reached the age of 4 years by 30 September of that year, but the plan called for increasing the number of spaces and gradually (year-by-year) lowering the age of admission. Existing fee-waiving and financial aid programs would also be gradually discontinued in step with the new plan.

Thus, in 1997, Quebec began to commit significant resources to the consolidation and development of its child care network. In July, the new Ministry of the Family and Children assumed the responsibilities of the former Secrétartiat à la famille (family secretariat and office for child care services) and set out to build its network from existing services, namely, non-profit child care centres, regulated home-based child care, and for-profit centres. For-profit centres were given the option to convert their legal status and become non-profit or to sign agreements with the government to offer reduced-contribution child care spaces. In fact, the government reached agreements with most of the licensed for-profit centres in operation in June 1997 to retain their for-profit status and to sign contracts to provide reduced-fee child care spaces. But the main thrust of the new child care policy was the development of early childhood centres (Centres de la petite enfance, CPEs) from the non-profit centres and the child care agencies that had formerly been responsible for home-based services. The CPEs, non-profit organizations whose boards of directors include parent users (who hold the majority of the seats along with two members of the personnel and one member representing the community), would oversee two branches of child care services: those offered in child care centres and those offered in home-based settings.

Quebec's change in policy represented a real commitment by the government to both early learning and child care programs. Quebec is, therefore, unique in Canada in the number of available regulated, fixed-fee, reduced-contribution child care spaces: in 2008, the number of regulated child care spaces in Quebec represented about 37 per cent of all regulated spaces in Canada (Beach et al., 2009). The province is also unique in its method of funding spaces: cash payments or refundable tax credits to families were largely replaced by a system of direct funding of services. In 2009, direct grants to child care services represented about 37 per cent of the provincial budget for families, or $2.4 billion (Ministère des Finances, 2009). Making regulated child care spaces more affordable for the majority of families led to a significant increase

Table 10.1. Growth in Regulated Child Care Spaces in Quebec from 1997 to 2009

	CPE Centre-Based	CPE Home-Based	For-Profit Centres	Total Number of Spaces	Number of Children Aged 0 to 4 in Quebec
1997–98	36,606	21,761	23,935	82,302	428,297
1998–99	38,918	32,816	24,964	96,698	412,161
1999–00	44,735	44,882	24,936	114,553	397,971
2000–01	51,570	55,979	25,701	133,250	382,727
2001–02	58,525	62,193	25,882	146,600	373,191
2002–03	67,163	71,365	25,882	164,410	366,619
2003–04	69,672	83,970	30,613	184,255	371,028
2006	75,660	88,545	33,799	202,487	379,658
2007	76,213	88,645	34,095	203,721	389,661
2008	77,405	91,253	35,340	209,827	400,605
2009	77,864	91,582	36,377	212,777[a]	416,043

Source: Ministère de la Famille et des Aînés (2010) and Institut de la statistique du Québec (2010).
CPE = early childhood centre.
[a]This number includes 6,954 spaces in for-profit day care centres that are regulated but not subsidized.

in demand that, in turn, stimulated the rapid growth of the sector (see Table 10.1).

As Table 10.1 illustrates, in 1997 Quebec had 82,302 regulated child care spaces (Japel, Tremblay, & Côté, 2005). More than ten years later, by March 2009, this number had reached 212,777 with the objective of bringing the total number of funded spaces to 220,000 by 2012 (Ministère de la Famille et des Aînés, 2010). At present, more than half of Quebec's pre-school-aged children have access to home- or centre-based child care that is regulated and affordable (currently, the parental contribution is $7/day per child) – *a more than two and one-half–fold increase* since the implementation of the policy in 1997 (Institut de la statistique du Québec, 2010).

More than ten years after the inception of the new family policy, how does the child care system in Quebec fare with respect to the QUAD principles?

Quality and Developmental Components of ECEC Programs

The concept of quality is multidimensional and is directly associated with the provision of developmentally appropriate early childhood learning opportunities (Bigras & Japel, 2008). But how can this complex concept be defined and its components evaluated? In the 1980s, the National Association for the Education of Young Children (NAEYC) in the United States developed an instrument for accrediting child care services. This instrument was based on a definition of the parameters of a program appropriate to the different stages in the development of young children (Bredekamp, 1984, 1986). The criteria that a service must meet in order to qualify for accreditation are based on scientific knowledge and evidence related to conditions that foster the physical, social, cognitive, and emotional development of young children. The criteria relate to interactions between staff and children as well as staff and parents, activity programs, staff skills, staff:child ratios, health and safety conditions, food, physical environment, and management of the service. The elaboration of the Accreditation Program by the NAEYC (1984) and the development of a series of instruments to measure the quality of child care settings, created by Thelma Harms and her colleagues, sparked new interest in such evaluations. In Quebec, in the late 1980s, the child care services office set up a committee to explore the guiding principles and general thrust of an instrument to evaluate the quality of child care services, as well as the elements to be included in this instrument. One result of that initiative was the publication of *Le kaléidoscope de la qualité* (Gagné, 1993), a self-administered evaluation instrument whereby child care centres could examine, on the basis of key criteria, the quality of their services; this was the NAEYC tool adapted for use in Quebec. The concept of quality championed by the department thus mirrored that elaborated by the NAEYC and served as a reference point for the government in applying the concept of quality within the network of child care services.

In both North America and Europe, commonly used instruments for evaluating the quality of child care settings are the scales developed by Harms, Clifford, and Cryer – the Infant/Toddler Environment Rating Scale (ITERS; Harms, Cryer, & Clifford, 1990), the Early Childhood Environment Rating Scale (ECERS; Harms & Clifford, 1980), and the Family Day Care Rating Scale (FDCRS; Harms & Clifford 1989) – and their updated (revised) versions, the ITERS-R (Harms, Cryer, & Clifford,

2006), the ECERS-R (Harms, Clifford, & Cryer, 1998), and the FDCRS-R (Harms, Cryer, & Clifford 2007). These scales, whose validity and reliability are well established, measure parameters similar to those elaborated by the NAEYC to ascertain whether a particular setting is conducive to child development. The scales measure several dimensions of the quality of a child care environment, such as interactions between staff and children, interactions among children, activities, and provisions related to health and safety. These dimensions, which are at the core of the educational approach to child care, relate directly to the daily life of the children. In addition, the scales developed by the same authors assess elements not directly linked to the immediate experience of the children, such as the quality of furnishings and arrangement of rooms, the program structure, the role of parents, and the working conditions of staff. These elements are strongly associated with overall quality, since they define the physical and human context in which care is provided (Cassidy et al., 2003). These scales enable researchers to obtain a global quality rating (all of the sub-scales are weighted equally, since the global rating is the mean of the scores for the sub-scales), as well as a quality profile for each item and sub-scale.

A calculation based on the presence or absence of each of the indicators situates the child care setting on a scale of 1 to 7. A setting that obtains a score from 1 to 2.9 is considered *inadequate* in terms of quality; from 3 to 4.9 is *minimal;* and from 5 to 7 is *good:* within the *good* category, 6 or higher is *very good* to *excellent*, and 7 means that all of the criteria are being met.

Child Care Quality in Quebec

Over the past decade three studies have provided information on child care quality in Quebec. The first study, *You Bet I Care!* (YBIC) was an evaluation of the quality of caring and learning environments using the ITERS (Harms et al., 1990), the ECERS-R (Harms et al., 1998) and the FDCRS (Harms & Clifford 1989). The sample included 234 centres and 231 family child care providers across Canada (Doherty et al., 2000; Goelman et al., 2000). Forty-eight of the observed centre-based groups and forty-two of the family child care settings were located in Quebec. Given the relatively high refusal rates among the settings initially contacted and the sampling procedure, which included centres and family child care settings in and around Montreal and Quebec City, the sample cannot be considered representative of the province's child care settings.

Table 10.2. Average ITERS and ECERS-R Total and Sub-scale Scores YBIC and QLSCD

	Furnishings and Display	Personal Care Routines	Listening and Talking	Learning Activities	Adult–Child Interaction	Program Structure	Adult Needs	Total Score
YBIC ITERS N = 16	4.0	2.8	4.3	3.2	5.4	4.3	3.5	3.6
YBIC ECERS -R N = 32	4.9	4.6	5.3	4.0	5.5	5.3	4.3	4.7
QLSCD ECERS -R CPE N = 728	4.5	4.3	4.8	4.1	5.2	5.3	4.7	4.6
QLSCD For-profit N = 296	3.7	3.4	4.0	3.4	4.4	3.9	3.6	3.7

CPE = early childhood centre; ECERS-R = Early Childhood Environment Rating Scale-Revised; ITERS = Infant/Toddler Environment Rating Scale; QLSCD = Quebec Longitudinal Study of Child Development; YBIC = You Bet I Care!

The quality scores obtained within this study are presented in Tables 10.2 and 10.3. The most comprehensive evaluation of the quality of child care settings was undertaken within the Quebec Longitudinal Study of Child Development (QLSCD), a joint initiative of the Direction Santé Québec of the Institut de la statistique du Québec and an interdisciplinary team of researchers from several universities. Since 1998, the QLSCD has conducted annual surveys on the development of 2,223 young children. This cohort, selected from the birth registry, is a representative sample of children born in Quebec between 1 October 1997 and 31 July 1998. This particular time span was chosen because this cohort of children would all enter school in the same year (Jetté & Des Groseilliers, 2000). The goal of the study, which commenced when the children were 5 months old, is to determine the various factors that, during a crucial period in children's development, might

Table 10.3. Average FDCRS Total and Sub-scale Scores YBIC and QLSCD

	Space and Furnishings	Basic Care	Language and Reasoning	Learning Activities	Social Development	Adult Needs	Total Score
YBIC N = 42	5.0	3.9	4.3	4.5	4.4	5.6	4.5
QLSCD CPE N = 337	4.3	3.8	4.5	4.5	4.4	5.4	4.4
QLSCD Unregulated N = 179	3.6	3.1	3.8	3.7	4.2	3.5	3.6

CPE = early childhood centre; FDCRS = Family Day Care Rating Scale; QLSCD = Quebec Longitudinal Study of Child Development; YBIC = You Bet I Care!

compromise or facilitate their adaptation to school. The vast quantity of data collected served as the basis for a detailed profile of (1) the socio-demographic context in which the children were evolving as well as their social, emotional, and cognitive development; and (2) the different child care services that their parents have used since the children's births. The time span during which the cohort was born coincided with the adoption and implementation of Quebec's new family policy. Given the potential contribution of quality child care services to the children's cognitive and social development, an evaluation of the child care settings attended by the QLSCD children was incorporated into the study. Since the goals of the QLSCD parallel those of the new family policy, it was important that the quality of the child care services be assessed. This provided an up-to-date portrait of the child care network and, subsequently, a link between the quality of the services and children's development could be drawn. Additional grants to carry out an observational study of child care quality were obtained by the research group in 1999 when the children were about 2 years old. Since the QLSCD is a longitudinal survey, a sample of child care settings was evaluated on four occasions, starting in 2000 when the children were 2.5 years of age. The fourth data collection, undertaken in pre-school settings, was carried out in the spring of 2003, the year in which the children reached age 5 years, prior to starting kindergarten. From 2000 to 2003, a total of 1,540 child care settings were evaluated: 728 centre-based CPEs, 337 home-based CPEs, 296 for-profit daycares, and 179 unregulated home-based settings (Japel et al., 2005).

Using French versions of the ECERS-R (Harms et al., 1998) and the FDCRS (Harms & Clifford, 1980), this study provides a comprehensive profile of the different child care services, whether centre- or home-based, attended by the QLSCD children aged 2.5 to 5.0 years. A particular advantage of this study was the inclusion of unregulated home-based settings, a type of child care used by a significant number of parents unable to obtain a subsidized space in CPEs or for-profit daycares. Tables 10.2 and 10.3 show the average total and sub-scale quality scores obtained within this study.

The third study on child care quality in Quebec is the Grandir en qualité survey. Commissioned in 2003 by the Ministère de l'emploi, de la solidarité sociale et de la famille (MESSF) to evaluate the educational quality of Quebec's child care settings, this study comprised 356 groups of children in CPEs, 200 home-based CPEs, and 349 groups of children in for-profit daycares (Drouin et al., 2004). The MESSF decided to develop its own observational scales, which measure the following four dimensions: (1) space, furnishings, and materials; (2) structure and variety of activities; (3) adult–child interaction; and (4) child care provider–parent interaction. A calculation based on the presence or absence of a variety of indicators within each dimension situated the child care setting on a scale of 1 to 4. A setting that obtains a score of 1 is considered *inadequate* in terms of quality; a score of 2 is indicative of *minimal* quality; a score of 3 falls within the *good* category; and a score of 4 is *very good* and means that most of the criteria are being met. Table 10.4 shows the average quality score obtained by the various settings and age groups observed within the Grandir en qualité survey.

Although the three studies on child care quality in Quebec used different instruments, their results converge and indicate that overall quality of child care is minimal. These scores reflect a situation where the majority of settings meet custodial care needs but offer few activities that would stimulate children's social, language, or cognitive development. Figure 10.1 illustrates the QLSCD results for all of the settings that were evaluated except child care services in schools, stopover centres (occasional care not exceeding twenty-four consecutive hours), and nursery schools. Of the settings, 61 per cent have a score indicating a global quality rating of minimal, about 12 per cent have a rating of inadequate, and only 27 per cent have a score of 5 or higher, indicating a rating of good or better.

Table 10.4. Average Quality Score by Type of Child Care Setting and Age Group, Grandir en qualité Survey, 2003

	Space, Furnishings, and Material	Structure and Variety of Activities	Adult–Child Interaction	Child Care Provider– Parent Interaction	Total Score
CPE 0 to18 months N = 128	2.91	3.02	3.12	3.38	3.05
CPE 18 months to 5 years N = 228	2.89	3.02	2.85	3.18	2.93
For-profit daycares 0 to 18 months N = 124	2.33	2.66	2.76	2.96	2.62
For-profit daycares 18 months to 5 years N = 225	2.47	2.69	2.54	2.83	2.58
CPE home-based N = 200	2.65	2.78	2.78	2.97	2.75

CPE = early childhood centre.

Quality by Type of Service

The results of the QLSCD and the Grandir en qualité survey also converge regarding significant differences in quality between commercial and non-profit settings. (The *You Bet I Care!* study does not provide a breakdown by auspice for the settings observed in Quebec.) As Tables 10.2, 10.3, and 10.4 demonstrate, centre-based care is generally of higher quality in CPEs than in for-profit child care centres. Similarly, as the QLSCD data reveal, children in home-based CPEs receive better care than those in unregulated home-based settings (see Table 10.2).

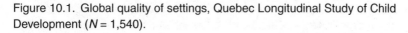

Figure 10.1. Global quality of settings, Quebec Longitudinal Study of Child Development (*N* = 1,540).

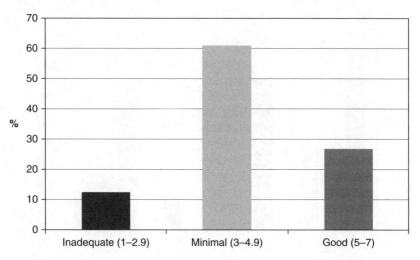

Figure 10.2 shows the percentage of different types of settings observed within the QLSCD that rank above or below the minimal quality rating. Among those with a score of 5 or higher, the majority are CPEs. Thus, 35 per cent of centre-based and 29 per cent of home-based CPEs provide a service that is considered good. Outside of the CPEs, only 14 per cent of for-profit centres and 10 per cent of unregulated home-based centres obtain this rating. The inverse is true for the services that score below 3: only 6 per cent of centre-based and 7 per cent of home-based CPEs are rated as inadequate, compared with 27 per cent of for-profit centres and 26 per cent of unregulated home-based centres.

Developmentally Appropriate Practices

Child care settings of higher quality provide children with learning opportunities that are appropriate to their developmental stage and, thus, foster their social, language, and cognitive development. Although in the three studies the scores reported for care (provider–child interactions and associations with social development and language and reasoning) are among the highest, the frequency and variety of educational activities are a critical dimension. The YBIC and QLSCD scores on the

Figure 10.2. Global quality: Percentage of settings of inadequate and good quality, by type of setting, Quebec Longitudinal Study of Child Development.

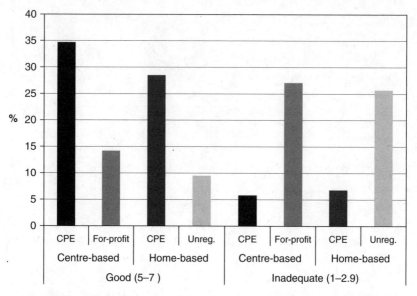

CPE = early childhood centre
Source: Japel et al. (2005, p. 16)

sub-scale *Activities* of the ECERS-R (Harms et al., 1998) show, for example, that quality is generally mediocre and needs to be improved (see Table 10.2). More precisely, scores on items pertaining to the availability of materials and the frequency of activities that would assist children to develop an understanding of nature, basic scientific concepts, mathematics, and numbers are particularly low. Furthermore, there is relatively little provision of guidance and activities that promote creativity through music and movement or the acceptance of diversity (Goelman et al., 2000; Japel et al., 2005). Although the scores on the sub-scale *Structure and variety of activities* in the Grandir en qualité survey (see Table 10.4) cannot be compared with those of the ECERS-R, the results of this study are similar, namely, low scores on items pertaining to the variety of activities offered during the day, the educators' planning and observation of activities, and their organization of materials necessary for the different activities (Drouin et al., 2004).

Figure 10.3 shows how the different settings observed within the QLSCD fared with respect to the quality of the activities offered to

Figure 10.3. Quality of activities: Percentage of settings of inadequate and good quality, by type of setting, Quebec Longitudinal Study of Child Development.

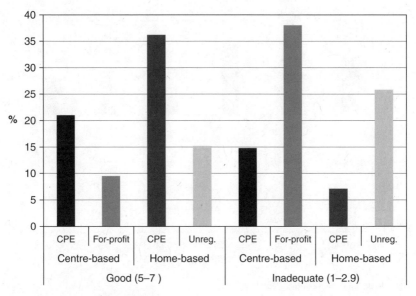

CPE = early childhood centre
Source: Japel et al. (2005, p. 22)

children. Only 21 per cent of centre-based CPEs received a rating of good on this sub-scale, but the proportion rises to 36 per cent for home-based CPEs. It should be pointed out that the evaluation criteria for activities and materials in centre-based services are more stringent than those for home-based services; for example, a centre-based service can obtain a score of 5 only if the children have access to sand and water play for at least one hour each day, while for home-based centres the minimum requirement is once per week. Very few for-profit and unregulated home-based centres have a score of 5 or higher. Only one in ten for-profit centres and one in six unregulated home-based centres obtained a rating of good.

A significant number of settings have a very low rating on this sub-scale. For one out of six centre-based CPEs and almost four out of ten child care centres, serious failings were observed with respect to the content and variety of activities. In the case of home settings, 26 per cent of unregulated home-based centres but only 7 per cent of home-based CPEs fail to meet the minimal level of quality (Figure 10.3).

Figure 10.4. Mean socio-economic status (SES) of families and their use
of child care services, by children's age (in years), Quebec Longitudinal
Study of Child Development, 1998–2003.

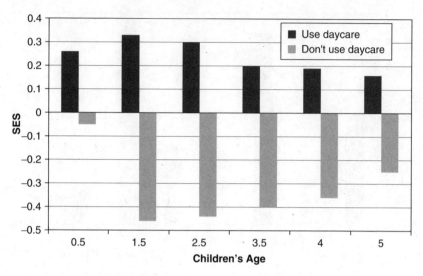

Source: Japel et al. (2005, p. 28)

Universality and Accessibility

In 1997, Quebec set out to put in place a child care system that provides
access for all without discrimination based on income or other criteria.
This universal system is publicly funded with a parental contribution
of $7 per day per child. A universally inclusive system should be open
to all children without discrimination. However, as Table 10.1 shows, in
2009, only about half of Quebec's pre-school-aged children had access
to home- or centre-based child care that is regulated and affordable.
Given that labour force participation among mothers with pre-school
aged-children has increased significantly in Quebec, and at present, at
least three-quarters of these mothers work (Lefebvre & Merrigan, 2008),
a significant proportion of the latter are left to find child care arrangements outside the regulated and more affordable sector. The QLSCD
allows for an examination of the question of accessibility by drawing
a portrait of the socio-economic characteristics of families that do and
do not use child care services. This information is extremely important given that Quebec's family policy of 1997 is intended to enhance

equality of opportunity through the creation of a network of high-quality child care services accessible to all children, irrespective of the socio-economic status of their parents.

Figure 10.4 clearly shows that parents whose children attended a child care centre at the time of the study were in general more socio-economically privileged than parents whose children did not attend a day care centre. The gap is narrower for young children, but this probably reflects the fact that many mothers had not yet returned to work following maternity leave. Although it diminishes gradually over time, the gap is, nonetheless, quite striking from the time the children reach the age of 1.5 years: the socio-economic status (SES) of parents who do not use child care services is lower than the mean of zero, which represents the standardized average SES of the population in this study. The SES of parents who do use these services is higher than the mean. Given that children's cognitive, social, and emotional development is strongly associated with the SES of their parents (Willms, 2002), these results suggest that a large number of potentially vulnerable children do not attend child care, a potential protective factor in their lives (Japel et al., 2005; Japel, 2008).

Discussion

Quebec is unique within Canada: It has the highest number of regulated child care spaces, and it allocates the largest amount of government spending to early childhood education and care of any of the provinces or territories. Almost fifteen years after the implementation of the family policy, what benefits can we detect from this investment in ECEC? First, we observe a sharp rise in the number of children in regulated child care. There is also evidence that this attendance is having beneficial effects on the behaviour and cognitive development of the children. These benefits are particularly evident among vulnerable children (Côté et al., 2007; Japel, 2008). Second, available and affordable child care accompanied by a generous parental leave program may have had an impact on Quebec's demographic profile: compared with the other provinces and territories, Quebec has had the largest increase in its birth rate over the past five years (Statistics Canada, 2009a). Furthermore, families have greatly benefited from Quebec's child care model: the increased availability of spaces has facilitated mothers' attendance at an educational institution or their return to work; in fact, provincial statistics indicate that labour force participation among mothers of pre-school-aged children has increased significantly over the past ten years and has surpassed the percentage of mothers' labour force participation observed in the rest of Canada (Statistics Canada, 2009b). Compared with mothers in the rest of Canada, mothers in Quebec work more hours and weeks per year and have a higher annual income (Lefebvre & Merrigan, 2008). This improves the socio-economic conditions in which their children grow up, conditions that have been shown to have an influence on children's development including health outcomes, school readiness, and psychosocial adjustment (Duncan & Brooks-Gunn, 1997). Finally, families are not the only ones to benefit from the return of mothers to the workforce and subsequent increases in family income and spending power. There are also positive repercussions on the economy through the creation of child care jobs, so that the government is able to recover through taxes some of the costs associated with ECEC.

Despite the striking advantages of these policy changes for children, families, and society, the Quebec experience teaches us lessons that are not so positive. Three studies have found that child care quality is minimal overall; in other words, Quebec's child care network has not attained the general level of quality needed to foster the social, emotional, and cognitive development of all children (Drouin et al., 2004; Goelman et al., 2000; Japel et al., 2005).

The QLSCD was the first large survey to draw a portrait of the quality of child care settings in Quebec. Its results, presented to the Social Affairs Committee of the Quebec National Assembly as well as to the Association québécoise des centres de la petite enfance (Tremblay, Japel, & Côté, 2003), raised issues related to child care practices in the various types of settings and have led to regional initiatives to improve the quality of the services offered by early childhood centres (CPEs). The individuals charged with implementing these initiatives have to deal with the ongoing changes to the funding and the structure of the child care network. Since the election of the Charest government in 2003, several measures have been adopted: a fee increase (from $5 to $7 per day per child), imposition of budgetary restrictions on all child care settings (both non-profit and for-profit), and the claw-back of any surpluses accumulated by the CPEs. Furthermore, in 2005, the government adopted a law that resulted in the restructuring of the network of home-based CPEs – henceforth, they were no longer affiliated with nor supported by the centre-based CPE of their neighbourhood but regrouped to be accredited and supervised by a reduced number of coordinating offices. The role of the latter consists of three annual inspections to assure health and safety measures. However, support to the care provider for the implementation of the pedagogical program in family-based settings is only offered on demand. This diminished support on a voluntary basis is most likely to have negative repercussions on the quality of services offered in these settings.

The above-cited surveys were carried out a number of years ago and may not represent the present state of quality in Quebec's child care system. However, with all the measures adopted since 2003, it is most unlikely that overall child care quality has improved. In fact, several smaller studies carried out in Quebec since 2004 have found a significant decrease in quality and observed particularly low scores in environments that offer care for infants and toddlers (Côté, 2005; Japel & Manningham; 2008; Japel & Welp, 2009).

Quality levels vary significantly according to the type of child care setting: non-profit centres generally offer better quality services than for-profit centres. In the late 1990s, a moratorium was imposed on the creation of new for-profit daycares. When the moratorium was lifted in 2003 by the incoming government, the for-profit sector experienced a surge in growth, despite the fact that there is compelling and consistent evidence that this sector is generally of lower quality than the non-profit sector. Furthermore, almost half of the children attending child care in Quebec are in home-based settings. Although regulated home-based care (accredited, supervised, and coordinated by CPEs) is superior in quality to the unregulated home-based service – still used by a large number of parents because demand for regulated and subsidized spaces is far greater than supply – the proportionally large expansion of the home-based child care sector has had questionable repercussions. The required qualifications of staff are minimal, so there is no guarantee that home-care providers are well-equipped and sufficiently supported to offer the high-quality environment that stimulates children and responds adequately to their developmental needs.

Quebec's 1997 family policy intended to enhance equality of opportunity through the creation of a network of high-quality child care services accessible to all children, irrespective of the socio-economic status of their parents. However, only about half of pre-school-aged children have access to regulated and subsidized care, and there are still waiting lists for CPEs of one to two years. Furthermore, the most vulnerable children are the least likely to attend child care services that provide a potential protective factor in their lives. One of the reasons for this unfortunate reality is that child care services are not sectorized as are schools. CPEs located in disadvantaged neighbourhoods, which are generally of better quality than other types of child care (Japel et al., 2005), are not obliged to provide services for children living in the immediate surrounding area, that is, those who most need it. There is a clear need to set aside more spaces for children from disadvantaged circumstances. In addition, although children of families receiving social assistance may attend a child care service free of charge on a part-time basis (up to a maximum of 23.5 hours per week), many child care services prefer full-time attendance for administrative reasons and, therefore, do not give priority to children from these families (Tougas, 2002). If more spaces were reserved for these children, and if schedules were more flexible, more parents of at-risk children might be encouraged to use the services. Note, however, that since 2002 some Quebecers living in disadvantaged areas have had free access to full-time child care. Because of intersectoral agreements and agreements between CLSCs (community health and social service centres) and CPEs, the parental contribution for a family receiving social assistance can be waived when an organization designated by the health and social services network recommends full-time attendance. CPEs that have signed such an agreement are committed to setting aside 5 per cent of their spaces for children who are being followed by a CLSC (Ministère de la Famille et de l'Enfance, 2002). However, although nearly half of the province's CPEs are party to such an agreement, about two-thirds have reported that they do not accept all the children recommended by the CLSC because they lack sufficient day care spaces (Ministère de la Famille et des Aînés, 2008). Information on the exact number of at-risk children who have benefited from this initiative is not currently available. A lesson from this might be that CPEs using public funds should be required to set aside more spaces for vulnerable children and to offer flexible part-time attendance to make their services more equitable.

Despite much criticism of Quebec's family policy, the Quebec model has resulted in a network of child care centres that aims to offer high-quality care to all children. Since 1997, this network has expanded rapidly to meet parental needs. As these are not yet fully met, the emphasis in the development of child care services in Quebec still seems to remain focused on the number of spaces available rather than on the quality of the services offered. Aware of the mediocre quality of its services, the government announced in 2004 an Ongoing Quality Improvement Plan, which included a self-evaluation tool for child care services (Ministère de l'Emploi, de la Solidarité Sociale et de la Famille, 2004). This plan requested that child care settings sign a commitment to quality and clearly stated that any improvement was the responsibility of the child care setting; however, no funds were allocated for these endeavours.

If we are to create a network of child care services that offer higher than minimal quality, the Act Respecting Childcare Centres and Childcare Services, as well as the regulations stemming from it, need to be re-examined. Areas of particular concern are educator:child ratios, facilities and interior and exterior space for various activities, and staff training (see chapter by Ellen Jacobs and Emmanuelle Adrien in this volume). Staff training is a critical component of the quality of daily life for children in a child care setting. In fact, educator competence is a core element in the creation of a high-quality environment. In order for children to engage in activities that enhance their social, emotional, motor, and cognitive skills, educators in both centre-based and home-based daycares must be better trained and equipped to deal with the many aspects of child development. Only with improved staff training, supervision, and ongoing support will child care settings be able to implement educational programs that enhance the global development of children and, thus, be able to offer high-quality services.

A society that strives for universal equality of opportunity and that is committed to addressing problems related to poverty, which in 2007 was a reality for close to one in six children in Quebec (Campaign 2000, 2009),[1] must recognize that child care is an essential service – a public good – and that its cost, like the costs of education and health care, must be borne collectively. We must ensure that all children, particularly those living in disadvantaged environments, get a fair start in life. This will be possible only through a high-quality publicly funded child care system that is accessible to all parents and children and that allocates resources sufficient to respond to the needs of the most vulnerable in society, while also striving to achieve and maintain the highest standards of quality. Such a system will help ensure equality of opportunity and thus move us one step closer to eliminating poverty, a problem that is passed from one generation to the next.

---

1 The percentage reported here is based on Statistic Canada's Low Income Cut-Offs (LICOs), before tax. The percentage of children living in poverty varies according to the measures of poverty that are used. If the LICOs, after tax, or the Market Basket Measures are used, child poverty rates in Quebec are below 10 per cent.

Quebec has laid the groundwork for an important social structure that is beneficial to children and their families. Yet its child care system must be seen as a work-in-progress, and we must continue striving to improve its quality and accessibility. The development and maintenance of a network of high-quality child care services will require a large investment of public funds, as well as policies that promote a global and long-term perspective on human development. There is sufficient proof that the long-term benefits of investing in human capital far outweigh the costs (Heckman & Carneiro, 2003). The need to devote more funds to support our human capital has never been greater, and investment in a universal, subsidized, and not-for profit early childhood education and care system staffed by qualified workers would benefit not only children and families but also the economy, stimulating our economic recovery.

References

Beach, J., Friendly, M., Ferns, C., Prabhu, N., & Forer, F. (2009). *Early childhood education and care in Canada 2008*. Toronto: Childcare Research and Resource Unit. Retrieved from http://www.childcarecanada.org/ECEC2008/index. html#toc.

Bigras, N., & Japel, C. (Eds.). (2008). *La qualité dans nos services de garde éducatifs à la petite enfance: La définir, la comprendre, la soutenir*. Quebec: Presses de l'Université du Québec.

Bredekamp, S. (Ed.). (1984). *Accreditation criteria and procedures. Position statement of the National Academy of Early Childhood Programs, A Division of the National Association for the Education of Young Children*. Washington, DC: National Association for the Education of Young Children.

Bredekamp, S. (Ed.). (1986). *Developmentally appropriate practice*. Washington, DC: National Association for the Education of Young Children.

Campaign 2000. (2009). *2009 report card on child and family poverty in Canada: 1989–2009*. Retrieved from http://www.campaign2000.ca/reportCards/nati onal/2009EnglishC2000NationalReportCard.pdf.

Cassidy, D.J., Hestenes, L.L., Hedge, A., Hestenes, S., & Mims, S. (2003). *Measurement of quality in preschool child care classrooms: The Early Childhood Environment Rating Scale-Revised and its psychometric properties*. Paper presented at the biennial meeting of the Society for Research in Child Development, 24–27 April, Tampa, Florida.

Côté, S. (2005). *Family risks and young children's mental health: The role of non-maternal care*. Grant application to CIHR/IRSC.

Côté, S.M., Boivin, M., Nagin, D.S., Japel, C., Xu, Q., Zoccolillo, M., Junger, M., & Tremblay, R.E. (2007). The role of maternal education and non-maternal care services in the prevention of children's physical aggression problems. *Archives of General Psychiatry, 64*(11), 1304–1312.

Doherty, G., Lero, D.S., Goelman, H., Tougas, J., & LaGrange, A. (2000). *You bet I care! Caring and learning environments: Quality in family child care across Canada.* Guelph, ON: Centre for Families, Work and Well-Being, University of Guelph.

Drouin, C., Bigras, N., Fournier, C., Desrosiers, H., & Bernard, S. (2004). *Grandir en qualité 2003: Enquête québécoise sur la qualité des services de garde éducatifs.* Quebec: Institut de la statistique du Québec.

Duncan, G., & Brooks-Gunn, J. (Eds.). (1997). *Consequences of growing up poor.* New York: Russell Sage Foundation.

Gagné, M.-P. (1993). *Le kaléidoscope de la qualité: Outil d'évaluation des services de garde en garderie.* Quebec: Publications du Québec.

Goelman, H., Doherty, G., Lero, D.S., LaGrange, A., & Tougas, J. (2000). *You bet I care! Caring and learning environments: Quality in child care centres across Canada.* Guelph, ON: Centre for Families, Work and Well-Being, University of Guelph.

Harms, T., & Clifford, R.M. (1980). *Early Childhood Environment Rating Scale.* New York: Teachers College Press.

Harms, T., & Clifford, R.M. (1989). *Family Day Care Rating Scale.* New York: Teachers College Press.

Harms, T., Clifford, R.M., & Cryer, D. (1998). *Early Childhood Environment Rating Scale.* Rev. ed. New York: Teachers College Press.

Harms, T., Cryer, D., & Clifford, R.M. (1990). *Infant/Toddler Environment Rating Scale.* New York: Teachers College Press.

Harms, T., Cryer, D., & Clifford, R.M. (2006). *Infant/Toddler Environment Rating Scale.* Rev. ed. New York: Teachers College Press.

Harms, T., Cryer, D., & Clifford, R.M. (2007). *Family Day Care Rating Scale.* Rev. ed. New York: Teachers College Press.

Heckman, J., & Carneiro, P. (2003). *Human capital policy.* NBER working paper 9495. Washington, DC: National Bureau of Economic Research.

Institut de la statistique du Québec. (2010). *Population par année d'âge et par sexe, Québec, 1er juillet 2008.* Retrieved from http://www.stat.gouv.qc.ca/donstat/societe/demographie/struc_poplt/201_08.htm.

Japel, C. (2008). Factors of risk, vulnerability and school readiness among preschoolers: Evidence from Quebec. *Choices, 14*(16), 1–42. Montreal: Institute for Research on Public Policy.

Japel, C., & Manningham, S. (2008). L'éducatrice au cœur de la qualité: Un projet pilote visant l'augmentation des compétences. In N. Bigras & C. Japel

(Eds.), *La qualité dans nos services de garde éducatifs à la petite enfance: La définir, la comprendre, la soutenir* (pp. 75–100). Quebec: Presses de l'Université du Québec.

Japel, C., & Welp, C. (2009). *Cap Qualité! Les premiers resultats.* Presentation at the Regroupement des centres de la petite enfance des regions de Québec et Chaudière- Appalaches, 16Dec., Quebec.

Japel, C., Tremblay, R.E., & Côté, S. (2005). Quality counts! Assessing the quality of daycare services based on the Quebec Longitudinal Study of Child Development. *Choices, 11*(5). 1–42. Montreal: Institute for Research on Public Policy.

Jetté, M., & Des Groseilliers, L. (2000). Description and methodology. In *Quebec Longitudinal Study of Child Development (QLSCD 1998–2002), 1*(1). 1–60. Quebec: Institut de la statistique du Québec.

Lefebvre, P. & Merrigan, P. (2008). Child-care policy and the labor supply of mothers with young children: A natural experiment from Canada. *Journal of Labor Economics, 26*(3), 519–548.

Ministère de l'Emploi, de la Solidarité sociale et de la Famille. (2004). *L'engagement qualité. Plan d'amélioration continue de la qualité en service de garde.* Quebec: Gouvernement du Québec.

Ministère de la Famille et des Aînés. (2008). *Rapport d'évaluation de l'entente-cadre et des protocoles CLSC-CPE.* Quebec: Author.

Ministère de la Famille et des Aînés. (2010). *Portrait des services de garde.* Retrieved from http://www.mfa.gouv.qc.ca/fr/services-de-garde/portrait/places/Pages/index.aspx.

Ministère de la Famille et de l'Enfance. (1997). *Nouvelles dispositions de la politique familiale.* Quebec: Gouvernement du Québec.

Ministère de la Famille et de l'Enfance. (2002). *Protocole CLSC-CPE: Guide d'implantation, entente-cadre et protocole-type.* Quebec: Author.

Ministère des Finances. (2009). *Budget 2009–2010. La politique familiale du Québec: Où en sommes-nous?* Quebec: Gouvernement du Québec.

National Association for the Education of Young Children (NAEYC). (1984). *Accreditation criteria and procedures of the National Academy of Early Childhood Programs.* Washington, DC: Author.

Statistics Canada. (2009a). *Births and birth rate, by province and territory.* Retrieved from http://www40.statcan.gc.ca/l01/cst01/demo04b-eng.htm.

Statistics Canada. (2009b). *Canadian Economic Observer.* Retrieved from http://www.statcan.gc.ca/pub/11–010-x/00606/9229-eng.htm.

Tougas, J. (2002). *La restructuration des services éducatifs et de garde à l'enfance au Québec: Les cinq premières années.* Toronto: Childcare Resource and Research Unit, University of Toronto.

Tremblay, R.E., Japel, C., & Côté, S. (2003, 9 Sept.). *Les jeunes enfants du Québec sont-ils bien gardés? Vers une politique intégrée pour le développement des ressources humaines.* Brief presented at individual consultations and public hearings, Committee on Social Affairs, Quebec National Assembly.

United Nations Children's Fund (UNICEF). (2008). *The child care transition, Innocenti Report Card 8.* UNICEF Innocenti Research Centre, Florence. Retrieved from http://www.unicef.ca/portal/Secure/Community/502/WCM/HELP/take_action/Advocacy/rc8.pdf.

Willms, J.D. (2002). Socioeconomic gradients for childhood vulnerability. In J.D. Willms (Ed.), *Vulnerable children* (pp. 71–104). Vancouver: UBC Press.

11 Community-Based Early Child Development Projects

RAY DEV PETERS, ANGELA HOWELL-MONETA,
AND KELLY PETRUNKA

During the past twenty years, there has been increased interest in Canada concerning the influence of the early years of life on children's social-emotional well-being, health, development, and 'readiness to learn.' This interest has prompted a focus on the effects of prevention and early intervention programs designed to facilitate the healthy development and well-being of young children and their families, with special attention to those who are socio-economically disadvantaged. These early childhood development (ECD) programs have the potential to alter children's trajectories by providing a protective influence to compensate for risk factors, which can compromise healthy development. Programs may affect children directly through structured experiences, or indirectly by enhancing the caregiving environment. In this chapter, we first review the historical backdrop against which ECD programs have been developed and implemented. Many of the earliest programs were initiated in the United States in the 1960s, were very small scale in terms of the number of children involved and driven by university-based researchers who developed, implemented, and evaluated the programs using a 'top-down,' highly prescriptive project intervention model. Some of these early programs are briefly described.

More recently, especially in Canada, there has been a growing interest in including parents of young children and other interested residents in the planning, design, and implementation of ECD programs, particularly in disadvantaged neighbourhoods. The first of these large-scale community-based programs was the Ontario Better Beginnings Better Futures/Partir d'un Bon Pas pour un Avenir Meilleur initiated in 1991. In the next section of this chapter, the processes by which the Better Beginnings Better Futures (BBBF) project was developed and implemented are described. Following this, we review several federally and provincially funded community-based ECD programs that have been initiated since the BBBF project.

Each of the community-based programs is examined from an epidemiological and social policy point of view by attempting to identify the number of children and families involved in each project, and the 'spread' of the project in terms of the percentage of eligible children and families who actually participate in the programs. Also, an attempt is made to relate government resources allocated to each project compared with the number of participants in order to estimate an average cost of economic resources available per child and/or family. The main research questions for the review are:

- How many children and families participated in each project and for what period of time?
- How many of the intended target population of eligible children actually participated in the project (i.e., the project's 'reach')?
- What are the financial resources provided by the funding government in terms of project costs per child and/or family?

History of the Better Beginnings Better Futures Project

In 1987, the large-scale epidemiological Ontario Child Health Study, funded by the Ontario government was released (Offord et al., 1987). Results indicated that 18 per cent of children aged 4 to 18 years showed major emotional or behavioural problems (i.e., psychiatric disorders or mental problems). Of those showing major mental health problems, only one in six (17%) had received any contact with a service-providing agency or special education program in the past year. It was concluded that even if treatment for children's mental health problems were 100 per cent effective, such treatment would have little impact on the population prevalence of these mental health problems in children and young adolescents.

Based on these findings, in 1988 the Ontario government convened a Technical Advisory Group of program experts and researchers to carry out a review of successful prevention programs for young children in Canada and internationally. In this review, it was concluded that relatively few studies had been carried out on programs for children younger than 6 or 7 years of age that were adequately designed, implemented, and evaluated. Even fewer studies existed that followed the children or parents after the program ended to determine long-term effects. The costs of implementing the programs were seldom reported. It was further noted that most of the 'model' programs that existed in the late 1980s had been carried out in the United States, were very small scale, and had a narrow focus, primarily on the intellectual and cognitive development of developmentally delayed children or on improving the quality of life for their mothers. The earliest of these programs was the Carolina Abecedarian Project, an intervention for very high-risk children. Children received year-round, full-day educational day care from soon after birth through age 5 years (Ramey & Campbell, 1984). Another well-known project from this period was the Perry Preschool Project, a centre-based program that targeted 3- and 4-year-old African-American children who were living in poverty (Schweinhart et al., 1993). Both of these interventions enhanced cognitive outcomes for participating children as compared with non-participating peers. However, both had very small sample sizes and it was not known how well the program models would work for larger and more heterogeneous groups of participants. Also, both programs were very expensive to implement. Costs of these and other ECD programs are discussed later in this chapter. Attempts to expand small-scale 'efficacy' trials to multiple sites and to more children have been disappointing (e.g., the Comprehensive Child Development Project reported in St Pierre et al., 1997).

Another concern of the Technical Advisory Group was that there were virtually no well-researched programs for young children that were comprehensive, ecological, community-based, and integrated. At that time, there was a call for more community involvement in social services. The vision was that local residents and service providers would work together to integrate services, provide programs that were tailored to local needs, and ultimately, improve children's lives by changing entire neighbourhoods. None of the programs reviewed by the Technical Advisory Group included a focus on the child's neighbourhood, involved parents or other local residents in program or research planning and implementation, or attempted to integrate the project with other services or organizations in the community. The Technical Advisory Group recognized the need for a model that could be implemented in diverse Ontario communities and tailored to local needs. Based on their review, the Technical Advisory Group recommended to the Ontario government a project model for preventing serious emotional and behavioural problems and fostering optimal social, cognitive, and physical development in young children living in disadvantaged neighbourhoods in the province. It was in this context that the Ontario Better Beginnings Better Futures Project (BBBF) was conceived. In 1990, the BBBF was announced by the Ontario government as 'a 25-year longitudinal prevention policy research demonstration project to provide information on the effectiveness of prevention as a policy for children' (Government of Ontario, 1990).

Two variations of the BBBF have been implemented in eight disadvantaged Ontario neighbourhoods since 1991. In five *younger-child* project sites, prenatal/infant development programs link with pre-school programs for children 0 to 4 years of age and their families. In three *older-child* project sites, pre-school programs link with primary school programs for children between the ages of 4 and 8 years of age and their families.

The BBBF in each site was funded by the Ontario government to be bottom-up, community-based programs that were locally owned and operated jointly by community residents and professionals. Thus, BBBF is the first government-funded, community-based longitudinal research project of its kind in Canada. The development and evaluation of the BBBF from 1990 to the present will be described later in this chapter. Extensive research has been conducted to determine the impact and costs of the BBBF in the eight project sites.

Since the initiation of the Ontario Better Beginnings Better Futures Project in 1990, several other federally and provincially government-funded, community-based ECD projects have been undertaken in many Canadian jurisdictions. Examples of these community-based initiatives will be described in this chapter (see Table 11.1; see the Appendix for a summary of these initiatives including details about the targeted population, objectives, and funding). Following the descriptions of these projects, we return to a focus on the BBBF including project outcomes and implications for Canadian public policy on government-funded, community-based ECD programs.

Federally Funded Community-Based ECD Programs

Community Action Program for Children

The federally funded Community Action Program for Children (CAPC) began in 1993 to mobilize community-based groups to form coalitions

Table 11.1. Community-Based Programs

Program and Source	Jurisdiction
Community Action Program for Children (PHAC, 2007a)	PHAC
Canada Prenatal Nutrition Program (PHAC, 2007b)	PHAC
Early Childhood Development Agreement (First Ministers' Communiqué, 2000)	Government of Canada
Alberta Parent Link Centre Program (Government of Alberta, 2004)	Government of Alberta
B.C.'s Children First Initiatives (Government of British Columbia, 2009)	B.C. Ministry of Children and Family Development, regional budget allocations
Manitoba's Parent Child Coalitions (Government of Manitoba, 2008)	Government of Manitoba
New Brunswick's Communities Raising Children and Excellence in Parenting Development (Government of New Brunswick, 2006, 2009)	Government of New Brunswick
Ontario's Best Start Programs (Government of Ontario, 2006)	Government of Ontario

PHAC = Public Health Agency of Canada.

and/or partnerships that would enable them to design prevention and intervention programs for vulnerable families and young children in their communities. Often these families did not participate in mainstream health services or social programs. CAPC was designed to be culturally appropriate and sensitive to the unique needs of community members such as literacy levels, language, and cultural differences. For example, programs involved home visiting and family resource centres designed to provide information and support for parents and improve parenting skills and coping strategies (Public Health Agency of Canada [PHAC], 2007a).

EVALUATION

CAPC projects have demonstrated innovation and expertise in reaching women, children, and families who are most at risk. Evaluation findings from a recent measure of national program reach reflected the diversity of CAPC in the demographic characteristics of the participants (PHAC, 2007a). This analysis revealed that for every risk factor, CAPC participants exhibited these characteristics to an equal or greater extent than the Canadian population as a whole. For example, 42 per cent of CAPC households had incomes of less than $15,000, 35 per cent of CAPC participants were lone parents, and 38 per cent of CAPC parents had not finished high school (PHAC, 2007a).

CAPC projects have mutually beneficial partnerships with an average of thirteen partner organizations. More than 85 per cent of projects partner with health organizations, 60 per cent with educational institutions, 50 per cent with child protection services, 59 per cent with community associations, and 50 per cent with early childhood or family resource centres. Participants are actively involved in program development, management, delivery, and evaluation. Over half (53%) of the projects involve participants as members of a governing body (PHAC, 2007a). In 2005, there were approximately 450 CAPC projects across 3,000 communities in Canada providing services to more than 67,000 children 0 to 6 years of age and their caregivers (PHAC, 2007a). With an annual budget to CAPC communities of $52.9 million each year, this results in an average allocation of $790/child per year.

Friendly and colleagues (2007) provide population data for 2006 indicating that there were approximately 2.3 million children 6 years of age and younger living in Canada. If Willms' (2002) estimate that 28.6 per cent of children younger than age 6 years in Canada are vulnerable is accurate, then there would have been approximately 667,333 vulnerable children aged 6 years and younger in Canada in 2005. Of this number, 67,000 or one in ten vulnerable children were involved in CAPC programs. From a population health perspective, it is doubtful that this level of program reach is adequate to successfully impact the overall national prevalence rate of childhood vulnerability, even if all programs are extremely successful. Furthermore, Boyle and Willms (2002) reported no significant effects of CAPC programs on participating children or their families on a variety of outcomes. According to PHAC (2007a), a summative evaluation is planned that will consider the success, impact, relevance, and cost effectiveness to provide clarity on the full scope of program contribution. However, we have been unable to access information on the PHAC website about these evaluations (PHAC, 2010).

Canada Prenatal Nutrition Program

The Canada Prenatal Nutrition Program (CPNP) was initiated in 1994 as long-term funding for community groups and coalitions to provide services for at-risk pregnant women. CPNP is managed by the federal, provincial, and territorial governments. Protocols for joint management, such as establishing regional priorities and allocating funds, were signed at the ministerial level for the CAPC and later included the CPNP. Programs vary by region in terms of size, sponsorship, and geographical distribution, but all programs follow a common set of guiding principles, objectives, and essential elements to form a national foundation across Canada. Collaborative partnerships at all levels of government enable communities to decide on their unique needs and goals, and to monitor their programs to obtain positive results.

EVALUATION

According to PHAC (2007b), 60 per cent of CPNP projects are the community's only source of prenatal nutrition services. Often, other available prenatal nutrition services do not meet the needs of the CPNP target population. A comparison of socio-demographic characteristics illustrated that CPNP participants faced greater conditions of risk compared with the general population (i.e., lower income and education, younger age, more smoking, greater food insecurity). Despite these differences, the comparison found key birth outcomes (birth weight, breastfeeding initiation) to be identical between the two populations. This result suggests that the program has likely contributed to helping at-risk families achieve the same positive birth outcomes as the general population, despite their additional challenges. A 2008 assessment of the economic impact of CPNP examined data gathered from the regions receiving CPNP, in relation to control groups established from a variety of sources across Canada (McMurchy & Palmer, 2008). The costs of the program and the cost impact of its effect on rates of low birth weight and breastfeeding were reported. CPNP was found to reduce rates of low birth-weight babies and increase breastfeeding rates among its target at-risk population compared with the control groups (McMurchy & Palmer, 2008).

The annual budget for the program is $27.2 million, which goes directly to communities in the form of grants and contributions. Approximately 330 CPNP projects serve more than 50,000 women annually in

2,000 communities across Canada (PHAC, 2007b). This allocation provides approximately $540 per year of program dollars for each mother involved in CPNP.

In 2007, a total of 367,864 births were registered in Canada (Statistics Canada, 2007). If CPNP involves only pregnant women, then the program involves approximately 14 per cent of pregnant Canadian women annually. It is difficult to determine how many pregnant women in Canada would be considered high risk so the actual spread of CPNP may be difficult to determine. However, given the data on the high-risk nature of many women participating in CPNP, the impact of the program on the national prevalence of low birth-weight babies and breastfeeding initiation rates may be substantial. Countering this conclusion, however, is a recently released report by the Organisation for Economic Co-operation and Development (OECD, 2009) indicating a sharp increase in infant mortality in Canada, dropping from 6th to 24th place ranking among OECD countries (OECD, 2009). This is a surprising finding given the apparent success of CPNP. Clearly, more research is required on this issue.

Provincially Funded Projects: The Early Childhood Development Agreement

In 1999, the Government of Canada partnered with the provincial and territorial governments to work on a National Children's Agenda. In September 2000, Canada's first ministers released a communiqué pledging to work together so that young children in Canada can reach their potential. They committed to improve and expand early childhood development programs and report progress regularly. They agreed to continue to build knowledge and share information with parents, service providers, and communities to improve children's early years (First Ministers' Communiqué, 2000).

The ECD Agreement focuses on children 0 to 6 years of age and their families. Its objectives are to help children develop optimally and to help families support their children within strong communities. To meet these objectives, the following four key areas for action that build on prior government investments were agreed upon: (1) promote healthy pregnancy, birth, and infancy; (2) improve parenting and family supports; (3) strengthen early childhood development, learning, and care; and (4) strengthen community supports. The first ministers agreed that these investments should be incremental, predictable, and sustained in the future. A transfer of $2.2 billion was made from the federal to provincial and territorial governments over five years, beginning in April 2001, to support these initiatives.

A broad range of ECD programs for children from 0 to 6 years of age and their families were developed through these government funds. Since strengthening community supports for young children and their families was one of the four major pillars in the ECD Agreement, many jurisdictions developed community-based initiatives. A few examples are presented in the following section. This information was extracted primarily from annual ECD reports from various provinces.

The Alberta Parent Link Centre Program

Alberta's Parent Link Centres (PLCs) are one of the many community-based programs in Alberta that are designed to support and strengthen families. Staff at the centres are community members who actively participate in local planning groups to build networks and partnerships with parents, schools, and community agencies. For example, centres partner with schools that provide school readiness training and agencies that provide child protection, literacy training, and housing assistance (Government of Alberta, 2004).

In 2004–05, $11 million was provided by Children's Services to establish PLCs in communities throughout Alberta (Government of Alberta, 2004). In 2008–09, 69,000 Albertans across 160 communities received PLC programs and services through main centres, satellite sites, and outreach services in community locations such as schools and libraries (Government of Alberta, 2008).

EVALUATION

No evaluation of the PLCs was provided in the 2008 annual ECD report. Also, we could find no indication of dollars allocated to PLCs for 2008. However, if the $11 million allocation outlined in the 2004–05 report continued in 2008–09, then the average amount of program dollars for each of the 69,000 Albertans participating in the program would be approximately $160 per year. There were 228,400 children from 0 to 6 years of age in Alberta in 2005. According to the 2008–09 annual ECD report, 34,100 children were involved in PLC programs, representing approximately 15 per cent of all Alberta children younger than 6 years of age.

British Columbia's Children First Initiatives

Children First (CF) involves forty-five initiatives throughout British Columbia designed to increase the capacity of communities to meet the unique needs of children aged 0 to 6 years and their families and promote healthy development. Children First provides funds for community-driven programs rather than delivering services directly; it also seeks to mobilize and engage community members in programs designed to improve ECD. As described in the Early Years annual report (Government of British Columbia, 2009): 'Since 2000, CF has grown from three pilot "learning sites" to 45 distinct and active initiatives throughout the Fraser, Interior, Northern, Vancouver Coastal and Vancouver Island regions of B.C. In 2007–8, supports and services to children and families across British Columbia were strengthened with the increased collaboration between CF and other ECD community development initiatives such as Success by 6®, the Human Early Learning Partnership, and the Community Action Program for Children, and with regional funding received from the Ministry of Children and Family Development' (p. 26).

EVALUATION

The collaborative ECD Evaluation Project, initiated in 2005, is focused on creating an integrated evaluation and reporting system for ECD programs and services in British Columbia that support the following four long-term outcomes: (1) mothers are healthy and give birth to infants who remain healthy; (2) children experience healthy early child development, including optimal early learning and care; (3) parents and families have the knowledge, resources, and support they need to help their children develop to their full potential; and (4) communities support the development of all children and families.

No evaluations have been conducted related to the first and second outcomes concerning maternal health during pregnancy, healthy births, and healthy ECD. An evaluation process has begun for the third outcome: parents and families. For the fourth outcome, communities' support of the development of all children and families, a province-wide evaluation was implemented in 2008, with the participation of sixty communities, represented by their early years planning initiatives, and over 800 community-based stakeholders. A significant increase in community planning, coordination, community ECD awareness and continued improvements in service delivery were reported (Government of British Columbia, 2007).

According to the British Columbia annual report, $4,011,000 was spent on CF programs in 2007–08. There were 233,200 children in the province aged 0 to 6 years in 2005. This indicates that the average annual allocation for the CF initiative was approximately $17 per child. No data were provided regarding participation rates of children or families, so it was not possible to evaluate the reach of the program (Government of British Columbia, 2009).

Manitoba's Parent Child Coalitions

Parent Child Coalitions (PCCs) involve community members such as parents, early childhood educators (ECEs), health providers, and representatives from other community organizations. These members cooperate to develop and implement programs that support young children and their caregivers. There are twenty-six PCCs in Manitoba; twelve are in communities within Winnipeg, eleven are within regional health authority boundaries outside of Winnipeg, and three are cultural organizations (e.g., Indian and Métis Friendship Centre of Winnipeg). The activities of each PCC differ according to the unique needs of the community, and goals are determined through community consultation (Government of Manitoba, 2008).

EVALUATION

As outlined by the Manitoba Government (Government of Manitoba, 2008), there are plans to evaluate PCCs: 'As part of a Manitoba model for measuring progress in child-centred public policy, HCMO [Healthy Child Manitoba Office] is developing a provincial strategy that integrates the evaluations of programs in the HCM [Healthy Child Manitoba] continuum, including Healthy Baby, Families First, Triple P, and the Parent-Child Centred Approach. Key components of the strategy include HCM program surveys, administrative data from Manitoba departments, the Early Development Instrument (EDI), the National Longitudinal Survey of Children and Youth (NLSCY), and the development of a Manitoba Longitudinal Survey of Children and Youth (MLSCY), modelled after the NLSCY' (Government of Manitoba, 2008, p. 19).

No specific budget data regarding numbers of young children or parents participating in the twenty-six PCCs in the Manitoba ECD report could be found. Instead, numbers are provided for Healthy Child Manitoba, which includes many programs. Specific measures of progress for the PCCs were also not found.

New Brunswick's Capacity-Building Programs for Children and Families

Two major initiatives have been launched in New Brunswick to build the capacity of families and communities to promote healthy child development (Government of New Brunswick, 2006, 2009). Communities Raising Children (CRC) provides funding, resources, and capacity building for neighbourhoods to create programs that support their children and families. Excellence in Parenting involves support services and information aimed at increasing parental confidence and providing strategies for parents to raise healthy children.

EVALUATION
No information about evaluation efforts for either CRC or Excellence in Parenting is available. Also, the actual numbers of young children and parents involved in these two programs are not provided, so it is difficult to draw conclusions concerning the reach, cost, or cost effectiveness of these community-based programs. However, investment by the New Brunswick government for these two programs was reported to be $776,000 for 2006–07. There were 43,800 children aged 0 to 6 years in New Brunswick in 2005. This yields an average per child allocation of $18 per year for the two programs, a figure strikingly similar to the allocation of British Columbia's Children First initiative.

Ontario Best Start Centres

Ontario's Best Start was developed to prepare children for success in school by the time they start Grade 1. By enhancing and integrating key early years programs and services, Best Start gives children in Ontario the opportunity to develop and learn optimally in life (Government of Ontario, 2006). As of 2005–06, Best Start was implemented in forty-seven community-based networks; these networks submitted their plans to move towards an Ontario-wide integrated system that provides children and their families with seamless access to the supports and services they need. There are three demonstration communities (in the District of Timiskaming, Hamilton's east end, and the rural areas of Lambton and Chatham-Kent) where the Ontario government has accelerated the implementation of the full Best Start vision; these three demonstration communities established twenty-four Neighbourhood Early Learning and Care hubs in convenient neighbourhood locations, providing families with access to a continuum of services.

EVALUATION

No specific details on program reach, budget, or evaluation were available in the 2005–06 annual report. The Best Start Centres are discussed in Janette Pelletier's chapter in this volume, including a description of the recent Full-Day Kindergarten Early Learning Program announced by the Ontario government.

Summary

Over the past two decades, there has been a tremendous expansion of government-funded, community-based programs in Canada to support the healthy development of young children and their families, particularly for those living in socio-economic disadvantage and other conditions of risk. We have reviewed several examples of these initiatives, both at the federal and provincial levels. Similar ECD initiatives exist or are being developed in other Canadian jurisdictions. Our review is not meant to be an exhaustive list of all such initiatives, but rather to present examples to demonstrate the current state of government-funded, community-based ECD initiatives in Canada early in the twenty-first century.

Despite the existence of many programs throughout Canada, the lack of evaluation data on program costs and participation rates is disappointing. Few initiatives have apparently built in a requirement for evaluating the outcomes of the programs offered or the cost per participant of program involvement. This is the case despite recommendations in social policy discussions that highlight the critical importance of accountability in ECD programs for the overall social and economic health of our society (see chapters in this volume by Martha Friendly and Susan Prentice and by Gordon Cleveland on related social policy and economic issues). Currently, more information is available for the two large federal initiatives, CAPC and CPNP. The fact that these two projects have been in place since 1993 and 1994, respectively, may have allowed more time to develop and implement information systems. For the community-based provincial ECD projects reviewed, little evaluation data are currently available. However, where data are available, the spread and the resources allocated to these projects appear to be limited, at least as reflected in the annual ECD reports from the various jurisdictions across the country. This issue will be discussed in conjunction with the BBBF research described in the following section of this chapter.

Ontario's Better Beginnings Better Futures Project

Beginning in 1991, eight BBBF projects have implemented programs designed to impact components of an ecological model of human development (Bronfenbrenner, 1979), which emphasizes a comprehensive view of children's development. The model encompasses children's physical, social-emotional, and cognitive development, as well as an awareness of the multitude of parent, family, neighbourhood, school, and cultural/societal factors that directly and indirectly influence children's development. The BBBF guidelines are ambitious. Each selected community was funded to develop a local prevention project designed to (1) reduce emotional and behavioural problems of young children; (2) strengthen the capacity of parents, families, and the neighbourhood to respond to the needs of their children; (3) develop a local organization to provide programs for children from 0 to 4 or from 4 to 8 years of age that respond effectively to local needs; (4) encourage parents and neighbours to participate as equal partners with service providers to develop and carry out programs; and (5) establish partnerships with existing and new service providers and schools and to coordinate programs with these partners.

Program Activities

The BBBF model required each community to develop and deliver high-quality programs that could be expected to produce positive child, family, and neighbourhood outcomes. High-quality programs were defined as paying careful attention to the following: (1) staff recruitment, training, adequate compensation, and participation in decision making; (2) favourable child:staff ratios; (3) curriculum development relating program activities to goals and objectives; and (4) providing time for staff to develop close relations with the families and communities in which they work.

The five younger-child sites, focusing on programs for children aged 0 to 4 years and their families, were required by the government funder to provide home visiting programs, plus supports to increase the quality of local child care (e.g., additional staff and resources to existing child care and pre-school programs). The three older-child sites were required to provide in-classroom or in-school programs, plus supports to increase the quality of local child care, through, for example, before and after school and summer holiday care, homework support, and recreation programs.

Each site provided a variety of programs tailored to local needs, either by themselves or in partnership with other education and service providers. Examples include parent–child drop-in programs, toy-lending libraries, parent training and support groups, nutrition supports, neighbourhood safety initiatives, cultural awareness activities, recreation, and mentoring programs. The five younger-child sites provided an average of twenty-six different programs, whereas the three older-child sites provided an average of sixteen different programs for the children, their families, and the local neighbourhood.

The Better Beginnings Better Futures Project is neither a service nor a program. It is an initiative to mobilize disadvantaged neighbourhoods to foster resilience by promoting positive functioning in young children, their families, and their neighbourhoods. Some children and families were touched directly by these improved resources (e.g., home visitors, classroom programs, before and after school programs, parent training, play groups). Some attended programs on a regular basis, others on a very random or part-time basis. Some did not attend any programs but may have been influenced indirectly, for example, by a neighbour who attended programs and offered advice and/or support, or by safer streets and parks, or by increased community participation. Larry Schweinhart (personal communication, 2000), a researcher with the High/Scope Perry Preschool Study, described BBBF as being not a program but a 'meta-program' or general strategy for fostering resilience in children, families, and communities.

Program Costs per Child and Family

Program costs for BBBF funded directly by the Ontario government include labour, facilities, equipment, materials, and any items necessary to implement the programs successfully at each BBBF site. Since BBBF programs were available to and potentially accessed by all children and their families in the respective site locations, the cost of the programs has been related to the *total* number of children in each of these areas; that is, we have calculated a 'cost per capita' based on an 'intent to treat' analysis.

Approximately $2.8 million was spent on programs by the five BBBF sites combined each year. The program cost per child and/or family was based on 1996 census data of children age 0 to 4 years living in the BBBF sites; this age range directly corresponds to the main programming focus of the younger-child sites. According to the census data, there were approximately 3,785 children aged 0–4 years in the five BBBF sites. Thus, the average annual cost per child and/or family in the five younger-child sites combined for 1996–97 was $733.

In the three older-child sites, approximately $1.7 million was spent on BBBF programs by the three sites combined each year. The program cost per child and/or family was based on the number of children eligible to participate in the BBBF programs based on school participation records; in 1996–97, there were approximately 1,549 children attending junior kindergarten to Grade 2 in the three sites. Thus, the average annual cost per child and/or family in the three older-child sites combined for 1996–7 was $1,130.

Research Methods

A team of multidisciplinary researchers from seven Ontario universities and field researchers in each local site was responsible for the research design, data collection, analysis, and reporting. All research activities were coordinated by the BBBF Research Coordination Unit with central offices at Queen's University in Kingston, Ontario.

QUALITATIVE, DESCRIPTIVE RESEARCH ON PROJECT
DEVELOPMENT AND ORGANIZATION

Local site researchers were trained to write descriptive reports on program development and implementation at each site using a common protocol. These local site reports were summarized in comprehensive cross-site reports describing the following: (1) how the BBBF initiative was developed; (2) how communities generated proposals for the original competition in 1990; (3) how local residents were involved in project decision making; (4) how local service providers and educators were involved in project decision making and resource provision; (5) specific program activities and components, as well as staffing patterns; (6) the formal and informal decision-making structures and values; and (7) personal stories from program participants, staff, and local residents concerning their experiences with Better Beginnings Better Futures.

QUANTITATIVE OUTCOME RESEARCH

Information about children, parents, families, and neighbourhoods was collected in a variety of ways including annual two-hour in-home parent interviews and direct child measures carried out by local site researchers employed by the Research Coordination Unit; annual teacher reports; and federal and provincial databases (e.g., Statistics Canada Census data, Ontario Principals' Reports of Special Education Instruction).

In 1992–93, three comparison sites were selected using Statistics Canada Census data. Comparison sites were similar to the BBBF sites in terms of average annual family income, single-parent status, parent education and employment, and cultural identity.

For the first phase of the research (evaluation of the short-term findings; see section below for more details), 1,536 children and their families in the eight BBBF sites and three comparison neighbourhoods agreed to participate in a longitudinal research group. At the younger-child sites, the longitudinal research sample consisted of children born in 1994, and at the older-child sites, children who were 4 years old in 1993. Data were gathered regularly over a five-year period in the younger-child project and comparison sites when the children were 3, 18, 33, and 48 months of age, and in the older-child sites every year from age 4 years until the children turned 8 in 1997–98.

The quasi-experimental control-group design examined how changes in children and families in the BBBF neighbourhoods over five years of programming differed from changes in those from the demographically similar comparison sites that did not receive BBBF funding.

Results

SHORT-TERM OUTCOMES

The results presented in this section summarize the data collected in 1998 when the BBBF children in our longitudinal research sample ended their four years of program eligibility. For detailed reports of these data, see Peters et al. (2000, 2003). A positive impact of BBBF on children's social-emotional functioning and physical health was found. The project had little impact on children's cognitive and academic performance, except for the decreased rates of special education in schools at three older-child BBBF sites.

Reduced smoking by mothers was found across all sites. This finding is encouraging since smoking levels tend to be high in disadvantaged communities, and the long-term health effects of smoking are well known. The change in smoking rates in BBBF sites may be related to the fact that parents had increased opportunities to meet other parents, participate in support groups or committees, and to volunteer in community activities, especially since meetings and events were often held in public locations such as schools, where smoking is restricted or discouraged.

For neighbourhood outcomes, in each younger-child BBBF site, parents reported increased safety when walking at night. In the three older-child sites, parents reported greater satisfaction with the general quality of their neighbourhoods and housing. In all eight BBBF sites, parents perceived an improvement in the quality of life in their neighbourhoods more than parents from the comparison sites.

In summary, both the younger- and older-child BBBF sites yielded similar positive outcomes. Thus, there was little support for the prediction that programs starting earlier in children's development, in this case immediately after birth, would be more effective than programs starting later in children's development, in this case age 4 years corresponding with the beginning of public school–provided half-day junior kindergarten in Ontario.

MEDIUM-TERM OUTCOME

The same measures of child, parent, and neighbourhood outcomes were used to collect data four years after children and their families completed program participation in all eight BBBF sites and the three comparison sites. These data were collected when children in the younger cohort were in Grade 3 and those in the older cohort were in Grade 6. BBBF has the most extensive and intensive longitudinal database involving children and families from disadvantaged neighbourhoods in Canada.

The analyses of these data yielded a picture in stark contrast to that of the short-term findings described above. At Grade 3, children and families from the five BBBF younger-child sites showed no positive outcomes relative to those from the comparison sites on any measures. In contrast, children from the three older-child BBBF sites showed significantly more positive outcomes relative to those from the comparison sites, including better child social functioning, less hyperactivity, fewer school suspensions, higher scores on a standardized math test, less use of special education services, and better child nutrition. Also, parents from the three older-child BBBF sites reported higher levels of social support, better family functioning, more community involvement, and greater neighbourhood satisfaction than parents from the comparison neighbourhoods.

LONG-TERM OUTCOMES

Due to the positive findings in favour of the three older-child BBBF sites when the children were in Grade 6, a further longitudinal follow-up study has been completed when the children were in Grade 9 (seven years after ending program involvement). These results, along with extensive descriptions of the project history and complete methodology of the BBBF, are presented in Peters et al. (2010) and in a less technical publication (Roche, Petrunka, & Peters, 2008). To briefly summarize the Grade 9 findings, youth from the three older-child BBBF neighbourhoods continued to show superior school and academic performance relative to youth from the comparison neighbourhoods. Grade 9 teachers rated youth from the BBBF sites as being better prepared for school, using fewer special education services, showing more adaptive functioning in school, repeating fewer grades, and displaying fewer emotional problems and hyperactive/inattentive behaviours in the classroom. Also, parents from these BBBF neighbourhoods were more satisfied with their marital relationship and reported more positive family functioning, as well as greater social support.

Also at Grade 9, a cost-savings analysis was carried out contrasting the cost to the Ontario government of providing BBBF programs for up to four years with the cost of providing government services to children and their families from both the project and comparison communities. This cost-savings analysis employed twelve measures that could be assigned a dollar figure and that cost the government money to provide. These measures included various health services (e.g., physician visits, emergency room and overnight hospital use), educational services (e.g., special education services, grade repetition), and social services (e.g., social welfare assistance, disability supports). The cost associated with the BBBF program such as health, educational, and social services for youth and their parents were approximately $1,000 less per family than the cost of those services provided to youth and families from the comparison sites. Therefore, the investment that the Ontario government made to provide BBBF programs in these older-child project sites returned nearly $1,000 per family on the investment.

Analyses of longitudinal follow-up data collected when the youth were in Grade 12 have recently been conducted. Results indicate that the cost savings to the Ontario government associated with BBBF involvement increased substantially to over $4,500 per family (Peters et al., 2010).

Discussion

The analyses of data collected four years after termination from program involvement indicate that BBBF programs implemented for older children (4–8 years of age) had longer lasting positive effects on children and their families than did the BBBF programs implemented with younger children (0–4 years of age). These findings are inconsistent with a 'starting younger is better' view of ECD programs. How can these results, especially the lack of enduring effects from the younger child programs, be explained?

One possible reason for these differences is the greater amount of program involvement that occurred in the older-child BBBF sites. Since all children attended primary school during the four years of program implementation (kindergarten through Grade 2), and many of the BBBF child-focused programs were delivered either in the school or immediately before and after school hours, we found that 100 per cent of the children participated in BBBF programs. In two of three sites, 98 per cent of children attended programs eighty times or more over the four years. For younger children aged 0 to 4 years, there is no universal learning environment equivalent to the primary school system available or mandated for children or their parents. Consequently, it is more difficult to develop and implement prevention programs that have a high probability of reaching all infants and pre-school children and their families; for example, in one BBBF younger-child site only 15 per cent of families participated eighty times or more. The lower program exposure of children and their families in the younger-child BBBF sites relative to those in the three older-child sites may help to explain the absence of durable medium-term outcomes in the younger-child sites. To maintain the advantage of children from the younger-child BBBF sites through kindergarten and Grade 1, they likely would have benefited from extra support, such as educational assistants in the classroom and coordinators working to involve parents in the child's education. These latter activities have been used successfully in the older-child BBBF sites.

We can also compare the cost of the BBBF program with that of several other ECD programs for children aged 0 to 5 years (all costs are reported in 2005 Canadian dollars). For example, Olds' Nurse Home Visiting Program (Olds et al., 1998) cost over $5,000 per family per year for 2.5 years of home visits (six months prenatal and two years postnatal). The Abecedarian Project cost $20,000 per child/family per year for five years (Barnett & Masse, 2007), the Infant Health and Development Project cost over $23,000 per child/family per year for three years, Early Head Start cost approximately $10,000 per child/family per year for three years (Ludwig & Phillips, 2007), the Perry Preschool Project cost over $14,000 per child per year for two years (ages 3 and 4 years; Barnett, 1996), and the Chicago Child-Parent Centers Project cost on average over $7,500 per child per year for two years (ages 3 and 4 years; Reynolds et al., 2002). Contrast these figures with approximately $700 per child/family of resources available each year in the local younger-child BBBF budgets. This relative lack of resources likely contributed to the less than maximum participation rates and desirable outcomes in the younger-child program sites.

Also, differences in resources may not be the only reason for lack of lasting positive outcomes for the younger children. The results of a large, multi-site project (the Comprehensive Child Development Program, CCDP) implemented in the early 1990s in the United States provided up to $10,800 annually per child/family for five years to fund programs for children from birth to school entry at 5 years of age and their families; totalling over $50,000 per family over the five years (St Pierre et al., 1997). Despite this generous program funding, there were no significantly positive outcomes at age 5 on any of the wide array of child, parent, and family measures. St Pierre et al. comment: 'One of the findings that is emerging from studies of child development with some degree of consistency is that the best way to achieve positive effects is to provide intensive services directly to the individuals that you hope to affect. CCDP did not take this approach. Rather, CCDP funds were used to provide a wide variety of services to all family members, and the approach was broad-brush rather than intensive in nature. The idea of "comprehensive services" as implemented in CCDP meant that a great number of services were provided, but none of the services may have been provided with sufficient intensity to be effective' (1997, Chapter 8, p. 10).

The broad mandate for the BBBF programs (i.e., to improve all aspects of children's development, provide programs for parents and the neighbourhood while involving community residents in all project activities, and collaborate with other service providers) may have been asking too much of the younger-child sites. The older-child BBBF programs were organized in and around the neighbourhood schools attended by all children. These schools are funded by the Ontario Ministry of Education at the level of approximately $7,000 per child annually. The older-child BBBF programs were able to add their programs before, during, and after school hours, engaging virtually every child in ongoing programs during the school year for up to four years. The relatively modest BBBF program resources of $1,130 per child/family, then, represents 'value added' to the well-financed primary school system. For children younger than four years of age, there exists no comparable universal, well-financed service system with which to connect. If a universal, high-quality, affordable, optional early learning and child care system existed, similar to those in many European countries, the BBBF programs could be organized in conjunction with such a system. This could possibly provide 'value added' outcomes for children and their families similar to those of the BBBF programs in the three older-child sites.

Conclusion

Several conclusions arise from the BBBF longitudinal evaluation study. First, the outcome data collected immediately after the program ended indicated positive effects on children, families, and neighbourhoods in the BBBF sites relative to data collected from demographically matched comparison groups. This was true for both the younger-child (0–4 years) and older-child (4–8 years) projects.

Second, the longitudinal follow-up data collected from participants four years after the project ended (Grade 3 for younger-child programs, and Grade 6 for older-child programs) yielded no positive outcomes for the younger-child sites, but a wide range of positive child, family, and neighbourhood outcomes for the older-child sites. Similar positive outcomes were found three years later when youth from the three older-child BBBF sites were in Grade 9.

The failure to find durable effects for the younger-child BBBF programs may be related to low rates of participation, since it was difficult to identify and maintain contact with children between the ages of 0 and 4 years and their parents. Alternatively, in the older-child BBBF programs, it was possible to encourage parental participation and access families through schools starting at age 4 years. The modest investment by the Ontario government of $1,130 per family annually for four years, when added to the already substantial investment of $7,000 per child annually for primary education, appears to have provided 'value added' in terms of improved outcomes for young children and their families. No such universal government investment for children aged 0 to 4 years is currently available in Ontario in the form of, for example, a universal, high-quality, affordable early learning and child care program through which very young children could also be involved in an enrichment program such as BBBF.

Finally, economic analyses carried out for both Grade 9 and Grade 12 BBBF data collection periods suggested a return on the Ontario government's investment in the BBBF of approximately $1,000 per family at Grade 9, and over $4,500 per family at Grade 12. The costs to government of several of the best ECD programs with demonstrated long-term outcome effectiveness and positive cost savings were described previously. These model programs were carried out in the United States, most with small samples of very high risk or developmentally delayed young children. None were community based. Costs for these programs ranged from a low of $5,000 per family per year for 2.5 years to a high of $20,000 per family per year for five years.

These costs contrast sharply with the resources currently available for community-based ECD programs in Canada, often involving hundreds or thousands of young children and their families. This raises serious questions regarding the wisdom of implementing ECD programs such as those reviewed in this chapter, where the resources allocated to programs are less than $1,200 per family per year, (e.g., BBBF and CAPC). In several examples of provincially funded community-based ECD programs described for British Columbia, Alberta, and New Brunswick, the resources allocated were less than $200 per family annually. This leads one to wonder whether with so few resources, many community-based ECD initiatives are doomed to fail unless a universal, high-quality, and affordable early learning and child care system is established for children younger than 4 years of age. This would need to be a system funded to the level of current primary education systems (McCain, Mustard, & Shankar, 2007). If such a system existed, then community-based ECD programs for young children might be able to generate the added value that the BBBF programs are demonstrating in Ontario today.

Appendix

Program Objectives, Activities, Target Population, and Funding Source

Program/Source	Objectives and Program Activities	Target Population	Funding Source
Community Action Program for Children (PHAC, 2007a)	Funding for community-based groups to provide culturally competent prevention and intervention programs. Emphasizes building coalitions/ partnerships with community agencies. Recognizes all members of a community (e.g., prison-based parenting programs, street-level programs for mothers using substances).	Vulnerable children aged 0–6 years and families who often do not participate in mainstream health services and programs	PHAC
Canada Prenatal Nutrition Program (PHAC, 2007b)	Develop new or enhance existing prenatal health programs. Reduce incidence of low birth weight, strengthen community supports for women and build partnerships. Lifestyle counselling, food preparation training, transportation, child care and referral to other services. Programs offered include: food supplements, vitamin supplements, breastfeeding support, nutrition counselling.	Pregnant women facing conditions of risk (poverty and/ or family violence), adolescents, socially or geographically isolated, recently immigrated mothers	PHAC
Early Childhood Development Agreement (First Ministers' Communiqué, 2000)	Promote healthy pregnancy, birth and infancy (prenatal programs and screening). Improve parenting and family supports (family resource centres, parent information, and home visiting). Strengthen early childhood development learning and care (child care and targeted developmental programs for young children). Strengthen community supports (community-based planning and service integration).	Children 0–6 years and caregivers	Government of Canada

Program Objectives, Activities, Target Population, and Funding Source

Program/Source	Objectives and Program Activities	Target Population	Funding Source
Alberta Parent Link Centre Program (Government of Alberta, 2004)	Community-based centres partner with parents, schools, and community agencies to promote healthy child development (e.g., centres partner with agencies to provide housing assistance, job training, public health services, primary health care). Family services include parent education; early childhood care; family support; information and referrals.	Children aged 0–18 years and caregivers	Government of Alberta
British Columbia's Children First Initiatives (Government of British Columbia, 2009)	To increase community capacity, improve effectiveness of service delivery, engage hard-to-reach families, increase opportunities for early identification, and improve outcomes for children and families. Activities within core areas: coalition and partnership building, public awareness, research, advocacy, resource allocation, and evaluation Identify barriers that limit access for some populations.	Aboriginal and multicultural populations, hard-to-reach families, and those who must overcome barriers to access services	B.C. Ministry of Children and Family Development, regional budget allocations
Manitoba's Parent-Child Coalitions (Government of Manitoba, 2008)	Core priorities are: positive parenting, nutrition and physical health, literacy and learning, and community capacity building. Centre-based models include family resource centres, school hub models, home-based models such as home visiting programs and outreach services, workshops and training in parenting and literacy, community knowledge exchange forums, and mobile services such as book- and toy-lending programs.	Children 0–6 years and family members	Government of Manitoba

Program/Source	Objectives and Program Activities	Target Population	Funding Source
New Brunswick's Communities Raising Children and Excellence in Parenting Development (Government of New Brunswick, 2006, 2009)	To help communities develop strategies to support young children and provide information for parents. Provides information and support for parents to increase confidence and parenting skills (e.g., parenting information in libraries, information sessions, home visiting by early intervention specialists or nurses).	Children 0–6 years and their families and community partners	Government of New Brunswick
Ontario's Best Start Programs (Government of Ontario, 2006)	Provides prevention and intervention to prepare children for success when entering school. Services include: infant hearing programs, pre-school speech and hearing programs, licensed child care, services for children who are blind or have low vision, screening for new mothers in hospitals, home visit or phone call from nurse post-delivery of baby, referrals to services such as breastfeeding, nutrition and health services, play and parenting programs, and child screening tools.	Children prenatal to age 6 years and family members. Special focus on families facing conditions of risk	Government of Ontario

PHAC = Public Health Agency of Canada

References

Barnett, W.S. (1996). *Lives in the balance: Age-27 benefit-cost analysis of the High/Scope Perry Preschool Program*. Monographs of the High/Scope Educational Research Foundation, 11. Ypsilanti, MI: High/Scope Press.

Barnett, W.S., & Masse, L.N. (2007). Comparative benefit-cost analysis of the Abecedarian program and its policy implications. *Economics of Education Review, 26,* 113–125.

Boyle, M.H., & Willms, J.D. (2002). Impact evaluation of a national, community-based program for at-risk children in Canada. *Canadian Public Policy,*
28, 461–481.

Bronfenbrenner, U. (1979). *The ecology of human development.* Cambridge, MA:
Harvard University Press.

First Ministers' Communiqué. (2000). *First ministers' meeting communiqué on*
early childhood development. Retrieved from http://www.ecd-elcc.ca/eng/
ecd/ ecd_communique.shtml.

Friendly, M., Beach, J., Ferns, C., & Turiano, M. (2007). *Early childhood education*
and care in Canada 2006. 7th ed. Retrieved from http://childcarecanada.org/
ECEC2006/ index.html#toc.

Government of Alberta. (2004). *Parent Links: A network of resource centres serv-*
ing parents, caregivers and children in Alberta. Alberta Children's Services.
Retrieved from http://www.child.alberta.ca/home/documents/parenting/
ParentLinksGuidelineandBestPracticesExcerpt.pdf.

Government of Alberta. (2008). *Alberta Children's Services annual report.* Retrieved from http://www.child.alberta.ca/home/documents/ministry/
CS_AnnualReport20080919.pdf.

Government of British Columbia. Ministry of Children and Family Development. (2007). *British Columbia's Early Years' annual report 2006/2007.* Retrieved from http://www.mcf.gov.B.C.ca/early_childhood/pdf/ecd_an
nual_06_07.pdf.

Government of British Columbia. Ministry of Children and Family Devel-
opment. (2009). *British Columbia's Early Years' annual report 2007/2008.*
Retrieved from http://www.mcf.gov.B.C.ca/early_childhood/pdf/Early-
YearsAnnualReport2009_Web.pdf.

Government of Manitoba. (2008). *2007/08 annual report of the Healthy Child*
Manitoba Office. Retrieved from http://www.gov.mb.ca/healthychild/
about/annual_report_2007_08.pdf.

Government of New Brunswick. (2006). *Greater opportunities for New Brunswick*
children: An early childhood development agenda. Update: Investments and activi-
ties 2004/05 and 2005/06. Retrieved from http://www.gnb.ca/0017/Chil
dren/ECDInvestmentsActivities-e.pdf.

Government of New Brunswick. (2009). *For our children's well-being. Early child-*
hood services in New Brunswick: Investments and Outcomes (2006/07). Retrieved
from http://www.gnb.ca/0017/children/ECD0607-e.pdf.

Government of Ontario. (1990). *Better Beginnings, Better Futures: An integrated*
model of primary prevention of emotional and behavioural problems. Toronto:
Queen's Printer.

Government of Ontario. (2006). *Ontario's investments in early childhood develop-*
ment. Early learning and child care 2005/2006 annual report. Retrieved from
http://www.ontla.on.ca/library/repository/ser/245177/2005–2006.pdf.

Ludwig, J., & Phillips, D. (2007). The benefits and costs of Head Start. *SRCD*
Social Policy Report: Giving Child and Youth Development Knowledge Away,
21(3), 3–18.

McCain, M.N., Mustard, J.F., & Shankar, S. (2007). *Early Years Study 2: Putting*
science into action. Toronto: Council for Early Child Development. Retrieved
from http://www.councilecd.ca/cecd/home.nsf/7F1B.CE63A330D01785257
2AA00625B79/$file/Early_Years_2_rev.pdf.

McMurchy, D., & Palmer, R.W.H. (2008). *An assessment of the economic impact*
of the Canada Prenatal Nutrition Program. Prepared for the Public Health
Agency of Canada. Summative evaluation of the Canada Prenatal Nutrition
Program 2004–2009. Retrieved from www.phac-aspc.gc.ca.

Offord, D.R., Boyle, M.H., Szatmari, P., Rae-Grant, N.I., Links, P.S., Cadman,
D.T., et al. (1987). Ontario Child Health Study. II: Six month prevalence of
disorder and rates of service utilization. *Archives of General Psychiatry, 44,*
832–836.

Olds, D.L., Henderson, C.R., Cole, R., Eckenrode, J., Kitzman, H., Luckey, D.,
et al. (1998). Long-term effects of nurse home visitation on children's
criminal and antisocial behavior. *Journal of the American Medical Association,*
280(14), 1238–1244.

Organization for Economic Co-operation and Development (2009). *OECD*
Factbook 2009: Economic environmental and social statistics. Paris: Author.

Peters, R.D., Arnold, R., Petrunka, K., Angus, D., Brophy, K., et al. (2000).
Developing capacity and competence in the Better Beginnings, Better Futures
Communities: Short-term findings report. Technical Report. Kingston, ON:
Better Beginnings Research Coordination Unit. Retrieved from http://bbbf.
queensu.ca/pdfs/r_stfr.pdf.

Peters, R.D., Bradshaw, A.J., Petrunka, K., Nelson, G., Herry, Y., Craig, W.M.,
et al. (2010). The 'Better Beginnings, Better Futures' ecological, community-
based early childhood prevention project: Findings from Grade 3 to Grade 9.
Monographs of the Society for Research in Child Development, 75(3).

Peters, R.D., Nelson, G., Petrunka, K., Pancer, S.M., Loomis, C., Hasford, J.,
et al., (2010).
Investing in our future: Highlights of Better Beginnings, Better Futures research
findings at Grade 12. Kingston, ON: Better Beginnings, Better Futures Research Coordination Unit, Queen's University.

Peters, R.D., Petrunka, K., & Arnold, R. (2003). The Better Beginnings, Better
Futures Project. A universal, comprehensive, community-based prevention

approach for primary school children and their families. *Journal of Clinical Child and Adolescent Psychology, 32,* 215–226.

Public Health Agency of Canada (PHAC). (2007a). *Formative evaluation of the Community Action Program for Children* (TBS File No. 999843). Retrieved from http://www.phac-aspc.gc.ca/dca-dea/programs-mes/comm-eval/index-eng.php.

Public Health Agency of Canada (PHAC). (2007b). *The Canada Prenatal Nutrition Program: A decade of promoting the health of mothers, babies and communities.* Retrieved from http://www.phac-aspc.gc.ca/dca-dea/publications/pdf/mb_e.pdf.

Public Health Agency of Canada (PHAC). (2010). *Community Action Plan for Children.* Retrieved from http://www.phac-aspc.gc.ca/dca-dea/programs-mes/capc_goals-eng.php.

Ramey, C.T., & Campbell, F.A. (1984). Preventive education for high-risk children: Cognitive consequences of the Carolina Abecedarian Project. *American Journal on Mental Deficiency, 88,* 515–523.

Reynolds, A.J., Temple, J.A., Robertson, D.L., & Mann, E.A. (2002). Age 21 cost-benefit analysis of the Title I Chicago Child-Parent Centers. *Educational Evaluation and Policy Analysis, 24,* 267–303.

Roche, J., Petrunka, K., & Peters, R.D. (2008). *Investing in our future: Highlights of Better Beginnings, Better Futures research findings at Grade 9.* Kingston, ON: Better Beginnings, Better Futures Research Coordination Unit. Retrieved from http://bbbf.queensu.ca/pdfs/BB%20Report%20O31.pdf.

Schweinhart, L.J., Barnes, H.V., Weikart, D.P., Barnett, W.S., & Epstein, A.S. (1993). *Significant benefits: The High/Scope Perry Preschool Project through age 27.* Ypsilanti, MI: High/Scope Press.

Statistics Canada. (2007). *Births.* Statistics Canada Catalogue no. 84F0210X. Ottawa: Author. Retrieved from http://www.statcan.gc.ca/pub/84f0210x/2007000/aftertoc-aprestdm1-eng.htm.

St Pierre, R.G., Layzer, J.I., Goodson, B.D., & Bernstein, L.S. (1997). *National impact evaluation of the Comprehensive Child Development Program: Final report.* Cambridge, MA: Abt Associates.

Willms, J.D. (2002). *Vulnerable children: Findings from Canada's National Longitudinal Survey of Children and Youth.* Edmonton: University of Alberta Press.

12 Federal Investments in Strengthening Indigenous Capacity for Culturally Based Early Childhood Education and Care

JESSICA BALL

Many Indigenous children in Canada, as around the globe, experience inequities in infant mortality, health, development, education, and prospects for social inclusion throughout their lives. Despite explicit recognition of this situation by the federal government and rhetoric about commitments to remedy it (Assembly of First Nations, 2006), these disparities persist. They result from a combination of risk factors, especially poverty and associated poor quality of life and social stigma, colonial history and associated depletion of cultural and family assets, racism, and lack of awareness on the part of the general public about how colonial policies created hardships for Indigenous families that continue to the present day (Hackett, 2005). This lack of awareness contributes to a lack of political will to invest in structural reforms and deliver on promises made in Canada's Aboriginal Action Plan (Minister of Indian Affairs and Northern Development, 1997) – and reiterated in the federal government's second apology to Indigenous Peoples in 2008 (Office of the Prime Minister of Canada, 2008).

Early childhood education and care (ECEC) provisions can mitigate risks for disadvantaged children and enhance their opportunities for health, development, and social belonging while equalizing readiness for school. Indigenous Peoples in Canada have long recognized the crucial importance of the early years for nurturing a child's capabilities, and have identified culturally based ECEC as a priority for federal investments. Generally, funding for the health, education, and welfare of children living on reserves is the responsibility of the Government of Canada, while for other Aboriginal children, meeting these needs may be a federal or provincial responsibility depending on the specific sub-population and geographical location. The federal government's growing commitment to ECEC provisions is a bright light in an otherwise gloomy landscape of federal government support for young Indigenous children. Federal funding committed in 1995 for Aboriginal Head Start (AHS) programs on reserves and in 1999 for programs off reserves, has resulted in a growth of capacity in First Nations, Métis, and Inuit communities to create and operate culturally based ECEC programs over the past fifteen years. The model developed for AHS programs is particularly effective and instructive in its use of a centrally mandated set of program dimensions and a decentralized approach to program design and curriculum decision making.

This chapter discusses challenges facing Indigenous children that can be ameliorated to some extent by ECEC provisions. The discussion describes how the Aboriginal Head Start program provides scope for local identification of needs and goals for children in order to design well-utilized, effective programs. Outcome research undertaken to date is reviewed, including a study that illustrates how some Indigenous communities have used initiatives like AHS as a central organizing point, or *hook*, in a larger community development strategy, and have incrementally introduced social, health, and education programs that are co-located or coordinated with the ECEC program to form a community service hub (see also chapter by Janette Pelletier in this volume). While federal investments have delivered rudimentary ECEC training, federal funds for post-secondary education that yields early childhood education (ECE) credentials have not been deployed. This chapter describes a bicultural, community-based post-secondary education program that has documented success in supporting the growth of ECEC provisions for young Indigenous children. The development of a fully qualified Indigenous ECE workforce is identified as an outstanding need, as well as expanded access to Aboriginal Head Start and other quality ECEC programs for Indigenous children.

Indigenous Children in Canada

Who Are Indigenous Children?

In Canada, Indigenous Peoples are commonly known as *Aboriginal*; they make up about 4 per cent of the Canadian population, with 1,311,200 self-reporting on the 2006 census form that they have an

Aboriginal identity (Statistics Canada, 2006).[1] The 1982 Canadian Constitution Act recognizes three separate peoples as original inhabitants: Inuit, Métis, and North American Indians, known as First Nations. Between 1996 and 2006, the Aboriginal population in Canada grew by 45 per cent, nearly six times faster than the 8 per cent increase of the non-Aboriginal population (Statistics Canada, 2006). The population across all three Indigenous groups is much younger than the Canadian average, with a median age in 2006 of 26.5 years, compared with 39.5 years for all Canadians. The 2006 census enumerated 130,000 Indigenous children under 6 years old, including approximately 7,000 Inuit, 35,000 Métis, 48,000 First Nations children living off reserves, and 40,000 First Nations children living on reserves.[2] Demographers project that the Indigenous population will remain significantly younger and maintain its high growth rate relative to the non-Aboriginal population for at least the next twenty years, with an increase of about 47 per cent by 2026 (Indian and Northern Affairs Canada & Canadian Housing and Mortgage Corporation, 2007; Steffler, 2008). Although Aboriginal children and youth currently comprise less than 5 per cent of the population, they are a growing proportion of all Canadian children, particularly in the Yukon, Northwest Territories, Nunavut, Saskatchewan, and Manitoba. For example, in 2006 in Saskatchewan, Aboriginal children made up 20 per cent of all children under 6 years old.

Challenges Faced by Indigenous Children

Indigenous children are arguably the most socially disadvantaged population in Canada. Indigenous Peoples in Canada have the lowest quality of life and the shortest life expectancies (Cooke, Beavon, & McHardy, 2004; Salee, 2006). Indigenous children suffer from significantly higher incidence rates on nearly every health indicator, especially chronic middle ear infections and early hearing loss, respiratory tract disorders and asthma, fetal alcohol spectrum disorder (FASD), and accidental

---

1 People designated by the federal government as Aboriginal are increasingly favouring the term *Indigenous* because it serves to identify them with Indigenous Peoples worldwide, who face many similar issues.

2 A reserve is land set apart and designated for the use and occupancy of an Indian group or band. As such, the terms *on-reserve* or *off-reserve* are generally not applicable to Métis or Inuit peoples.

injury (Adelson, 2005; Canadian Institute for Health Information, 2004; Kohen, Uppal, & Guevremont, 2007; Smylie & Adomako, 2009).

As a population, Indigenous children begin to show difficulties early on in their educational trajectories. For example, in a study of ten schools across Canada, between 40 per cent and 50 per cent of Indigenous students failed to meet the requirements of Grades 4, 7, and 10 literacy tests (Bell et al., 2004).[3] During the 1996 to 2006 period, secondary school completion among Indigenous youth has stayed the same or declined (Mendelson, 2008). The gap in high school attainment is highest for Inuit (3.6 times higher than the Canadian average).[4] Low levels of formal education are associated with higher unemployment and lower lifetime income (Riddell, 2006), poorer physical and mental health, inadequate life skills, lack of social support systems, dependence on welfare, and incarceration (Howe, 2002; Stearns & Glennie, 2006). Compared with the Canadian average, labour market outcomes for the Indigenous population are significantly poorer, including lower incomes and higher unemployment (Sharpe & Arsenault, 2009). There is increasing recognition of the failure of the education system to drive Indigenous Peoples' recovery from the devastations of past colonial policies – including the Indian residential schools and the prohibition against Indigenous participation in post-secondary education except in limited vocational fields.

Poor education outcomes tend to be multigenerational. Canada's shame is that, until recently, Indigenous Peoples were actually excluded by federal government policies from educational opportunities equivalent to those offered to non-Indigenous Peoples. Thus, many Indigenous young people today live in families that have been more harmed than helped by mainstream education, and in communities

---

3 British Columbia is unique because it is the only province, to date, to organize educational assessments in a manner that provides evidence on the relative performance of Aboriginal students in the provincial school system. For example, in 2003, the Ministry of Education in British Columbia found that Aboriginal students in Grade 4 were 'not meeting expectations' at a rate 16 per cent higher than non-Aboriginal students. In Grade 7, this figure rose to 21 per cent. J. Richards and A. Vining, *Aboriginal off-reserve education: Time for action* (Ottawa: C.D. Howe Institute, 2004).

4 Significantly, one of the primary reasons Inuit students now state for leaving high school is to care for a child (Government of Nunavut and Nunavut Tunngavik Inc., 2004).

that have not even had school-aged children and youth living in the community until quite recently when the era of enforced residential schooling finally ended. Many Indigenous parents understandably are unsure whether to trust the public education system, and unsure of how to support their children's engagement in formal schooling, including what kinds of early stimulation may help to prepare them for school. Indigenous leaders and agencies across Canada have long argued that overall lack of services before children enter formal schooling and during the primary school years, as well as culturally inappropriate tools for monitoring, screening, assessing, and providing extra supports, frequently result in serious negative consequences for Aboriginal children (British Columbia Aboriginal Network on Disability Society, 1996; Canadian Centre for Justice, 2001; First Nations Child and Family Caring Society, 2005; Royal Commission on Aboriginal Peoples, 1996). Negative outcomes that have been identified include over- and under-recognition of children with developmental challenges, early intervention services introduced too late, undermining Indigenous language and cultural goals for development through an overvaluing of standard urban English and of monolingualism, cultural alienation, low levels of school readiness, and high rates of early school failure and premature school leaving. Overall, indicators of developmental challenges and negative outcomes experienced by many Aboriginal children, combined with their high rates of health problems, are so alarming that the Council of Ministers of Education state: 'There is recognition in all educational jurisdictions that the achievement rates of Aboriginal children, including the completion of secondary school, must be improved. Studies have shown that some of the factors contributing to this low level of academic achievement are that Aboriginals in Canada have the lowest income and thus the highest rates of poverty, the highest rate of drop-outs from formal education, and the lowest health indicators of any group' (2004, p. 22).

This recognition should be enough to make family supports, prevention, and early intervention services for Indigenous children a priority for federal, provincial, and territorial governments. Given the impact of school readiness and educational success on labour market participation and the overall economy, quality ECEC programs are a low-hanging fruit with far-reaching and considerable economic and social benefits for a country as a whole. Early learning experiences in a safe, stimulating environment at home or in an early learning program can help children develop cognitive and language skills so that they encounter the world with confidence in their ability to manage themselves and solve simple problems. With this kind of early experience, when children start school they are likely to see themselves as capable and feel they belong. On the other hand, early experiences of being unable to handle the learning challenges in school are associated with low self-esteem, and can lead to years of poor academic performance and culminating in early school dropout (Audas & Willms, 2001; Lee & Burkam, 2003).

Unlike most high-income countries, Canada lacks a national strategy to ensure access to quality programs to actively support optimal development during the early years for all children or for children in an identified risk category. Early childhood programs for all children are part of a piecemeal collection of programs and services. However, the situation is vastly bleaker for young Indigenous children (Bennett, 2003). Many young Indigenous children with chronic health problems, developmental delays, or disabilities are never seen by developmental specialists such as infant development consultants, occupational therapists, paediatricians, or speech-language pathologists (deLeeuw, Fiske, & Greenwood, 2002). Only about 18 per cent of Indigenous children in Canada have access to any ECEC program (Leitch, 2008).

A Multisectoral Approach to Improve Outcomes for Indigenous Children

Health and education inequalities of Indigenous children are understood to reflect primarily the cumulative effects of pervasive poverty and social exclusion (Ball, 2008; Canadian Institute of Child Health, 2000; Salée, 2006). Several studies have shown that up to 50 per cent of the variance in early childhood outcomes is associated with socioeconomic status (SES; Canada Council on Learning, 2007; Case et al., 2002; Dearing, 2008; Raver et al., 2007; Weitzman, 2003). Closing gaps in health and education outcomes for Indigenous children requires a multisectoral approach at all levels of government. First, the conditions of life for Indigenous children must be improved through structural reforms and infrastructure development that reduces poverty, food insecurity, lack of road access to programs and services, exposure to racism, and other social exclusions. Second, since health and nutrition impact attention, language development, and capacity for learning, provisions of nutritious foods and timely, accessible health care, early intervention, and ongoing services for children with chronic health conditions must be secured. Third, when Indigenous children attend school, the language of instruction, teaching methods, curriculum content, and expectations for parents' involvement must be linguistically and culturally appropriate. Fourth, quality ECEC programs that reflect the values, goals, and needs of the parents of Indigenous children, such as the Aboriginal Head Start program described below, must be provided so that communities can address these needs.

The Role of Early Childhood Education and Care

Policy makers around the world increasingly recognize the importance of early childhood education and care as foundational for lifelong learning. Research on the developing brain, the human genome, and the impact of early childhood experiences on later learning, behaviour, and health has converged to create a compelling argument for investing in programs to provide optimal conditions for children's growth and development before formal schooling (Shonkoff & Phillips, 2000). The early years lay the foundation for a lifetime of learning, physical and mental health, responsible citizenship, economic productivity, and parenting the next generation. High quality early childhood care and development programs have been shown to be a powerful equalizer in nurturing the social adjustment and communication skills needed for participation in schooling, promoting excitement about learning, and engendering a sense of oneself as a capable learner (Irwin, Siddiqi, & Hertzman, 2007). Extensive research shows that targeted investments in a range of community-fitting or locally designed programs during the early years can make a difference in short- and long-term health, development, educational achievement, economic success, and subsequent parenting of the next generation of offspring (Cleveland & Krashinsky, 2003; Doherty, 2007; Heckman, 2006). Most research on early childhood programs has investigated centre-based programs. Evidence supports the potential cognitive benefits of centre-based early childhood programs for children 3 years of age and older if these programs are of high quality and congruent with children's language and culture (Canadian Council on Learning, 2007). Although almost no outcome research has focused on Indigenous children, families who are impoverished, facing high stress, and/or who lack access to safe, reliable, nurturing care for infants and young children appear to be most likely to benefit from such programs (Grantham-McGregor et al., 2007; Jolly, 2007; Magnuson, Ruhm, & Waldfogel, 2006).

Indigenous Calls for Investments in Culturally Based Early Childhood Education and Care

Beginning in 1990 with a statement from the Native Council of Canada (1990), Indigenous community representatives, leaders, practitioners, and investigators have vocalized the need for an adequately resourced, sustained, and culturally based national strategy to improve supports for young Indigenous children's development as part of a program of efforts to equalize their readiness for school and increase school retention, achievement, and completion. Stakeholders call for resources to enable children to acquire skills valued by Indigenous parents, such as learning their Indigenous language, and services to address health and developmental difficulties, such as ear infections and hearing loss, before children start school. The Royal Commission on Aboriginal Peoples (1996) called for these supports to be delivered within the contexts of children's families and cultural communities through community-driven programs operated by Indigenous practitioners with relevant professional education. It recommended that 'federal, provincial, and territorial governments co-operate to support an integrated early childhood funding strategy that: (a) extends early childhood education to all Aboriginal children regardless of residence; (b) encourages programs that foster the physical, social, intellectual and spiritual development of children, reducing distinctions between child care, prevention and education; (c) maximizes Aboriginal control over service design and administration; (d) offers one-stop accessible funding; and (e) promotes parental involvement and choice in early childhood education options' (vol. 3, chapter 5.2, 3.5.3).

Federal Investments in Aboriginal Head Start

Program Scope

In most of Canada's ten provinces and three territories, the provision of ECEC for First Nations children living on reserves and for Inuit children is the responsibility of the federal government or a First Nation government. Over the past fifteen years, federal investments have supported a groundswell of Indigenous ECEC capacity, including many promising culturally based program innovations. Human Resources and Social Development Canada funds a First Nations and Inuit Child Care Initiative, which, in 2010, supported 462 sites in First Nation and Inuit communities, providing child care to 8,538 children of parents who were working or training for the labour market. Federal spending on the First Nations and Inuit Child Care Initiative increased from $41.0 million in 2000 to $57.1 million in 2010. Indian and Northern Affairs Canada funds approximately 812 child care spaces on eighteen First Nation reserves in Alberta, and approximately 2,850 child care spaces on fifty-two First Nation reserves in Ontario. These programs are intended to provide ECEC services that are comparable to those offered by the respective provincial governments to people living off reserves. Federal spending through Indian and Northern Affairs Canada for these child care spaces in Alberta and Ontario totalled approximately $20.4 million in 2010. Regulation of federally funded child care spaces is patchy: not all provinces carry out regulation of on-reserve child care. Some First Nations communities do not recognize provincial jurisdiction on reserves. Generally, First Nations and Inuit organizations have responsibility for the administration of funds and delivering services. Several provinces and territories have also invested in important ECEC initiatives in the areas of home-visiting programs targeting infants' and toddlers' wellness and development, parent education and support, as well as networking and resource exchange.

By far the largest impact on the availability and cultural appropriateness of ECEC provisions for Indigenous youngsters has been through the inception and steady expansion of Aboriginal Head Start (AHS). Since 1995, for First Nation, Inuit, and Métis children living in urban and northern communities, the Public Health Agency of Canada (PHAC) has funded the delivery of Aboriginal Head Start in Urban and Northern Communities, including approximately 140 pre-school programs in 2010. Federal spending on the Aboriginal Head Start in Urban and Northern Communities program in 2010 was approximately $29 million. Since 1999, for First Nation children living on reserves and Inuit children, the federal government has funded Health Canada's Aboriginal Head Start On-Reserve program, delivered in 383 communities in 2010. Federal spending on the Aboriginal Head Start On-Reserve program in 2010 was approximately $51 million. The two branches of the federal government that fund AHS also support the training of Indigenous community members to staff AHS and other federally funded programs. However, as will be discussed later in this chapter, federal commitments for post-secondary programs in early childhood education (ECE) lag far behind commitments to non-accredited, short-term training, and to expanding pre-school spaces.

Program Overview

Following the inception of the AHS program, increases in Indigenous participation in ECEC were indicated in parents' reports on the 2001 Aboriginal Peoples Survey. Of Aboriginal children entering Grade 1, 16 per cent had participated in Aboriginal-specific programs during their pre-school years, compared with only 4 per cent of 14-year-olds (Statistics Canada, 2001). The survey also indicated that the proportion of Aboriginal children living off-reserve and attending early childhood programs specifically designed for them had increased fourfold over an eight-year period, reflecting in large measure the federal investment in AHS. In 2008, a review by the child and youth adviser to the federal health minister estimated that 18 per cent of Indigenous children across Canada have access to an ECEC program (Leitch, 2008). AHS was the program most commonly accessed and that seemed to have the most support among Indigenous families and community representatives; the special adviser recommended increasing federal investment to enable 25 per cent of Indigenous pre-schoolers to access AHS programs.

AHS is for children up to 6 years of age, and most programs focus on pre-schoolers aged 3 to 5 years. Criteria for selecting children to attend the program vary from one community to another. Some programs reserve a number of spaces for children referred by child welfare or by community social service agencies. Depending on staff qualifications and appropriate facilities, most programs reserve spaces for children with special needs; some set aside a day for children with special needs and their primary caregivers. Some programs give priority to siblings of children who have attended or are currently enrolled in the program.

AHS programs typically operate on a part-time basis three or four days a week. Most operate primarily in English or French, with some effort to expose children to one or more Indigenous language(s). In a minority of programs, an Indigenous language is the primary language, with English or French used as a second language or not at all.

AHS directly involves parents and communities in project management and operations. Programs are locally operated by Aboriginal,

Métis, or Inuit non-profit community organizations (in the case of the Aboriginal Head Start in Urban and Northern Communities program) or First Nation governing bodies (in the case of the Aboriginal Head Start On-Reserve program). A community group that receives funding for program delivery works with parents and other stakeholders to decide on program specifics. National and regional committees of Aboriginal representatives oversee program implementation, and each program has a parent advisory committee. Provisions for parental involvement vary: some programs require parents to volunteer; some ask parents to either volunteer or donate money, food, or other supplies; some programs have no expectation of direct parental involvement.

A majority of staff in both the on-reserve and urban and northern AHS programs are Indigenous. Staff typically include early childhood practitioners who may or may not have formal ECE credentials, managers, administrative support, and in some programs, parent outreach workers, bus drivers, and cooks (Health Canada, 2002). Staff work with community Elders, Indigenous language specialists, and parents to enhance child development, school readiness, and children's cultural pride. As well, staff typically coordinate the AHS program with other services for young children and families in the area, and often work closely with professional service providers who periodically visit the community to conduct screening and diagnostic assessment, deliver early intervention services, or monitor children who have ongoing health or developmental needs.

AHS in Canada is similar to the Head Start approach developed in the United States (Zigler & Valentine, 1979) insofar as the program integrates provisions for children's health, nutrition, education, and family development; however, important differences exist. While both programs share the overall goal of preparing children for successful transition from home to school learning environments, the focus of Head Start in the United States is on school readiness for low-income children, and the federal government establishes eligibility for enrolment largely based on family income. The U.S. program uses a prescribed curriculum with standardized tools for measuring and reporting on children's early learning; in Canada, holistic development, cultural pride, and eagerness for learning are emphasized. The programs focus on culturally fitting, community-specific elaborations of the following six program components, as shown in Figure 12.1: (1) culture and language; (2) education and school readiness; (3) health promotion; (4) nutrition; (5) social support; and (6) parent/family involvement.

Figure 12.1. Six mandated program components of Aboriginal Head Start.
© Jessica Ball, 2012.

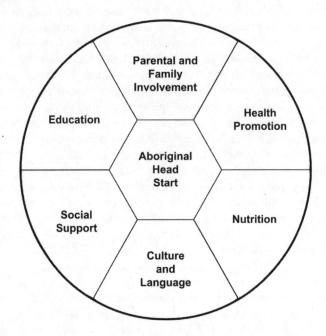

In Canadian program literature, AHS is more often described in terms of early intervention than school readiness, a recognition both that the long era of Indian residential schools created multigenerational obstacles to school success and that a high level of need exists among Indigenous children. For example, early reports (e.g., Health Canada, 2005 and later evaluations (e.g., Public Health Agency of Canada, 2006; Western Arctic Aboriginal Head Start Council, 2007) indicate that at least one-quarter of the children enrolled in AHS have developmental delays or specific learning difficulties such as Fetal Alcohol Spectrum Disorder and language-related disorders.

Local control of AHS programs allows for innovation to find the best curricula and staff for each community and child. No standard early learning curriculum for children or training curriculum for staff is required or commonly used across programs. High/Scope training and curricula were used as a platform to launch the AHS program and as a starting point for community-based programs to deliver developmentally appropriate early learning activities. Over time, AHS programs have diversified and incorporated curriculum ideas and resources from various sources; they have also involved community members in creating culturally informed learning resources such as stories, songs, books, arts and crafts, science projects, and activities to promote at least rudimentary exposure to the local Indigenous language. As well, national and regional workshops and conferences have provided an array of opportunities to AHS staff to consider different kinds of learning objectives, approaches, curricula, and materials that might suit the objectives, needs, and interests of children and families involved in their particular program.

Programs use various approaches to monitoring program quality and children's learning. Some programs do not use a structured approach, while others employ a regimen of developmental or learning assessment tools at regular intervals. For example, a survey of AHS programs in urban and northern communities in British Columbia indicated that the Ages and Stages Questionnaire (Bricker et al., 1995), especially the tool's social and emotional scales, was used in a majority of programs and received favourable reviews (Ball, 2006). However, the manner in which the tool was used varied widely; some programs reported simply offering it to parents to review if they wished, while other programs used it as a guide for staff to have a conversation with a parent about their child. No programs reported scoring the tool or using it as a screening instrument for referral or early identification. Most programs reported using some kind of checklist to track each child's progress on developmental milestones or learning tasks. Often these checklists are tailor-made at the program site to fit locally defined learning objectives. In a study involving four Indigenous communities (Ball & Janyst, 2008), including three with AHS programs, the staff, and especially parents expressed strong views that standardized developmental or learning assessment tools would not be appropriate for their ECEC programs at this time. They saw the primary objective of the programs as providing safe and stimulating environments for young children to develop their cultural knowledge, confidence as learners, and readiness to learn, including focusing attention, listening, and learning by observing. Equally important, they emphasized parent involvement with the program as instrumental in rebuilding their confidence and skills to support their child's well-being, including nutritious food preparation; health and dental care; indoor and outdoor activities that promote learning, language, and literacy stimulation, and encourage learning through play. Standardized assessment tools were seen as imported and imposed, not as a priority for achieving local program goals.

Evaluation

Enormous variability across AHS programs in the way each of the six program components is delivered presents challenges for evaluation. To date, no program of controlled empirical research has evaluated the impact of AHS. Beyond annual evaluations for purposes of operational accountability, no known research has focused on evaluating the Aboriginal Head Start On-Reserve program. The Aboriginal Head Start in Urban and Northern Communities program has been the focus of some evaluation efforts, including a descriptive evaluation released in 2002 (Minister of Public Works and Government Services, 2001) and a three-year national impact evaluation completed in 2006 (Public Health Agency of Canada, 2007). The 2002 evaluation focused mostly on demographic characteristics of the children served, parents' involvement, and information about program facilities and components. The overall impression from this evaluation was that AHS was extremely well received and was seen by parents as beneficial to their children and themselves in many respects; however, no systematic assessment was made of the impact on specific areas of child development, health, or quality of life.

Approaches to measuring the impact of the program have been fraught with difficulties, partly due to a lack of appropriate tools to measure Aboriginal children's development in ways that are readily amenable to standardized scoring and composite analysis. The national impact evaluation of the Aboriginal Head Start in Urban and Northern Communities program appears to have encountered several problems, including widely varying interpretations across evaluation sites concerning dimensions to be evaluated and scoring criteria. The evaluation did not include procedures with established validity or reliability for measuring baseline, exit, or longitudinal levels of children's health, development, cultural knowledge, or quality of life, nor parents' confidence, competence, or social support. Qualitative data collected in the program sites would have been difficult to interpret and analyse across the research sites. The evaluation did not ask exactly what sites were doing to promote various measurable developmental outcomes. Also, the research design did not include comparison or control groups, which is always ethically and practically challenging in small communities.

While a detailed report of the findings of the Aboriginal Head Start in Urban and Northern Communities national impact evaluation has not yet been released, a brief overview of the results is available. Researchers used the Work Sampling System (Meisels et al., 2001), which draws on practitioners' assessment of the child's performance in various skill areas, to obtain data. They reported that children in ten participating program sites had low baseline scores on language and literacy when they started the program and showed 'moderate proficiency' in these areas after one year (Public Health Agency of Canada, 2007). Children showed greatest proficiency in physical development and health. Parents reported increases in their children's practice of their Indigenous cultural traditions and in Indigenous language acquisition. No direct measurement of children's behaviours was used. Given the limitations of the study design and data analyses, it is not possible to draw conclusions about the effects of children's participation in AHS on their health or development nor the effectiveness of AHS as an early intervention for vulnerable children or parents.

An evaluation of AHS sites in the Northwest Territories, undertaken from 1996 to 2006 by the Western Arctic AHS Council (2007), used a somewhat more robust and practical evaluation method. From 2000 to 2001, and again in 2004, data were collected on various child outcomes identified as important by local program staff, using measures of each child's overall health and development, social skills, and vocabulary that were seen by local advisers as having potential validity for First Nations children. The investigator concluded that children came to the program with a wide variety of skill levels; many children had developmental delays in language and social skills, and most children showed some improvement after one year in AHS. Many children improved their scores on the Brigance (1998) pre-school and kindergarten screening scales after one year, but one-third to one-half were still delayed in terms of school readiness skills. The most positive findings came from parent and community ratings of the program's culture and language components. The evaluation concluded that one of the strongest features of the AHS movement in the Northwest Territories is the site-specific identity, focus, and dedication to the promotion of local culture, language, and traditions. This community collaboration on a multisite program evaluation is a promising first step upon which to build future impact evaluation research.

Another perspective on the impact of AHS comes from the Regional Health Survey conducted by the First Nations Centre (2005). The findings, based on reports by children's primary caregivers, indicate that AHS helped children to become ready for school as measured by reduced risk of repeating a grade: 11.6 per cent of AHS attendees repeated a grade, compared with 18.7 per cent of non-attendees who repeated a grade.

Although efforts to evaluate the impact of AHS do not yield a very differentiated view of how AHS affects children, the findings are encouraging. Clearly, independent research evaluating AHS using quasi-empirical designs involving comparison groups and culturally appropriate measures amenable to comparative analysis would be timely and informative for future refinements of AHS.

Promising Features

While more work is needed to establish research-based evidence of the ways in which AHS impacts Indigenous children's quality of life and developmental outcomes, the AHS model has a number of positive and promising features that are highly congruent with principles advocated by many Indigenous organizations.

For example, AHS programs provide safe, supervised, stimulating environments for young children. This is especially important for children whose home environments may be crowded, chaotic, or contaminated. Many programs provide nutritional supplementation; cognitive stimulation; socialization with Indigenous peers, adult role models, and Elders; and exposure to Indigenous language and spirituality. These opportunities promote children's health, development, cultural knowledge and pride, and are valued by Aboriginal parents.

AHS programs also help to fill gaps in services to support families during the early stages of family formation when parents – many of them very young and with few resources – need social support and practical assistance. The programs are mandated to provide opportunities for parent involvement and support. Program reports describe a wide range of ways that programs reach out to parents (e.g., involving them in children's activities, parenting education, home economics, food preparation, cultural events, community fairs, language and literacy facilitation programs, resources to assist with job searches, and social and health service referrals; Health Canada, 2002).

AHS has been a timely and effective vehicle to enable communities to deliver ECEC programs in culturally congruent ways to children who need them most. AHS programs have the flexibility to develop in ways that are family-centred, act to preserve families, and are delivered within a community development framework. The programs are informed by communities' internally identified needs and vision for improving the quality of life of young children and their families.

AHS programs are increasing the numbers of Aboriginal people who are skilled in delivering programs for Aboriginal children and families. Each site employs community members who receive pre- and in-service training through a number of training workshops convened annually by AHS regional and national offices (see chapter by Nina Howe and Ellen Jacobs on in-service professional development in this volume).

Some AHS programs have the potential to reduce the high rates of removal of children from their families and communities for government care. Anecdotal reports in the non-formal or 'grey' literature (e.g., unpublished reports within agencies) and at AHS training conferences often describe how the programs help the families of participating children to access food, warm clothing, income assistance, and needed health, mental health, and social services. This bridging function is significant because one of the challenges for ensuring Indigenous children's access to needed supports is that they often do not make it as far as the entry point in mainstream service delivery systems set up to meet the needs of children in middle-class families in urban centres.

As well, some communities that host AHS effectively use it as a starting point for developing the hard and soft infrastructure to host other community-based programs. Program descriptions describe how many AHS programs have become community hubs where additional programs are integrated or co-located to streamline children's access to specialists, including speech-language pathologists, physiotherapists, occupational therapists, dental hygienists, and other services. The potential for early childhood programs to become an entry point for young children and their caregivers, gradually introducing families to a range of other services and opportunities, has been documented in First Nations early childhood programs in British Columbia, as shown in Figure 12.2 (Ball, 2005, 2009).

Another positive feature of the AHS model is that it combines both structural and conceptual integration.[5] The model is an exception to

---

5 The Integration Network Project (Colley, 2006) defines integration as both 'structural and conceptual.' Structural integration enables a child to receive a range of services from different programs without repeated screening, referral, registration, and wait-time processes for each program. Integration usually involves programs with common philosophies, human resource practices, and coordinated or combined funding systems. The conceptual aspect of integration is key to an effective integration process. Programs leave behind previously independent identities and become consolidated entities. In ECEC programs this often means incorporating options for extended days operating full year.

Figure 12.2. 'Hook and Hub': Integration and coordination of multisectoral programs with early childhood education and care (ECEC) as an initial and central organizational and community focal point. © Jessica Ball, 2012.

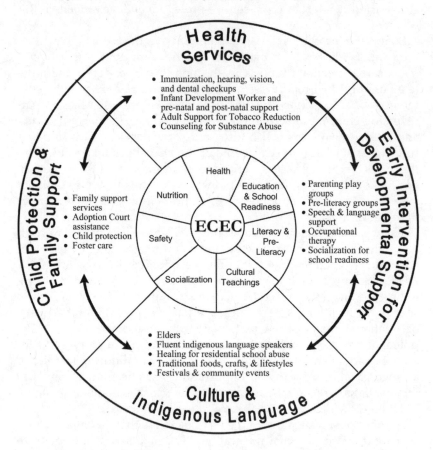

the persistently fragmented patchwork currently available to children in Canada. Outside of the AHS program, *if* children's diverse needs are addressed, this is typically done by separate programs with distinct conceptual identities, practice philosophies, physical facilities, eligibility requirements, registration procedures, waiting periods, licensing, and human resource practices, often in separate ministries, with structural and conceptual integration only a distant dream. For children living on reserves, whose provisions are the responsibility of various federal ministries, many of these needs are minimally supported, if at all. While coordinated and collaborative program delivery among services is often discussed among different funding agencies, it rarely happens, and it can be costly in terms of human effort and financial expenditures, with fewer benefits to children and families compared with consolidated program delivery (Corter et al., 2006). After a national consultation process with leaders in non-Aboriginal ECEC and kindergarten education, the Integration Network (Colley, 2006) concluded that achieving integration of early childhood education and care services will require a major paradigm shift. In the interim, because the quality of life and well-being of many Indigenous children remain, for now, a matter of federal fiduciary responsibility, and because Indigenous Peoples share a holistic view of the child and a belief that children's needs must be embedded within family and community values and language, AHS presents an inspiring example of integration.

In contrast to quick fix innovations rolled out and back with the turning of political tides, for over a decade, AHS has established credibility in Aboriginal communities, built a cadre of trained and experienced program staff, accumulated a wealth of anecdotal reports and program examples, and taken some initial steps towards documenting outcomes for children. Many ECEC programs around the world struggle to embody core principles of community development, such as customizing curricula to meet community-specific needs and goals and integrating typically fragmented supports such as nutrition, health, and education. AHS is built upon these ideals, and is unquestionably the most extensive, innovative, and culturally based initiative in Aboriginal ECEC in Canada. Although solid evidence of its impact on child health and developmental outcomes has yet to accumulate, qualitative evidence abounds that AHS is working in complex ways to gather the strength within communities to enhance the quality of family and community environments for Aboriginal young children.

Consolidating and Expanding Indigenous ECEC Capacity

Practitioner Training: The Need for Expanded, Long-Term Investments

Communities with an AHS program typically have long waiting lists; in many communities that do not have a program, receiving funding to develop one is identified as a top priority. Among the challenges for communities to obtain approval and funding to implement AHS is a shortfall of trained community members to staff the program. The call for more Indigenous early childhood education practitioners is consistently heard at Indigenous education conferences and community gatherings. When Ball and Simpkins (2004) asked First Nation ECE staff and parents what program elements made their First Nation–designed and operated ECEC programs distinctively *First Nation*, a majority response was that First Nation practitioners staffed the program.

While significant gains have been made in Indigenous capacity for delivery of ECEC programs over the past fifteen years, shortfalls in availability of qualified ECE practitioners remain an outstanding barrier to expanding the reach of AHS and other ECEC programs and to keeping some programs open. Some programs are not able to meet provincial or territorial standards for numbers of staff with ECE credentials. Many programs, especially on reserves, repeatedly ask officers charged with licensing child care facilities for 'variances' that allow programs to operate without a full complement of certified ECE staff[6] (see chapter by Ellen Jacobs and Emmanuelle Adrien on regulations in this volume).

Merely recruiting and retaining Indigenous staff for ECEC programs is challenging enough in many communities, and may overshadow concerns about ensuring that staff has post-secondary training in early childhood education. It is generally acknowledged that as many as half of the staff in federally funded Indigenous ECEC programs on reserves lack training and qualifications (Whiteduck Resources Inc., 2007). They also lack ready access to post-secondary ECE programs with Indigenous content or relevance for programs operating in rural or remote settings. Of 107 ECE programs identified in public and private post-secondary institutions across Canada, only seventeen had an Indigenous focus; of those, only one course was offered with Inuit content (Bridgeworks Consulting, 2007). Some Indigenous community leaders have expressed the view that post-secondary ECE programs in most colleges and universities promote dominant European-heritage

---

6 In many jurisdictions, regulations allow a centre to be licensed without the required number of employees with early childhood credentials, provided the centre is able to demonstrate its efforts to recruit staff with training. This 'variance' allows the centre to continue to operate as a licensed program, and generally requires an employee without a credential to complete the required post-secondary education for an ECE credential within a specified period.

concepts and methods pertaining to young children's development and care, and they and their constituents want to resist their wholesale adoption. Some leaders advocate for federal investment in creating an Indigenous training program designed by and for the Indigenous child care sector. In addition to the lack of culturally based post-secondary education, the current shortage of trained staff is a consequence of the rural and often remote location of many Indigenous communities, especially First Nations on reserves and Inuit villages.

A need exists for ECE training opportunities that provide scope for communities' particular culture, language, goals, and needs to be considered by trainees in their course work. Further, training needs to be readily accessible through innovative approaches involving flexible course scheduling and blended course delivery modalities, including virtual classrooms and distance education. A targeted, coordinated approach that draws on partnerships between Indigenous organizations and post-secondary institutions could respond to the needs and goals of Indigenous learners and communities to expand the number of qualified Indigenous ECE practitioners. Improving the education of the workforce would promote the well-being of Indigenous children through expanded program capacity and would enhance the Indigenous economy. ECEC programs can generate community development with immediate economic returns.[7] According to one series of community economic analyses, every dollar of investment in ECE generates about $1.58 in economic activity, and every job in an ECEC program creates or sustains 1.49 jobs (Prentice, 2007a, 2007b, 2007c).

Federal funds for the development of post-secondary education, specifically for the Indigenous early childhood workforce, could build upon promising practices in a handful of community colleges and universities that have been effective for strengthening the number and qualifications of Indigenous ECE practitioners. One model with documented success is the First Nations Partnership Programs (FNPP) offered for twenty years by the University of Victoria (see commentary by Alan Pence in this volume). This program was instigated by the Meadow Lake Tribal Council (MLTC) in Saskatchewan in 1989. Aiming to provide ECEC

---

7 For example, reports from Manitoba underscore employment effects: there are as many jobs in child care as in the biotechnology and health research sector or the energy and environment sector, both of which are priority areas for the government.

training for Cree and Dene community members, the Meadow Lake Tribal Council could not find an existing program with room for culturally specific knowledge to become centrally integrated into the students' course work, and no colleges or universities were prepared to deliver post-secondary courses in the community or involve community members, including Elders, in the teaching and learning process. The MLTC applied successfully for federal funding through the Child Care Visions program of Human Resources Development Canada and entered into a partnership with the University of Victoria's School of Child and Youth Care to create a career-laddered program of course work. The courses introduced an innovative 'generative curriculum' approach (Pence et al., 1993), which incorporated, in equal measure, university- and community-generated content. Twenty co-scripted courses were delivered entirely in the partnering First Nation communities, enabling Elders to be involved in teaching alongside university-appointed instructors. Community-based delivery also enabled students to undertake practica in local settings and allowed community members and service staff in local agencies to observe and be involved in the students' learning journeys. The program was a demonstrated success in ten university–community partnerships, with 151 First Nation graduates at the ECE certificate or diploma level. A program evaluation funded by Human Resources Development Canada found that 95 per cent of graduates remained in their communities; 65 per cent introduced new programs for children, youth, and families; 21.5 per cent joined the staff of existing programs; and 11.5 per cent continued on the education ladder towards a university degree (Ball & Pence, 2006). A career-laddered approach increases access to accredited post-secondary education, enabling students first to obtain preparatory training to ensure their success in post-secondary courses; second, to complete an ECE certificate; third, to upgrade certification with additional course work in special needs and infant and toddler care, which are separate levels of certification in some jurisdictions; fourth, to complete a diploma in ECE or a related field such as child and youth care; and finally, to apply to continue with third- and fourth-year Bachelor's degree–level education in early years or a related field.

Following the program's pilot delivery, the Meadow Lake Tribal Council passed their co-ownership of the program over to Saskatchewan Indian Institute of Technologies, which carried on the traditions of community-based, cohort-driven delivery of the career-laddered program through partnerships that incorporate Indigenous as well as

Euro-Western–based curricula. Recognized by UNESCO as a *best practice* for incorporating Indigenous knowledge, the program has served as a model for Indigenous and other culturally specific education programs around the world, not only in early childhood education but in other professional fields as well (UNESCO/MOST, 2002). Over the past decade, other community colleges and universities have explored new approaches to making their ECE programs more accessible, for example, through blended program delivery that offers some opportunity to complete courses online, through work-based practica and course delivery, community-based program delivery, and course scheduling that takes into account weather-related transportation issues and seasonal activities in communities.

Beginning in 2005, federal funding was made available to First Nations communities on reserves to support co-location, co-planning, and joint training of front-line practitioners in ECEC programs in the Aboriginal Head Start On-Reserve programs, First Nations and Inuit Child Care Initiative, and in Alberta and Ontario, child care sites funded by Indian and Northern Affairs Canada. The Public Health Agency of Canada has also demonstrated a commitment to deliver training and is currently exploring the development of a post-secondary education and certification strategy for Indigenous early childhood educators. But while significant federal investment has been made in various kinds of ECE training to strengthen Indigenous capacity, most of the training has been short term, non-accredited, and not career-laddered insofar as generating course credits from accredited post-secondary institutions that learners can use to progress towards a post-secondary credential. The professional identity and retention of Indigenous ECE practitioners can be secured, in part, through national and regional conferences and local workshops that provide in-service training, but a sustained commitment on the part of the federal government is needed to enable this. And, while discussions are underway about developing a career-laddered, accredited post-secondary program to support the expansion of a fully qualified Indigenous ECE workforce, there remains an urgent need to train and retain more staff to keep programs open and strong.

Conclusion

Through the synergy of advocacy on the part of national Indigenous organizations, long-term federal investments, grassroots vision and commitment, and parent demand, tremendous momentum for Indigenous

ECEC capacity has been built across Canada's First Nation, Inuit, and Métis communities over the past fifteen years. Continued momentum to support expansion and Indigenization of community-driven ECEC programs will support the burgeoning population of young Indigenous children and help to equalize their readiness for formal schooling.

A valuable next step would be to undertake a methodologically sound longitudinal research study with comparison groups to determine the extent, nature, and sustainability of Indigenous children's gains that are attributable to AHS participation. Also, to achieve equity for Indigenous children through ECEC, the federal government should prioritize the following actions:

- Invest in community-based, culturally relevant, accredited, career-laddered training for Indigenous ECEC practitioners, incorporating non-traditional delivery models (e.g., blended, cohort driven) and supports (e.g., Indigenous mentors, preparatory and ongoing learning skills supports, transportation, computer hardware).
- Develop ECEC leadership that encompasses Indigenous knowledge.
- Expand access to holistic, locally fitting ECEC programs like AHS for Indigenous children from birth to 8 years of age.
- Support Indigenous children's transitions to school and early experiences of success.
- Fund longitudinal and comparative research on innovative Indigenous ECEC programs such as AHS and others.

Other stakeholders also have a role to play. Policy makers can commission program evaluations by early development researchers and encourage innovative, community-driven early learning programs over standardization and best practices. Communities can host government-funded programs in existing community organizations (e.g., Native Friendship Centres, learning centres, adjuncts to health centres, and band-operated and independent schools). They can build community awareness, strengthen the demand for ECEC, and consolidate Indigenous knowledge and goals for children's early learning and formal education. Secondary and tertiary institutions can build institutional capacity for innovative ECEC training for Indigenous students. Of particular value would be compulsory courses for pre-service teachers on (1) meeting the needs of Indigenous learners and (2) intercultural awareness and engagement aimed at improving Indigenous/non-Indigenous student relations.

As Colley (2006) has argued, effective structural and conceptual integration of early childhood education and care services requires a major paradigm shift. Programs like Aboriginal Head Start provide an inspiring example of what effective integration can look like. Indigenous Peoples are determined to close the gaps in their children's educational achievement, but they require the support of all parties to make this happen. Investing in early education will have significant positive impacts on Indigenous children, families, and communities as well as on Canada's broader social fabric and economy.

References

Adelson, N. (2005). The embodiment of inequity: Health disparities in Aboriginal Canada. *Canadian Journal of Public Health, 96*, S45–S61.

Assembly of First Nations. (2006). Royal Commission on Aboriginal People at 10 years: A report card. Ottawa: Author.

Audas, R.P., & Willms, J.D. (2001). *Engagement and dropping out of school: A life-course perspective.* Ottawa: Applied Research Branch, Strategic Policy, Human Resources Development Canada.

Ball, J. (2005). Early childhood care and development programs as hook and hub for inter-sectoral service delivery in Indigenous communities. *Journal of Aboriginal Health, 2*(1), 36–49.

Ball, J. (2006, Nov.). *Developmental monitoring, screening and assessment of Aboriginal young children: Findings of a community-university research partnership.* Paper presented at the Aboriginal Supported Child Care Conference, Vancouver.

Ball, J. (2008). Promoting equity and dignity for Aboriginal children in Canada. *Choices, 14*(7), 1–30. Montreal: Institute for Research on Public Policy.

Ball, J. (2009). Centring community services around early childhood care and development: Promising practices in Indigenous communities in Canada. *Child Health and Education, 1*(4), 183–206. Retrieved from http://journals.sfu.ca/che/index.php/english/index.

Ball, J., & Janyst, P. (2008, Nov.). *Screening and assessment with Indigenous children: Community-university partnered research findings.* Policy Brief for Early Years Policy Forum, Vancouver.

Ball, J., & Pence, A. (2006). *Supporting Indigenous children's development: Community-university partnerships.* Vancouver: UBC Press.

Ball, J., & Simpkins, M. (2004). The community within the child: Integration of Indigenous knowledge into First Nations childcare process and practice. *American Indian Quarterly, 28*, 480–498.

Bell, D., with Anderson, K., Fortin, T., Ottoman, J., Rose, S., Simard, L., & Spencer, K. (2004). *Sharing our success: Ten case studies in Aboriginal schooling.* Kelowna, BC: Society for the Advancement of Excellence in Education. Retrieved from http://www.artssmarts.ca/media/fr/sharingoursuccess. pdf.

Bennett, J. (2003). *Early childhood education and care policy: Canada, country note.* Paris: Organisation for Economic Co-operation and Development Directorate for Education. Retrieved from http://www.oecd.org/datao ecd/42/34/33850725.pdf.

Bricker, D., Squires, J., Dichtelmiller, M.K., & Twombly, E. (1995). *Ages and Stages Questionnaires: A parent-completed, child monitoring system.* Baltimore, MD: Paul H. Brookes.

Bridgeworks Consulting. (2007). *ECD/ECE training programs in Canada.* First Nations Inuit Health Branch. Ottawa: Health Canada.

Brigance, A.H. (1998). *Preschool screen, kindergarten screen and first grade screen.* North Billerica, MA: Curriculum Associates.

British Columbia Aboriginal Network on Disability Society. (1996). *Identification of barriers to post-secondary training and employment.* Vancouver: Author.

Canadian Centre for Justice. (2001). *Aboriginal peoples in Canada. Statistics Profile Series.* Ottawa: Minister of Industry.

Canadian Council on Learning. (2007). *State of learning in Canada: No time for complacency.* Ottawa: Author.

Canadian Institute of Child Health. (2000). *The health of Canada's children.* 3rd ed. Ottawa: Author.

Canadian Institute for Health Information. (2004). Aboriginal peoples' health. In *Improving the health of Canadians* (pp. 73–102). Ottawa: Author.

Case, A., Lubotsky, D., & Paxson, C. (2002). Economic status and health in childhood: The origins of the gradient. *American Economic Review, 92,* 1308–1334.

Cleveland, G., & Krashinsky, M. (2003). *Starting strong: Financing ECEC services in OECD countries.* Paris: Organisation for Economic Co-operation and Development.

Colley, S. (2006). *The integration kit: Policy papers. How can integrated services for kindergarten-aged children be achieved?* Toronto: Integration Network Project, Institute of Child Study, University of Toronto.

Cooke, M., Beavon, D., & McHardy, M. (2004). *Measuring the well-being of Aboriginal people: An application of the United Nations Human Development Index to registered Indians in Canada, 1981–2001.* Ottawa: Strategic Research and Analysis Directorate, Indian and Northern Affairs Canada.

Corter, C., Bertrand, J., Pelletier, J., Griffin, T., McKay, D., Patel, S., & Ioannone, P. (2006). *Evidence-based understanding of integrated foundations for early childhood.* Toronto: Atkinson Centre at OISE/University of Toronto.

Council of Ministers of Education. (2004). *Quality education for all young people: Challenges.* Retrieved from: http://www.cmec.ca/international/ice/47_ICE_report.en.pdf.

Dearing, E. (2008). Psychological costs of growing up poor. *Annals of the New York Academy of Sciences, 1136,* 324–332.

deLeeuw, S., Fiske, J., & Greenwood, M. (2002). *Rural, remote and north of 51: Service provision and substance abuse related special needs in British Columbia's hinterlands.* Prince George, BC: University of Northern British Columbia Task Force on Substance Abuse.

Doherty, G. (2007). Ensuring the best start in life: Targeting versus universality in early childhood development. *IRPP Choices, 13*(8).

First Nations Centre. (2005). *First Nations Regional Longitudinal Health Survey 2002/03: Results for adults, youth and children living in First Nations communities.* Ottawa: Assembly of First Nations/First Nations Information Governance Committee. Retrieved from: http://www.naho.ca/firstnations/english/regional_health.php.

First Nations Child and Family Caring Society of Canada. (2005). Wen: De: We are coming to the light of day. Ottawa: Author. Retrieved from http://www.fncfcs.com/docs/WendeReport.pdf.

Grantham-McGregor, S., Cheung, Y., Cueto, S., Glee, P., Richter, L., & Strupp, B. (2007). Developmental potential in the first 5 years for children in developing countries. *Lancet, 369*(9555), 60–70.

Government of Nunavut and Nunavut Tunngavik Inc. (2004). *Background paper submitted to the Canada-Aboriginal Peoples Roundtable.* Iqaluit and Ottawa: Author.

Hackett, P. (2005). From past to present: Understanding First Nations health patterns in a historical context. *Canadian Journal of Public Health, 96,* 17–21.

Hanushek, E.A., & Wolfmann, L. (2007). *Education quality and economic growth.* Washington, DC: World Bank.

Health Canada. (2002). *Children making a community whole: A review of Aboriginal Head Start in urban and northern communities.* Ottawa: Author.

Health Canada. (2005). *First Nations comparable health indicators.* Retrieved from http://www.hc-sc.gc.ca/.

Health Canada and First Nations/Inuit Health Branch. (2003). *A statistical profile on the health of First Nations in Canada.* Ottawa: Author.

Heckman, J.J. (2006). Skill formation and the economics of investing in disadvantaged children. *Science, 312*(5782), 1900–1902.

Howe, E. (2002). *Education and lifetime income for Aboriginal people in Saskatch-ewan.* Regina: University of Saskatchewan, Department of Economics.

Indian and Northern Affairs Canada & Canadian Housing and Mortgage Corporation. (2007). *Aboriginal demography: Population, household and family projections, 2001–2026.* Ottawa: Author.

Irwin, L.G., Siddiqi, A., & Hertzman, C. (2007). *Early child development: A powerful equalizer.* Final report for the World Health Organization's Commission on the Social Determinants of Health. Geneva: World Health Organization.

Jolly, R. (2007). Early childhood development: The global challenge. *Lancet, 369*(9555), 8–9.

Kohen, D., Uppal, S., & Guevremont, A. (2007). Children with disabilities and the educational system: A provincial perspective. *Education Matters, 4*(1). (Statistics Canada, Catalogue 81–004-X20070019631). Retrieved from http://www.statcan.gc.ca/pub/81–004-x/2007001/9631-eng.htm.

Lee, V.E., & Burkam, D.T. (2003). Dropping out of high school: The role of social organization and structure. *American Educational Research Journal, 40*(2), 353–393.

Leitch, K.K. (2008). *Reaching for the top: A report by the advisor on healthy children and youth.* Ottawa: Health Canada.

Magnuson, K.E., Ruhm, C., & Waldfogel, J. (2006). The persistence of preschool effects: Do subsequent classroom experiences matter? *Early Childhood Research Quarterly, 22,* 18–38.

Mendelson, M. (2008). *Improving education on reserves: A First Nations Education Authority Act.* Ottawa: Caledon Institute of Social Policy.

Meisels, S.J., Marsden, D.B., Jablon, J.R., & Dorfman, A.B. (2001). *The Work Sampling System.* New York: Pearson Early Learning.

Minister of Indian Affairs and Northern Development. (1997). *Gathering strength: Canada's Aboriginal action plan.* Ottawa: Public Works and Government Services Canada.

Minister of Public Works and Government Services. *Aboriginal Head Start in urban and northern communities: Program and participants 2001.* Retrieved from http://www.hc-sc.gc.ca/hppb/childhoodyouth/acy/ahs.h.

Native Council of Canada. (1990). *Native child care: The circle of care.* Ottawa: Author.

Office of the Prime Minister of Canada. 'Prime Minister Offers Full Apology on Behalf of Canadians for the Indian Residential Schools.' Press release, 11 June 2008. Retrieved from http://pm.gc.ca/eng/media.asp?id+2149.

Pence, A.R., Kuehne, V., Greenwood, M., & Opekokew, M.R. (1993). Generative curriculum: A model of university and First Nations cooperative post-secondary education. *International Journal of Educational Development, 13,* 339–349.

Prentice, S. (2007a). *Franco-Manitoban childcare: Childcare as economic, social and language development in St-Pierre-Jolys.* Winnipeg: Child Care Coalition of Manitoba.

Prentice, S. (2007b). *Northern childcare: Childcare as economic and social development in Thompson.* Winnipeg: Child Care Coalition of Manitoba.

Prentice, S. (2007c). *Rural childcare: Childcare as economic and social development in Parkland.* Winnipeg: Child Care Coalition of Manitoba.

Public Health Agency of Canada. (2007, June). *Aboriginal Head Start in urban and northern communities: National impact evaluation.* Paper presented to the International Union for Health Promotion and Education, Vancouver.

Raver, C.C., Gershoff, E.T., & Aber, J.L. (2007). Testing equivalence of mediating models of income, parenting, and school readiness for White, Black, and Hispanic children in a national sample. *Child Development, 78,* 96–107.

Riddell, C. (2006, Feb.). *The impact of education on economic and social outcomes: An overview of recent advances in economics.* Paper presented at An Integrated Approach to Human Capital Development, Canadian Policy Research Networks, School of Policy Studies, Queen's University, Kingston, Ontario.

Royal Commission on Aboriginal Peoples. (1996). *Report of the Royal Commission on Aboriginal Peoples,* vols. 1 and 3. Ottawa: Minister of Supply and Services Canada.

Salée, D., with Newhouse, D., & Levesque, C. (2006). Quality of life of Aboriginal people in Canada: An analysis of current research. *Choices, 12*(6), 1–38. Montreal: Institute for Research on Public Policy.

Sharpe, A., & Arsenault, J.-F. (2009). *Investing in Aboriginal education in Canada: An economic perspective.* Ottawa: Canadian Policy Research Networks.

Shonkoff, J., & Phillips, D. (Eds.). (2000). *From neurons to neighborhoods: The science of early childhood development.* Washington, DC: National Academy Press.

Smylie, J., & Adomako, P. (2009). *Indigenous children's health report: Health assessment in action.* Toronto: St Michaels Hospital. Retrieved from http://www.stmichaelshospital.com/crich/indigenous_childrens_health_report.php.

Statistics Canada. (2001). *A portrait of Aboriginal children living in non-reserve areas: Results from the 2001 Aboriginal Peoples Survey.* Ottawa: Statistics Canada. Retrieved from http://www.statcan.gc.ca/pub/89-597-x/89-597-x2001001-eng.pdf.

Statistics Canada. (2006). *Census of the population 2006.* Ottawa: Author.

Stearns, E., & Glennie, E.J. (2006). When and why dropouts leave high school. *Youth and Society, 38*(1), 29–57.

Steffler, J. (2008). Aboriginal peoples: A young population for years to come. *Horizons* (Policy Research Initiative), *10*(1), 13–20. Retrieved from http://www.policyresearch.gc.ca/doclib/HOR_v10n1_200803_e.pdf.

UNESCO/MOST (United Nations Educational, Scientific and Cultural Organization/Management of Social Transformations). (2002). *Best practices using Indigenous knowledge.* The Hague: Author.

Weitzman, M. (2003). Low income and its impact on psychosocial child development. In *Encyclopedia on Early Childhood Development* (pp. 1–8). Montreal: Centre of Excellence for Early Childhood Development.

Western Arctic Aboriginal Head Start Council. (2007). *Ten years of Aboriginal Head Start in the Northwest Territories 1996 to 2006.* Yellowknife, NWT: Author.

Whiteduck Resources Inc. (2007). *Aboriginal Head Start On-Reserve standards and licensing overview.* First Nations Inuit Health Branch. Ottawa: Health Canada.

Zigler, E., & Valentine, A. (Eds.). (1979). *Project Head Start: A legacy of the war on poverty.* New York: Free Press.

13 Integrated Early Childhood Services in School-as-Hub Models: Lessons from Toronto First Duty and Peel Best Start

JANETTE PELLETIER

This chapter highlights new directions in integrated early childhood services with a focus on 'school-as-hub' models. In these models, schools serve in the role of 'hubs' in which education, care, parenting, and community services can be accessed in a one-stop model. Here, parents can find integrated full-day child care and kindergarten from 7 a.m. to 6 p.m., along with other supports for parenting such as family literacy, early intervention, public health services, and recreation programs. This chapter describes findings from two Ontario demonstration projects that feature the integration of kindergarten, child care, and parenting supports. These initiatives began through partnerships between municipal governments and school boards, along with other service organizations. As the projects evolved, evidence has informed the development of new provincial early childhood policy, most notably, Ontario's adoption of the Pascal (2009) report to the premier in which full-day early learning and kindergarten including extended-day care was recommended. A unique aspect of the new policy is that the full-day early learning program is being delivered by a team of early childhood educators (ECEs) and kindergarten teachers. In both projects, research and evaluation were designed to study the effects of implementing the integrated model. The research team wanted to know how integrated early childhood services would affect children's and parents' experiences as well as professional teamwork and program quality. Evidence on feasibility, positive findings from the front line, and details of the significant challenges to combining services and reform have contributed to the context for policy development by the Ontario government.

The first project described in this chapter, Toronto First Duty (TFD), began in 2001 as five demonstration sites were co-developed and supported by the municipal government, the district school board, community service organizations, and a charitable foundation. A central aim of the TFD partners was to use evidence from the project to improve early childhood policies, particularly in relation to integrated services, at the local and provincial levels. Toronto First Duty predated and informed Ontario's comprehensive early years' initiative, Best Start, which began in 2005. It also contributed to the context for extending provincial policy into the universal school-based full-day early learning/kindergarten programs for 4- and 5-year-olds beginning in September 2010. The chapter moves from describing a demonstration project in Toronto First Duty to replication and scaling up in the second project, Peel Best Start. The research features the implementation of five Best Start sites in the region of Peel, Ontario, and the integration of early childhood staff teams, early learning programs, governance, seamless access to services, and parent engagement, in comparison with a control group. The chapter concludes with a discussion of commonalities across the projects and of differences that relate to contextual factors and the implications for improving and implementing government policies on service integration for young children and families. Finally, applications to changing policy highlight the uniqueness, and some of the new challenges facing Ontario, of the school-as-hub model for combined child care, kindergarten, and child and family centres.

Integrated Services in Early Childhood

In the current societal quest for better ways to support children's early learning and development, many variations on traditional services have been tested. These include improving the quality of pre-school child care (Bryant et al., 2003), offering school-based learning in pre-kindergarten classes (e.g., Gormley et al., 2005), using innovative instruction in kindergarten (e.g., Pelletier, Reeve, & Halewood, 2006), and involving parents of pre-school children in school-based programs (e.g., Pelletier & Corter, 2005a). Another dimension of innovation occurs when these kinds of services are integrated in school-based hubs, as advocated by Edward Zigler in the model of Schools for the 21st Century (Desimone et al., 2004; Zigler, Finn-Stevenson, & Stern, 1997) or in other community school arrangements (Dryfoos, Quinn, & Barkin,

2005). Service integration often includes additional aims that go beyond child development and learning. Integrative service arrangements may be designed to support parents' needs to work and study, as well as their parenting skills (e.g., Zigler et al., 1997). Although ambitious innovations such as early service integration hold real promise, they are extremely complex; providing evidence about their effectiveness and fine-tuning these innovations for diverse communities is a thorny challenge.

In the literature, a strong conceptual argument for integrated services has been made on the basis of a social-ecological analysis of how complex social systems affect child development and parenting (Lerner et al., 2002). Conceptual models such as Lerner's borrow heavily from Bronfenbrenner's (1979) ecological model of development with multiple levels of influence on children and parents, beginning with immediate bidirectional exchanges between individuals in microsystems, such as the family, service setting, or neighbourhood. These microsystems are linked dynamically at the level of the mesosystem; for example, home-service connections can mean that parents feel more confident in helping their children learn at home after participating in integrated service programs (Patel & Corter, 2006, 2010). Furthermore, events in settings in which the child does not directly participate may influence interaction in the child's microsystem. For example, parent–child interaction may suffer if the parent has difficulty negotiating the work and child care connection (Arimura & Corter, 2010). This level of influence is labelled the *exosystem*. Finally, all of these interconnected systems are influenced by the societal macrosystem including culture, subcultures, public attitudes, and government policies and funding. Bronfenbrenner's ecological model has been helpful in framing our analyses of early childhood programs, processes, and outcomes (e.g., Pelletier & Corter, 2005a, 2005b, 2006), but other models are also useful in examining influences at the community level; in particular, the developmental or population health approach provides an important conceptual perspective in Canadian government policy (Dunn et al., 2006; Irwin et al., 2007; Keating & Hertzman, 1999).

Aside from theoretical arguments about children's and parents' needs for a more coherent and supportive social ecology, it is clear that there are broader societal forces promoting service integration in many service sectors and in many countries. These forces range from accountability measures, to the use of community or social-level indicators, to government cuts in services and a search for efficiencies, to a quest for more effective and cohesive community-oriented services (e.g., Corbett, 2006; Pelletier & Corter, 2006). From an early childhood practice standpoint, arguments for integration have often been made on the basis of the importance of continuity for fostering children's security and learning (Saracho & Spodek, 2003). Integration with continuity can mean fewer transitions for the child, greater recognition of the child's individual needs, better and more consistent programming, and more consistent expectations and support from adults in the home and in programs. From a parent support standpoint, integrating child care and education in a school-based hub is a strategy for reducing the gap in availability of quality child care and reducing the fragmentation of care, education, and family life (Zigler et al., 1997).

Despite the theoretical and practical arguments, empirical evidence on the value of early childhood service integration is limited and not always positive, depending on how integration is defined. For example, a study of integration as 'coordination' of service and referrals through an individual case manager who facilitated access across otherwise disconnected services, found no developmental benefits (St Pierre et al., 1999). On the other hand, recent United States and United Kingdom studies have begun to produce empirical evidence for the benefits of other forms of integrated early childhood services (Henrich et al., 2006; James-Burdumy et al., 2005; Melhuish et al., 2007; Melhuish et al., 2008; Selden, Sowa, & Sandfort, 2006). In Canada, as elsewhere, evidence on an integrated services approach is limited (Cleveland et al., 2006; Siraj-Blatchford & Siraj-Blatchford, 2009). Canadian evidence on service integration is provided by the evaluation of the Better Beginnings Better Futures Project, an ambitious comprehensive, community-based research demonstration program for children and their families living in eight disadvantaged Ontario communities (see chapter by Ray Peters, Angela Howell-Moneta, & Kelly Petrunka in this volume), as well as the TFD and Best Start research described here.

In a broad international perspective, Helen Penn and colleagues (Penn et al., 2004) reviewed international studies of integrated early learning and care and found some evidence that these programs benefited children, but cautioned that conclusions about integration as a general approach are limited by the different contexts in which early care and education are combined. In some countries, integration occurs in an established national system, and in others, it is a targeted program established as part of a local evaluation. In most cases, evidence on the process of integration is not brought together with evidence on the impact on children and families. In this chapter, the focus is on community-level examples of service integration via school-based hubs and how research on *implementation* and *process*, as well as *outcomes*, may help to move provincial government policy forward. Before presenting the TFD and PBS projects, some ideas are reviewed about schools as hubs for integrated early childhood services and about the context for the development of school hubs in Ontario.

Schools as Hubs

At the broad policy level there are strong arguments for merging child care and education; accordingly, the disconnect between early care and education in Canada is viewed as a problem (OECD, 2004). At the community level, there are also arguments for basing integrated early childhood services in schools, and these services may go beyond care and education to include other programs such as family support, parent education, and health-related services (Pelletier & Corter, 2006; Zigler et al., 1997). Connecting care to education may improve the status of child care as a basis for child development and learning. Connections to the formal education system may foster public understanding of the value of economic investment in a range of early childhood services. Furthermore, elementary schools are local, universal, and normative; schools foster equity of access since nearly all parents enrol their children beginning with kindergarten, even when programs are not mandatory (Beach et al., 2009).

On the negative side, schools have strong organizational cultures and are structured in ways that may not foster collaboration with other service sectors (Crowson & Boyd, 1995). There is also mounting fear that the 'schoolification' of child care will lead to inappropriate academic programming for young children that will be counterproductive to children's development and learning (Moss, 2008). Nevertheless, some of the traditional principles of high-quality child care practice are finding new support that may help stem inappropriate academic programming being pushed down from the elementary school curriculum. For example, the value of play in programming and the importance of supporting whole child development are part of the emerging evidence on the development of self-regulation as a basis for educational and life success (e.g., Diamond et al., 2007). A hopeful view is that early childhood service integration might lead to the 'careification' of schools. In addition to fostering engaging programming and whole child development, there should be other contributions that extend beyond children. Thus, child care and pre-school programs represent points of contact for parents and have unique potential to bridge parents into other service connections as described later in this chapter.

As noted above, there is little Canadian evidence on service integration, and very little on school hubs. However, Mathien and Johnson (1998) conducted a study of integrated care and school programs for kindergarten children in several Canadian provinces. They found evidence of benefit, including some cost efficiency and higher program quality ratings in integrated programs. The study also surveyed general attitudes about the desirability of integrated care and education among parents and professionals. Interestingly, while parents were very supportive, both child care and kindergarten professionals were less enthusiastic about integration. Both sets of professionals believed that early childhood educators 'care' and teachers 'teach.' This finding foreshadows the difficulties of bringing together professionals and organizations that have long received training and work in separate service silos.

The Ontario Context for Early Childhood Service Integration

Integrative approaches to young children and families have a long history in the City of Toronto and the Province of Ontario, as well as elsewhere. In 1981, the idea of schools as community hubs was heralded by a provincial royal commission as the answer to the best educational approach for the young child (LaPierre, 1981). Into the 1980s and early 1990s, Ontario provincial policy supported the provision of child care in schools, and child care space was part of the design in newly constructed schools. However, this approach was not sustained, and its full potential was explored only in some pilot sites. Co-location does not often lead to integration and program continuity even for kindergarten children who might spend half of the day in school and half of the day in care in the same site (Corter et al., 2009).

A Conservative provincial government elected in 1994 ended the development of ideas for integrating services and universal early education beginning at age 3 years. Nevertheless, some years later, the Early Years Study (McCain & Mustard, 1999), commissioned by the same government, set out an ambitious plan for the integration of early childhood programs into a network of community-based early child development and parenting hubs, which would be available to all young children and their families. The report documented the need for a system of early child development supports with an extensive research rationale. The provincial government subsequently took steps to implement the recommendations, but without involving core programs of kindergarten and child care. As an example, a centrepiece of the government's implementation was the establishment of a limited number of Ontario Early Years Centres, which were initially geared towards information dissemination and parenting programs; these were not generally situated in schools, nor did they include child care and other services. In fact, the government of the day was described by some key informants in our research as having an ABC strategy (Anything But Child Care) based on ideological grounds (Corter et al., 2002). Despite the unfavourable provincial climate for child care, Toronto First Duty (TFD) was conceived in 2000 by the Atkinson Charitable Foundation, the City of Toronto, and the Toronto District School Board (TDSB) as a way of demonstrating first-hand how a quality system for early childhood could be created through the integration of currently existing services. As the TFD project and its evaluation unfolded, consultation and key informant interviews with provincial and municipal government officials were part of the demonstration project strategy. The provincial context changed dramatically in 2003 with the election of a new government and the subsequent establishment of the Ministry of Children and Youth Services (MCYS). As the only ministry with a specific focus on children from birth to age 6 years, MCYS was responsible for core early childhood programs, such as child care, Ontario Early Year Centres, Preschool Speech and Language, and Healthy Babies, Healthy Children. The MCYS established an integrative Best Start Plan for Early Childhood, with a multi-billion dollar commitment over a five-year period starting in 2005–06. The plan for full implementation included:

- A massive expansion of child care, predominantly in Ontario's publicly funded schools
- More child care subsidies so that more families could access child care spaces
- Best Start neighbourhood early learning and care hubs that would provide one-stop services for families
- Universal newborn and ongoing screening and services to identify needs and provide supports
- A comprehensive 18-month well-baby check-up program.

Early efforts to realize Best Start goals included the establishment of Best Start Networks across the province with municipalities as 'consolidated' service managers in the lead along with other service organizations and school boards at the table. A 2005 MCYS Implementation Planning Guide stipulated that a key goal of Best Start Networks should be to 'develop a plan to implement early learning and care hubs' (Ministry of Children and Youth Services, 2005, p. 38) and that 'schools are seen as the most appropriate sites' (p. 65) for the location of the hubs. Key informants in government and other observers suggested that Toronto First Duty contributed to the Best Start policy developments by showing how an integrated system could work on the ground (Corter et al., 2009).

A major setback for achieving the initial Best Start goals occurred in 2006 when the newly elected federal government cancelled funding that would have supported child care expansion. Nevertheless, the Ontario MCYS continued to support initial goals through Best Start community panels across the province. Best Start Networks responded to the call for integration in different ways, but in the Peel Region, the TFD model of school-based hubs was replicated and extended, beginning in 2008, using some of the technical tools and lessons learned from the TFD evaluation. Results from research and evaluation of the school-based hub model are described later in this chapter.

Toronto First Duty Project

Aims of the Toronto First Duty Project

Toronto First Duty (TFD) and its evaluation began in 2001 as a demonstration project to test an ambitious model of service integration across early childhood programs of child care, kindergarten, and family support in school-based hubs. Phase 1 of TFD, with implementation of the model in five community sites, concluded in 2005. Phase 2 (2006–08) focused on knowledge mobilization, policy change, and further development of the TFD model in one of the original five sites. Currently, Phase 3 continues the work with an emphasis on understanding the implementation of integrated curriculum approaches.

The aspirations of the partners who came together to design and implement the TFD model went beyond those in many pilot or demonstration projects. The first aspiration was to design the project to lead to system change and improvement, not merely in the participating organizations and at the local Toronto level, but also at other levels, including facilitating provincial policy change. The second aspiration was to embed research and evaluation into the project and to mobilize the knowledge in several ways. One way was to feed findings back to the participating organizations and to the project sites to enable reflection and continuous improvement of the implemented program (see Corter et al., 2008; Pelletier & Corter, 2006). A second way was to mobilize findings to support practice and policy change beyond the TFD project (Corter et al., 2007a). This aspiration for knowledge building and mobilization meant that the partners supported research and evaluation for the university-based TFD research team and that they worked within their own organizations to contribute to and use the information and ideas for improvement in the early years' programs, their management, and links to other programs. The buy-in to research and knowledge building by the municipality, school boards, and other community partners continued in the Peel Best Start project and its evaluation.

The Toronto First Duty Model

The integrated early childhood service delivery model in Toronto First Duty (TFD) combines regulated child care, kindergarten, and family support services consolidated into a single, accessible program, located in primary schools and coordinated with early intervention and family health services. In this delivery model, a professional team of kindergarten teachers, early childhood educators (ECEs), family support staff, and teaching assistants plan and deliver the program. Space and resources are combined. There is a single intake procedure and flexible enrolment options. Children and families are linked to specialized resources as required. The goal of TFD is to develop a universal, accessible service that promotes the healthy development of children from conception through primary school, which assists parents to work or study and offers support to their parenting role. The project is designed to inform public policy by demonstrating the feasibility of a comprehensive approach to the transformation of the existing patchwork of programs into a single, integrated, and comprehensive early childhood program embedded within the education system and in communities.

Toronto First Duty Methods and Findings

Phase 1 of the project was a four-year period with funding for development and coordination at five school sites to operate as integrated service hubs. Evaluation described the implementation process and project outcomes at three levels of analysis cutting across the levels of social ecology: (1) programs, professionals, and policy; (2) children and families; and (3) community impacts and awareness.

TFD allocated significant resources to developing a comprehensive research approach that would document both process and outcomes. The partners who came together to plan and implement TFD wanted to have a detailed description of how programs and people came together, what the obstacles were on the front lines, and what policies might best support a coherent early childhood system. They also wanted to understand how an integrated delivery model affected young children, their families, and communities. The partners wanted the research to report on what happened but they also wanted to know how it happened. The research team thus adopted a program-process-outcome approach to evaluation, with understanding of process and implementation as the key elements to demonstrate the feasibility of the model to policy makers and practitioners. A theory-of-change model was developed that viewed outcomes for children as a function of two process pathways between service integration efforts and improvements in children's development. One pathway was improvement in the quality of learning environments through staff teamwork and continuity. The other pathway was through parent engagement, including connections to services, feelings of empowerment, and parent education.

The overall approach for the study was a mixed-methods, longitudinal, case study analysis, which combined quantitative and qualitative data to understand the design, implementation, and possible effects of TFD as in previous research on early childhood and parenting programs (Pelletier & Corter, 2006). The narrative information helped to explain the quantitative data. Each of the five sites was treated as a separate case study to explore how a common approach would work in five different communities. Each case study combined information about changes in service access and delivery over time, evidence about the impact on children and families, and descriptions of the community context. In addition, the implementation and management of the project were treated as a case study of organizational development, placed in the context of the city, school board, and charitable foundation working together in a complex social and policy context. Quasi-experimental designs also assessed effects on parents (Arimura & Corter, 2010; Patel & Corter, 2010) and children (Corter et al., 2008). In these designs, the functioning of children and parents in TFD sites was compared with families in matched community sites without integrated services.

The research team used a variety of techniques to gather data, including document collection, meeting notes and observations, focus groups, interviews, direct observation, and surveys. Continuous monitoring of program utilization also took place; the City of Toronto developed a sophisticated intake and tracking system that included more than 2,500 families by the end of Phase 1. In this report, several measures of process and outcome are featured: The Toronto First Duty Indicators of Change was a tool developed to identify specific integration benchmarks for each of the key elements (site level governance, seamless access, early learning environment, early years' staff team, and parent participation) that define the service integration goals of the TFD model. The indicators were assessed through a group interview with leaders and staff at the sites (Corter et al., 2007a, 2007b). The Early Childhood Environmental Rating Scale-Revised (ECERS-R; Harms, Clifford, & Cryer, 2005), a standard measure of program quality, was used across time in various program settings within each of the sites. Although programs became more integrated over time, some programs retained separate physical space. Thus, in several sites a parent–child literacy drop-in centre was housed separately from the merged care and kindergarten space. The Early Development Instrument (EDI), a community-level measure of kindergarten children's readiness for school (Janus & Offord, 2007) was also administered in the Toronto schools, including TFD sites, at several points between 2003 and 2005.

The Phase 1 research described the implementation process in terms of variations and adaptations of the model across the five communities, as well as common struggles and successes across the sites. Predictable challenges to local integration efforts were found. Struggles included issues related to professional turf, space, funding, staffing, leadership turnover, and working without system support across sectors that were siloed at higher levels of government. At the same time, remarkable process success was achieved in staff teamwork across professional groups in several sites. In the early days of the TFD project, there was some confusion about the process of integrating staff in a school-as-hub model. Professionals who had not worked together before were being asked to plan and implement programs as a team. Child care staff had held separate space either in the child care centre in the schools or at the local community centre that provided care for children in the local schools. Parenting and Family Literacy Centre workers had run their own programs down the hall with little to no interaction with kindergarten teachers and child care educators. Kindergartens were located in a separate space where school board teachers implemented programs based on the provincial curriculum. For the first time, these separate professions would try to become one integrated team with the strong involvement of parents, who may have had little involvement up to that point. The initial experiences were characterized by role confusion, territorial claims, and interpersonal misunderstandings. However, with time and support, improvements were noted. One strong lesson was that the newly integrated team needed time to meet, some top-down encouragement and guidance from the school board and municipal partners, and a commitment to move forward. The importance of this commitment was demonstrated in the TFD research findings that improved staff integration was directly related to the quality of the program, using a standardized quality rating scale (Harms et al., 2005): 'Staff committed themselves to working together more closely, to making explicit efforts toward integration. Thus, as integration increased, program quality increased' (Corter et al., 2009, p. 13). Indeed, over time, the staff reported more often that they benefited professionally from working as a team in the school-as-hub model (see Figure 13.1).

Of course, integration itself was not the ultimate goal. Did the increased integration relate to improvement in program quality and positive outcomes for children and parents? Comparisons across the implementation period showed that progress was made in each of the five sites on service integration (as indexed by the Indicators of Change tool; Pelletier & Corter, 2005b), as well as on program quality improvement (as assessed by the ECERS-R; Harms et al., 2005).

We also found evidence of positive effects on parents' engagement with school and learning, using comparisons with matched communities without TFD programs and on children's social-emotional development on the Early Development Instrument (Corter et al., 2007b; Janus & Offord, 2007). Thus, the findings from Phase 1 bear out the theory-of-change model in which service integration fosters professional teamwork leading to higher program quality along with increased parent engagement. These professional/program and parent changes may facilitate more positive outcomes for children.

A benefit of the integrated TFD approach, which may have contributed to positive outcomes, was that project outreach was successful in

Figure 13.1. Toronto First Duty staff team: Early childhood educator (ECE), kindergarten teacher (KG), and family support worker (FS) reports of professional benefits of working as an integrated staff team.

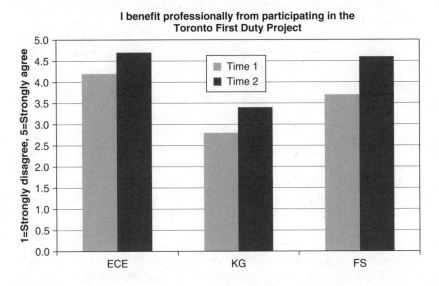

bringing underserved groups into the TFD programs. The TFD neighbourhoods were characterized for the most part by lower socioeconomic status (SES) families and high immigration, factors often associated with lack of school connection. Outreach efforts brought more of these families into school as partners in their children's learning (Patel, 2009; Pelletier & Corter, 2005b). This may have explained the benefits seen in the EDI data. Nevertheless, there was little evidence of awareness of TFD programs in the communities surrounding them. In 'person-on-the-street' interviews and in surveys of parents without young children, community members indicated that they had not heard of the TFD initiative even though they supported tax dollars going to early childhood programs and the aim of encouraging separate programs to work together (Corter et al., 2007a, 2007b).

The general purpose of TFD Phase 2 was to promote system change through continued research and knowledge mobilization. Questions addressed by the research team included: Was the TFD blueprint informing the transformation or evolution of early childhood service delivery in Toronto, in Ontario, and elsewhere? What were the new lessons from the Bruce/WoodGreen site (Bruce/WoodGreen Early Learning Centre), which served as a prototype for further development of integration and as a demonstration site for scores of international visitors?

Analysis and reporting in Phase 2 took an inside-out perspective. It began with the on-the-ground case study of the Bruce/WoodGreen site, which continued as a demonstration site and as a test-bed for ways to move closer to ideal levels of integration in staff teamwork and in the early learning environment. In the Bruce/WoodGreen site case study, front-line observations in TFD2 reinforced the connection between integrated teamwork and quality improvement, although in a somewhat unexpected way. Early in Phase 2 both integration and quality declined with changes in leadership, staffing, and sense of mission, along with the expansion of on-site programming for older children. But upon learning about the research findings, the site leadership and staff pushed both integration and quality indicators back to very high levels by the end of 2008. Once again, integrated work and program quality moved together. In addition to shared resolve and problem solving, a number of factors coincided with this renewed success: common beliefs and an articulated site vision, monitoring of integration, and using quality measurement tools (Indicators of Change and ECERS-R), teamwork that aimed at children's development but that also included respect among blended professionals, joint professional development and common principles, clean-up of space and materials, and a focus on curriculum developed by an expert provincial panel (Ministry of Children and Youth Services, 2007). The Bruce/WoodGreen community of practice, thus, benefited from feedback on program quality assessments and the Indicators of Change technical tool as they solved problems and improved programs. Their accomplishments underscore the need for *ongoing* reflection and knowledge building in-service improvement and reform.

The follow-up observations on the four TFD Phase 1 sites that did not receive special supports for continuing integration in Phase 2 were also instructive. Findings illustrated that local-level service integration efforts were hard to sustain without mandates and supports flowing from integrated policies and mandates at higher levels. They also suggested that community steering groups were important; collaborative work continued only in communities with steering groups that continued to meet. On the theme of leadership, the observations reaffirmed the struggles of individual leaders who sought to make integration work in the face of many competing demands. Despite the challenges, middle levels of service integration were being maintained at several TFD1 sites. Furthermore, reports from the sites strengthen our earlier conclusion that TFD early childhood services build capacity for parents' engagement with the school and other services. In several cases, current school councils boast large numbers of diverse parent 'grads' of the integrated child care, kindergarten, and family support programs. Also, at the on-the-ground level, a quasi-experimental study (Arimura & Corter, 2010) described the impact of service integration in reducing stress in family life, providing additional evidence that the parent-family pathway is important for facilitating beneficial effects of service integration on children and parents. This study asked whether seamless early childhood services in a school-as-hub model improved family life and children's experiences, beyond the direct experience in early childhood programs. The quasi-experimental design compared the daily experiences of parents and children accessing integrated TFD services and families using traditional, disconnected forms of kindergarten and child care services. Comparison group participants were recruited from sites that matched TFD sites on the TDSB Learning Opportunities Index (TDSB, 2007). Integrated school-as-hub services were associated with lower levels of daily parenting hassles, greater satisfaction with some forms of support, and greater levels of continuity in children's days. In TFD sites, parents named both kindergarten teachers and early childhood educators as part of their social support network. In comparison sites, only early childhood educators were named. Children in TFD sites spoke about the seamless nature of their experiences. In contrast, several children from the non-integrated sites noted differences between their experiences at school and at the child care centre (e.g., 'We have to learn a lot in kindergarten but we mostly play at day care'). Compared with TFD parents, parents in the comparison group reported more frequent and intense hassles on the Parenting Daily Hassles – Early Childhood Services scale (PDH-ECS), a new measure developed to assess everyday stress associated with service use (Arimura, 2008).

Moving beyond the front line and the mix of young children, professionals, parents, and programs in local sites, research in TFD2 analysed the project's contribution to organizational and policy change, with a focus on the local and provincial levels. The perspectives of the TFD partners, including the Atkinson Charitable Foundation, the Toronto District School Board, and the City of Toronto were described through the reports of key informants and through document analysis. The descriptions extended to the Toronto Best Start Network where the City and TDSB joined a host of other partners in the integrative aims and plans of Best Start. At the next level, perspectives of Ontario Ministries of Education and Children and Youth Services were reported.

Reports from the TFD partners – the Atkinson Charitable Foundation, the TDSB, and the City – suggested that the organizations themselves changed as a result of participating in Toronto First Duty. The TDSB has made particularly impressive organizational changes over the course of TFD. It pulled together fragmented early years' operations and created a cohesive early years team working incrementally on a number of fronts to improve and integrate early years' programs. Despite the remarkable progress, it was still a challenge for a relatively small early years' team to reach across hundreds of schools, particularly without a mandate and support from the provincial Ministry of Education.

In Phase 2 the City of Toronto and TDSB also worked on knowledge building to inform improvement of programs and policy. For example, they both provided public data portraying problems in accessibility to programs. Toronto Children's Services reports showed the continuing shortfall of subsidized child care spaces for Toronto's children. A TDSB document showed the uneven access of pre-school programs by different minority groups. The City and the TDSB joined in a number of knowledge-building exercises with the other Toronto Best Start partners. A major project in Phase 2 was turning the TFD Indicators of Change into a survey and using it to assess service integration levels across hundreds of Toronto communities.

The Toronto Best Start (TBS) Network and its Implementation Steering Committee also developed concrete technical supports to foster integrative work. A major accomplishment has been the development of the *Working Together* support documents for child care, education (including both the Toronto Catholic District School Board and the Toronto District School Board), and family support programs. Despite the efforts of the TBS Network, and the carry-forward lessons of TFD, in the long run, it is likely that good will is not enough to maintain even modest incremental movement towards an improved system of early childhood services without major support from higher levels of government.

Scaling Up in Peel Best Start

In 2008, the Region of Peel municipal government, human services division, in partnership with the district school boards and the Peel Best Start (PBS) Network, began the implementation of integrated early childhood services in the school-as-hub model at five English-language and two French-language sites, with lessons from Toronto First Duty to guide them. The research design employed the same methodology and research tools, adapted minimally for Peel, but had the advantage of funding to support a control group of five matched, non-integrated sites. Further, the Peel Best Start research employed elaborated child experience and outcome measures including children's drawings, puppet interviews, and parent ratings along with the standard academic outcomes. Four- and 5-year-old children were followed longitudinally to the next grade, and a second cohort of incoming children was added and followed in Year 2. The Parent Daily Hassles and Parent surveys used in TFD were included in PBS.

Peel Best Start: Staff

Staff in Peel Best Start looked to Toronto First Duty research to help them begin implementation of the integrated staff team in the school-as-hub model. Municipal and school board administrators, along with a significant number of front-line staff, visited the Bruce/WoodGreen Early Learning Centre site in order to see integration in action. As a result, Peel Best Start was able to get off the ground more quickly due to a greater understanding of the school-as-hub model, and it had the benefit of research findings and measures from TFD to assist in implementation. For example, the Indicators of Change tool, developed as part of the TFD project (Pelletier & Corter, 2005b) was used with PBS staff to guide their thinking and goal planning. Thus, it was possible to see substantial growth in the PBS sites even within the first year of implementation. The Indicators of Change focus groups were carried out twice, towards the beginning and end of the first year of implementation. Figure 13.2 illustrates change in integration at one site, but represents the kind of change seen at all five sites. Figure 13.2 illustrates movement of one site from a state of coexistence, coordination, and collaboration to full integration across five domains: (1) the early learning environment, (2) the early childhood staff team, (3) site governance, (4) seamless access to services, and (4) parent participation. The change was recorded by researchers during the staff team focus groups as team members discussed the indicators for each domain and collaboratively arrived at an indicator of their current state in each domain. In a similar pattern to that of the TFD staff who over time reported more often that they benefited professionally from working in a collaborative

Figure 13.2. Indicators of change at Time 1 and Time 2 in one Peel Best Start site.

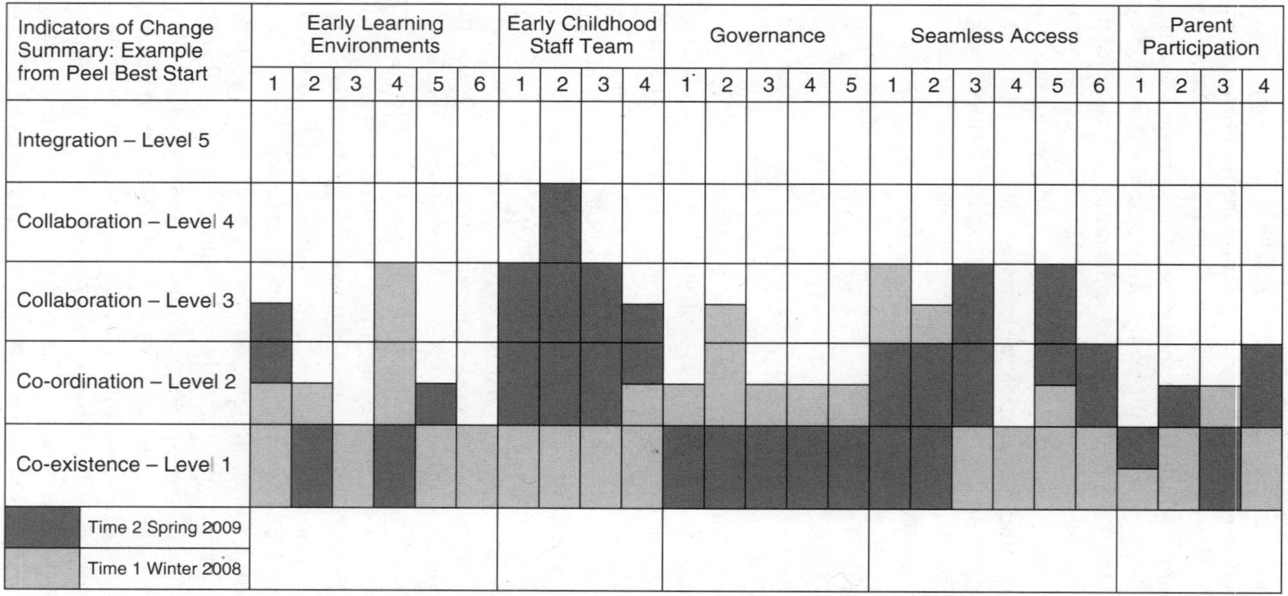

Figure 13.3. Peel Best Start early childhood educator (ECE) and kindergarten teacher (KG) reports of professional benefits.

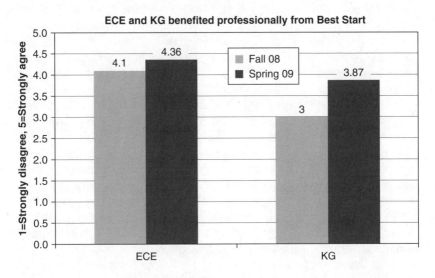

school-as-hub model, Peel Best Start staff likewise became more positive about working in an integrated early years' setting. The most notable change, as was the case for TFD, was in kindergarten teachers' views about collaboration (see Figure 13.3).

Peel Best Start: Parents

Of the 237 parents who participated in the Peel Best Start research during the first year, 210 reported their employment status. Almost 50 per cent of parents were employed full-time ($n = 104$), 13 per cent were employed part-time ($n = 27$), 5 per cent were on parental leave ($n = 10$), 6 per cent were unemployed ($n = 13$), 26 per cent were stay-at-home parents ($n = 54$), and 1 per cent of respondents were students ($n = 2$).

Peel Best Start and control group parents completed the Parent Survey developed for use in TFD. The survey asked parents about knowledge of and need for services in their community.[1]

---

1 Copies of the Parent Survey may be obtained from the author.

As one example, parents were asked if they knew about programs and services that were available in their community. One analysis compared parents who were employed (full-time, part-time, or students) with those who were not employed (stay-at home, parental leave, and unemployed). This comparison showed that parents who were employed ($n = 128$) were significantly more aware of programs than were parents who were not employed ($n = 76$), $F(1,202) = 5.24$, $p < .05$.

The Parenting Daily Hassles Survey, adapted for use in the TFD project (Arimura, 2008), was completed by parents of children at the five English-language Peel Best Start sites and at five control group sites. Parents rated their experiences of daily hassles on a scale of 1 to 5 with 5 being 'a great hassle,' across a number of daily experiences. It was evident that parents whose children had been attending the on-site child care and/or were taking advantage of the child and family centres in the new school-as-hub model were already experiencing fewer daily hassles in some areas. For example, in response to the item, 'It's difficult understanding how things work at my child's school,' control group parents reported significantly ($p < .05$) greater hassles ($M = 1.72$, $n = 94$) than Best Start parents ($M = 1.32$, $n = 72$). In response to the item, 'It's difficult to know whether my child's behaviour is a problem or whether he/she is behaving like other kids his/her age,' control parents reported significantly ($p < .01$) greater hassles ($M = 2.07$, $n = 92$) than Best Start parents ($M = 1.55$, $n = 73$). Similar significant patterns were found for the items, 'It's difficult finding the time to read with my child' and 'It's difficult finding the time to play with my child.' These findings within the first year of the Peel Best Start program parallel the TFD finding that parents who have access to integrated school-as-hub early childhood services experienced fewer daily hassles than parents who did not have access.

Parents who were working full- or part-time or attending school experienced more daily hassles than parents who were not. There were significant differences in many items on the Parenting Daily Hassles Survey (Arimura, 2008), The following are a few examples: Working parents found it to be significantly (all $p < .05$) more of a hassle to (1) make special arrangements to get their child from school to child care or the reverse, (2) worry about their child's safety being taken back and forth from child care to school, (3) be separated from their child during the day, (4) make alternate child care arrangements when their child was sick, (5) find time to read with their child, (6) find time to play with

Figure 13.4. Children's spontaneous mention of transitions in their reports of their day.

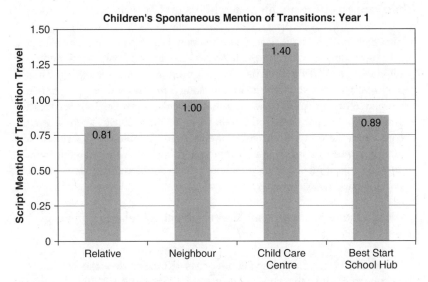

their child, (7) stay in touch with child care staff, (8) discuss issues of concern with child care staff, (9) worry about the quality of their child's experience, (10) find out about their child's day due to multiple care arrangements, and (11) avoid spending money because they have to pay for child care. Also of interest, parents who reported not speaking English at home found it significantly more of a hassle to communicate with their child's school.

Peel Best Start: Children

Of the children who were in some form of child care (153/315), whether with a relative, a child-minder (parents referred to this as 'babysitter'), a child care centre, or in the Best Start child care in the school, Best Start children in the school-as-hub model reported fewer transitions than children who went to a non-relative babysitter or to a child care centre, $F(5,309) = 3.2$, $p < .05$. Children who were cared for by a relative reported approximately the same number of transitions as children in the Best Start school hubs (see Figure 13.4). To bring to life what this looks and sounds like, the following transcripts are examples of children's spontaneous scripts when asked to talk about their day. A Best Start (child care on-site in an integrated hub) child reported:

> First welcome and have snack and then play Lego, read, make something for your mom. Then clean up, play outside, come in, wash hands, and do the message. And then we have large group and play something. Then after that we have small group and do something. Then we plan and then we play with our friends and after that it is clean-up time. Then we recall and tell the teacher what you did and then we have lunch. Then we play lego. Then we go to JK. After JK, the [daycare] people pick you up and after that we have snack and do anything you want. And then your mom and dad might pick you up soon and I get to stay long because Mommy picks me up late. Mommy is a teacher.

A child from the control site (travels to babysitter and child care centre) said:

> I wait for Jason and Isaiah to get out of Ms. [Kindergarten teacher's] class so we can get into the car . . . And then we drive to [babysitter]'s house and then we have snack . . . and then we go to the basement and play . . . and then we come back upstairs to do some work and then we wait for our mommy to come and then we go. Jason stays at [the babysitter's]. Me and Isaiah go to a daycare.

Thus, as can be seen, in parallel to the TFD children's reports of more seamlessness and fewer disruptions, children in the Peel Best Start sites reported fewer transitions than did children who attended child care or who were cared for by a babysitter. In both cases, children whose days flowed seamlessly in school-as-hub models, both recognized and talked about it.

Conclusion

Common Findings from the Two Projects

The findings across school-as-hub sites in these two demonstration studies produced corroborative evidence for a theory of change in which two process pathways linked school-based service integration to better outcomes for young children. In one pathway, integrated professional work provided coherent programming and improved program quality in the care-school microsystem where children spend much of their day. In the second process pathway, parents become more engaged with the school and with learning at home, while family life was less stressful via seamless services. Thus, the second pathway improves the child's home microsystem as well as family connections to services. From the longer-running Toronto First Duty project, there is evidence that these pathways translated into better child outcomes in TFD sites as compared to matched community sites without integrated services. In particular, community level comparisons showed TFD advantages on the social and emotional dimensions of the Early Development Instrument (Corter et al., 2008). An important part of the findings is that these pathways and outcomes are not limited to particular demographic groups. For example, minority-language parents reported considerably lower levels of use of a variety of pre-school services prior to TFD, but this gap was eliminated in patterns of enrolment in TFD. Furthermore, analysis of intake and tracking data from the TFD project also showed that continuing participation was not adversely affected by minority language status or lower levels of parental education (Patel, 2009).

Although we do not yet have all the evidence on child outcomes from the more recent PBS project since it is currently underway, there is emerging evidence on the value of integrated services for child outcomes in the U.S. 21st Century Initiative (Heinrich et al., 2006) and the U.K. National Sure Start Strategy (Melhuish et al., 2008). For example, in a large-scale quasi-experimental comparison, the U.K. research team found advantages for children's social and emotional development in integrated service sites. Interestingly, they also found advantages on some measures of parenting as well, providing further support for parenting as a potential pathway of program influence on children's development. These findings were more positive than the results of an earlier shorter-term evaluation, prompting the investigators to suggest that complex change initiatives like Sure Start take time to mature.

Similar points about the importance of allowing time for changes to occur have emerged from the evaluation of the 21st Century program (Heinrich et al., 2006), along with some support for the effects of the school-as-hub model on parent and staff pathways as important in achieving benefits for children (Finn-Stevenson et al., 1998). Additional evidence on professional collaboration in early childhood service integration as a pathway was provided in a U.S. study showing that greater levels of integration and intensity of professional relationships were associated with higher levels of program quality (Selden, Sowa, & Sandfort, 2006).

Policy Impact

From our analysis of knowledge mobilization in the Toronto First Duty and Peel Best Start projects, we believe that the research emphasis on process and implementation has helped policy makers, politicians, service organization leaders, and practitioners to visualize how some of the big ideas on service integration and an early childhood system would look on the ground, starting with the bringing together of existing services. A quote from a foundation official who was involved in advocacy efforts with the province illustrates the value of studying implementation, 'We would not be here today with an Early Learning Advisor, considering full-day early learning care, without TFD . . . Best Start is really all about coordinating services and systems change, and until they (the government) could see what it looked like on the ground as TFD, they would not have been able to move forward' (Corter et al., 2009, p. 24).

In addition to TFD's influence on the development of provincial Best Start policy, including Peel Best Start, the government has now committed to implementing Full-Day Early Learning/Kindergarten for 4- and 5-Year-Olds in Ontario schools. The approach is integrative in several ways. One is that child care professionals and certified teachers jointly deliver a unified, play-based program. Another way the approach is integrative is the plan for the continuation of the Best Start approach via Child and Family Centres, which will complement the school-based Early Learning Program for children. This commitment follows a report from the Premier's Special Advisor on Early Learning (Pascal, 2009), which outlined a visionary integrated system to support children and families from the period before birth to age 12 years. TFD was cited in the report as providing evidence supporting the development of the kind of system being envisioned. Although the government's initial commitments are only a first step towards achieving the vision, it is interesting that the key research piece from TFD and PBS on building programs through teamwork is being written into law. The Education Act has been amended to mandate the new province-wide Full-Day Early Learning/Kindergarten Program, to require school boards to designate and fill early childhood educator positions for the full-day early learning classes, to make provisions for the extended day program and to provide additional recognition of the important new role that early childhood educators play, including a 'duty to cooperate' in the expectation that teachers and early childhood educators will collaborate on shared professional activities. Although the Ministry of Education has been appointed the lead ministry and schools are to be Early Learning Program hubs, for the first time in Ontario's Education history, early childhood educators have been given a key role in developing and delivering early learning in partnership with teachers in schools.

Of course, the messiness of implementation, tests of wide-scale effectiveness and long-term political commitment lie ahead. Furthermore, these demonstration projects do not provide answers for systemic problems such as inequitable pay for early childhood education professionals or the gap in availability of child care spaces in publicly funded, high quality programs beyond the Early Learning/Kindergarten Program (e.g., Children's Services Division, City of Toronto, 2008). Nevertheless, the first step towards an integrated system is afoot in Ontario. In his analyses of education reform, Michael Fullan (1993) popularized the 'ready, fire, aim' antidote for postponing action until the perfect plan is agreed upon, a point that is rarely reached. In Ontario the provincial government has 'fired' its first shots at reforming the foundations for early childhood. Hopefully, it will have the opportunity to continue to sharpen its aim with the benefit of further debate, informed by evaluation of process and outcomes of the developing school-as-hub model.

References

Arimura, T. (2008). *Daily routines, parenting hassles, and social support: The role that early childhood services play in parents' and children's daily life.* Unpublished M.A. thesis, University of Toronto.

Arimura, T., & Corter, C. (2010). School-based integrated early childhood programs: Impact on the well-being of children and parents. *Interaction,* 24(1), 23–28.

Beach, J., Friendly, M., Ferns, C., Prabhu, N., & Forer, B. (2009). *Early childhood education and care in Canada, 2008.* Retrieved from http://www.childcare canada.org/ECEC2008/index.html#toc.

Bronfenbrenner, U. (1979). *The ecology of human development.* Cambridge, MA: Harvard University Press.

Bryant, D., Maxwell, K., Taylor, K., Poe, M., Peisner-Feinberg, E., & Bernier, K. (2003). *Smart Start and preschool child care quality in North Carolina: Change over time and relation to children's readiness.* ED 473699, 22 pages. Chapel Hill, NC: FPG Child Development Institute. Retrieved from http://www.fpg.unc.edu/smartstart/reports/Child_Care_Quality_2003.pdf.

Children's Services Division, City of Toronto (2008). *Children's services fact sheet.* Retrieved from http://www.toronto.ca/children/pdf/factsheet_oct2008.pdf.

Cleveland, G., Corter, C., Pelletier, J., Colley, B., J., & Jamieson, J. (2006). *A review of the state of the field of early childhood learning and development in child care, kindergarten and family support programs.* Prepared for the Canadian Council on Learning. Toronto: Atkinson Centre for Society and Child Development, University of Toronto. Retrieved from http://www.ccl-cca.ca/NR/rdonlyres/67F194AF-8EB5-487D-993C-7CF9B565DDB3/0/SFREarlyChildhoodLearning.pdf.

Corbett, T. (2006). The role of social indicators in an era of human social reform in the United States. In A. Ben-Arieh, & R.M. Goerge (Eds.), *Indicators of children's well-being: Understanding their role, usage and policy influence,* vol. 27 (pp. 3–20). New York: Springer Science & Business Media.

Corter, C., & Pelletier, J. (2005). Parent and community involvement in schools: Policy panacea or pandemic? In N. Bascia, A. Cumming, A. Datnow, K. Leithwood, & D. Livingstone (Eds.), *International handbook of educational policy* (pp. 295–327). Dordrecht: Springer.

Corter, C., Bertrand, J., Griffin, T., Endler, M., Pelletier, J., & McKay, D. (2002). *Toronto First Duty Starting Gate Report: Implementing integrated foundations for early childhood.* Toronto. (81 pages). Retrieved from http://www.toronto.ca/firstduty/reports.htm.

Corter, C., Bertrand, J., Pelletier, J., Janmohamed, Z., Brown, D., Arimura, T., & Patel, S. (2007a). *Toronto First Duty Phase 2 research progress report: December.* Retrieved from http://www.toronto.ca/firstduty/tfd_research_progress_report_dec07.pdf.

Corter, C., Bertrand, J., Pelletier, J., Griffin, T., McKay, D., Patel, S., & Ioannone, P. (2007b). *Toronto First Duty Phase 1 Final Report: Evidence-based understanding of integrated foundations for early childhood.* Retrieved from http://www.toronto.ca/firstduty/tfd_phase1_finalreport.pdf.

Corter, C., Patel, S., Pelletier, J., & Bertrand, J. (2008). The Early Development Instrument as an evaluation and improvement tool for school-based, integrated services for young children and parents: The Toronto First Duty Project. *Early Education and Development, 19,* 1–22.

Corter, C., Pelletier, J., Janmohamed, Z., Bertrand, J., Arimura, T., Patel, S., Mir, S., Wilton, A., & Brown, D. (2009). *Toronto First Duty Phase 2, 2006–2008: Final research report*. Retrieved from http://www.toronto.ca/firstduty/TFD_phase2_final.pdf.

Crowson, R.L., & Boyd, W.L. (1995). Integration of services for children. In L. Rigsby, M. Reynolds, & M. Wang (Eds.), *School-community connections*. San Francisco, CA: Jossey-Bass.

Desimone, L., Payne, B., Fedoravicius, N., Henrich, C., & Finn-Stevenson, M. (2004). Comprehensive school reform: An implementation study of preschool programs in elementary schools. *Elementary School Journal, 104,* 369–389.

Diamond, A., Barnett, W. S., Thomas, J., & Munro, S. (2007). Preschool program improves cognitive control. *Science, 318,* 1387–1388.

Dryfoos, J.J., Quinn, J., & Barkin, C. (Eds.). (2005). *Community schools in action: Lessons from a decade of practice*. New York: Oxford University Press.

Dunn, J.R., Frohlich, K.L., Ross, N., Curtis, L.J., & Sanmartin, C. (2006). Role of geography in inequalities in health and human development. In J. Heymann, C. Hertzman, M.L. Barer, & R.G. Evans (Eds.), *Healthier societies: From analysis to action* (pp. 237–263). New York: Oxford University Press.

Finn-Stevenson, M., Desimone, L., & Chung, A. (1998). Linking child care and support services with the school: Pilot evaluation of the school of the 21st century. *Children and Youth Services Review, 20,* 177–205.

Finn-Stevenson, M., & Zigler, E. (1999). *Schools of the 21st century: Linking child care and education*. Boulder, CO: Westview Press.

Fullan. M. (1993). *Change forces: Probing the depths of educational reform*. London and New York: Falmer.

Gormley, W.T., Gayer, T., Phillips, D., & Dawson, B. (2005). The effects of universal pre-K on cognitive development. *Developmental Psychology, 41,* 872–884.

Harms, T., Clifford, R.M., & Cryer, D. (2005). *Early Childhood Environment Rating Scale-Revised*. New York: Teachers College Press.

Henrich, C., Ginicola, M., Finn-Stevenson, M., & Zigler, E. (2006). *The School of the 21st Century is making a difference: Findings from two evaluations* (issue brief). New Haven, CT: Zigler Center in Child Development and Social Policy, Yale University.

Irwin, L., Johnson, J., Henderson, A., Dahinten, V., & Hertzman, C. (2007). Examining how contexts shape young children's perspectives of health. *Child Care, Health & Development, 3,* 353–359.

James-Burdumy, S., Dynarski, M., Moore, M., Deke, J. Mansfield, W., Pistorino, C., & Warner, E. (2005). *When schools stay open late: The national evaluation of the 21st century community learning centers program – final report.* Washington, DC: U.S. Department of Education.

Janus, M., & Offord, D. (2007). Psychometric properties of the Early Development Instrument (EDI): A teacher-completed measure of children's readiness to learn at school entry. *Canadian Journal of Behavioural Science, 39,* 1–22.

Keating, D.P., & Hertzman, C. (1999). *Developmental health and the wealth of nations: Social, biological, and educational dynamics.* New York: Guilford.

LaPierre, L. (1981). *To herald a child.* Toronto: Ontario Public School Men Teachers' Federation.

Lerner, R., Rothbaum, F., Boulos, S., & Castellino, D. (2002). Developmental systems perspective on parenting. In M. Bornstein (Ed.), *Handbook of parenting,* vol. 2 (pp. 407–437). Englewood Cliffs, NJ: Erlbaum.

Mathien, J., & Johnson, L. (1998). *Early childhood services for kindergarten-age children in four Canadian provinces: Scope, nature and models for the future.* Ottawa: Caledon Institute of Social Policy.

McCain, M., & Mustard, F. (1999). *Early Years Study: The real brain drain.* Toronto: Government of Ontario.

McCain, M.N., Mustard, J.F., & Shanker, S. (2007). *Early Years Study 2: Putting science into action.* Toronto: Council of Early Child Development.

Melhuish, E., Belsky, J., Anning, A. Ball, M., Barnes, J., Romaniuk, H., & Leyland, A. (2007). Variation in community intervention programmes and consequences for children and families: The example of Sure Start Local Programmes. *Journal of Child Psychology and Psychiatry, 48,* 543–551.

Melhuish, E., Belsky, J., Leyland, A., & Barnes, J. (2008). Effects of fully-established Sure Start Local Programmes on 3-year-old children and their families living in England: A quasi-experimental observational study. *Lancet, 372,* 1641–1647.

Ministry of Children and Youth Services. (2005). *Implementation planning guidelines for Best Start networks.* Toronto: Author. Retrieved from http://www.london.ca/Child_Care/PDFs/Implementation_Planning_Guidelines_Re visedJuly1.pdf.

Ministry of Children and Youth Services. (2007). *Early learning for every child today: A framework for Ontario early childhood settings.* Toronto: Ontario Ministry of Children and Youth Services. Retrieved from http://www.gov.on.ca/children/graphics/stel02_183342.pdf.

Moss, P. (2008). What future for the relationship between early childhood education and care and compulsory schooling? *Research in Comparative and International Education, 3,* 224–234.

Organization of Economic Cooperation and Development (OECD) (2004). *Canada Country Note. Thematic review of early childhood education and care.* Paris: Author.

Pascal, C. (2009, June). *With our best future in mind: Implementing early learning in Ontario*. Early Learning Advisor's report to the Premier. Retrieved from http://www.ontario.ca/en/initiatives/early_learning/ONT06_018865.

Patel, S. (2009). *Integrated early childhood program participation, parenting, and child development outcomes: The Toronto First Duty Project*. Doctoral dissertation, University of Toronto, 2009.

Patel, S., & Corter, C. (2006). *Parent-school involvement, diversity, and school-based preschool service hubs*. Paper presented at the annual meetings of the American Educational Research Association, April, San Francisco.

Patel, S.. & Corter, C. (in press). Building capacity for parent involvement through school-based preschool services. *Early Child Development and Care.*

Patel, S., Corter, C., & Pelletier, J. (2008). What do families want? Understanding their goals for early childhood services. In M. Cornish (Ed.), *Promising practices for partnering with families in the early years* (pp. 103–135). Family School Community Partnership Monograph series. Charlotte, NC: Information Age Publishing.

Pelletier, J., & Corter, C. (2005a). Design, implementation and outcomes of a school readiness program for diverse families. *School Community Journal, 15,* 89–116.

Pelletier, J., & Corter, C. (2005b). Toronto First Duty: Integrating kindergarten, childcare and parenting supports to help diverse families connect to schools. *Multicultural Education Journal, 15,* 89–116.

Pelletier, J., & Corter, C. (2006). Integration, innovation, and evaluation in school-based early childhood services. In B. Spodek & O. Saracho (Eds.), *Handbook of research on the education of young children* (pp. 477–496). Matwah, NJ: Erlbaum.

Pelletier, J., Reeve, R., & Halewood, C. (2006). Young children's knowledge-building and literacy development through Knowledge Forum®. *Early Education and Development, 17,* 323–346.

Penn, H., Barreau, S., Butterworth, L., Lloyd, E., Moyles, J., & Potter, S., & Sayeed, R. (2004). *What is the impact of out-of-home integrated care and education settings on children aged 0–6 and their parents?* Research Evidence in Education Library, London: EPPI-Centre, Social Science Research Unit, Institute of Education. Retrieved from http://eppi.ioe.ac.uk/EPPIWebContent/reel/review_groups/early_years/EY_rv1/EY_rv1.pdf.

Saracho, O., & Spodek, B. (2003). Recent trends and innovations in the early childhood education curriculum. *Early Child Development and Care, 173,* 175–183.

Selden, S., Sowa, J., & Sandfort, J. (2006). The impact of nonprofit collaboration in early child care and education on management and program outcomes. *Public Administration Review, 66,* 412–425.

Siraj-Blatchford, I., & Siraj-Blatchford, J. (2009). Improving development outcomes for children through effective practice in integrating early years services. *Knowledge Review 3*. London: Centre for Excellence and Outcomes in Children and Young People's Services.

St Pierre, R., Layzer, J., Goodson, B., & Bernstein, L. (1999). The effectiveness of comprehensive, case management interventions: Evidence from the National Evaluation of the Comprehensive Child Development Program. *American Journal of Evaluation, 20*, 15–34.

Toronto District School Board (2007). *TDSB Learning Opportunities Index*. Toronto: Author.

Zigler, E., Finn-Stevenson, M., & Stern, B. (1997). Supporting children and families in the schools: The School of the 21st Century. *American Journal of Orthopsychiatry, 6*, 396–407.

Part III Commentary: Government Roles in Early Childhood Education and Care in Canada: Patchwork, Perils, and Promise of New Directions

CARL CORTER

In Canada, the story of government roles in early childhood programs has been told mainly in words like 'fragmented' and 'underfunded,' certainly not 'foundational' for providing coherent supports to children's development and to their families. Education in Canada is a provincial/territorial responsibility, and Canada's federal government has provided neither leadership, nor the funding to establish a coherent approach to early education, care, and family support. The federal–provincial–territorial (FPT) agreements dating back to the Early Childhood Development (ECD) Agreement in 2000 and the 2003 Multilateral Framework on Early Learning and Child Care had established a framework that led to some progress and federal funding, but the election of a Conservative federal government in 2006 derailed movement towards a national approach. The lack of coherence and limits on policy development and government resolve show up graphically in international comparisons. Nevertheless, new initiatives at the local and provincial levels hold real promise for the future.

Canada made the news late in 2008 with its last place showing in early childhood service provision in the UNICEF report, *The Childcare Transition: A League Table of Early Childhood Education and Care in Economically Advanced Countries* (United Nations Children's Fund, 2008). In terms of achieving ten critical early childhood education and care benchmarks, Canada met only one and was tied for last place among Organization for Economic Co-operation and Development (OECD) countries with Ireland. This failing report card spotlighted the need to improve child care in Canada and to critically examine public policy against that of highly ranked countries. The failing mark was not surprising given that Canada had previously defined the bottom of the scale in financial commitment to early childhood among OECD countries. In 2004, estimated expenditures on early childhood services as a percentage of gross domestic product were lower for Canada than for any other country surveyed in the OECD's *Starting Strong* reviews (Bennett, 2008). The OECD's 2006 report also criticized Canada's service provision for the lack of connection between kindergarten education programs and child care programs for working parents. A subsequent Canada Senate report (Standing Senate Committee on Social Affairs, Science and Technology, 2009), presented a national call to action to address Canada's shameful showing in supporting its youngest members. That action has not yet emerged at a national level, but there is promise at other levels of government.

Quebec has not waited for a national approach and began its own move to an early childhood system in 1997. Other provincial governments are now awakening to the possibilities for coherent systems, building in part on the initiatives spawned by the earlier FPT agreements. Of course no amount of funding and FPT policy development will improve the lives of children and families without local levels of governance and management that orchestrate effective policy implementation and service delivery. Much of the evidence presented in Part III shows the critical roles played by municipalities, other local and regional governing bodies, local service delivery organizations and school boards, parents, and other community members.

The chapters in this part take us across examples of roles for different levels of government. Christa Japel's chapter leads off with a research-informed report on the successes and limitations of the ground-breaking Quebec provincial government policy to provide universal 'educare' to pre-schoolers and their families as part of a larger family policy. Ray Peters, Angela Howell-Moneta, and Kelly Petrunka describe community-based programs originating at both the provincial and federal levels; they describe in detail the community role in developing coherent and comprehensive programming for children and families through the twenty-five-year provincially funded Better Beginnings Better Futures (BBBF) demonstration and research project in Ontario. Jessica Ball catches the federal government doing something right in its gradually increasing support of the community-centred and culturally respectful Aboriginal Head Start Program. Janette Pelletier's chapter concludes with research descriptions of municipal-level demonstration projects, Toronto First Duty and Peel Best Start, with stories of implementation at the community level and implications and impacts on provincial-level policies.

The Quebec Child Care System:
Research Results and Lessons to Be Learned

Standing in contrast to the Canadian patchwork of early childhood programming, the Quebec provincial government's creation of a universal child care system has been a national milestone. Japel's chapter describes some of the context for the work of the provincial government and its ministries in the establishment and continuing development of the system. She also reviews research from three major studies of the implementation and effects of the system, two of which were commissioned by the provincial government. The research points out that the system is a 'work in progress,' with important shortcomings that need to be addressed in further policy development and in improved professional training. Nevertheless, research also shows broad benefits of the system as a wise investment and a 'social good.' Part of the good news is that the system has survived provincial government change and remains a stable enough platform to invite realistic suggestions for improvement, some of which are offered in Japel's chapter.

The child care system was established in 1997 as one component of a new Quebec family policy. It had multiple aims of supporting work and family balance for parents and whole-child development and school readiness for children. It established low-cost, directly publicly funded care for young children via the creation of CPEs (Centres de la Petite Enfance), which incorporated existing non-profit centres and home-based care. Contracts were also negotiated with existing licensed for-profit daycares, but with a subsequent moratorium on the opening of new for-profit centres. Provincial government change in 2003 contributed to challenges in terms of ongoing funding and structural supports to the system, including reduced programming support to home-based CPEs. Policy change also ended the moratorium on the creation of new for-profit centres, which expanded the number of for-profit centres, with presumably lower levels of quality, according to converging findings from the Quebec experience, reviewed here, and from other jurisdictions (see Gordon Cleveland's chapter in this volume). Given the multiple aims of the Quebec child care system, it may not be surprising that multiple government ministries have worked on the development of the child care system. What may be more surprising is that a coherent system has resulted.

Although this is a story of Quebec's provincial government leadership, Japel does allude to the federal government's role in child care (see Martha Friendly and Susan Prentice's chapter in this volume), with the 2003 Multilateral Framework on Early Learning and Child Care and subsequent 2004 Speech from the Throne enunciating foundational principles for the establishment of a national child care system. Quebec did not take part in negotiations on bilateral FPT agreements to implement the multilateral framework, but it did negotiate federal funding for its existing system. And Japel uses the foundational QUAD principles (quality, universality, accessibility, and developmental appropriateness) to review research on how the Quebec system is performing.

There is converging evidence across studies on quality, universality, and accessibility concerns. For example, Japel reports data from the Quebec Longitudinal Study of Child Development (QLSCD) showing that a rating of 'good' is obtained by 35 per cent of centre-based and 29 per cent of home-based CPEs. Outside of the CPEs, this rating is obtained by only 14 per cent of for-profit daycares and 10 per cent of unregulated home-based daycares. Although the Quebec system is built on principles of universality and accessibility, only about half of pre-school children have access to affordable regulated centre- or home-based care. Furthermore, higher SES families are overrepresented among users of child care. In terms of developmental appropriateness, data show that some CPEs lag behind in terms of structured activities and developmentally appropriate materials.

Revisions of provincial policies could correct some of these weaknesses. For example, accessibility for the most vulnerable families is limited because there is no policy obligation for CPEs to serve children in their immediate neighbourhoods. Furthermore, intentions to link vulnerable families targeted for support from community health and social service centres (CLSCs) with CPEs have not worked well due to inadequate policy articulation. Although the government has worked on increasing universality and the number of children served, the policy of expansion may have contributed to problems in quality. And although the government developed a 2004 Ongoing Quality Improvement Plan, it turned the responsibility over to child care settings with no funding attached.

Despite the problems, there are clear markers of overall success for the Quebec system. It leads the country in providing affordable, regulated care for young children. The system benefits children's development and readiness, particularly vulnerable children. In concert with other family policy, such as generous parental leaves, birth rates, and labour participation have climbed in Quebec compared with other provinces.

Community-Based Early Child Development Projects

The Peters et al. chapter describes the rationale and the fruits of findings from Better Beginnings Better Futures (BBBF), a twenty-five-year demonstration project designed to inform prevention policy established by the Ontario government in 1990. To set the stage for the unique community intervention approach in BBBF and the remarkably broad and deep research design embedded in the project, Peters et al. review a number of Canadian federal and provincially funded early childhood community initiatives, including the federally funded Community Action Program for Children (CAPC) and Canada Prenatal Nutrition Program (CPNP). Peters et al. also note how federal funding for the joint federal, provincial, territorial Early Childhood Development Agreement contributed to province-wide initiatives for community-level service delivery across a number of projects before the Harper government cancelled funding.

These initiatives represent a range of intervention approaches; in some provinces they also include an array of sub-initiatives. The approaches range across universal and targeted programs, service delivery in child and family centres or community/professional networks, and more and less comprehensive and integrated approaches. According to Peters et al., they do have some features in common: they often do not reach a large proportion of the populations they aim to serve, even when these are targeted groups. A second common feature is that evaluation on the implementation and effects of these programs is often not available. Even when it is, the results are not always promising. In particular, one national evaluation of CAPC found no evidence of effects even though the premise of the program shared community-building aspects with BBBF, which has yielded strong evidence for lasting effects. As in many cases of complex initiatives, other investigations of CAPC are still underway.

A very useful feature of the analysis in this chapter is the attention to the economic dimensions of government initiatives including the BBBF demonstration project. Costs and benefits and other types of economic analyses of early childhood programs are an important part of the government policy context at all levels. The analysis also calls attention not only to cost, but also to patchy provision in terms of numbers of children served out of target populations.

This historical context for BBBF is particularly interesting in light of the current interest in population health perspectives on early childhood policy and programs in Canada (Patel & Corter, 2011). The project had its roots in an Ontario Child Health Study released in 1987. The study showed that a significant proportion of children in the general population had mental health problems and that only a small fraction of these children had contact with special services over the preceding year, particularly among disadvantaged children. In the context of these findings, BBBF was a promotion and prevention approach targeted to eight relatively disadvantaged communities, but all young children and families in the eight communities were eligible to participate. Five of the BBBF sites focused on younger children (birth to age 4 years) by offering home visiting, enriched child care programs, and additional programs for children and their families based on locally identified needs and available resources; whereas three BBBF sites focused on children from 4 to 8 years of age. The aim was to support all aspects of child development and prevent later mental health problems through community-level development of services for parents and children. The bottom-up development of supports through the participation of residents and professionals was paired with top-down design principles, or requirements, such as the establishment of local organizations to develop and coordinate community-level services. The longitudinal investigation of the intervention and its participants has examined outcomes over a twenty-year span.

The results describe both the process of how community development of BBBF worked and the outcomes from short term to long term. For children from the sites focusing on 4- to 8-year-olds, the results demonstrate long-term outcomes consistent with the child development and mental health promotion aims of the project. The calculation of BBBF costs to benefits shows a significant repayment on program costs, even though the per child cost is less than many other effective early childhood interventions. Remarkably, however, mid- to long-term effects were not found for children from sites focused on birth to 4 years of age. This finding is inconsistent with conventional policy wisdom that 'the earlier the intervention, the better the payoff.' Peters et al. discuss several interpretations of this finding. One is that the modest investment in support per child was not enough to reach a critical-level of intensity for younger children, but in the case of older children, the investment was on top of the thousands invested in every child via the public school system, so that BBBF programming was 'value added.' A related argument is that schools provide a platform for coordination of services and new supports, but there is no equivalent universal platform for effective and integrated service in the pre-school period. In other words, there is no 'system' for early childhood. Although service coordination was a design principle in BBBF, it must have been challenging to pull off in communities where an average of twenty-six different programs were delivered to younger children and families without a common platform.

Federal Investments in Strengthening Indigenous Capacity for Culturally Based Pre-school

Jessica Ball's chapter puts the shameful inequities for Canada's Aboriginal children in the modestly promising context of federal government early childhood education and care (ECEC) funding that supports the Aboriginal Head Start (AHS) program, which is grounded in community-based and culturally competent (bi-cultural) approaches. While the AHS is promising and has grown over the past fifteen years, Ball takes us through some of the historical and contemporary barriers to more substantial progress on addressing barriers to equity, and the real limits on current outreach and funding for AHS and other ECEC programs, as well as the need to embed them in broader approaches. In particular, she makes a case for ECEC practitioner training at the post-secondary level that is also community-based and bi-cultural, and federally supported. Although Ball's chapter is focused on the federal level, where most policy and funding in the area rests, she notes that there are some targeted provincial programs for services such as parent education and home visiting. She also outlines in more detail some of the arrangements for local community governance of AHS, which appear to be critical to the success of culture-fitting and buy-in to the program through community participation. Programs are locally operated by Aboriginal, Métis, or Inuit non-profit community organizations (in the case of the Aboriginal Head Start in Urban and Northern Communities program) or First Nation governing bodies (in the case of the Aboriginal Head Start On-Reserve program). Local parent groups are also involved. These groups have input into management and operations, including program 'specifics,' as general design principles are adapted to local communities. The chapter presents evidence that rallying around early childhood programs can be a 'hook' for a wider community-building agenda. It also shows the AHS works in an integrated fashion at the community level, often as a community 'hub,' reinforced by 'conceptual' agreement on the importance of integrative approaches.

Nevertheless, part of the challenge in addressing the inequities may be the dim public awareness of the shameful gaps in the lives of Aboriginal children and the current ecologies creating them, not to mention the history of government oppression, with residential schooling destroying trust in education and other community capacities. If there were more awareness, there might be more funding and resolve to force different levels of government to stop passing the buck on health and intergenerational problems in the context of poverty and racism; and there might be more government action to actually implement Canada's Aboriginal Action Plan released more than a decade ago. Where is the national outcry for more government funding?

Another substantial part of the problem is the lack of integration and cohesive strategies across different levels of government. There is the usual patchwork of government initiatives, management, and jurisdictional boundaries across FPT regional and community levels. Even within the federal level, multiple branches are involved and AHS is funded by two different branches. Across FPT boundaries, in some cases, federal programs fall under provincial regulation of child care, but in other cases they do not.

Ball briefly reviews the litany of vulnerability gaps for young Aboriginal children in health and education. Indigenous groups themselves have asked for culturally based ECEC programs to address the inequities in school readiness. Even though ECEC programs can help, Ball cites evidence that 16 per cent of Aboriginal children have had Aboriginal-based pre-school programs and an estimate that only 18 per cent have access to any pre-school programming. AHS is a targeted program available to some Aboriginal children, but not others. Other federal ECEC programs are also 'targeted.' For example, the First Nations and Inuit Child Care Initiative provides child care for parents who are working or in training. Since these parents may include those who are better off, the net effect of providing these programs could be to increase gaps for children who are not eligible. As Ball observes, a 'multisectoral' approach at all levels of government is needed.

Integrated Early Childhood Services in School-as-Hub Models: Lessons from Toronto First Duty and Peel Best Start

The Pelletier chapter describes research from two demonstration projects that integrate child care, kindergarten, and other traditionally separate pre-school services in seamless school-based hubs. The design and implementation of the projects were based on collaborations between municipalities, school boards, and other community-level service providers. However, other levels of government entered into the context for the development of both projects. Provincial government change in Ontario in the early 1990s wiped out an established agenda for service integration and building child care space into schools, but the Early Years Study in 1999, commissioned by the same government, put new evidence for integrative approaches and the importance of the early years back in the forefront. It also set the stage for the establishment of the Toronto First Duty (TFD) Project.

It is notable that this project was designed with the explicit aim of influencing practice and policy at the local agency, municipal, and provincial government levels, as well as beyond. Part of the influence strategy was funding a broad-scale evaluation with a focus on the process of implementation, as well as on the outcomes of the new service model. Giving politicians concrete evidence that implementation of the new approach was feasible in local contexts, starting with services that already exist, may have been as important in moving policy as evidence on positive outcomes. Of course, there was some of that evidence, indirectly from related early childhood interventions in other provinces or countries such as Quebec or the U.K.'s Sure Start (Melhuish, Belsky, & Barnes, 2010), as well as directly from TFD. In setting the stage for her studies, Pelletier reviews some of the international evidence on both small-scale studies of early childhood service integration, as well as broader policy analyses of integration at the federal government level in other countries.

With another government change and ideas from TFD and elsewhere, Ontario's Best Start Initiative in 2004 (also described in the Peters et al. chapter) set out integrative principles for early childhood services, goals for school-based hubs, and increases in child care provision.

However, full implementation of provincial plans was predicated on federal funding, which was eliminated after government change in Ottawa. Nevertheless, enthusiasm for the integrative vision of Best Start persisted in many communities, including the Peel Region, where the municipal government and the local school boards replicated and extended the design and evaluation of school-based, integrated service community hubs. Replication of results is an important science principle but this project also reflects the appetite for locally based research results that can be mobilized with local practitioners and administrators in a formative evaluation approach that improves local programs and practice. The Ontario government has now moved to the phased implementation of a very ambitious universal approach to providing integrated care and education in full-day early learning kindergarten programs for 4- and 5-year-olds. Hopefully, research will help to guide and improve the development and implementation of the emerging system, and not just deliver a future verdict on outcomes.

Conclusion

Across the varied government levels, roles, and initiatives represented in these chapters, some common themes emerge. Regarding the broad issue of *aims* of early childhood programs and policy, it is clear that school readiness, with the presumed long-term economic returns, is not the only aim driving policy development of Canadian governments. Each of the initiatives portrayed here focuses on broader child development aims and other aims as well. Better Beginnings Better Futures was designed as a mental health promotion and/or prevention approach that would also build community. Aboriginal Head Start aims to strengthen Aboriginal culture and language, parental engagement, and other pathways that may also strengthen communities. The Quebec 'educare' system and the Toronto First Duty model of integrated care, kindergarten, and other services, aim to support both child development and parents in balancing work and family.

Each of the chapters in Part III illustrates how research can contribute to government policy development and improvement with support for new directions. Governments look for encouraging program and policy outcomes for child development, and several of these chapters provide such evidence. The chapters also describe evidence showing the value of early childhood education and care for some of the other aims noted above. Both the chapter on Quebec and on the municipal demonstration projects in Peel and Toronto, for example, suggest benefits for parents and family-work balance.

The chapters show the value of research in understanding the *processes*, as well as *outcomes* of programs and policy implementation. For example, program quality and professional work are important mediators of success featured in the chapters on the Quebec system and the Toronto area school-as-hub models. Japel shows that the Quebec government has recognized issues in program quality of the Quebec system but more substantial policy adjustments are needed. As another important example, both the Ball and Peters et al. chapters describe the processes involved in local governance and communities coming together in successful implementation of Aboriginal Head Start and Better Beginnings Better Futures community programs.

Nevertheless, the Peters et al. review of research on government early childhood initiatives also shows the very limited research and evaluation on many government initiatives and the need to do more (see also Cleveland et al., 2007); there is clearly a need for a systematic review of many of the existing programs. The Manitoba efforts noted in the Peters et al. chapter appear to be a shining example of a systematic approach to provincial government data coordination to evaluate new initiatives, with presumed benefits for public knowledge building and policy improvement. While research and evaluation are important to policy building and improvement in ECEC, understanding and 'evaluation' by the public are also critical to the political will to improve programs and policies.

A major theme running through these chapters and their analyses of current roles of governments in Canadian ECEC is the crying need for more coherence along many dimensions: across and within different levels of governance, across traditionally separate service types and professions, and between services and families and their communities.

Underfunded, disconnected interventions may be more than inefficient and hard to navigate for families. They actually have iatrogenic effects; for example, child outcome and equity gaps may increase if less advantaged families use ECEC services at lower rates, or if targeting misses large numbers of vulnerable children (Willms, 2002), or if patchwork provision misses whole sub-populations. A stark example came to light as Ontario began to roll out universal full-day early learning kindergarten across the province. It was pointed out in the press (Talaga, 2010) that many Aboriginal children on reserves will remain in half-day kindergarten programs since their programs are federally funded and managed while more advantaged children elsewhere move ahead with full-day programs. Some of these kinds of gaps are noted in the chapters here but the problem goes beyond made-in-Canada examples. In the U.S. ECEC service context Sharon Kagan (2009) surveyed the fragmented service picture in the United States and concluded that longer-term benefits on a policy shift to integration, which brings together schools, communities, and higher quality early childhood programs, achieve better results. In fact, she argued that any new proposals for early childhood funding should be required to include a 'linkage impact statement,' similar to environmental impact statements, and designed to avoid further pollution by service fragmentation.

The success of joining education and care in Quebec and similar steps in other provinces signals new directions and more coherent approaches. More comprehensive approaches for creating community ECEC platforms to support young children and families, as described in Part III of this book, are also a promising direction of the government policy mix.

References

Bennett, J. (2008). *Early Childhood Services in the OECD Countries: Review of the literature and current policy in the early childhood field.* Innocenti Working Paper No. 2008–01. Florence, UNICEF Innocenti Research Centre.

Cleveland, G., Corter, C., Pelletier, J., Colley, Bertrand, J., & Jamieson, J. (2006). *A review of the state of the field of early childhood learning and development in child care, kindergarten and family support programs.* Prepared for the Canadian Council on Learning. Toronto: Atkinson Centre for Society and Child Development, University of Toronto. Retrieved from http://www.ccl-cca.ca/pdfs/StateOfField/SFREarlyChildhoodLearning.pdf.

Kagan, S. (2009). Moving from 'transitions' to policy change: Next steps for linking ready kids to ready schools. In *Linking ready kids to ready schools.* Kellogg Foundation and Education Commission of the States. Retrieved from http://www.wkkf.org/DesktopModules/WKF.00_DmaSupport/ViewDoc.aspx?Lang uageID=0&CID=168&ListID=28&ItemID=5000607&fld=PDFFile.

Melhuish, E., Belsky J., & Barnes J. (2010). Sure Start and its evaluation in England. In R.E. Tremblay, R.G. Barr, R.D. Peters, & M. Boivin (Eds.), *Encyclopedia on early childhood development* [online]. Montreal: Centre of Excellence for Early Childhood Development; 2010: 1–6. Retrieved from http://www.child-encyclopedia.com/documents/Melhuish-Belsky-

BarnesANGxp.pdf. http://www.child-encyclopedia.com/documents/ Melhuish-Belsky-BarnesANGxp.pdf.

Patel, S., & Corter, C. (2011). Early intervention research, services, and policies. In A. Slater, M. Lewis, G. Anzures, & K. Lee (Eds.), *Introduction to infant development* (pp. 268–285). Toronto: Oxford University Press.

Standing Senate Committee on Social Affairs, Science and Technology. (2009). *Early Childhood Education and Care:* Next Steps. Final Report, April. Retrieved from http://www.parl.gc.ca/Content/SEN/Committee/402/soci/rep/ rep05apr09-e.pdf.

Talaga, T. (2010, 10 Oct.). Reserves lack full-day kindergarten; First Nations children left out of Ontario plan, as Ottawa covers their education. *Waterloo Region Record* (Kitchener, ON), p. A4.

United Nations Children's Fund (UNICEF). (2008). *The childcare transition: A league table of early childhood education and care in economically advanced countries.* Innocenti Report Card 8. UNICEF Innocenti Research Centre, Florence. Retrieved from http://www.unicef.ca/portal/Secure/Community/502/ WCM/HELP/take_action/Advocacy/rc8.pdf.

Willms, J.D. (2002). Socioeconomic gradients for childhood vulnerability. In J.D. Willms (Ed.), *Vulnerable children* (pp. 71–102). Edmonton: University of Alberta Press.

Postscript: Early Childhood Education and Care in Canada

HELEN PENN

In Canada, it has been a 'slow road' to achieving a comprehensive early education and care (ECEC) system – and, as the editors of this book say, there is still a long way to go. This book has been conceived as a hopeful summary of the achievements so far, and as an illustration of what can be achieved with more political will. I have been following ECEC developments in Canada for more than twenty-five years, and as the rapporteur for the OECD report on ECEC in Canada, published in 2004, I have more than a passing acquaintance with Canadian ECEC actors, policies, statistics, and traditions. So I am very pleased to be given an opportunity to comment on these chapters, and to relate what is here to some current international developments.

Each country has its own ECEC trajectory. Schweie and Willekens (2009) argue that current ECEC research and theory, in any country, is dominated by relatively short-term policy perspectives, but that policy always has roots in the past. They explore the notion that

> preschool organizations have their roots in different national traditions, themselves having their origins in different eras of social and economic development. These traditions have been crystallized in different institutions, in socially and legally structured ways of doing things which tend to facilitate the introduction of some innovations and to stand in the way of others. To understand the development of public childcare and preschool organizations and the range of accessible solutions for contemporary social policy issues it is imperative to see how these institutions create openings at the same time as being obstacles for certain kinds of solutions. (Schweie & Willekens, 2009, p. 2)

The notion of *path dependency* has been used to illustrate how decisions made in the distant past still influence decisions in the present; and the term *policy stickiness* describes a situation where policy stagnates partly because efforts to change it fail to recognize what really needs to be changed. This book is important as an opportunity to describe institutions and innovations and pinpoint both their successes and their limitations. But standing back from one's own experiences and seeing them in a broader perspective, especially an international perspective, is never easy.

The European Union (EU) represents a contrast to current ECEC policy making in Canada. The EU, at its Barcelona summit in 2002, agreed on child care targets: 'Member States should remove disincentives to female labour force participation and strive, taking into account the demand for childcare facilities and in line with national patterns of provision, to provide childcare by 2010 to at least 90% of children between 3 years old and the mandatory school age and at least 33% of children under 3 years of age' (European Union, 2008).

Subsequently the EU commissioned a report on child care from the perspective of women's rights, which shows clearly the relationships between child care provision, women's employment, and parental leave arrangements across Europe (Plantenga & Remery, 2009).

The policy rationale is that women's labour is crucial to a vibrant and successful economy, and child care, in turn, is an essential measure in reconciling work and family responsibilities. There is also another rationale underpinning European policy about lifelong learning, citizenship, and social inclusion. From this point of view, too, it is important to provide ECEC experiences for *all* children, irrespective of their circumstances, in order to promote social cohesion (European Commission/NESSE, 2009). Most European countries have tried to enact these EU goals, although their routes to doing so have been markedly different. Nevertheless, there is not much dissention about the legitimacy of these EU goals. They are reflected, to a greater or lesser degree, in the agendas of other transnational organizations – the OECD and UNICEF-IRC among them.

In Canada, by contrast, these goals of sufficient child care to enable families to reconcile work and family life, universal pre-school education, and the governmental coordination required to deliver them do not seem to be reasonable or achievable, with the possible exception of Quebec. ECEC is essentially a matter for families to resolve as best they can. Federal and state interventions are at a relatively low level and targeted at the most needy families. As an outside observer, my questions are why is Canada so slow in accepting that ECEC is part of a modern-day society? Using the notions of path dependency and policy stickiness, can we learn anything from the chapters presented here?

The first four chapters in particular address policy issues. As Goelman comments, these chapters provide a 'geological' view of Canada's policy position, uncovering the strata beneath the surface. Other chapters flesh out the picture, and give the details of current policies and initiatives. But these other chapters, too, make assumptions about policy and about possibilities and routes for changing policy. In discussing the book, it is these assumptions that I have attempted to uncover, from my privileged perspective as an international observer.

Prochner and Robertson explore the history of ECEC in Canada. In tracing the details of ideas about early education in Canada, they acknowledge that developments in child care, nursery school, and kindergarten education in Canada have closely followed those in the United States. The United States has had a very particular history of maternalism – a mother's place is in the home – and of minimal state intervention or support for the vulnerable (Michel, 1999). While Canada has had a more interventionist social policy stance than the United States, for example, in health care, American research and policy on ECEC, in some senses, is deeply parochial and has not been seriously challenged, or even critiqued, by policy makers or, for the most part, by academics.

The chapter by Friendly and Prentice foregrounds social policy issues. They argue that the particular federal structure of Canada, as well as the neo-liberal stance held in common with the United States, has mitigated against the development of ECEC services in Canada. They give a detailed account of how Canadian policies can be said to fall short in comparison with the benchmarks generated by international bodies such as UNICEF-IRC and OECD.

Gordon Cleveland presents an account of the economic arguments for supporting child care and early education, drawing on human capital theory. This is a succinct account of some powerful and widely used arguments.

However, recent OECD work presents a rather different emphasis. The influential Stiglitz report *The Measurement of Economic Performance and Social Progress* (2009) has stressed the importance of a wide range of micro-financial data – household-level information in understanding and predicting outcomes across a range of indicators. In particular, the report stresses the economic well-being of families and the importance of reducing income inequalities in order to achieve such well-being. As a result, there are a series of publications in the OECD Family Database Series that refer to various aspects of ECEC usage, ECEC costs and the relationship of ECEC policy to employment and income distribution and family life. The focus is on present benefits for families rather than on possible future outcomes for children.

The most recent OECD (Verbist et al., 2012) and EU work (Atkinson & Marlier, 2012) has drawn on household panel data to explore in more detail how public funding for ECEC services lessens the impact of poverty; and in particular how the poorest children in society benefit from ECEC provision. Verbist et al. (2012) point out that ECEC provision has a number of complementary functions. Access to affordable child care is one of the key elements of strategies to reconcile work and family life, promote equal opportunities, and combat social exclusion. Investment in early education in particular can protect children from further social and educational disadvantages and contribute to more equality. Using OECD data from the family database, and without recourse to human capital theory, the authors are able to demonstrate how different countries use ECEC services to impact positively on family well-being in low income families.

The OECD approach is likely to influence future work in this field, and possibly diminish the emphasis currently placed on the human capital approach, which focuses on outcomes for individual children over the long term.

Jacobs and Adrien provide a very detailed account of regulation procedures across Canada, and how training affects compliance. They point to the factors – structural and process variables – determining quality, which have been identified by American research and consider how they have been incorporated into the regulatory framework. This is interesting and very comprehensive. But, again, it takes the status quo for granted, and a poor system of ECEC – even poorer in the United States than in Canada in many respects, as the OECD (2000) suggests – is perhaps not the best, or only basis for considering what works. The chapter does not speculate on the wider question of why regulation is necessary, and whether there are circumstances in which it might not be necessary. An ongoing study of regulation of child care across Europe, in which I am currently involved, suggests that there is a spectrum of regulatory requirements, varying from self-evaluation at a local or municipal level (as in the Nordic countries and some regions of northern Italy) to highly centralized and highly specified regulatory and monitoring requirements, as in England.

Similarly, the content of the regulatory requirements varies considerably – in some countries, it may include, for example, the pay and working conditions and right to trade union representation of the workers in the service and also specify the amount that parents can be expected to pay. Very generally, the better qualified the staff, and the better the level of funding, the more relaxed the regulatory system. Regulation is a form of accountability, and demonstrating the worth of a service or institution to its stakeholders (including children as well as taxpayers) is an important issue. But regulation is also a reflection of the broader way in which ECEC is conceived and delivered in a country, whether it is an integral and relatively minor part of a coherent well-funded system or whether it is a necessary tool in the struggle to hold the line on standards in a fragmented and underfunded system.

Pacini-Ketchabaw and Bernhard highlight the very particular nature of Canadian society – an immigrant society and a large Indigenous population who have been badly treated and disregarded in the past. They argue that those working with young children and their families generally take a normative stance, and overall may not have the concepts and theoretical tools to be sufficiently sensitive to Canada's diverse population. This is an important perspective but it gives rise to a further question: is such a perspective more or less difficult to put into practice in a policy vacuum or where services are irregular and fragmented? Is their argument directed at individual practitioners and those who train them, in which case, in a fragmented system, the efforts can only be hit and miss; or is it part and parcel of a wider effort to reform ECEC services?

Heydon discusses her research in documenting an intergenerational program bringing together the very old and the very young. This is an outstanding and moving account, and it raises some profound questions about age segregation across all institutional life. From an anthropological perspective, such age segregation is highly unnatural, but it has become a feature of modern life. Are different skills required to live with and work across different age groups? Heydon discusses 'cross-training' and argues for some kind of curricular coherence across the different age groups in institutions and illuminates these discussions with details from her observations. It is interesting to compare this approach with the social pedagogue training in a number of European countries, most notably Denmark. This is based on the assumption that practical entrepreneurial social skills are required for work with people of any age. Danish pedagogues are trained to be 'animateurs,' literally to animate the groups with which they work by their familiarity with a range of resources – art, drama, dance, storytelling etc – and through their emphasis on creating a good emotional atmosphere and caring for others (Cameron & Petrie, 2009).

Langford locates her analysis of attempts across Canada to introduce curricular frameworks in a wider international setting. She discusses, for example, the radical bicultural Te Whāriki curricular framework from New Zealand, which deliberately avoids standard child developmental categories such as physical, intellectual, and social development, and instead, emphasizes the well-being of children within a community of others. Certainly, ECEC curricula across the world differ in the extent to which they emphasize individual progress and outcomes or stress communal activities and solidarity with others. In Sweden, for example, 'solidarity' with those who are weaker and more vulnerable is written into national curricula at all levels. Nevertheless, it is very difficult to develop curricula, however wide the consultation process, that deviate very much from accepted ideas in the education system as a whole. In New Zealand, the much admired and influential Te Whāriki curriculum was achieved partly because New Zealand is such a small country, and partly because the ECEC curriculum was 'under the radar.' Although provision for the early years in New Zealand is relatively well funded, it is all independently provided, and there is no direct state provision before the age of 5 years. The independence and unity of professionals working in the sector meant that it was possible to develop a relatively independent curriculum, although there are certainly problems of meshing with the state education system (May, 2010).

Pence and Pacini-Ketchabaw report on their Investigating Quality Project in British Columbia. This is based on the idea that arriving at any definition of quality involves comprehensive discussions with stakeholders. Such definitions are necessarily transitory, depending on who takes part in the discussions and at what point. The documentation of this project was over a five-year period. Although I accept that different stakeholders may have different views about what constitutes quality in early childhood services, and differing views have somehow to be reconciled, I also consider that the wider policy framework (or its absence) substantially affects how practitioners and policy makers formulate, interpret, and enact ideas about quality. Practitioners live in a very real world of instructions and restraints – the regulatory system, for example – and have to dovetail their everyday practice into these wider structural requirements. They can never act in a vacuum (Penn, 2011). The authors hint at this with their very brief discussion of evaluation and measurement at the end of their chapter.

Howe and Jacobs focus on mentoring as an aspect of practitioner in-service training. They document the work of a skilled mentor in several settings, and match this up with the comments of two women being mentored in delivering a constructivist curriculum. Here, again, the focus is on the actions of individuals, of the mentor promoting change, and of the women being mentored in enacting her suggestions. Clearly, there is room for considerable discussion about the process and how it can be adjusted, and the chapter offers insightful comments. But focusing on the micro-level limits any macro-level considerations. It may be the case that in early education settings, given the fragmentation of provision and the range of skills and qualifications of practitioners, successful procedures and processes vary considerably – what works in one place may not work in another.

The last four chapters in the book report on evaluations of ECEC projects in Canada. They offer empirical evidence of what has worked and what has not worked. Japel's excellent chapter discusses policies in Quebec, and shows in careful detail how these have impacted on practice. The Quebec government accepted the universalistic arguments being put forward outside of North America. A policy document issued in 1997 stated the Quebec government's aim of providing for all children at a fixed-fee rate irrespective of need or parental income. But, in doing so, the policy emphasized quantity over quality. The funding made available for the initiative, although a considerable step forward in Canadian terms, was not enough to guarantee quality, as measured by scales such as the revised Early Childhood Environment Rating Scale (ECERS-R). (Whatever one thinks about the limitations of measurement scales such as ECERS-R, they do give a useful indication of what kind of facilities exist for children and what activities the children typically engage in.) The result of the policy has been that uptake has been more patchy than expected and quality is low. But, at least, Japel argues, Quebec is on the right track: 'Quebec has laid the groundwork for an important social structure that is beneficial to children and their families. Yet its child care system must be seen as a work-in-progress, and continually striving to improve its quality and accessibility. The development and maintenance of a network of high-quality child care services will require a large investment of public funds, as well as policies that promote a global and long-term perspective on human development.'

Peters, Howell-Moneta, and Petrunka write about their evaluation of community-based early child development programs. They show, by examining the funding, that whatever the rhetoric about meeting the needs of children, the amounts allocated to the projects were woefully inadequate – in some cases as low as $17–$18 dollars per child per year compared with, for example, the $20,000 per child allocated to the Abecedarian project, a key longitudinal study in the United States. These authors question the value of community-based programs, with different funders, scarce resources, different modes of operation, different target groups, and inadequate evaluation frameworks. They conclude that not only have projects been grotesquely underfunded for what they have been designed to do, but that even if funding were more generous, such projects are less likely to be effective in a fragmented system. This is harsh criticism, indeed, since these kinds of community-based initiatives have been justified by policy makers as the main thrust of ECEC policy in Canada.

Ball reviews the initiatives to support Aboriginal ECEC. Here there have been some good results, in that Aboriginal communities became involved in the projects and saw them as compensating, at least marginally, for past injustices. But these initiatives, too, have been fragmented, and it is not clear which approaches are likely to produce the best outcomes. Ball argues for clearer evaluative frameworks and longitudinal research.

Finally, Pelletier reports on her evaluation of a 'school-as-hub' initiative for promoting an integrated school-based model of ECEC. The model appears promising but is undermined by 'the messiness of implementation.' However enterprising and promising individual initiatives may be, they are dependent on wider policy frameworks – the system as a whole needs to work better for such initiatives to succeed.

This is a rich collection of essays, by concerned and articulate researchers, working across a wide range of issues. Together, directly and indirectly, they present a strong argument for change. No human service, of any kind, is unchanging. But ECEC in Canada is wedged in the past at a policy level, and however good individual efforts to develop or challenge aspects of it, they founder against this policy inadequacy. It is reasonable, in global terms, to expect a better funded and comprehensive policy environment, which both acknowledges the importance of lifelong learning and the need for families to reconcile work and family life. The experience of most wealthy countries (but not the United States) is that it is economically and politically possible to implement such policies. The policy stickiness and path dependency that Canada displays does not mean that failure is inevitable, but it does require an energetic and coherent effort by the research community to address policy shortfalls. This book is an outstanding contribution to the debate.

References

Atkinson, A., & Marlier, E. (2012). *Income and living conditions in Europe.* Brussels: Eurostat/EU Commission.

Cameron, C., & Petrie, P. (2009). Importing social pedagogy? In J. Kornbeck & N. Rosendal Jensen (Eds.), *Social pedagogy in Europe today* (pp. 145–168). Bremen: Europaischer Hochschulverlag.

European Commission/NESSE (Network of Experts in Social Sciences of Education and Training). (2009). *Early childhood education and care: Key lessons from research for policy makers.* Brussels: Author. Retrieved from http://www.nesse.fr/nesse/activities/reports/activities/reports/ecec-report-pdf.

European Union. (2008, 8 Oct.). Child care services in the EU. Europa Press Release, MEMO/08/592. Brussels: Author. Retrieved from http://europa.eu/rapid/pressReleasesAction.do?reference=MEMO/08/592&format=HTML&aged=0&language=EN&guiLanguage=en.

May, H. (2010, Sept.). *Recent policy shifts in early childhood policy in New Zealand.* Paper given at a seminar in the International Centre for the Study of the Mixed Market Economy of Childcare (ICMEC) series, London.

Michel, S. (1999). *Children's interests/mothers' rights: The shaping of America's child care policy.* New Haven, CT: Yale University Press.

Noailly, J., & Visser, S. (2009). The impact of market forces on the provision of childcare: Insights from the 2005 Childcare Act in the Netherlands. *Journal of Social Policy, 38,* 477–498.

OECD, Directorate for Education. (2000). *Early childhood education and care policy in the United States of America: OECD country note.* Paris: Author.

OECD. (2011). *Family Database.* Paris: Author.

Penn, H. (2011). *Quality in early childhood services: An international perspective.* Maidenhead, UK: Open University Press/McGraw-Hill.

Plantenga, J., & Remery, C. (Eds.). (2009). *The provision of childcare services: A comparative review of 30 European countries.* Brussels: European Commission's Expert Group on Gender and Employment Issues, Directorate for Employment, Social Affairs and Equal Opportunities.

Schweie, K., & Willekens, H. (Eds.). (2009). *Child care and preschool development in Europe: Institutional perspectives.* Basingstoke: Palgrave Macmillan.

Stiglitz, J., Sen, A., & Fitoussi, J. (2009). *Report of the Commission on the Measurement of Economic Performance and Social Progress.* Paris. Retrieved from www.stiglitz-sen-fitoussi.fr.

Verbist, G., Förster, M., & Vaalavuo, M. (2012*). The impact of publicly provided services on the distribution of resources: Review of new results and methods.* Paris: OECD.

Contributors

Emmanuelle Adrien, graduate student, Department of Education, Concordia University

Jessica Ball, professor, School of Child and Youth Care, University of Victoria

Judith K. Bernhard, professor, School of Early Childhood Education, Ryerson University

Gordon Cleveland, senior lecturer, Department of Management, University of Toronto, Scarborough

Carl Corter, professor, Human Development and Applied Psychology, University of Toronto, OISE/UT

Martha Friendly, executive director, Childcare Research and Resource Unit, Childcarecanada.org

Hillel Goelman, professor, Educational and Counselling Psychology, and Special Education, University of British Columbia

Rachel Heydon, associate professor, Faculty of Education, Western University

Nina Howe, professor and Concordia University Research Chair in Early Childhood Development and Education, Department of Education, Concordia University

Angela Howell-Moneta, adjunct assistant professor, Department of Psychology, Queen's University

Ellen Jacobs, professor emeritus, Department of Education, Concordia University

Christa Japel, professor, Éducation et formation spécialisées, Université du Québec à Montréal

Rachel Langford, associate professor, School of Early Childhood Education, Ryerson University

Veronica Pacini-Ketchabaw, associate professor, School of Child and Youth Care, University of Victoria

Janette Pelletier, associate professor, Human Development and Applied Psychology, University of Toronto, OISE/UT

Alan Pence, professor, School of Child and Youth Care, University of Victoria

Helen Penn, professor, Cass School of Education, University of East London

Ray DeV Peters, professor emeritus, Department of Psychology, Queen's University

Kelly Petrunka, research associate, Better Beginnings, Department of Psychology, Queen's University

Susan Prentice, professor, Department of Sociology, University of Manitoba

Larry Prochner, professor, Department of Elementary Education, University of Alberta

Lynne Robertson, PhD student, Department of Elementary Education, University of Alberta

Index

Following a page number, the letter *f* refers to a figure and the letter *t* refers to a table.